CHALLENGING
FRONTERAS

CHALLENGING FRONTERAS: STRUCTURING LATINA AND LATINO LIVES IN THE U.S.

An Anthology of Readings

Edited by

Mary Romero, Arizona State University

Pierrette Hondagneu-Sotelo,
   University of Southern California

Vilma Ortiz, University of California, Los Angeles

Routledge
New York & London

Published in 1997 by
Routledge
29 West 35th Street
New York, NY 10001

Published in Great Britain by
Routledge
11 New Fetter Lane
London EC4P 4EE

Copyright © 1997 by Routledge

Printed in the United States of America on acid-free paper.

Library of Congress Cataloging-in-Publication Data
     Challenging fronteras : structuring latina and latino lives in the U.S. / edited by Mary Romero, Pierrette Hondagneu-Sotelo, Vilma Ortiz.
       p. cm.
     Includes bibliographical references and index.
     ISBN 0-415-91607-0 (alk.   er). — ISBN 0-415-91608-9 (pbk. : alk. paper)
     1. Hispanic Americans—Ethnic identity. 2. Hispanic Americans—Cultural assimilation. 3. Latin America—Emigration and immigration. 4. United States—Emigration and immigration. 5. Hispanic Americans—Social conditions. I. Romero, Mary. II. Hondagneu-Sotelo, Pierrette. III. Ortiz, Vilma, 1954-EE184.S75C467   1996
305.868—8820   96-34287
                                                          CIP

CONTENTS 🦋

INTEGRATING LATINO STUDIES INTO THE CURRICULUM

RACE RELATIONS AND SOCIAL INEQUALITY COURSES IN SOCIOLOGY, economics, psychology, and other social sciences have only recently begun to recognize the limitations of a binary, White/Black paradigm to include the multiple experiences of other groups of color in the U.S. While it is likely that today's college students have some knowledge of Latinos, that knowledge is usually fragmentary—grounded in news reports of social "problems"—crime, drugs, AIDS, gangs, and high school drop-out rates. Images are likely to be profoundly influenced by stereotypes portrayed in motion pictures, beginning with western movies and continuing with such "cultural" offerings as *American Me, Miami Vice, Scarface,* and, most recently, an explosion of gang movies. Generally, the information students have about Latinos is inaccurate, biased, or simply superficial and facile. Students rarely receive a comprehensive introduction to the Latino experience in the U.S. that moves beyond sweeping generalizations. Frequently course materials treat Latinos as a monolithic cultural group, sharing the same language and neighborhood, and struggling for the same political goals. We feel that it is important to expose students to the diversity of the various groups encompassed in the pan-ethnic term—"Latino." In place of stereotypes, it is critical to examine each group's entry to the United States, and the different historical paths each group has traversed. In order to gain a sociological perspective of Latinos, students should be exposed to sophisticated background information that provides historical specificity and up-to-date research that employs the conceptual and analytical tools of social science.

This edited volume was designed to give students a comprehensive overview of the Latino experience in the U.S. The collection benefited from increasing interest in the Latino population in the social sciences and humanities, and drew strength from the growing number of Ethnic Studies, Chicana/o Studies, and Latina/o Studies programs. These multidisciplinary programs have nurtured and allowed the production of research and writings by and about Mexican Americans, Puerto Ricans, Cuban Americans, Dominican Americans, and other groups classified as Hispanic in the U.S.

Challenging Fronteras: Structuring Latina and Latino Lives in the U.S. grew out of the editors' involvement in establishing the Latina and Latino Section of the American Sociological Association. In 1993, several of us participated in a workshop on "Teaching Latino/a Studies in Sociology" at the annual conference. Our colleagues expressed their desire for a social science reader focusing on the diversity of Latino experiences. We began thinking about the structure for a reader by reviewing forty-nine course syllabi that appeared in "Chicano and Latino Studies in Sociology, Syllabi and Instructional Material."[1] Our selection of topics and readings was informed by that survey of existing courses in the field. Over the last year, we designed new courses and incorporated the readings in existing courses to "test" their use in the classroom setting. This included courses taught in Sociology, Ethnic Studies, and Chicano Studies at Arizona State University, the University of Oregon, Colgate University, the University of Southern California, and the University of California at Los Angeles. These settings presented different teaching environments: required "diversity" classes of predominately white students at the University of Oregon; classes with students from diverse Latino backgrounds at UCLA, USC, and Colgate; as well as predominately Mexican American students at Arizona State University.

In selecting material for the reader our objective was to present writings and research that identified specific Latino groups rather than homogenizing the group as a pan-ethnic group. We drew heavily on the work of authors that attend to important historical and social differences between groups and research that provided sophisticated analyses of pan-ethnicity. At the same time, we were also limited by the available social science research on smaller groups, particularly those groups of recently arrived immigrants. We hope that our colleagues and their students will respond to the absence of various groups as a call for future research in Latino Studies.

The book is organized into five topics: concepts and theories, immigration, ethnic identity, work and family, and economic and political restructuring. The topics reflect major areas of social science research integrating race, ethnicity, gender, class, and citizenship. We believe that the interrelationship between these categories of experience captures the structural constraints that continue to shape Latino lives in the U.S. today. The intersectionality of race, ethnicity, class, and citizenship affects individual consciousness, intra- and inter-group interaction, and each group's access to institutional power and privileges. Each section contains articles about several Latino groups, followed by suggested readings and discussion questions.

ACKNOWLEDGMENTS

Although we are all sociologists, our own ethnic backgrounds, research interests and methodologies, and teaching experiences are quite diverse. We used this diversity as a resource in developing an inclusive approach to the study of Latino and Latina lives in the U.S. Many hours were spent discussing books and articles, outlining new directions for research in the social sciences, and developing conceptual and pedagogical frameworks. The work of preparing this reader allowed us to share, challenge, argue, and learn from each other. As a result of our collaboration, we have not only become friends but better researchers and teachers.

We are deeply indebted to the scholars, teachers, and students who are the pioneers in Latino Studies, Chicano Studies, Puerto Rican Studies, and Ethnic Studies. Originally laboring in the interstices of academia, the work of interdisciplinary scholars studying the Latino experience can no longer be ignored by mainstream disciplines. The recent attention to Latinos by publishers, funding agencies, and traditional disciplines is due largely to their persistent struggle and important contributions. We wish to acknowledge the efforts of our colleagues who worked with us in establishing the Latina/o Section of the American Sociological Association, who generously contributed syllabi and teaching materials for the ASA publication, and who continue to work towards transforming the curriculum, the discipline, and academia.

We are grateful to the students who shared their reactions to various articles and topics. We acknowledge the support we received from Arizona State University, University of Southern California, and University of California, Los Angeles. We are particularly appreciative of Kris Zentgraf who provided help in the early stages of obtaining permissions and assistance in editing.

We thank Jayne Fargnoli for her interest in a social science reader in Latino Studies. We appreciate her encouragement and support of this project.

We also wish to thank our families for their encouragement and support in this project: Eric Margolis, who provided editing and computer assistance; Mike Messner, who offered kindness and occasional release time; and Antonio Scrrata, who provided encouragement. Lito, Sasha, and Miguel enriched our meetings and gave work meaning.

NOTES

1. Mary Romero (ed.). 1994. *Syllabi and Instructional Materials for Chicano and Latino Studies in Sociology.* Washington, D.C.: American Sociological Association Teaching Resource Center. Previous editions were also consulted: *Syllabi and Instructional Materials for Latino Studies in Sociology.* Washington, D.C.: American Sociological Association Teaching Resource Center (1990); *Syllabi and Instructional Materials for Chicano Studies Courses in Sociology.* Washington, D.C.: American Sociological Association Teaching Resource Center (1985).

INTRODUCTION ❦

Mary Romero

LATINOS COMPRISE THE FASTEST GROWING RACIAL ETHNIC GROUP in the United States. In the past, Latino presence was concentrated in specific geographic areas: Chicanos and Mexicanos in the Southwest, Puerto Ricans in New York, Cubans in Miami, and so on. This is no longer the case; Latino communities can be found almost everywhere. Moreover, aspects of Latino cultures are becoming integrated into popular culture and have become well known to the general public: tacos, tortillas, salsa, and margaritas are as common as pizza, bagels, ketchup, and kool-aid. Spanish television and radio stations are broadcast throughout the country. Spanish radio stations are challenging monolingual English stations for the number one spot in Los Angeles, and Spanish media offers significant competition in New York City, Miami, and Houston. Many industries are redesigning advertising campaigns to attract the Latino market. However, while food, music, clothing, and other elements of Latino material culture have become incorporated into the mainstream, little is known about the history, socio-economic conditions, politics, family life, and educational experiences of Latinos.

It is unfortunate that the national discussion of race continues to be dominated by a White/Black paradigm in the face of current events like Proposition 187, student movements for the continuation of affirmative action and the establishment of ethnic studies programs, the Cuban/Black conflict in Miami, and the increase of hate crimes against Latinos. By 2010 Latinos will outnumber African Americans, yet leading scholars continue to frame racial tensions in the U.S. without including or incorporating them. The presence of sizable communities of Puerto Ricans, Chicanos, South and Central Americans (as well as related groups identified as American Indians, Caribbean, or Asian Americans) contradicts White/Black conceptualizations of race. Multiracial diversity gives evidence to the limited value that a binary paradigm has in explaining the complex social, political, and economic realities found in cities such as Boston, Denver, San Francisco, Los Angeles, Miami, Houston, Phoenix, Chicago, New York, or Washington, D.C. All of these cities are home to growing Latino communities and their numeric and economic clout is profoundly influencing political realities.

The U.S. Census Bureau's classification of the population illustrates the difficulties that result from attempts to force Latino groups into America's dualistic race category. The U.S. Census has a long history of classifying Americans according to race. The government's construction of race as White or Black is of little utility when applied to Anglo Americans and African Americans who fall into a broad continuum of skin shades and cultural allegiances; but it completely falls apart when forced upon Puerto Ricans, Cubans, Chicanos, Nicaraguans, Dominicans, and Guatemalans. Throughout the years the way that Latinos see themselves, and the way that the Census attempted to record their race have frequently been incompatible. Probably the most accurate count taken of Mexican Americans was in the 1930 Census, when enumerators were instructed to classify "all persons born in Mexico, or having parents born in Mexico, who were not definitely White, Black or Indian, Chinese, or Japanese" as Mexican. In 1940, the classification changed. This time Mexicans and other persons of "Latin descent" were to be classified as "White" unless they were definitely Black or Indian. In 1980, Mexicans, like Puerto Ricans, were left in the "other race" category. And in the 1990 census, the choices under race did not include Mexican or Latin descent. Respondents were expected to select one of the following race categories: White, Black, American Indian (fill-in the affiliation), Native Alaskan, Asian and Pacific Islander, or other race. Separate from race was Spanish/Hispanic origin. Here, persons could identify as Mexican American, Puerto Rican, Cuban, or print "other Spanish/Hispanic" group. The limited options available in the 1990 census reflect the inadequacy of the European American and African American experience in capturing the Latino experience.

Latinos are a physically, as well as culturally, heterogenous group. Five hundred years of conquest, immigration, and intermarriage have brought together peoples from Europe, the Americas, Africa, and Asia. Thus, Mexicans, Puerto Ricans, Cubans, Dominicans, Nicaraguans, Panamanians, Peruvians, and Guatemalans are not easily classified into any one racial category. Within each group one finds the entire human range of physical characteristics: tall and short, fair, brown and black skin tones, hair ranging from blond to black and from straight to kinky, blue, brown, and black eyes. Even within families, skin colors often range from dark to light. Latinos challenge the social construction of both "whiteness" and "non-whiteness." Research on the social construction of racial identity among Latinos suggests that Latinos do not construct racial identity simply on genetic and physical characteristics but include social class, language, phenotypic variation within families, and neighborhood socialization. It is not that uncommon to find Latinos who claim a dual or tri-racial heritage, a combination of African, European, and indigenous ancestors.[1]

Clearly, we cannot continue to rely on the dominant culture's notions of "whiteness" or "blackness" to assess racial identity among Latinos in the U.S. The binary thinking of race relations in this country is so ingrained in the dominant culture that it continues to shape what we see. Take the 1994 Los Angeles Riots, for example. National coverage of the event reported it as a Black riot. Yet the majority of persons arrested were Latinos, many of whom were Mexican and Central American immigrants. Moreover, the academic press is not much better than the popular press in conceptualizing the issue. Prominent recent books such as Cornel West's *Race Matters* and Andrew Hacker's *Two Nations Black and White, Separate, Hostile, Unequal* perpetuate the White/Black racial paradigm for analyzing race relations in the U.S.

It is also important to analyze the distinction between racial groups and ethnic groups. However, in the case of Latinos, the more accurate classification is racial ethnic group. For example, police commonly identify Latino suspects not as white, black, or even brown or red for that matter, but as Hispanic. If the labels Latino and Hispanic were actually being used as simply an ethnic term, then we would have to question how the police knew the suspect was Latino. Is it because the suspect has a Spanish-surname, speaks Spanish, or speaks English with a Spanish accent? Was the suspect reported to be eating Mexican food at the time of the crime, listening to *novelas*, or maybe engaging in other cultural practices? Most likely the description of the suspect was not a cultural description but a physical description. The terms Latino and Hispanic are most commonly generated by phenotypical appearance. Most people have an image of what Latinos or Hispanics look like (regardless of how inaccurate the image may be); and it has less to do with culture than it has to do with skin color and other physical characteristics. Identifying who is Latino in a crowd is usually done in the same way that Whites or Blacks are identified, not by acting White or acting Black but by physical characteristics. It is not surprising, then, that more and more

Latinos understand Hispanic origin to be a racial classification in the U.S. because their experience is a racial one. Hispanic functions as a racial classification, just as Mexican or Puerto Rican did a decade ago.

The emphasis on binary racial identification poses an additional obstacle to the development of Latino identity and consciousness. Unlike other pan-ethnic groups in the United States, we are divided by race. Asian Americans, for example, may be Japanese American, Chinese American, Vietnamese American, or Korean American, but all are perceived as "Asian." In the case of Latinos, however, we are asked first to classify ourselves as White, Black, American Indian, or Other, and then to select "Hispanic" ethnicity. Forcing racial distinctions on Latinos may hinder the development of a Latino consciousness, particularly when the official label, "Hispanic," was not entirely a voluntary designation. The Spanish/Hispanic origin classification was invented by the federal Office of Management and Budget in the '70s and later adopted throughout the government. The Bureau of Census adopted "Hispanic" as the official Census category in an attempt to eliminate the problem of undercounting and to provide more accurate statistics for the Bureau of Census.[2] While the "Hispanic" population was initially a political construct, it seems to have acquired a facticity of its own among social scientists, policy makers, and the mass media. One no longer hears about the drop-out rates among Chicano, Mexican American, or Puerto Rican students. School districts and universities now report the performance of their "Hispanic" students and worry about recruiting "Hispanic" teachers, while the mass media reports what "Hispanic" politicians or "Hispanic" gang members do.

The reduction of Mexicans, Chicanos, Puerto Ricans, Cubans, Dominicans, Salvadorans, Nicaraguans, Costa Ricans, and other groups to the single category of "Hispanic" has met with resistance. There are two main objections: one is the depoliticization of each group's distinct history with the U.S. (colonized, conquered, exploited, etc.); the other is the emphasis upon Hispanic (European) culture and ancestry, rather than African and indigenous cultures. An analysis of U.S. foreign policy is essential in understanding the economic role that each group experiences. The comprehension of the socio-economic conditions of Chicanos in Albuquerque is incomplete without the context of the Mexican-American War and the violations of the Treaty of Guadalupe Hidalgo. An analysis of Puerto Ricans in New York would be incomplete without considering the causes of unemployment on the island. Understanding the migration and immigration patterns of the various Latino groups to the U.S., and the classification of political and economic refugees, requires attention to U.S. foreign policy towards Central and South America.

The label "Hispanic" may have begun as a political construct developed by the government, but it appears to have developed a life of its own. While a preference for the term "Latino" remains among many Chicanos, Puerto Ricans, and others, there is an increasing use of the term "Hispanic" to self-identify. There is significant evidence that Hispanics do not perceive the term as restricted to a cultural classification, but instead interpret "Hispanic" as a racial designation in itself; that is, a multi-racial category. There are also signs that a Latino consciousness is developing. Several recent attempts at coalition building have occurred in cities with large Latino populations, such as Los Angeles, Chicago, Boston and New York City. Coalition building among Latino groups has been successful in getting Latino representation in city councils and other political office. Long time civil rights organizations in the Mexican American community (e.g., MALDEF and LULAC) have broadened their mission to include other Latino groups. There are also signs of an emergent Latino culture that blends various cultures. This includes the appearance of remarkable musical fusions, Mexican and Salvadorean restaurant combinations in San Francisco, Miami, and Washington, D.C., and the transformation of Cinco de Mayo from a holiday for Mexican Americans into a Dia de la Raza, a celebration of Latino culture. Even in the presence of groups claiming a pan-ethnic identity, many also retain a strong national origin identity.

In selecting articles for this anthology, we tried to be inclusive of all Latino groups, excluding writings that ignore the distinct history and culture among groups. However, we were limited by the available research on various groups. Books and articles on Chicanos, Mexican immigrants, and Puerto Ricans dramatically outnumber available writings on Guatemalans, Dominicans, Salvadorans, Nicaraguans, Colombians, Peruvians, and Costa Ricans. We also tried to find articles that focused on the interaction between Latino groups and the changing demographics that have diversified Chicano and Puerto Rican communities into Latino communities. The sections focus on immigration experiences, the social construction of racial, ethnic and pan-ethnic identities, negotiating work and family life, and the impact of political and economic restructuring on urban Latino communities. Together these sections point to the dual *fronteras* facing Latinos in the U.S. today. On the one hand, *fronteras* evoke the possibilities of and potentialities symbolized by wide open frontiers and uncharted panoramas. On the other hand, *fronteras* are borders, sober reminders of the concrete divisions and limits between the dominant U.S. society and Latinos. This book is an exploration of these challenging *fronteras*.

DEMOGRAPHIC OVERVIEW OF LATINOS

Vilma Ortiz

Latinos are a diverse population including people from various national origins, each of which have a unique immigration and socio-economic history in the U.S. Latinos include persons from Mexico, Central and South America, and the Spanish speaking Caribbean. The largest Latino group, the Mexicans, have the longest history in the United States, and comprise 64 percent of all Latinos. Puerto Ricans make up 11 percent of all Latinos, and Cubans comprise 5 percent. These various groups are dispersed geographically throughout the U.S. Mexicans reside primarily in the Southwest (California, Texas, Colorado, New Mexico, and Arizona). In contrast, Puerto Ricans reside in the Northeast (New York, New Jersey, Pennsylvania) and Cubans in the Southeast (especially Florida). Central and South Americans constitute 13 percent of all Latinos, and include people from diverse countries of origin. For instance, significant numbers of Salvadorans and Guatemalans reside in California, while Dominicans and Colombians are mostly in New York. There are also communities of Nicaraguans and other Central Americans in Washington D.C., and Florida.

The characteristics of the Latino population presented in Table 1 convey the diversity of this population. Latinos tend to be younger than non-Latinos. On the average Latinos are 27 years old, while non-Latino Whites are 36 years old. This is due to two factors: the high percentage of Latinos that are immigrants (who tend to be younger) and to higher fertility (more of the population are young children). Among Latinos, Cubans are the only group that is considerably older, 44 years of age on average. The reason for this is that few

Table 1. Characteristics of the Latino Population

	Total	Non-Latino White	Latinos	Mexicans	Puerto Ricans	Cubans	Central & So. Americans
General Characteristics							
Median Age	34	36	27	25	27	44	29
% High School Graduate	80	84	53	46	60	62	63
% Immigration (1990)		5	35	26	51	78	
Latino Workers							
Labor Force Participation							
Men	75	75	79	81	69	67	84
Women	57	58	52	52	46	48	57
Unemployment Rate							
Men	8.5	7.1	12.4	12.1	17.2	7.6	12.4
Women	6.2	5.0	11.1	11.1	11.0	7.3	14.4
Median Earnings							
Men	$22,171	$24,994	$14,706	$13,622	$18,366	$18,416	$14,358
Women	$13,675	$14,241	$10,813	$10,098	$14,200	$14,117	$10,249
Latino Families							
% Married	58	61	56	57	50	61	57
% Headed by Women	18	13	23	19	40	18	25
Median Income	$36,811	$40,420	$23,912	$23,714	$20,301	$31,015	$23,649
Poverty Rate	12	7	26	26	32	15	27
% Own Home	65	70	40	44	23	53	26

Cubans came to the U.S. after the initial migration wave in the late 1950s and early '60s, consequently most are older settled immigrants.

Latinos have lower levels of education than non-Latinos. While 84 percent of non-Latino Whites are high school graduates, only about 50 percent of Latinos have graduated from high school. Mexicans have the lowest educational level with only 46 percent having graduated in contrast to 60 percent among other Latino groups. This is partly due to especially low levels of education among Mexican immigrants (about six to eight years of schooling). In contrast, Puerto Ricans have more years of school because educational levels are higher in Puerto Rico, while Cubans and Central and South Americans have more schooling because higher educated individuals are more likely to immigrate from those countries.

As Section II of this volume will indicate, immigration is an important aspect of the Latino experience. While only 5 percent of non-Latino Whites are immigrants, over one-third of Latinos are immigrants. Among Mexicans, one-fourth are immigrants, although this varies considerably by geographic location. For instance, half of the Mexicans in the greater Los Angeles area are estimated to be immigrants.[3] Half of Puerto Ricans are born on the island while half are born in the continental U.S. Three-fourths of Cubans were born in Cuba, although most of these Cuban immigrants came to the U.S. over 30 years ago.[4]

Overall, Latino workers are more disadvantaged than other workers. They have higher unemployment, are concentrated in lower status occupations, experience worse working conditions, and earn less. Table 1 shows that participation in the labor force is similar among non-Latino Whites, Mexicans, and Central and South American men (approximately 80 percent). In contrast, Puerto Ricans have lower levels of participation in the labor force, which is considered to be the result of pressures of a restructured economy (see Section V). Cubans similarly have a low level of labor force participation but this is due primarily to their older age and greater likelihood of being retired. The especially high rate of labor force participation among Central and South Americans is probably due to their more recent immigrant status, since recent immigrants are especially likely to work. Labor force participation among women is lower than men since women are more likely to devote considerable labor to caring for children and other dependents. Nevertheless, over half of Latinas still participate in the paid labor force.

Unemployment is significantly higher for all groups of Latinos than non-Latino Whites, with the exception of Cubans. Twelve percent of Latino men are unemployed in contrast to 7 percent of non-Latino White men. Puerto Rican men have an especially high rate of unemployment which is comparable to their lower rate of labor force participation observed above. Similarly large racial/ethnic differences are also observed among women.

Annual earnings among Latino men, $15,000, are lower than among non-Latino White men which average $25,000. Puerto Rican men, interestingly have higher earnings than other Latino men. This is a result of their being concentrated in the Northeast region of the U.S. where wages are generally higher. However, this contrasts sharply with their being less likely to work and more likely to be unemployed. Thus while Puerto Ricans who work earn more, fewer work. Because they came to the U.S. with high levels of education, professional, and business experience, Cuban men report higher earnings. Racial/ethnic differences in earning among women are smaller than among men. In other words, all groups of women, including non-Latino White women, earn lower wages. This is partly related to the fact that they hold lower status jobs, but is also due to the fact that women earn less than men even when they hold similar status jobs to those of men.

Latino families are also relatively disadvantaged. More Latino families are headed by women and fewer Latino adults are married than among non-Latino Whites. Among Latinos, Puerto Ricans are most likely to live in female headed households. The economic disadvantage of Latino families is similarly reflected in their lower likelihood of owning a home. Puerto Ricans have the lowest rate of home-ownership because they are geograph- ically concentrated in the Northeast region that has lower rates of owning a home and higher property values. Home ownership data has important implications for the future economic outlook for Latinos, because home-ownership is the major mechanism by which Americans experience mobility, accumulate wealth, and transmit status to their children.

NOTES

1. Clara E. Rodriquez, Aida Castro, Oscar Garcia and Analisa Torres. 1991. "Latino Racial Identity: In the Eye of the Beholder?" *Latino Studies Journal* 2:33-57.

2. David E. Hayes-Bautista. 1980. "Identifying 'Hispanic' Populations: The Influence of Research Methodology on Public Policy," *American Journal of Public Health* 70:353-56; David E. Hayes-Bautista and Jorge Chapa. 1987. "Latino Terminology: Conceptual Basis for Standardized Terminology," *American Journal of Public Health* 77:69-72.

3. Ortiz, Vilma. 1996."The Mexican Origin Population: Permanent Working-Class or Emerging Middle-Class." In Roger Waldinger and Medhi Bozorgmehr (eds.) *Ethnic Los Angeles*. New York: Russel Sage.

4. There have been more recent waves of Cuban immigrants, notably in the early eighties. While this group has very different characteristics than long-term settlers, they are a small percentage of all Cubans in the U.S.

PART ONE

CONCEPTUALIZING THE LATINO EXPERIENCE

Mary Romero

IN JUNE OF 1995, Judge Samuel Kiser decided in favor of a father's "right" to prohibit the mother of his daughter from speaking Spanish to the child. The judge claimed that teaching the child to speak Spanish would condemn her to a future of servitude as a maid: "What are you trying to do? Make her a maid for the rest of her life?" Although the judge received considerable criticism from the Mexican American community, his statement exposed a number of important taken-for-granted beliefs about race, ethnicity, social class, and gender. In the first place, while seldom stated overtly, many Americans believe that patriarchal authority should be supported by the state. In the second place, the claim that Mexican women in Texas are hired as private household workers because they speak Spanish, implies that culture constrains the individual's opportunities in the labor market. Claims of cultural determinism are consistent with the corollary view that assimilation is the path to upward social mobility. However, these commonly held beliefs do not explain two facts: bilingual and monolingual English-speaking Chicanas and Mexicanas dominate the occupation in Denver, Albuquerque, and other cities in the Southwest; English-speaking Latina immigrants in Los Angeles are able to negotiate higher wages than monolingual Spanish speakers, but are unable to find higher paying jobs outside of domestic service. The judge's ruling demonstrates, but does not explain, why domestic service is perceived as "Mexican women's work" in Texas, Colorado, New Mexico, and Arizona or "Latina's work" in California. Cultural determinism does not explain the relegation of Latinas to domestic service any more than it does the fact that the occupation has traditionally been treated as Black women's work in the South.

The central issue is this: Does a single variable—ethnicity, class, race, citizenship, or gender fully explain Puerto Ricans, Chicanos, Cuban Americans, Mexican, or Salvadoran immigrants' experiences in the labor market? Or more generally, is there an interrelationship of ethnicity, race, class, citizenship, and gender that explains the Latino experience in the U.S.?

In this section we examine conceptual frameworks that employ a structural perspective to explain the Latino experience. Theorists have debated how best to conceptualize the Latino experience: Is the process of integration of Latino immigrants similar to the assimilation of European immigrants? Or, do Latinos have more in common with African Americans? Is the Latino experience a racial experience? An ethnic experience? In either case, how can we understand class differences among the various Latino groups? Researchers have developed concepts and theories by analyzing employment and housing data in order to identify patterns of social mobility or discrimination. At the same time, Latinas and Latinos are engaged in the everyday life process of conceptualizing their experience. The ongoing development of social consciousness may contribute to the social construction of a "Latino" ethnic consciousness and identity, or to the development of a nationalistic identity that identifies an occupied homeland.

We have selected articles that analyze the experiences of two or more Latino groups from different conceptual frameworks. In the first article, "The Structuring of Hispanic Ethnicity: Historical and Contemporary Perspectives," Candace Nelson and Marta Tienda provide a thorough overview of theoretical frameworks employed in the analysis of ethnicity in the U.S. and critique their usefulness in explaining the historical experiences of Mexicans, Puerto Ricans, and Cubans. They begin by reviewing dominate themes in the conceptual frameworks of racial and ethnic stratification, highlighting distinctions between explanations that attribute ethnic groups' experiences to cultural factors or theories of social class. Applying William Yancey's concept of emergent ethnicity, they point to how the distinct histories of each group shaped their economic and cultural integration into American society. They argue that these unique experiences translate "Hispanic origin to a symbolic ethnicity for some and a minority status for others."

The second selection similarly argues for a historical perspective; however, unlike Nelson and Tienda, Suzanne Oboler does not employ the experiences of European immigrants as the point of reference in analyzing the experiences of Latinos. In her article, "'So Far from God, So Close to the United States': The Roots of Hispanic Homogenization," Oboler's historical overview draws attention to the social construction of race. Beginning with the history of Spain in Latin America, Oboler describes the establishment of a racial social order based on Spanish and Catholic colonial practices that discriminated against indigenous people and Blacks. However, unlike the rigid binary Black/White racial order established in the United States, racial classification in Latin America was interrelated with social status and honor. After the Mexican-American War, Mexicans in the Southwest became defined as racially and socially inferior to Anglos. Oboler discusses the ways that domestic boundaries excluding African Americans and Native Americans also functioned to exclude Mexican Americans and Puerto Ricans. Yet, unlike African Americans, Mexican Americans and Puerto Ricans continue to be perceived and treated as foreign born. Oboler's discussion of specific U.S. government policies demonstrates "the process of exclusion of people of Latin American descent from the American imagined community." Her analysis of the racial construction of Mexicans and Puerto Ricans in the U.S. identifies the limitations of assimilation policies while illustrating the racial construction of the "Hispanic other."

The last article in this section, "The Invention of Ethnic Origins and the Negotiation of Latino Identity, 1969-1981," Jorge Klor de Alva explores the ways that Chicanos and Puerto Ricans negotiated a regional identity during the early 1970s and invented a "nationalist ethnicity" which challenged the dominant "cultural narratives." Selecting pre-Columbian icons as their origins, Mexica and Tainos were adopted as symbolic weapons against "Anglo" American society and represented their legitimate claim to "being a nation rather than an ethnic minority." Politics of separatism, pluralism, and assimilation became closely linked with how Chicano, Puerto Rican, and Latino identity is negotiated. While debates over cultural nationalism and historical materialism are no longer as popular as they were in the '70s, significant fragments of the debate remain on university campuses and in grass-root organizations. Nationalistic symbols of Aztlán and Borinquen remain strong in our communities and nationalism remains a controversial issue among college students and community activists. Klor de Alva's analysis of levels of Latino identification highlights the constraints on the formation of a pan-ethnic identity, and points out the difficulties that, for example, immigrant and non-immigrant Mexicanos have in constructing a single identity.

DISCUSSION QUESTIONS:

1. Explain how Hispanic origin among Mexicans, Puerto Ricans, and Cubans functions as a symbolic ethnicity for some and a minority status for others. Discuss the factors impacting the classification of other Latino groups.

2. Compare and contrast the racial order of Spanish and Catholic conquest in Latin America to that of Anglo-Saxon Protestants in the U.S.

3. Discuss the pros and cons of cultural nationalism as a conceptual framework for empowerment.

SUGGESTED READINGS:

Almaguer, Tomas. 1994. Racial Fault Lines. *The Historical Origins of White Supremacy in California.* Berkeley: University of California Press.

Gutierrez, David G. 1995. *Walls and Mirrors. Mexican Americans, Mexican Immigrants, and the Politics of Ethnicity.* Berkeley: University of California Press.

Melendez, Edwin and Edgardo Melendez. (Ed.) 1993. *Colonial Dilemma: Critical Perspectives in Contemporary Puerto Rico.* Boston: South End Press.

Montejano, David. 1987. *Anglos and Mexicans in the Making of Texas, 1836-1986.* Austin: University of Texas Press.

Oboler, Suzanne. 1995. *Ethnic Labels, Latino Lives: Identity and the Politics of (Re)Presentation in the United States.* Minneapolis: University of Minnesota Press.

Rodriquez, Clara, E. 1989. *Puerto Ricans. Born in the U.S.A.* Boston: Unwin Hyman Press.

1

THE STRUCTURING OF HISPANIC ETHNICITY: HISTORICAL AND CONTEMPORARY PERSPECTIVES

Candace Nelson and Marta Tienda

A DOMINANT MYTH about the social and economic experiences of U.S. immigrants is that most groups confront similar opportunity structures and reception factors in the host society. Without regard for differences in the historical context of the migration, reception factors in the new society, or the migration process itself, ethnic groups are evaluated by how they fare in becoming American. Those who do not succeed socially or economically—the unmeltable ethnics—contribute towards the demise of the American "melting pot" as the dominant metaphor guiding our understanding of ethnic relations. Despite the plethora of alternative interpretations that have surfaced to explain the social significance of ethnicity and the persistence of racial and ethnic stratification in contemporary U.S. society, the melting pot metaphor has yet to be replaced.

One perspective of the persistence of racial and ethnic stratification maintains that ethnic bonds are promulgated as the natural extension of primordial ties. This view nurtures the idea that the disadvantaged, marginal position of certain ethnic and racial groups results from their cultural deficiencies which disappear as individuals assimilate into the dominant culture. At the opposite end of the spectrum, ethnic divisions are seen as mere reflections of class divisions. There exist several variants of the class interpretation of persisting ethnic differentiation, but the unifying theme is their focus on economic and social rather than cultural factors as determinants of ethnic inequality, and their emphasis on structural instead of individual explanatory factors.

The great diversity in the ethnic experience in the United States challenges both of these explanations and most that fall between them. Reducing ethnic stratification to a class phenomenon is reasonable only under the assumption that all members of an ethnic group are in the same class. Similarly, because ethnic identity and solidarity shift across groups and historical eras, it is equally inappropriate to deny the importance of social factors in molding ethnicity over time and place. By challenging widely held assumptions that high socioeconomic standing goes hand in hand with assimilation to the dominant culture, examples of ethnic groups who combine high levels of economic success with strong expressions of ethnic identity present a trouble spot for theories of race and class (Hirschman, 1982).

The complexities involved in interpreting ethnicity are aptly demonstrated by the case of the U.S. Hispanic population. While their presence in the United States predates the emergence of the American nation, their numerical strength and national visibility resulting from a high birth rate coupled with continuing inflows of new immigrants presents a challenge for students of ethnic stratification. "Hispanic" as a label combines colonized natives and their offspring, foreigner and political refugees under one ethnic umbrella, but the coherence of this label is questionable on theoretical and historical grounds. Unlike the European immigrants of the nineteenth and early twentieth centuries, the majority of Hispanics have not become structurally integrated into the broader society. And, in contrast to other white immigrants, use of Spanish has not disappeared among the second or third generations reared in the United States. Today Hispanic enclaves and the Spanish language thrive in diverse regions of the country, although there is evidence of linguistic acculturation among all Spanish-speaking national origin groups who have lived in the United States over a generation.

While common ancestral ties to Spain manifested in language, religion and various traditions suggest an underlying cultural commonality, the diverse incorporation experiences of Mexicans, Puerto Ricans and Cubans have contributed to significant social and economic differences that have remained intact over time. It is this persistence of socioeconomic differentiation among national origin groups that challenges the conception of "Hispanic" as a coherent ethnic category, and requires further specification of the underlying commonalities and divergences.

In an attempt to clarify the meaning of "Hispanicity" in contemporary U.S. society, this paper explores the roots of Hispanic ethnicity as it has emerged and evolved with the entry and social integration of each of the three major Hispanic national origin groups. It is a task that initially requires separating conceptually the structural elements of ethnicity from its cultural manifestations. In so doing, we emphasize historical comparisons between the Mexicans, Puerto Ricans, and Cuban origin populations, calling attention to the factors affecting their migration to this country and their incorporation into the labor market. Our ultimate goal is to critically evaluate the coherence of "Hispanicity" as an ethnic category as well as a social and political force in shaping the contemporary pattern of ethnic stratification.

To guide our interpretation of the historical circumstances that have shaped the integration of the Hispanic population into the U.S. society and economy, we first set forth the theoretical framework which outlines the processes underlying the emergence, consolidation and reformulation of Hispanic ethnicity. Following a brief historical vignette of the integration experience of the three major Hispanic origin populations, we summarize the contemporary socioeconomic position of each group through a descriptive analysis of selected social indicators derived from recent census data. These data are intended to illustrate empirically the extensive social and economic diversity among the national origin groups, and to highlight the direction of change among successive cohorts of Hispanic immigrants. We conclude with a reflection about the unifying and divisive elements inherent in the notion of "Hispanicity," and emphasize the distinction between symbolic identity and minority status.

ON THE SOCIAL CONSTRUCTION OF ETHNICITY: THEORETICAL CONSIDERATIONS

We choose to view ethnicity as a social construct rather than simply as a collection of ascriptive traits. While their importance as rallying points drawing people of similar cultural backgrounds together cannot be denied, the explanatory power of primordial ties for ethnic group solidarity conflicts with what is essentially a social phenomenon. This is demonstrated by the fact that ethnic group boundaries are not only defined by socially produced descent rules, but can be changed by group members themselves. One becomes an ethnic by virtue of leaving the homeland and by subsequent status vis-à-vis the dominant majority in the receiving society. Often it is only after immigration that a common sense of nationality emerges (Bonacich, 1980; Yancey et al., 1976).

Starting with the idea that ethnicity is a variable, William Yancey and his associates (1976) identified several factors that contribute to the emergence of ethnicity among immigrant groups, including: conditions affecting immigration; availability of wage labor; urban ecology; technology and the changing structure of industry. The impact that these structural variables have had on U.S. immigrants can explain their residential and occupational concentration better than the traditional notion of cultural disposition or preference to certain types of work. These two factors—residential and occupational concentration—are especially crucial to the formation of ethnic group solidarity in that they produce common class interests, lifestyles and friendships. When the ethnic experience includes rejection, discrimination and oppression, the elaboration of ethnic ties provides a ready system of support for groups distinguishable by race, national origin or language. As Yancey and his colleagues conclude, "Ethnicity may have relatively little to do with Europe, Asia or Africa, but much more to do with the requirements of survival and the structure of opportunity in this country" (Yancey *et al.*, 1976).

Yancey applied his notion of emergent ethnicity to European immigrants who settled in the eastern coastal cities. In order to distinguish between this early group of immigrants and later Hispanic waves, one must draw attention to the additional factors of timing of immigration, and modes of entry and integration of specific national origin groups. Like Yancey and his associates, we argue that these are more relevant to the understanding of Hispanic ethnicity than are the vestiges of Latin American or Spanish culture. Time of immigration is crucial because of temporal changes in employment opportunities and changing demand for various skills mixes. Europeans settled in large Eastern and Western cities during a period of industrial expansion. In contrast the Hispanic influx—at least the early Mexican immigration—began as a rural phenomenon (Tienda, 1981). As a predominantly urban population after the 1950s, Hispanics faced an economic system characterized by periods of restricted growth coupled with dramatic changes in the structure of production (Singelmann and Tienda, 1984). Race and racial discrimination must also be considered as a force shaping incorporation experiences even though a racial classification of Hispanics is complicated by the fact that they are brown, black and white. What is clear, however, is that predominantly white Europeans gave birth to the melting pot metaphor while the very different experience of Hispanics continues to destroy it. That most Hispanics have not assimilated and occupy the lower ranks of the stratification hierarchy brings into focus the issue of the convergence of ethnicity and low socio-economic position—an issue that needs to be explored in both theoretical and empirical terms.

Following the predictions of evolutionary theories of social change, Park (1950), an early prominent theorist on ethnic relations, maintained that the importance of ascriptive ties would eventually disappear under modern capitalism as industrial organizations recruited individuals based on universalistic criteria, such as skill and efficiency rather than ethnic origin. Using the same frame of reference—social changes resulting from the expansion of modern industrial capitalism—structural analysts and neo-Marxist theorists have reached diametrically opposed conclusions about the impact of capitalist expansion on race and ethnic relations. Bonacich (1972, 1980) and others (Portes and Bach, 1982) argued that ethnic stratification is the result of a split or segmented labor market that generates ethnic oppression from both capital and labor. By rooting ethnic segregation in labor competition that generates hostility from white workers while maintaining rates of profit for the employer, Bonacich provides a valuable insight into how ethnicity can override class consciousness. She also challenges the basic tenets of assimilationist ideology that faults individuals for their failures resulting from their lack of education, skills, and motivation and the persistence of culturally distinct values.

What both evolutionary and structural perspectives of ethnic inequality have left unexplained, however, is why certain ethnic groups are singled out for segregation in the least desirable low-skill, low-paying jobs, while others are not. A related and perhaps more central question for understanding the persistence of ethnic stratification is why some groups manage to experience mobility from low to high status jobs while others do not. Racism is an important element in this explanation, but it is a mistake to view the situation of European immigrants and racial minorities as polar opposites (Blauner, 1975). At the time of initial entry, European immigrants served many of the same functions that racial and ethnic minority workers currently do, and also were segregated residentially and occupationally by national origin. The key issue is why Europeans experienced social mobility from low status positions to the higher status, better-paying jobs while many blacks and Hispanics are seemingly unable to make this transition. These contrasting outcomes bring into focus a critical distinction between ethnic groups and minority groups. Although minority groups and ethnic groups are not coterminous, some ethnic groups become minorities. For example, Cubans are seldom identified as a minority group, but Mexicans and Puerto Ricans usually are. The reason, we maintain, has to do with their very different modes of incorporation and socioeconomic integration experiences.

Vincent (1974) has elaborated at some length the distinction between minorities and ethnics, and this is helpful for interpreting the Hispanic experience in the United States. A minority, according to Vincent, is a group whose members are subjected to unequal treatment through prejudice and discrimination by a dominant group. Ethnic groups, on the other hand, are a collectivity sharing common cultural norms, values, identities and behaviors, and who both recognize themselves, and are recognized by others as being ethnic. The extent to which ethnicity is a matter of individual choice depends on the group's access (or lack thereof) to the reward system of a dominant society. For the lower socioeconomic strata, choices to elaborate or conceal national origin are considerably more limited, if they exist at all. The convergence of ethnic origin and economic disadvantage requires an investigation of the circumstances that structures ethnicity into a disadvantaged minority position for some, and a symbolic identity for other (Gans, 1979). Such a pursuit might fruitfully uncover the areas of convergence and divergence among Hispanic origin groups, and help clarify the origins of the differential access to resources and social rewards that structure Hispanic ethnicity in different ways for Mexicans, Puerto Ricans, and Cubans.

THE EMERGENCE AND CONSOLIDATION OF "HISPANICITY"

Figure 1.1 maps the major historical and social processes describing the emergence, transformation and reformulation of ethnicity which we elaborate to interpret the diverse experiences of Hispanics. These processes are by nature interactive and the ways in which the social and historical dimensions intersect are central to understanding the relegation of Hispanics to a minority group status, or their eventual adoption of a more symbolic ethnicity, one less intertwined with economic and social standing.

The Hispanic population emerged as an ethnic group historically through international migration and conquest. The reasons for their entry to the United States, combined with the historical moment of that entry, determined both the composition of the ethnic population and its ultimate geographical configuration and socioeconomic position. Patterns of inter-ethnic contact, once established, were determined by occupational and residential segregation, and the changing climate of prejudice and xenophobic sentiment. Integration processes also changed in accordance with shifting economic conditions, the passing of generations, and legal prescriptions governing both immigration flows and labor practices.

Figure 1.1. STRUCTURING OF HISPANIC ETHNICITY: A CONCEPTUAL FRAMEWORK.

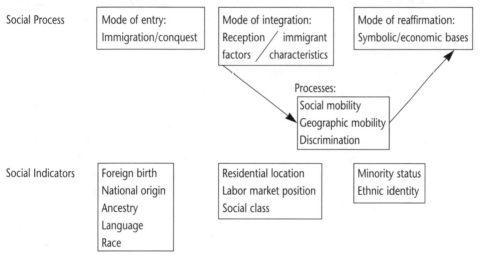

Once consolidated, ethnic groups can reformulate their position vis-à-vis the dominant society in response to any number of circumstances. Gordon (1964) has provided useful insights as to the diverse forms that any experience may assume, ranging from limited acculturation to structural and identificational assimilation. Which outcomes eventually emerge along this spectrum depends heavily on the preceding experiences of a group.

Hispanics having more "successful" integration experiences are more likely to maintain a symbolic connection to their ethnic heritage, as manifested by the continued observance of holidays, the revival of ethnic foods, the practice of cultural rituals, etc., while in the areas of occupation, education, language and residence they increasingly model Anglos. The elaboration of these ethnic traits acquires a symbolic character which constitutes the cultural pluralism dimension of the melting pot metaphor. Alternatively, for Hispanics who have not gained access to new opportunities, and for whom isolation within minority occupational and residential enclaves and systematic discrimination have remained the rule, their ethnicity has become coterminous with minority status. For ethnic minorities, the significance of ethnicity extends beyond the symbolic manifestation of cultural heritage. It also is more than a simple reflection of economic relationships. The survival of distinct ethnic cultures, while structurally determined, attests to the reflexive nature of ethnicity as it offers refuge to its adherents against the very system that produces stratification and oppression.

Theoretical constructs such as those abstractly presented thus far need to be translated into social experience with the stories of real people. It is to these that the focus now shifts. In discussing the very different experiences of Mexicans, Puerto Ricans and Cubans in the United States, the elements that translated Hispanic origin to a symbolic ethnicity for some and a minority status for others will become apparent.

MEXICANS

The structure of opportunity for Chicanos (encompassing both native- and foreign-born people of Mexican origin) is rooted in the history of the westward expansion, the geographical proximity and poverty of Mexico that facilitate continued immigration, and the historical labor functions of Mexican workers in the U.S. economy. Capitalist penetration of the Southwest dispossessed Chicanos of their land, created a cheap labor force and brought about the eventual destruction or transformation of the indigenous social systems governing the lives of the Mexican residents.

Immigration is the main vehicle by which the Mexican population grew and consolidated its regional and residential segregation in the Southwest; its significance cannot be understated. Most Mexican origin workers were channeled into the rural economy as a mobile, seasonal labor force subject to a colonial labor system whereby Mexican wages were paid for Mexican tasks in areas of agriculture, mining and railroad construction (Barrera, 1979; Alvarez, 1973; Tienda, 1981). Immigrant workers, however, were politically and socially vulnerable in that they could be deported. The history of Mexican immigration in the twentieth century is cyclical with the doors open in times of labor shortage, followed by massive deportations during periods of economic recession (Acuña, 1971; Samora, 1971; Barrera, 1979).

Immigrant vulnerability made them cheap workers and placed them in the position of a reserve labor force, exerting downward pressure on wages and undermining union organizing. The resulting hostility from Anglo workers combined with opposition from small farmers who were unable to compete with large enterprises employing cheap labor isolated Chicanos from class bases of support and further cut them off from potential avenues of integration into the social and economic mainstream. Racism was used by employers to pursue economic interests which resulted in a set of conditions that both structured the lives of Chicanos and gave racial and ethnic prejudice in the Southwest a life of its own. The continued entry of new immigrants maintains and renews this process.

The dimensions of immigration from Mexico to the United States in the twentieth century are so staggering that some have argued that the process has become self-sustaining via kinship ties and ethnic barrios which provide contacts and resources for incoming workers (Barrera, 1979; Tienda, 1980). This helps explain its "irrational" continuation despite stricter immigration policy and the shrinking job market of the 1970s and 1980s. The relationship between family networks and ongoing migration has several implications for Chicano ethnicity. Reliance of these workers on assistance from their families is a form of subsidy to employers in that their wages do not have to cover all of their maintenance costs (Burowoy, 1976; Tienda, 1980). Secondly, the influx of recent arrivals to the Mexican community reinforces and juxtaposes the values of Mexican culture against the corrosive forces of Anglo hegemony transmitted through the schools, mass media, industrial discipline, etc. (Saragoza, 1983).

Today, although the historical legacy remains, dramatic changes have occurred in the residence patterns and the structure of opportunity open to Chicanos. Mexicans as a group are principally an urban-based population, but one clear vestige of their rural origins is their disproportionate representation in agriculture—not as farmers, but as seasonal and permanent laborers. Unionization and legal sanctions against discriminatory practices have waged war on the colonial labor system while urban residence has provided access to a wider range of employment opportunities. Cultural manifestations of these changes include the trend toward a language shift away from Spanish (Gaarder, 1977; Arce, 1981), the declining isolation of the barrio (Moore, 1970) and indicators pointing to a greater degree of assimilation into Anglo society (Massey, 1981). Mario Barrera (1979) concedes that the segmentation line separating them from the majority culture across all classes has been weakening since World War II. This indicates that class divisions could become more salient than ethnicity as Chicanos become more integrated into the nonsubordinate part of the labor force, but the prospects of this occurring also depend on the process of immigration and the vitality of the economy.

PUERTO RICANS

The colonized position of Puerto Ricans on both the mainland and the island is more glaringly evident than that of Mexicans, but their labor experience is a similar one of ongoing deployment and circulation of both workers and capital across national borders (although fuzzy ones in the case of Puerto Rico). The island's Commonwealth status has obliterated economic boundaries and protective mechanisms that Third World nations are beginning to develop in order to defend local interests. United States hegemony on the island makes it difficult to define that society culturally or ethnically, for that which is Puerto Rican is partly North American as well. A dramatic illustration of this duality is the massive migration that has shifted one-third of the island's population to the U.S. mainland since World War II.

These intense demographic and economic changes are largely the result of a decision to transform and develop Puerto Rico's plantation economy through a program of rapid industrialization. The apparent success of the infamous Operation Bootstrap (in operation from 1948 to 1965) hinged on several key factors including unrestricted migration between the mainland and the island. Even with the help of the burgeoning Commonwealth bureaucracy (employing three out of ten workers by 1976), the new industrial order could not absorb the available workers, whose numbers rose steadily, owing to population growth and a severe decline in the plantation sector. The resulting movement of young urban dwellers toward blue-collar jobs in the northeastern cities of the United States gained momentum in the 1950s; migration flows from Puerto Rico to New York rose from an annual average of 18,700 in the 1940s to 41,200 between 1950 and 1960 (Centro de Estudios Puertoriqueños, 1979).

One would expect that the easy access of Puerto Ricans to the United States would, in comparison to other immigrants, carry over to their transition to mainland resident. In fact, the opposite occurred. Puerto Ricans were relegated to the lowest levels of the socioeconomic ladder, and often fared much worse economically than blacks who migrated to the North. Two features distinguish their mainland experience and strongly influence their class and ethnic identity. The first is a disproportionate representation in the secondary labor market. Three labor categories—clerical and sales, unskilled and semiskilled blue-collar workers and service workers—account for 70 percent of employed Puerto Rican men and 82 percent of employed women (Tienda, 1984). In addition, they are employed in industries with seasonal fluctuations and the declining manufacturing sector of the city. The suburbanization of industry, coupled with inadequate mass transit, has further restricted opportunities for those tied to their central city neighborhoods, a situation which seems to have worsened during the 1970s, as the flight of industry from the Frostbelt to the lower-wage Sunbelt progressed. Their marginal position in the labor market is reflected in other indicators of social well-being: of the three Hispanic groups considered, they have the lowest labor force participation rates, the highest unemployment levels, the highest incidence of poverty, and the lowest levels of education (Tienda, 1984).

The second feature in the ethnic structuring process for Puerto Ricans is the pattern of circular migration that emerged during the 1960s. In 1969-70 alone, 129,000 persons returned to Puerto Rico (Commission on Civil Rights, 1976); by 1972, 14 percent of the island's population consisted of return migrants (Lopez, 1974). The circular migration means that island population and mainland community are two parts of one whole, a situation which distinguishes Puerto Ricans from all former immigrants. It means that elements of both cultures thrive in both places, which requires a dual functional ability: children must be able to switch school systems, and must cope with competing value systems. It has resulted, as Frank Bonilla states, in "an unprecedented job of psychological and cultural reconstitution and construction that must rest on a very special political and economic infrastructure" (Bonilla, 1974:444).

The image of a single monolithic Puerto Rican community spanning the two locations is not entirely accurate, however. Members of the second generation raised in New York City have been dubbed "Nuyoricans," indicating their simultaneous separateness from Puerto Rico and their connection to it. Being caught between two value systems, especially with respect to race and ethnicity, is not only a feature of life on the mainland but also, given the U.S. hegemony over the island, plays an important role there as well, producing ideological divisions that transcend those of class hierarchy.

Thus Puerto Rican ethnicity can be interpreted as structurally determined by their colonial status, a pattern of migration that places Puerto Ricans between two worlds, and extreme occupational segregation, all of which contribute to their marginality vis-à-vis the rest of society. Their reaction is found in the maintenance of strong ethnic communities, low intermarriage rates (Fitzpatrick and Gurak, 1979) and the rejection of a quick transfer of cultural identity. Although in part a response to and protection against oppression, the persistence of ethnic distinctiveness, despite massive pressure towards homogeneous consumer culture, can also be interpreted as a form of protest. The settings for most Puerto Ricans—the schools, the streets, the military, the prisons and the sweatshops—are radicalizing contexts. That Puerto Rican ethnicity is reaffirmed here is "a sign of remarkable survival in the face of radical ambiguity" (Bonilla, 1974).

CUBANS

Three factors clearly distinguish the incorporation experience of Cubans from that of Mexicans and Puerto Ricans. They are primarily political refugees rather than economic migrants. Their reception in this country was not the tacit acceptance by employers hungry for cheap labor, but rather a public welcome by the Federal government eager to harbor the heroic victims of a communist dictatorship. And finally, among the exiles, those from professional, white-collar urban and more highly educated sectors were greatly over-represented, at least during the early phase of the exodus (Bach, 1980).

Until the Cuban refugees arrived, no other refugee group in this hemisphere had been so advantaged in terms of socioeconomic background and host country reception. In that sense the Cubans' "success" would not be surprising were it not for the serious obstacles they did face initially. Not the least of these were their widespread downward occupational mobility vis-à-vis the positions held in Cuba. Also, many believed that their stay in the United States would be temporary. A comparison of early occupational positions in the United States with the last occupations in Cuba showed that in Miami the percentage of unskilled laborers had doubled. Cubans who had been employed as professionals, managers and technicians dropped from 48 percent in Cuba to 13 percent in the United States (Casal and Hernandez, 1975).

In many ways, during the sixties Cubans found themselves in a situation similar to that of many other immigrants: residentially segregated; concentrated in blue-collar "ethnic" jobs; lacking English language skills; and tied to their ethnic communities. However, Cubans were never restricted to a position of second-class workers in an ethnically split labor market, nor was their success precedented by the assimilationist patterns of earlier European immigrants. In addition to the warm welcome and massive aid received under the auspices of the Cuban Refugee Program, two factors help explain their very different integration experience: these are class background and the emergence of an ethnic enclave economy in Miami.

Unlike Puerto Ricans and Mexicans, Cubans did not enter the United States as colonized or subordinate workers. They were fleeing the real and perceived persecution and harassment of a new regime. The same individualism that led upper- and middle-class Cubans to reject Castro provided both a cultural link to the socioeconomic orientation of the United States and the basis for effective competition. Therefore, the initial loss of occupational position was often compensated for by strong individualism and an orientation toward the future. Rogg and Cooney (1980) found that middle-class Cubans aggressively sought to learn English an new skills necessary for the socioeconomic rewards that would eventually signal their real integration. Furthermore, while occupational position in Cuba was unrelated to the first job acquired in this country, it was found to be a principal variable affecting subsequent upward mobility, along with education and age upon arrival. Clearly then, the current advantaged position of Cubans relative to other Hispanics is partly the result of the differential attitudes and resources derived from their class background.

The emergence of the Cuban enclave economy (also class related) is the other key factor in understanding the Cuban experience in the United States. Close to one-third of all businesses in Miami are Cuban-owned, while 75 percent of the workforce in construction is Cuban (Bach, 1980), and 40 percent of the industry is Cuban-owned. Twenty percent of the banks are controlled by Cubans (Wilson and Portes, 1980) who account for sixteen out of sixty-two bank presidents and 250 vice presidents. Other ethnic strongholds in the enclave economy include textiles, food, cigars and trade with Latin America.

In Miami, one can proceed from birth to death Cuban style (Bach, 1980). For the refugee with fewer marketable skills, the enclave not only provides a home, but also can shelter workers from the harsh realities of the open competitive market. Its success depends on low wages paid to Cuban workers, ethnic preference in hiring *and* the reciprocal obligation to help fellow ethnic members in their own financial ventures. The other crucial components are, of course, sufficient operating capital and entrepreneurial skills to initiate a successful enterprise, as well as an economic climate conducive to the flourishing of small-scale, private enterprises. The early Cuban exodus, with its upper-class bias and access to financial credit, was able to provide both elements. Later arrivals, however, became the working class for the "golden exiles" of the 1960s. As Bach concludes, "Thus there has been a total transplantation of the pre-revolutionary Cuban social structure to Miami, with all the implications of unequal wealth, power and prestige" (Bach, 1980:45).

REAFFIRMATION OF "HISPANICITY": ECONOMIC AND SYMBOLIC BASES

Our previous discussion not only emphasized the importance of economic factors in structuring the meaning of Hispanic origin as a coherent ethnic label, but also called attention to the distinction between symbolic ethnicity and minority status. In accordance with the predictions of evolutionary perspectives of ethnic integration, the cultural content of "Hispanicity" acquires a largely symbolic character as the different national origin groups move up the social hierarchy. While the continuing migration streams from Mexico and Puerto Rico will undoubtedly reinforce the cultural manifestations of the Hispanic presence in the United States for some time to come, the historical background of their integration experiences suggests that the ethnic fate of Cubans will differ notably from that of Mexicans and Puerto Ricans. This will occur not only because Cuban immigration is constrained by legal and political barriers, but also because their class background and differing reception factors provided them more favorable opportunities compared to Mexicans and Puerto Ricans. In contrast to Cubans, the substantially different incorporation experiences of Mexicans and Puerto Ricans resulted in the consolidation of their ethnicity with a disadvantaged economic position.

A recent snapshot of the three major Hispanic origin groups sharply illustrates the extent of socioeconomic diversity among the groups according to national origin and birthplace. Cubans have higher levels of formal schooling than either Mexicans or Puerto Ricans, but the differentials between the native- and foreign-born are themselves quite sharp. For Cubans, the educational differential according to nativity is just over one year, but for Mexicans and Puerto Ricans the difference is roughly three years.

A disaggregation of the educational composition of the foreign-born shows the more recent Cuban and Mexican immigrants to be of lower educational origins than their counterparts who arrived during the 1950s and 1960s. Nevertheless, for all cohort comparisons, Cuban immigrants exhibit notably higher educational levels than Mexican immigrants. The sharpest contrast occurred during the 1960-64 period, denoted the "golden exile" of Cuban emigration (Portes, 1969). During the seventies, the educational differentials between Mexican and Cuban immigrants have converged, stabilizing at about three years.

How these differences in educational attainment are economically significant is illustrated by the income and employment data. Despite the higher rates of labor force participation by Mexican origin men, particularly the foreign-born, average Mexican household

Table 1.1. SELECTED SOCIODEMOGRAPHIC CHARACTERISTICS OF THE HISPANIC CIVILIAN POPULATION AGE 16 AND OVER BY NATIONAL ORIGIN AND IMMIGRATION COHORT, 1980.

Selected Characteristics	Natives	Foreign-Born[a]	Before 1950	1950-59	1960-64	1965-69	1970-74	1975-80
			Mexicans					
Education[b]	10.0	6.9	6.0	8.0	7.5	7.2	6.8	6.6
Male LFPR[c]	77.6	82.3	46.8	84.9	85.5	86.8	88.9	86.2
Female LFPR[c]	51.6	43.2	22.1	46.8	49.0	48.7	48.0	42.6
Male unemployment rate	8.6	8.7	9.5	8.8	8.5	8.8	7.0	7.3
Female unemployment rate	8.7	12.6	8.9	10.1	13.2	12.8	13.6	13.7
Mean household income ('000)	19.0	16.8	15.0	19.7	18.2	17.6	16.7	15.5
Mean household size	4.2	4.6	3.3	4.5	4.9	5.0	5.1	4.8
% female headed household	13.2	9.2	12.2	9.7	9.7	9.6	8.3	8.1
% below poverty	17.8	24.0	21.2	17.0	20.7	21.6	23.1	31.3
% black	2.5	0.3	0.6	0.5	0.3	0.2	0.3	0.3
% speak English well	92.6	45.4	60.4	63.3	60.6	52.5	41.9	25.3
(N)	(177,149)	(93,422)	(11,438)	(11,253)	(9,916)	(12,856)	(21,724)	(26,235)

Table 1.1. Continued

SELECTED SOCIODEMOGRAPHIC CHARACTERISTICS OF THE HISPANIC CIVILIAN POPULATION AGE 16 AND OVER BY NATIONAL ORIGIN AND IMMIGRATION COHORT, 1980.

Selected Characteristics	Natives	Foreign- Born[a]	Before 1950	1950-59	1960-64	1965-69	1970-74	1975-80
					Immigration cohort			
			Puerto Ricans					
Education[b]	12.0	9.1						
Male LFPR[c]	64.6	72.7						
Female LFPR[c]	46.9	36.6						
Male unemployment rate	13.9	9.9						
Female unemployment rate	12.6	12.7						
Mean household income ('000)	16.6	14.2						
Mean household size	3.8	3.8						
% female headed household	24.3	23.4						
% below poverty	25.5	31.2						
% black	4.9	2.7						
% speak English well	96.1	69.5						
(N)	(19,078)	(43,677)						

Table 1.1. Continued

Selected Characteristics	Natives	Foreign-Born[a]	Immigration cohort					
			Before 1950	1950-59	1960-64	1965-69	1970-74	1975-80
			Cubans					
Education[b]	12.2	10.9	10.5	11.3	12.4	10.2	9.5	9.8
Male LFPR[c]	67.4	79.3	57.4	87.0	85.9	77.5	76.0	62.9
Female LFPR[c]	55.7	55.1	37.3	57.4	59.6	55.0	55.3	36.5
Male unemployment rate	7.8	4.5	4.2	3.9	3.4	4.5	4.5	13.8
Female unemployment rate	5.9	7.1	3.3	6.0	4.8	7.8	8.0	21.2
Mean household income ('000)	21.8	21.6	19.6	22.5	25.3	20.6	19.7	14.3
Mean household size	3.4	3.5	2.8	3.3	3.4	3.6	3.6	3.8
% female headed household	14.1	9.7	10.1	8.2	8.4	11.2	9.8	9.6
% below poverty	11.4	12.4	12.4	8.6	8.6	12.1	13.8	37.0
% black	10.6	1.9	4.5	3.1	1.0	1.5	2.3	2.9
% speak English well	94.3	58.0	79.0	1.6	72.4	52.2	43.5	29.3
(N)	(3,503)	(29,888)	(938)	(2,875)	(8,975)	(9,768)	(5,699)	(1,639)

Source: 1980 Census of Population, 5% PUMS, Sample A.

a   Puerto Ricans born on the island are considered native-born citizens, therefore the immigration cohort data are unavailable for them. For purposes of these comparisons, Puerto Ricans born on the U.S. mainland are classified as native-born and all others are foreign-born.

b   Refers to all individuals 25 years and over. Other characteristics are for all civilians 16 years and over.

c   Labor force participation rate.

income lags far behind that of Cuban households. While there was a negligible household income differential between units headed by native and immigrant Cubans, 1980 household income disparities between native and foreign Mexican and Puerto Rican adults were substantial. Puerto Ricans had the lowest household income levels, averaging between $16,600 and $14,200, respectively, for the U.S. mainland- and island-born heads. The highest rates of poverty, female headship and unemployment also correspond to Puerto Ricans, with the island-born population faring notably worse than the mainland-born population. In a socioeconomic profile Cubans emerge as the most advantaged, Puerto Ricans most disadvantaged, with Mexicans falling in between.

The only indicator of acculturation available in the 1980 Census is a measure of English proficiency. Although not a particularly precise measure of acculturation, when evaluated against indicators of socioeconomic status, this variable is nonetheless quite revealing. Puerto Ricans combine the highest levels of English proficiency with the lowest levels of socioeconomic achievement. Cuban immigrants, in contrast, are the least linguistically proficient, yet they are more successful in the labor market than either of the two "older" immigrant groups. A comparison of the changes in English proficiency between Mexican and Cuban immigrant cohorts suggests that the Cuban linguistic assimilation process may be more rapid, but it also may be tied to the educational background of the groups entering at different periods, as well as to their locational and associational patterns after their arrival to the United States.

That the mode of entry and integration of the Hispanic population has been of major consequence for the contemporary social and economic standing of the three major national origin groups is undeniable. As the data in Table 1.2 show, the advantaged class population of Cubans vis-à-vis Mexicans and Puerto Ricans has remained intact to the present time. The foreign-born Cuban population has consolidated its white-collar position while the foreign-born Mexican and Puerto Ricans continue to dominate in blue-collar jobs. Note that while recent Cuban immigrants—those who arrived during the 1970s—were largely blue-collar workers, members of this cohort were almost three times more likely to hold white-collar jobs in 1980 than Mexican immigrants who arrived at the same time. Thus, the significance of the differing class composition of Cuban compared to Mexican and Puerto Rican immigrants is that it is reproduced among the native-born generations. Although the data in Table 1.2 show that the disproportionate representation of native-born Mexicans and Puerto Ricans in blue-collar occupations had diminished relative to the foreign born generations, this may be more a reflection of the changing structure of industry than of a major improvement in their relative standing in the occupational structure (see Snipp and Tienda, 1982, 1984).

The higher representation of Cubans in managerial and professional jobs coincides also with their participation in an enclave economy consisting of Cuban owned and operated enterprises. As indicated in the historical discussion and affirmed by the data in Table 1.3, the emergence of the enclave is a direct consequence of the class composition of the early Cuban exiles. Two features of the data in Table 1.3 are noteworthy. First, the proportion of self-employed workers is substantially higher among the foreign-born Cubans as compared to Mexicans and Puerto Ricans who, for reasons elaborated above, were unable to reinforce their residential concentration in ethnic *barrios* with a viable economic base. The differential self-employment rate between native- and foreign-born Cubans arises largely because of the disproportionately higher share of self-employed workers among those who arrived

Table 1.2. DISTRIBUTION OF THE HISPANIC CIVILIAN LABOR FORCE BY WHITE AND BLUE COLLAR OCCUPATIONS, NATIONAL ORIGIN AND IMMIGRATION COHORT, 1980.

Immigration Cohort	Mexicans Blue collar	White collar	Puerto Ricans[a] Blue collar	White collar	Cubans Blue collar	White collar
Native-born	70.9	29.1	63.4	36.6	55.2	44.8
Foreign-born	87.4	12.6	79.4	20.6	62.7	37.3
before 1950	88.7	11.3			39.6	60.4
1950-59	78.8	21.2			39.6	60.4
1960-64	81.3	18.7			48.2	51.8
1965-69	85.7	14.3			67.6	32.4
1970-74	89.8	10.2			72.5	27.5
1975-80	91.8	8.2			78.0	22.0
Total	76.6	23.4	74.6	25.4	61.9	38.1
(N)	(207,259)	(63,312)	(46,785)	(15,970)	(20,676)	(12,715)

Source: 1980 Census Population, 5% PUMS, Sample A.

a Puerto Ricans born on the island are considered native-born citizens, therefore the immigration cohort data are unavailable for them. For purposes of these comparisons, Puerto Ricans born on the U.S. mainland are classified as native-born and all others are foreign-born.

prior to 1965. Subsequent cohorts continued to be more highly represented among the self-employed in 1980 than Mexicans who arrived during comparable periods, but the differentials were subsequently reduced.

A second noteworthy feature is that the prevalence of self-employed among the native-born was quite similar among Cubans and Mexicans, but not Puerto Ricans. This finding calls into question the long-term viability of the Cuban enclave sector, and supports claims about the deteriorating economic status of Puerto Ricans. It is conceivable that the relative under-representation of native-born Cubans among the self-employed simply reflects the lack of sufficient time to witness the inter-generational transfer of Cuban owned and operated enterprises from the immigrant generation to the second generation. However, it is also possible that the native-born generation may achieve its structural integration through employment in the private and public sector, especially if the existence of the enclave sector serves as a stepping-stone for more lucrative employment opportunities. It is too early to predict the fate of the Cuban economic enclave, but it viability may also hinge on the extent of cultural assimilation among the native-born, and its visibility as an ethnic enterprise may depend on the extent to which Cubans chose to elaborate the symbolic bases of their Hispanic ancestry.

Not only has the advantaged class position of Cubans vis-à-vis Mexicans and Puerto Ricans remained intact to the present time, but as a consequence of their greater socioeconomic success and middle-class orientations, the Cuban population may have experienced more extensive cultural assimilation than either Mexicans and Puerto Ricans, despite the fact that they have resided in the United States for a shorter period of time. Census data are not particularly suited to addressing questions about cultural reaffirmation and ethnic identity, but the data presented in Tables 1.4 and 1.5, albeit more suggestive than conclusive, provide some insights.

Consistent with the evolutionary perspective of ethnic assimilation, the pattern of Spanish language maintenance among Hispanics is lower among the native-born generations than among the foreign-born. What is striking, however, is that the retention of Spanish among U.S.-born Cubans—who, unlike Mexicans and Puerto Ricans, are essentially a second generation —is considerably lower than among Mexicans and Puerto Ricans. That the use of Spanish in the home should be lower among Puerto Ricans who were born on the island compared to foreign-born Mexicans is not surprising, because English is taught regularly in the island schools. However, the more rapid linguistic assimilation among Cubans is striking for it suggests that the socio-economic success of this group is creating class orientations that outweigh ethnic ones. Apparently the native-born generation is choosing *not* to elaborate the symbolic bases of its Hispanic ancestry.

Because of the predominance of immigrants among the Cuban population, it is not surprising that there is little variation in the extent of Spanish language use among those employed in various occupational categories. Nevertheless, Cubans employed as professionals and semi-professionals are less likely to use Spanish in the home than those employed in lower white-collar or blue-collar jobs. Although Mexicans and Puerto Ricans have lower rates of Spanish language retention overall than do Cubans, the aggregate statistic largely captures the higher prevalence of native-born individuals in the population. However, despite the higher rates of Spanish language retention among native-born Mexicans and Puerto Ricans, the corrosive forces of the Anglo environment are manifested in the lower levels of Spanish retention among the more successful members of the community—those whose incomes are well above the poverty levels, and who hold white-collar jobs.

Table 1.3. CLASS OF WORKER DISTRIBUTION OF THE HISPANIC CIVILIAN LABOR FORCE BY NATIONAL ORIGIN AND IMMIGRATION COHORT.

	Mexicans				Puerto Ricans[a]				Cubans			
	Wage private sector	Wage public sector	Self-employed	Unpaid workers	Wage private sector	Wage public sector	Self-employed	Unpaid workers	Wage private sector	Wage public sector	Self-employed	Unpaid workers
Native born	59.3	14.5	3.1	23.1	54.1	13.6	1.4	30.9	60.7	11.5	4.1	23.8
Foreign-born	65.2	5.2	2.7	26.8	50.3	10.4	2.0	37.2	61.6	7.1	6.8	24.5
1975-80	70.1	3.0	1.4	25.4					46.3	6.1	3.4	44.3
1970-74	73.4	3.8	2.0	20.8					62.0	5.2	5.3	27.5
1965-69	70.2	5.6	2.9	21.3					63.2	6.0	5.4	25.4
1960-64	67.2	7.6	3.3	21.8					64.1	9.4	8.6	17.9
1950-59	62.2	9.3	4.5	24.0					62.0	8.2	10.1	19.6
Before 1950	34.1	6.5	4.4	55.0					42.6	7.0	8.4	41.9
(N)	(166,003)	(30,566)	(8,050)	(65,952)	(32,305)	(7,147)	(1,160)	(22,143)	(20,527)	(2,523)	(2,173)	(8,160)

Source: 1980 Census of Population, 5% PUMS, Sample A.

a   Puerto Ricans born on the island are considered native-born citizens, therefore the immigration cohort data are unavailable for them. For purposes of these comparisons, Puerto Ricans born on the U.S. mainland are classified as native-born and all others are foreign-born.

Another indicator of the coherence of "Hispanicity" among the Mexican, Puerto Rican and Cuban origin populations is found in the extent to which they identify consistently as members of an ancestry group. For the tabulations reported in Table 1.5 we computed the proportion of individuals whose response to the ancestry question matched their response to the full-enumeration Spanish origin item. In other words, of the individuals who self-identified themselves as being of Spanish origin (specified by nationality), the figures reported indicate the proportions who also reported that their ancestry was either Mexican, Puerto Rican or Cuban. Although this measure is crude, it serves to illustrate the diversity in the extent of uniform ethnic identification among the groups.

Overall, the data indicate greater ethnic consistency among the two most disadvantaged groups, the Mexicans and Puerto Ricans, while the Cubans exhibit greater diversity in the extent to which they identify as ethnics. For Mexicans and Puerto Ricans, the use of Spanish in the home is the major factor differentiating those who are consistent in reporting their Hispanic ancestry, although poverty status and immigration status also contributes to the diversity in their Hispanic identity. Cubans present a different picture. Not only are the native-born notably less likely than their foreign-born counterparts to report an ancestry consistent with their self-reported Spanish origin, but they are also substantially less likely than individuals of either Mexican or Puerto Rican origin to identify consistently as Cubans. In part, this may reflect the homogenizing assimilation processes that often accompany rapid socioeconomic success, but it is noteworthy that this pattern has not been replicated by the native-born Mexicans or Puerto Ricans.

In the case of Hispanics, the overriding explanation for the pronounced differences in the cultural manifestations of ethnicity can only be class-based, or in Vincent's (1974) terms, grounded in the coincidence of ethnic origin with minority status. And, while the option of elaborating the symbolic bases of Cuban origin are certainly more open to the Cuban population by virtue of its relatively more advantaged position vis-à-vis Mexicans and Puerto Ricans, members of the native-born generation apparently are not choosing to elaborate their Hispanic ethnicity along cultural lines or nationality. Mexicans and Puerto Ricans, on the other hand, persist in their greater adherence to the cultural and nationality expressions of their ethnicity. In their experience, however, it is not only symbolism that maintains the cultural expressions intact, but also their disadvantaged minority position and the continued revitalization of ethnic symbols through the process of labor migration.

CONCLUSION

Mexicans, Puerto Ricans and Cubans each hold a distinct place within the range of experiences shaping their economic and cultural integration into American society. The Puerto Rican case provides the strongest support for the link between intense ethnic identity and lower class positioning. That Cubans have not remained segregated in a secondary labor market, have been the most successful of the three groups, and are demonstrating tendencies towards integration with Anglos lends positive support from the other direction. Their distinct status at entry and class resources are the most significant factors distinguishing Cuban refugees from Mexican and Puerto Rican immigrants. That the Mexican-American experience is more ambiguous and diverse can be explained by their numerical size and their longer history in the United States.

The indicators pointing to increasing assimilation of Chicanos must be weighed against the isolation, extreme poverty and lack of control over life as it exists in the *barrios*. In con-

Table 1.4. PERCENTAGE OF THE HISPANIC CIVILIAN LABOR FORCE WHO REPORTED SPEAKING
SPANISH AT HOME IN 1980 BY SELECTED SOCIODEMOGRAPHIC CHARACTERISTICS
AND NATIONAL ORIGIN.

Characteristic	Mexicans	Puerto Ricans[a]	Cubans
Immigration cohort			
Native-born	72.6	73.0	61.5
Foreign-born	96.8	94.8	96.8
1975-80	98.1		96.7
1970-74	98.0		98.4
1965-69	97.6		98.1
1960-64	96.2		96.4
1950-59	95.0		94.2
Before 1950	93.2		84.4
Occupation			
Professional	74.8	81.4	88.2
Semiprofessional	71.8	82.3	89.6
Farmer	81.3	83.8	81.5
Manager	75.9	81.8	91.0
Clerical	73.4	85.5	93.1
Sales	72.2	79.3	91.5
Craft	80.9	86.3	93.7
Operative	84.7	91.5	95.8
Service worker	79.7	85.3	91.8
Laborer	82.0	86.0	92.6
Farm laborer	93.8	87.2	94.6
Poverty status			
Non-poor	78.5	85.0	93.0
Near poor	86.4	91.5	94.1
Poor	84.9	92.6	92.6
Overall percentage	80.9	88.2	93.1
(N)	(270,571)	(62,755)	(33,391)

Source: 1980 Census of Population, 5% PUMS, Sample A.

a   Puerto Ricans born on the island are considered native-born citizens, therefore the immigration cohort
data are unavailable for them. For purposes of these comparisons, Puerto Ricans born on the U.S.
mainland are classified as native-born and all others are foreign-born.

trast to Barrera's claim to class integration, can the small rising Chicano middle class play the role of native elite within a formerly colonized group? (Almaguer, 1974). How is one to interpret the ongoing ethnic contact as it exists between classes (as Chicano businesses, for example, rely on Chicano clientele) or as it is affected by immigration? For Chicanos it is difficult to envision a future when ethnic distinctions within social class divisions will fade away. The cloudiness of what Barrera has labeled "the current period of confusion and redefinition" is maintained by the continuing influx of new immigrants during a period of economic instability as well as imprecise data to evaluate truly longitudinal comparisons of successive immigrant cohorts and generational transitions.

For Mexicans and Puerto Ricans, isolation in ethnic communities and other manifestations of ethnicity are structurally produced by their concentrations in minority labor markets and by the continued influx of immigrants who help to renew cultural traditions and subsequently elaborate them as a basis for social solidarity. In turn ethnically based solidarity serves as a protection and source of resistance against oppression. For Cubans, the cohesiveness of their ethnic community has been a key factor facilitating initial adjustment and success. Whether that success will ensure the survival of the ethnically enclosed community or lead to its decline remains to be seen. Initial evidence based on the most recent census suggests a decline as the first generation of native-born Cubans demonstrate an unusual ability to assimilate.

Our conceptual framework implies that ethnicity is structured by the relationship of a given national origin group to the system of production. Immigration history, reception factors in the United States and race shape this relationship over time. The elaboration of ethnicity as historically emergent further points to the intersecting nature of class and ethnicity as demonstrated by the diverse outcomes of the three Hispanic national origin groups. The labor market experience of Hispanics has been chosen as a key factor in the structuring of ethnicity because it strongly influences subsequent exposure to and interactions with other races, social classes and cultural forces.

On balance, the market experience of Hispanics has been chosen as a key factor in the structuring of ethnicity because it strongly influences subsequent exposure to and interactions with other races, social classes and cultural forces. Yet obviously, ethnicity is not simply a function of occupational and economic rewards. Ethnic identity as manifested by language, religion, race and national origin is only one part of a much broader, multidimensional social identity (Arce, 1981). For this reason, the process of integration cannot be unidirectional, proceeding from an unassimilated beginning to an assimilated end, from marginality to middle class. The complexities of the interaction between social and ethnic identities are beyond the scope of this paper which only provides a starting point for further exploration—an exploration urgently needed if a clearer conception of Hispanic ethnicity is to emerge from the distortions of the past.

NOTE

This research was supported by a grant from the Social Science Research Council and Russell Sage Foundation and by funds from the Graduate School Research Committee of the University of Wisconsin-Madison. Computational support is from a grant to the Center for Demography and Ecology from the Center for Population of NICHD (HD-05876). We acknowledge institutional support from the College of Agricultural and Life Sciences of the University of Wisconsin, and computational assistance from Ding-Tzann Lil.

Table 1.5. PROPORTION OF HISPANIC CIVILIAN LABOR FORCE WHO REPORTED CONSISTENT ANCESTRY AND ORIGIN RESPONSES IN 1980 BY SELECTED SOCIODEMOGRAPHIC CHARACTERISTICS AND NATIONAL ORIGIN.

Selected Characteristics	Mexicans		Puerto Ricans[a]		Cubans	
	Native	Foreign	Native	Foreign	Native	Foreign
Occupation						
Professional	.87	.90	.81	.88	.70	.91
Semiprofessional	.88	.89	.78	.90	.76	.91
Farmer	.77	.91	.44	.86	.40	.86
Manager	.87	.91	.84	.88	.69	.90
Clerical	.88	.91	.84	.89	.74	.92
Sales	.86	.92	.78	.85	.74	.90
Craft	.87	.94	.80	.89	.68	.91
Operative	.86	.94	.81	.88	.69	.92
Service worker	.84	.93	.78	.87	.70	.90
Laborer	.86	.94	.80	.87	.78	.90
Farm laborer	.85	.93	.69	.88	.36	.76
Spanish spoken[b]						
No	.68	.68	.63	.70	.51	.69
Yes	.92	.94	.88	.89	.85	.91
Poverty Status						
Non-poor	.81	.93	.80	.88	.73	.91
Near poor	.85	.94	.83	.89	.72	.91
Poor	.81	.93	.81	.88	.60	.90
Overall proportion	.86	.93	.81	.88	.72	.91
(N)	(177,149)	(93,422)	(19,078)	(43,677)	(3,503)	(29,888)

Source: 1980 Census Population, 5% PUMS, Sample A.

a   Puerto Ricans born on the island are considered native-born citizens, therefore the immigration cohort data are unavailable for them. For purposes of these comparisons, Puerto Ricans born on the U.S. mainland are classified as native-born and all others are foreign-born.

b   Spanish spoken at home.

REFERENCES

Acuña, Rudolfo. 1971. *Occupied America: The Chicano Struggle Toward Liberation.* San Francisco: Canfield Press.

Almaguer, Tomas. 1974. "Historical Notes on Chicano Oppression: The Dialectics of Race and Class Domination in North America." *Aztlán* 5 (1): 27–56.

Alvarez, Rodolfo. 1973. "The Psycho-Historical and Socioeconomic Development of the Chicano Community in the United States." *Social Science Quarterly* 53 (4): 902-944.

Arce, Carlos. 1981. "A Reconsideration of Chicano Culture and Identity." *Daedalus* 110 (Spring): 177-92.

Bach, Robert. 1980. "The New Cuban Immigrants: Their Background and Prospects." *Monthly Labor Review* 103 (October): 39-46.

Barrera, Mario. 1979. *Race and Class in the Southwest.* Notre Dame, Ind.: University of Notre Dame Press.

Blauner, Robert. 1975. "Colonized and Immigrant Minorities," in *Majority and Minority*, ed. Norman Yetman and C.H. Steele. Boston: Allyn & Bacon.

Bonacich, Edna. 1972. "A Theory of Ethnic Antagonism: The Split Labor Market." *American Sociological Review* 37 (October): 547-59.

_____. 1980. "Class Approaches to Ethnicity and Race." *The Insurgent Sociologist* 10 (1): 9-23.

Bonilla, Frank. 1974. "Por qué seguiremos siendo Puertorriqueños" in *Puerto Rico and Puerto Ricans*, eds. Alberto Lopez and James Petras. Cambridge, Mass.: Schenkman Publishing Co.

Burowoy, Michael. 1976. "The Functions and Reproduction of Migrant Labor: Comparative Material from Southern Africa and the United States." *American Journal of Sociology* 81 (5): 1050-87.

Casal, Lourdes, and Hernandez, Andres. 1975. "Cubans in the U.S.: A Survey of the Literature." *Cuban Studies* 5 (2): 25-51.

Centro de Estudios Puertorriqueños. 1979. *Labor Migration Under Capitalism.* New York: Monthly Review Press.

Fitzpatrick, Joseph P., and Gurak, Douglas M. 1979. *Hispanic Intermarriage in New York.* New York: Hispanic Research Center Monograph, Fordham University.

Gaarder, Bruce. 1977. *Bilingual Schooling and the Survival of Spanish in the United States.* Ralig, MA: Newbury House.

Gans, Herbert J. 1979. "Symbolic Ethnicity: The Future of Ethnic Groups and Cultures in America." *Ethnic and Racial Studies* 2 (1): 1-19.

Gordon, Milton. 1964. *Assimilation in American Life: The Role of Race, Religion and National Origins.* New York: Oxford University Press.

Hirschman, Charles. 1982. "America's Melting Pot Reconsidered." *American Review of Sociology* 9: 397-423.

Lopez, Alberto. 1974. "The Puerto Rican Diaspora," in *Puerto Rico and Puerto Ricans*, eds. Alberto Lopez and James Petras. Cambridge, Mass.: Schenkman Publishing Co.

Massey, Douglas. 1981. "Dimensions of the New Immigration to the U.S. and the Prospects for Assimilation." *Annual Review of Sociology* 7: 57-83.

Moore, Joan. 1970. "Colonialism: The Case of the Mexican Americans." *Social Problems* 17 (4): 463-72.

Park, R.E. 1950. *Race and Culture*. Glencoe, Ill.: Free Press.

Portes, Alejandro. 1969. "Dilemmas of a Golden Exile: Integration of Refugee Families in Milwaukee." *American Sociological Review* 34 (4): 505-19.

_____ and Bach, Robert L. 1980. "Immigrant Earnings: Cuban and Mexican Immigrants in the U.S." *International Migration Review* 14 (3): 315-37.

Rogg, Eleanor, and Cooney, Rosemary. 1980. *Adaptation and Adjustment of Cubans: West New York, N.J.* New York: Hispanic Research Center Monograph, Fordham University.

Samora, Julian. 1971. *Los Mojados: The Wetback Story*. Notre Dame, Ind.: University of Notre Dame Press.

Saragoza, Alex. 1983. "The Conceptualization of the History of the Chicano Family," in Albert Camarillo Valdez and Tomas Almaguer (eds.), *The State of Chicano Research in Family, Labor and Migration Studies*. Stanford, Calif. a Stanford Center for Chicano Research.

Singelmann, Joachim, and Tienda, Marta. 1984. "The Process of Occupational Change in a Service Economy: The Case of the United States, 1960-1980," in Ruth Finnegan, Duncan Gallie, and Bryan Roberts (eds.), *Labour Markets*. Manchester, England: University of Manchester Press.

Snipp, C. Matthew, and Tienda, Marta. 1982. "New Perspective on Chicano Intergenerational Mobility." *Social Science Journal* 19 (2): 37-49.

Tienda, Marta. 1980. "Familism and Structural Assimilation of Mexican Immigrants in the United States." *International Migration Review* 14 (3): 383-408.

_____. 1981. "The Mexican American Population," pp. 502-48 in Amos Hawly and Sara Mills Mazie (eds.), *Nonmetropolitan America in Transition*. Chapel Hill: University of North Carolina Press.

_____. 1984. "The Puerto Rican Worker: Current Labor Market Status and Future Prospects," in *Puerto Ricans in the Mid-Eighties: An American Challenge*. Washington, D.C.: National Puerto Rican Coalition.

U.S. Commission on Civil Rights. 1976. *Puerto Ricans in the Continental United States: An Uncertain Future*. Washington, D.C.: U.S. Government Printing Office.

Vincent, Joan. 1974. "The Structuring of Ethnicity." *Human Organization* 33 (4): 375-79.

Wilson, Kenneth, and Portes, Alejandro. 1980. "Immigrant Enclaves: An Analysis of the Labor Market Experiences of Cubans in Miami." *American Journal of Sociology*, 86: 2.

Yancey, William, Erikson, Eugene, and Juliani, Richard. 1976. "Emergent Ethnicity: A Review and Reformulation." *American Sociological Review* 41 (3): 391-403.

2

"SO FAR FROM GOD, SO CLOSE TO THE UNITED STATES": THE ROOTS OF HISPANIC HOMOGENIZATION

Suzanne Oboler

GIVEN THE DIVERSITY OF THE VARIOUS POPULATION GROUPS both in Latin America and in the United States, how *did* the culturally homogeneous representations of people identified as Hispanics become commonplace among scholars, government agencies, the media, and the public at large in this country? Popular reasoning about the origin of the term Hispanic usually locates it within the legacy of the Spanish conquest and colonization of the New World.[1] After all, the justification goes, Spanish colonial rule lasted for over three centuries, certainly long enough for the social, ethnic, linguistic, racial, and national experiences of the populations of Latin America and the Caribbean to establish a homogeneous heritage.

But in Latin America itself, the role of the Spanish legacy in shaping a common cultural identity on the continent has been the subject of ongoing debates since that region's independence in the early nineteenth century. Underlying these discussions is the recognition that in spite of the shared Spanish colonial heritage, there are profound differences in the various nations' postindependence histories and populations that often override cultural or linguistic commonalities they may also share. In many ways, then, the issue of the creation of a unified cultural—and even political and economic—"Hispanic identity" in the United States actually transports to this country a debate that Latin American intellectuals have themselves waged since the nineteenth century in historical essays, social science texts, and their respective national literatures.[2]

Thus I suggest that the definition and uses of the term Hispanic in the United States cannot be sought in its Spanish colonial heritage or even in Latin American antecedent debates. Instead, its meanings and social value must be found through exploring the specific context of U.S. society that fostered the emergence of this ethnic label as an ideological construct—a label that is thus specific to the political and daily life of this nation, to its past ideological self-image and identity as a "melting pot" of immigrants, and to its current redefinitions as an "ethnic mosaic."[3]

I begin with a brief overview of the racial and social dynamics developed during Spain's rule in the Americas, to explore the ways these shaped the social and racial hierarchies of colonial society, such that they continued to differentiate the image, status, and relations of various ethnic, social, and racial groups in post-independenced Latin America. Although a historical account is certainly not the aim of this chapter, it is important to note some of the ways that the significance of these differentiations was manifested in relation to the United States at different points during the nineteenth century—how varied social sectors within the Mexican and Puerto Rican populations, shaped in the context of the Spanish colonial heritage, responded to the expansionism of the United States in Mexico and the Caribbean, respectively. As I suggest in this chapter, internal social and racial group differentiations notwithstanding, people of Latin American descent in the United States have long been perceived homogeneously as "foreign" to the image of "being American" since the nineteenth century, regardless of the time and mode of their incorporation into the United States or their subsequent status as citizens of this nation.

Indeed, insofar as the understanding of the U.S. national identity is invariably defined and shaped in relation to those conceived as 'foreign Others" in the hemisphere, it is perhaps not surprising that in a period in which an increasing number of new nations were being established in the Americas, the contacts between this country and the newly formed Latin American national populations contributed toward creating representations in the United States of a unified image of the "American national community." Thus, I argue that the nation's identity was forged in the nineteenth century *partially* through the creation of racialized perceptions that homogenized Latin America's populations and that in turn set the context for the later emergence of the label Hispanic in the twentieth century. Based on the development of ideologies that justified the expansionist actions of the United States in Latin America and the Caribbean, these perceptions reflected a peculiar fusion of the social status, race, and nationality of "foreign Others" in the hemisphere.

Domestically, and particularly in the years following the Civil War, imagined boundaries of inclusion and exclusion in the national community were also being institutionalized through legalizing segregationist practices and customs in relation to previously enslaved African Americans. Thus, the community of *Americans* came to be imagined as white, Protestant, and Anglo-Saxon, despite the presence not only of non-Anglo-Saxon and Catholic Europeans, but also of native Americans and African Americans, as well as Asians, Caribbean, and Latin Americans of varying classes, races, and national origins.

The nineteenth-century fusion of the race and nationality of "foreign Others" both at home and in the hemisphere as a whole thus came to justify the systematic exclusion of nonwhite, non-Anglo-Saxon minorities from "being American." By the twentieth century, this was to ensure that regardless of citizenship status, non-white-European racial minorities born in the United States could continue to be conceived in the popular mind as outside of the "boundaries" of the "American" community.[4] It is important to reiterate that what follows is not intended to be a history of the period and that I am wary of oversimplification in intergroup relations, which perhaps inevitably arises from trying to synthesize complex ideas about the past. I am fully aware, for example, that the following discussion omits both the complex diversity within the "white European" population and an account of the multiple links and nuances that have always existed in individual relationships between white Europeans and minority groups in the United States. Similarly, I have omitted discussion on the complex relations between Mexicans and the various indigenous populations in the region. I want to emphasize, however, that my aim here is in no way to provide a history of the period or of the various groups' interrelations but rather to suggest some of the nineteenth-century issues that I believe should be considered in seeking to understand both the grounds for the mobilizations of the Chicanos/Mexican Americans and Puerto Ricans during the civil rights period and the emergence of and response(s) to the label Hispanic. More specifically, I want to show that the early fusion of race and nationality was to provide important grounds for defining the particular forms of mobilization that non-white-European minorities adopted in their struggles to achieve political and cultural inclusion during the 1960s.

THE LEGACY OF SPAIN IN LATIN AMERICA

There is no doubt that the newly formed Latin American republics of the early nineteenth century inherited a highly stratified social order from three hundred years of Spanish colonial rule.[5] The conquistadors who went to the New World were not the hidalgos or Spanish lords who, as unquestioned rulers of their feudal estates, owned large tracts of land and oversaw the labor and lives of serfs who in turn were born and died in servitude on their estates. But neither were they members of the poorest sectors in the Spanish society of their day. Rather like the law-school dropout Hernán Cortés (conqueror of Mexico) or Francisco Pizarro (conqueror of Peru), the son of a pig-herder, they were members of a small emerging middle sector of peasants and artisans who basically had very little, if anything, to lose and much to gain from leaving Spain to go to the New World.[6]

Once in the New World, the Crown provided them with both temporary land grants and indigenous laborers in recognition of their honor and bravery in their conquest and settlement of far-off lands. As Carlos Fuentes has noted, it is perhaps not surprising then that the Spaniards who settled in Latin America sought the privileges and status of the hidalgos and recreated the semifeudal hierarchical arrangements of the society they had left behind. But it is important to note that "*hidalguia* does not mean hard work. Quite the contrary, it means not having to labour with your hands; it means winning glory in the field of battle and then receiving the reward for your effort in lives and lands that should work for you."[7]

The Crown's control of this "new aristocracy" in the New World was partially guaranteed by its imposition of limits on the land grant terms, which meant both that these could eventually revert back to the Crown and that not all Spaniards remained at the top of the social hierarchy.[8] But it also meant that complex, regionally specific racial, social, and cultural arrangements were developed over three hundred years of colonial rule as the settlers and their descendants sought ways of reinforcing property ownership patterns and semifeudal labor relations on the agricultural haciendas, ranches, and mines.[9]

For the most part, distinctions between Christians and pagans had been erased early on by the relatively quick conversion of the indigenous populations. As these early religious grounds for separation between the ethnic groups disappeared, colonial master-slave relations were superimposed on a racial order that became increasingly diversified through both miscegenation and the introduction of the African slave trade.[10] Thus, exploitation of both the indigenous populations and the enslaved Africans was not limited solely to their labor, for the presence of both these groups also served to reinforce the class and racial status they and their offspring afforded the New World's Spanish rulers. Throughout the colonial period, factors such as the higher ratio of men to women and various laws addressing intermarriage and interracial relations as a whole did nothing to diminish the ongoing rap-ing and violation of indigenous and black women.[11] As Richard Morse and others have noted, however, they did ensure that the racial composition and the consequent rigid hierarchies of colonial Spanish America were ultimately determined not by strict segregation, but rather by *miscegenation*, the mixing of white Europeans, Indians, and Africans.[12] Indeed, to the extent that Spain's conquest of the Americas can also be seen as the conquest of women, as Magnus Morner suggests, the large numbers of "half-breeds" meant that the term *mestizo* in a deeply Catholic context was negatively appraised as a synonym for "illegitimate."[13]

As a result of extensive miscegenation throughout the colonies, racial classifications, social status, and honor evolved into a hierarchical arrangement that Alejandro Lipschütz has called a "pigmentocracy."[14] As Ramón Gutiérrez has described, this was a racial system whereby whiter skin was directly related to higher social status and honor, while darker skin was associated both with "the physical labor of slaves and tributary indians" and, visually, with "the infamy of the conquered."[15] Morner has explained that this extreme color consciousness was often accompanied by equally complex legal and social restrictions concerning marriage, taxes, residential settlement, and inheritance. Intermarriage among whites, "pure mestizos," and Indians, for example, was permitted—increasingly so, toward the end of the colonial period—but marriage of "pure bloods" to blacks and mulattoes required the authorities' permission. And, insofar as miscegenation, particularly among the lower sectors of the hierarchy, was also perceived as a real or potential threat to the established order, Afro-Indian marriages were strictly forbidden.[16] The Spanish notion of *pureza de sangre* or purity of blood was thus embedded in the New World aristocracy's understanding of the interrelated concepts of race, social status, and honor. And, although upper-class families adhered to it more rigidly, as Richard Griswold del Castillo notes, the patriarchal authority men derived from it, regardless of race or social status, was maintained through the corporativist ideology of the family's honor and respect—ensuring in the process the subordination of the women of all races and classes.[17]

As a result, Morner concludes that miscegenation in Latin America never necessarily meant either social or racial assimilation. Rather, as Morse explains, the graduated system of color prejudices was interwoven with the perceived status of different groups' social function in a highly rigid and entrenched corporativist hierarchy. Many of its remnants are still in evidence in Latin American societies even today.[18] Similarly, the colonies' semifeudal hierarchies and status arrangements, the disdain for racial and social inferiors, the continued violation of indigenous and black women, and the prevailing dominant ideology of contempt for manual labor ensured that the rancor between the races—although often disguised as class prejudice—was not to be so easily dismissed, even by the new Latin American republics formed in the early nineteenth century. Although at the end of the wars of independence several of the new national governments abolished all laws that made distinctions among the various ethnic and racial groups and some made concerted efforts to integrate their respective nations, the assessment of one Mexican intellectual in 1865 was to hold true for much of Latin America well into the twentieth century:

> The white is a proprietor, the Indian a proletarian. The white is rich, the Indian poor, and miserable. The descendants of the Spaniards have all the knowledge of the times within their reach . . . the Indian is ignorant of everything. . . . The white lives in the city in a splendid house, the Indian lives in iso-

lation in the countryside in a miserable hut. . . . There are two peoples in the same territory. What is worse, these peoples are to a certain degree mutual enemies.[19]

Almost one hundred years later, the commentary of race and ethnic relations in Peru by the famous novelist and anthropologist José María Arguedas reinforced this earlier observation and in many ways summarizes the racial, ethnic, social, linguistic, and regional divides that today continue at least partially to hinder both the integration of Latin America's respective nations and the construction of the unity of the continent's populations: "I believe there would be less distance between the czar of Russia and a peasant than between [an Andean] villager of Andahuaylas (my native village) and any of the presidents of Peru."[20]

It is perhaps not surprising then that several contemporary noted scholars insist that the unity of the continent hinges both on the social and economic incorporation into the Latin America nations of populations marginalized since colonial times and on the political recognition of the ethnocultural diversity of the region. While most agree that integration is an imperative, as Juan Odonne has stated, the "regional reality of the continent is a goal that is still far from being achieved."[21]

In many ways, Latin American's understanding of the racial and social hierarchy continues to be based on "a black-white continuum," to borrow Peter Wade's expression, one in which money can "whiten" people through intermarriage.[22] Yet this perception often undermines the extent to which lack of citizenship rights and continued discrimination has remained tied to historical prejudices against the racial and social status of indigenous people and blacks. The consequent articulation of race, social status, and religiously grounded beliefs of family honor and respect has thus at least partially contributed to the current problems in achieving the continent's full integration.

THE CLASH OF CULTURAL HIERARCHIES: RACE AND CLASS IN LATIN AMERICA AND THE UNITED STATES

The significance of the attitudes and perceptions about race and social status shaped in colonial Latin America for understanding the sudden and violent incorporation of Spanish-speaking populations into the U.S. social hierarchy can perhaps best be exemplified through pointing to some of the differences in the ways that rich and poor Mexicans responded to the conquest and penetration of what were once Mexico's territories in the Southwest. After all, the 1846-48 Mexican-American War and its aftermath contributed to setting the stage both for what has since become a continuous clash in the construction and cultural perception of the racial and social hierarchies of the United States and Latin America, and the consequent homogenizing of "Hispanics" in this country.

In political and economic terms, land ownership was certainly one key point of contention between Anglo settlers and conquered Mexicans—rich or poor—in the aftermath of the war. Many of the Mexicans who had decided to accept U.S. citizenship and stay in the United States, as stipulated by the Treaty of Guadalupe Hidalgo, sought to retain ownership of their lands, appealing to the U.S. courts of law to uphold their property rights. While many won their cases, hundreds were ultimately displaced from their lands—whether as a result of unscrupulous lawyers and unfair judicial practices, of pressure to give up the land, or of confusion about their titles and the new land laws and language.[23] At the same time, "Mexican hating" (to use Ronald Takaki's expression) also justified the systematic expropriation of many Mexican small village farmers' communally owned grazing lands (*ejidos*) and underlay the eventual political and social subordination of large sectors of the Chicano populations.[24]

But, as Mario Barrera noted, insofar as all Mexicans were not members of the upper echelons at the end of Spanish colonial society and thus did not have "an equal stake" in the land, "not all Mexicans were seen or treated as inferior" in the immediate aftermath of the war. In southern California, New Mexico, Arizona, along the Texas border, and elsewhere, sectors of the landed elite families (*los ricos*) struggled in different ways to remain in control of their power and wealth, reinforcing their commitment to the traditional castelike social hierarchy inherited from Spain. Early nineteenth-century Yankee immigrants in California, for example, had had to contend with the political and economic power of the two hundred ruling *Californio* families who controlled 14 million acres of land and thus the lives of a considerably larger number of agricultural laborers.[25] Many of the *ricos* forged alliances with the growing numbers of "Anglos," whether through their collaboration and political alliances with the new Anglo officials, through strengthening their economic ties with the emerging Anglo business classes in urban areas, or through intermarriage or court cases or both. Others essentially sought to become brokers for the communities of small farmers, shepherds, serfs, and villagers in the rural Southwest.[26]

Sectors of the latter in turn sometimes banded together to prevent the enclosure of their traditional communal lands by Anglos and their allies among the Mexican elites.[27] But by the end of the century, as Sarah Deutsch has recently shown, structural economic changes had forced many of the poorer Mexican populations to become seasonal migrant workers, establishing in the process new villages in which both kinship and shared economic and cultural ties were reinforced, particularly by women, in regional communities spread out over hundreds of miles. This too contributed to the development of villagers' strategies of resistance to the presence of Anglos throughout the Southwest, as the regionally based autonomous communities and economic systems allowed *los pobres* a relative independence from exploitative labor conditions, as well as the survival of their culture and language.[28]

Anglos in Texas, whether merchants or officials, were for their part, as David Montejano has noted, "quite adept at drawing the distinction between the landed 'Castilian' elite and the landless Mexican."[29] But although the old ruling families tried to protect their status and power in their respective communities, by the 1920s the continuous flow of new Anglo settlers in the region, along with the period's changed economic context, had made even this distinction obsolete. *Los ricos* often incorporated the prevailing Spanish-American "aphorism about color and class"—"money whitens"—in the strategies they developed to cope with the increasing decline of their fortunes during the second half of the nineteenth century and with the racial, segregationist-based attitudes that had developed in Anglo society. But it is important to note, as Montejano suggests, that this also meant that "the only problem for upper-class Mexicans was that this principle offered neither consistent nor permanent security in the border region."[30]

As their wealth decreased toward the end of the century, sectors of the elites of New Mexico increasingly began to refer to themselves as Hispanos—perhaps the earliest period in which the term was widely used in the United States, specifically as a response to the

American social and racial context. Although, as Gonzales suggests, they were not to fully deny their Mexican origins until the early years of the twentieth century, in adopting the term Hispano they were emphasizing not their racially miscegenated, mestizo origins, but rather their specific class-based descent from the original "pure-blooded" Spanish conquistadors who settled in New Mexico. The translation of Hispano in this case would thus *not* be Hispanic but rather, as Rodolfo Acuña states, "Spanish American," for "according to them, New Mexico was isolated from the rest of the Southwest and Mexico during the colonial era; thus, they remained racially pure and were Europeans, in contrast to the mestizo (half-breed) Mexicans."[31]

In this sense, what Carey McWilliams called the "fantasy heritage" of racial purity adopted by *los ricos* was, as Acuña suggests, more likely a strategy to retain power and status based on their understanding of the Anglo racial hierarchy than actual fact for, as in the rest of Spanish America, New Mexico's colonizers, too, had mixed with and exploited indigenous populations such as the Pueblo in the region.[32] By the early part of this century, prejudice and discrimination against Mexicans had increased such that the term "Spanish American" had become widely used among the Spanish-speaking elites in the United States, particularly by the New Mexican *ricos*. "Money whitens," and thus, insofar as they were rich and considered themselves to be white, by the early twentieth century the *ricos* had adopted it to distinguish themselves in the context of Anglo society from the *mexicanos pobres*: "You don't like Mexicans, and we don't like them either, but we are Spanish-Americans, not Mexicans."[33] Similarly, as David Montejano notes, the influx of Mexican farm laborers recruited to work in the expanding commercial farming industry of Texas ultimately "eroded the centuries-old class structure of the Mexican ranch settlements," reducing the Mexican populations of the region "to the status of landless and dependent wage laborers." He goes on to describe the bitterness of the Mexican elite as they responded to their process of exclusion from the national community. The cumulative effects on upper-class Texas Mexicans in the early decades of the century were recorded by Jovita Gonzales:

> We, Texas-Mexicans of the border, although we hold on to our traditions, are proud of our race, are loyal to the United States, in spite of the treatment we receive by some of the new Americans. Before their arrival, there were no racial or social distinctions between us. Their children married ours, ours married theirs, and both were glad and proud of the fact. But since the coming of the 'white trash' from the north and middle west we felt the change. *They made us feel for the first time that we were Mexicans* and that they considered themselves our superiors.[34]

Given the Spanish colonial legacy in the Americas, it is perhaps not surprising that the general disdain of some ruling elite families for "Mexicans"—understood in the pejorative class-based terms adopted from the Anglos—also prevailed in what were once Spanish colonies and later Mexico's northern territories. In cultural and racial terms, then, the postwar period was to bring a shift from an initial confrontation to a gradual overlapping of two very different social hierarchies, which reflected differences in the ways race relations and social status were understood. The postindependence Latin American hierarchy within which Mexican *ricos* and *pobres* were socialized was based on rigid social and racial hierarchical arrangements stemming from the Spanish and Catholic colonial heritage.

The social and status hierarchy in the United States was instead forged concomitantly with the construction of the nation's identity based on the belief in white, Anglo-Saxon, and Protestant superiority. As a result, and notwithstanding Mexicans' adherence to the social and racial dynamics that once differentiated their status and power in Spanish colonial and postcolonial societies, they, like other Latin American populations, came to be perceived homogeneously, and as culturally and racially inferior in the U.S. context. As Leonard Pitt noted, eyewitness accounts of the gold rush years in California, for example, documented the prevalence among Anglos of condescending Protestant attitudes toward Catholics, of the republican traditional loathing of aristocratic attitudes such as those held by the Mexican ruling elites, and of the idea of the nation's "manifest destiny," the upholding of the Protestant work ethic, and the general discomfort with interracial settings.[35]

In fact, as I argue in the following sections, this was partially due to the domestic boundaries of membership in the national community. These had been largely shaped by the presence and legalized segregation of native-born blacks, such that the nation's self-definition and public image in relation to "foreign Others" could be invoked primarily in white-only terms. The subsequent forms of incorporation of Mexicans and later of Puerto Ricans were also defined in these terms. At the same time, they simultaneously excluded people of Latin American descent from the Black/White framework through which the national community of citizens came to be imagined, and differentiated their experience from that of African Americans after the Civil War.

The underlying religious, racial, and social bases of colonial Latin America's history of miscegenation and consequent racial continuum were in sharp contrast to the black/white divisions. As Peter Wade points out, the latter divisions were to legitimize the oppression of blacks as a specific group in the United States and also to allow for their subsequent politization in those terms in the 1960s.[36]

CONSIDERATIONS ON IMAGES OF COMMUNITY OF THE UNITED STATES

As more new nations joined the United States in the hemisphere during the early nineteenth century, the problems of establishing the imagined community of the United States, defining its boundaries, ensuring its national integration, and constructing the identity of its racially diverse and hierarchically structured population also had to be addressed by the United States. Indeed, as Benedict Anderson suggested, nations are culturally constructed artifacts, imagined as communities by their populations. The way in which people imagine their national community is thus just as important in determining their experiences in their society as is their recognition of the limits of their nation set by its boundaries and the sovereignty that ensures them their freedom.[37]

But contrary to the nation-building policies adopted by some of the other emerging nations in the hemisphere, the issue of defining an American nationality was actually compounded by the fact that being an American had never really been solely conceived in terms of birthplace. The melting pot, a term first coined in 1909, had initially served to encapsulate the belief that the combined effects of the egalitarian ideals of the United States and the mixing of all immigrant and ethnic cultures during the previous centuries had in fact created a *new* "American" culture. But in the course of the twentieth century, it became increasingly clear that being "American"—and hence American culture, as symbolized by the term *melting pot*—had long been imagined exclusively in white Anglo-American cultural terms.[38] Insofar as "Anglo-conformity" had been the prevailing ideology of assimilation throughout much of the nation's history, as Milton Gordon suggested in 1964, the (racial) terms of exclusion of African Americans and Native Americans had in fact been established long before the term *melting pot* was actually popularized.[39] Hence, it is perhaps not surprising that the rejection by racial minority groups of the melting pot metaphor during the 1960s represented the *beginnings* of a struggle to shift the way the U.S. community of citizens had come to be imagined. "In the blunt words of one black intellectual: 'There never was a melting pot; there is not now a melting pot; there never will be a melting pot; and if there ever was, it would be such a tasteless soup that we would have to go back and start all over!'"[40]

Two years after Gordon's study, Joshua Fishman explained why the belief in assimilation and de-ethnization of immigrant populations has persisted for so long, suggesting that as a society of immigrants, the United States was essentially representative of a nation whose ("American") nationality had no ethnic roots itself. As a result, for all immigrants after the Puritans, "the Americanizing process itself takes on a central role in the formation of the national identity and the national self-concept of most Americans." Hence the relevance of negotiating the role of ethnicity in ensuring "assimilation," in creating an *American* national identity, an *American* ethnic-nationalism.[41]

Becoming an American has always also been, to use Eric Hobsbawm's apt phrase, "an act of choice" both by the individual and by the national society. But, while the former may decide to make the ideological choice to become Americanized, the latter could also "choose" whether to accept him or her into the national community and to support the extension of full citizenship rights. Throughout the nation's history, representatives of the society's institutions have emerged again and again with the power to recreate the "American public" and its "opinion" in their discourse. In the process they contributed toward setting the terms of the debates on individuals' inclusion or exclusion from various aspects of the national community and its social and political life.

Key to understanding these debates, as they were to affect both the meaning and value of ethnicity more generally and the development of the racialized basis of the incorporation of Latin American populations in the United States, is the role played by the particular form of exclusion of African Americans from the nation's population.[42] Unlike all other groups in this country, the very basis of African Americans' historical struggle for human and civil rights is rooted in slavery. Thus, the specificity of their history contrasts markedly with the terms of the historical public debates on inclusion of people of Latin American descent. Regardless of the prejudices and racialized discrimination against the latter, they did not have to contend with the political and socioeconomic consequences of enslavement. Instead, the situation of Latinos entailed the disentangling of the conflation of their race and national origins in their political struggle for political and civil rights. These have long been identified with various social economic policy issues, particularly as these impact on public opinion about their presence in the United States. As a report to the secretary of labor detailing each Latin American country's racial composition concluded in 1925:

> It is the economic argument which chiefly has made a welcome to these immigrants to the United States and the economic argument for immigration has always been dangerous. No man is a worker alone. He is also a citizen and must further be viewed as the father of more citizens also. The years of his ser-

vice as a wage earner are limited; not so the span of time in which those of his blood will play their parts in the country."[43]

And, more recently, educational questions closely tied to the historical debates on the national language have been added to long-held concerns about immigration. Ernest L. Boyer, president of the Carnegie Foundation for the Advancement of Teaching, appealed to American public opinion to once again rethink its stance on allowing non-English-speaking foreigners to immigrate into the United States. He noted that the national community's social tensions in the mid-1980s were now signified by bilingual education—a "code word," he argued, that had turned the schools into the "battle ground" of the nation.[44]

Although appeals to public opinion have often been used to cultivate national pride in the nation's self-image as a land of immigrants, instilling fear of the real or imagined consequences of introducing foreign ways into American life has at times also contributed to defining the national identity of the United States. In this sense, Hobsbawm's historical perspective perhaps provides a more useful approach than Boyer's to explain the issues involved in past and current debates on the question of immigrants and the "making of Americans," as well as in understanding the incorporation of racial minorities as "Americans" into the "national community." Focusing on the 1870-1914 period, Hobsbawm argues that the concept of Americanization as "an act of choice," as a "decision to learn English, to apply for citizenship—and a choice of specific beliefs, acts and modes of behavior"—implied the concept of "un-Americanism." Emphasizing the significance of distinguishing between people's status in the nation and their lack of patriotism, he notes that unlike the case in many other countries during that period in the United States (as in Germany), a person's lack of patriotism "threw doubt on his or her actual status as member of the nation"[45]—a doubt, one might add, that has often been raised throughout this century, regardless of the style in which the American nation's "public opinion" has variously reimagined "un-Americanism" over time.[46]

The forms of mobilization that minority groups adopted during the 1960s exemplify the response by specific racial groups to their status in the nation. While originally conceived in different ways, the response was embedded in the style in which mainstream society had imagined its boundaries in white Anglo-Saxon terms, and ensured their exclusion from full participation in the national community. Referring to the racial violence of the 1960s, Hannah Arendt pointed out that "the obvious dangers of domestic violence" in a multinational society such as the United States had historically been contained "*by making adherence to the law of the land, and not national origin, the chief touchstone of citizenship* and by tolerating a considerable amount of mutual discrimination in society." Consequently, she argued, the struggle of African Americans for political inclusion during the sixties raised the need to acknowledge that nationalism and racism are not the same. The solution to the racial violence could not be approached in the same way as it had been in the past.[47] Thus, while the civil rights and black liberation movement during the 1960s were certainly a struggle to get the "community of Americans" to *recognize* the political and civil rights of African Americans as equal citizens under the law, they also represented an attempt to shift the notion of *how* one is defined as an American with full citizenship rights away from ideological choice to one of native-born right to membership as citizens in the nation.

Indeed, although African Americans had been legally excluded from social mobility and freedom for centuries, there has not been any doubt—at least since the Civil War—that they were born in the United States.[48] For, however, reluctantly and in spite of their political and legal exclusion, the dominant society has acknowledged their existence—albeit negatively, through the Civil War, the passing of segregationist laws and practices, and consequent persistent discrimination. The question of ethnicity in the United States is thus rooted in the segregationist polices of the nineteenth century. These had the effect of excluding African Americans from the way the national community was imagined and simultaneously establishing the domestic "boundaries" in ethnic terms for those who *would* be included as members of the nation. As a result, the "black issue" in the United States became a question of trying to define empirically the distinction between nationality as their native-born right in relation to the society's right to exclude them (based on ideological notions of racial and moral superiority) from the national community's self-image.

In 1896, for example, in spite of a few attempts to protect the rights of African Americans (through, for example, the Civil Rights Act of 1875, revoked by the Supreme Court in 1883), segregation became "an established fact, *by law as well as by custom.*"[49] The *Plessy v. Ferguson* case challenged the constitutionality of an 1890 Louisiana law that reestablished segregation of blacks and whites in the state's railroad trains. Based on the Fourteenth Amendment guaranteeing equality to African Americans, this case was brought to the court by Homer Adolph Plessy, a man whom Richard Kluger has described as "exceedingly light-skinned," in a part of the country where the racial mixture of blacks, French, Indians, and Anglo-Saxons had created "a racial *bouillabaisse* unlike any other state in the union." The "separate but equal" decision thus brought to light issues of racial passing and the difficulties in disentangling racial origins. At the same time, it served to legally acknowledge the presence of blacks and simultaneously justify their segregation on the grounds that "social equality" could not be reached in the national community through what the court referred to as "laws which conflict with the general sentiment of the community upon whom they are designed to operate."[50]

Domestically, then, until the 1954 *Brown v. Board of Education* decision, the presence of blacks in the United States was acknowledged through the *Plessy v. Ferguson* decision, which legalized nineteenth-century customary practices of discrimination. As the next section illustrates, the enforced segregation of African Americans was paradoxically also to signal their partial political incorporation into the nation. At the same time, it contributed to establish the internal boundaries of the "national community" such that the public self-image of the American nation could be invoked primarily in white-only terms. In this sense it is not surprising that in demanding full participation and rights in the nation, the black movements of the sixties reinforced the "adherence to the law of the land" as one means of combating long-held "general sentiments" of the "national community."

FORGING THE EXCLUSION OF LATIN AMERICANS FROM THE AMERICAN IMAGINED COMMUNITY

The struggle of Mexican Americans and Puerto Ricans for civil rights and equality before the law has necessarily taken a different form from that of African Americans, precisely because, at least since the Civil War period, the exclusion of blacks has not been couched in distortion stemming from xenophobic portrayals of them as foreign born. Indeed, the experiences of Mexican Americans and Puerto Ricans in the United States (legally fellow citizens of Americans since 1848 and 1917, respectively) exemplify the ways that xenophobic nationalism and domestic racism have been conflated since the early nineteenth century.[51] This fusion has forged a public self-image of the "American people" in relation to racially perceived foreign "Others" not only in the United States but in the hemisphere as a whole.

The conflation of Latin Americans' race and nationality has shaped a different relationship between Mexican Americans and Puerto Ricans and the American imagined community—a relationship based primarily on de facto (rather than de jure) exclusion. Indeed, the Treaty of Guadalupe Hidalgo, signed at the end of the 1846-48 Mexican-American War, had ensured Mexicans, unlike African Americans, the full privilege of U.S. citizenship, including the right to appeal to the courts to maintain their ownership of their lands— making them the first non-Anglo-Saxons to have the rights and privileges previously reserved only to white, European men. As Tomás Almaguer recently suggested, legal access to these citizenship rights was to have important implications in the subsequent development of the various Mexican-American communities in the United States and was certainly a key factor differentiating their experience from that of African Americans and other racial groups—at least in terms of their legal recognition as members of the "national community."[52]

Nevertheless, while both citizenship rights and legal recourse to the courts of the nation were guaranteed, the fact that the populations of the Southwest were persistently perceived as foreign to the style in which the "national community" was imagined meant that, fifty years after the Treaty of Guadalupe Hidalgo, "the Anglo still considered the Mexicans as aliens and made attempts through the courts to exclude them from citizenship. In 1896 Ricardo Rodriguez was denied his final naturalization papers."[53] Thus although legalized segregation of African Americans had shaped the *domestic* definitions of exclusion from the imagined community of Americans, segregationist customary practices were gradually extended to ("foreign") Mexicans and sometimes even served as the basis from which to challenge the dictates of the "laws of the land."

It is ironic that Rodriguez brought his case to the courts in 1896. For as discussed above, it meant that the very year the Plessy verdict legally sanctioned the segregation of African Americans in the society was also the year when the recognition that blacks were present— albeit segregated—in the national community was clearly being affirmed in the courts against "foreign" Mexicans who sought to assert their legal right to become naturalized. As Acuña notes, in making their case against Rodriguez "the authorities argued in court that *Rodriguez was not white or African and 'therefore not capable of becoming an American citizen.'*" Noting that "They wanted to keep 'Aztecs or aboriginal Mexicans' from naturalization," Acuña tells us that nevertheless Rodriguez himself eventually won his case for naturalization through invoking the terms prescribed by the Treaty of Guadalupe Hidalgo.[54] But the very fact that he had had to assert his right to citizenship against a prosecution using racial terms shows that the definition of the domestic boundaries of the national community in black/white terms had also become a legitimate justification for reinforcing nationality to render Mexican Americans invisible both as *citizens* and as *native-born members* of the nation.

By the turn of the century, this definition, initially shaped in relation to Mexican Americans, was further reinforced through the relations the U.S. established with all the Latin American nations. In fact, the form in which nationality and race were fused in the treatment of Mexican Americans, Puerto Ricans, and indeed of all Latin Americans in the United States is best exemplified in some of the expansionist policies and ideologies of the nineteenth century. As early as 1823, the Monroe Doctrine determined that the entire hemisphere was to come under the sphere of influence of the United States. Initially an economic rather than political declaration, the doctrine aimed at preventing the intervention of European nations in the affairs of the hemisphere. But as Victor Valenzuela bluntly states, "By the end of the XIX century, the Monroe Doctrine was used freely by the United States to seize, to control or to intervene openly in the affairs of Latin American countries."[55] Thus the Monroe Doctrine had in effect early on begun to establish a homogeneous approach to relations between the United States and Latin American nations and was to have far-reaching implications in forging a public American identity in relation to the other emerging nations in the hemisphere.

At the same time, the fusion of Latin Americans' race and nationality was also furthered by the development of the ideology of the nation's "manifest destiny," which substantiated the doctrine's clearly expansionist intent at home.[56] The term was initially coined in 1845 by John O'Sullivan, then editor of the *Democratic Review*, who apparently drew his own conclusions about the nation's future mission and destiny from early Puritan beliefs of Providence. In so doing, he provided the Polk government with the rationale for both the Mexican-American war and the subsequent annexation of more than half of Mexico's territory.[57] Effectively declaring the superiority of the white Anglo-Saxon, the ideology of the nation's manifest destiny was widely used by journalists to spread the justification of expansion and the subsequent exclusion of "foreign" Mexicans from the way the national community was imagined.[58] While competing commercial concerns and economic interests were, as Mario Barrera has argued, more probable causes for the conquest of Mexico's northern territory than the pure adherence to the belief in the nation's manifest destiny, the ideological terms of the debate are also essential for explaining the process through which popular support for the war was galvanized and justified by politicians and journalists to the American public.[59]

Among politicians, there was much discussion about the merits of declaring war on Mexico and on its aftermath. Both those in favor and those against the war and annexation struggled with the conflict between economic interests and the racial concerns about Mexico's Spanish and Indian *mixed* populations. According to Reginald Horseman, the latter seem to have caused much soul-searching among some antiexpansionists, particularly among those who were not English but rather of proud Scottish and Irish descent. Confronted by the serious issue of what to do with the "mongrel" Mexicans, they were nevertheless not willing to accede to the claims of Anglo-Saxon superiority. This led them to affirm the superiority of "Americans" of northern European descent, thus relegating the Spanish southern European heritage of Mexicans to "second place" in the white European hierarchy in the hemisphere. Thus, while some could then praise the European side of Mexico's heritage in these terms, almost all could use racial arguments to deny their rights as equal citizens of a national community in which the superiority of white northern Europeans was rarely challenged.[60]

In setting the style of reestablishing the boundaries of the nation of Americans, nineteenth-century American opinion makers came to construct a "white only" public, which, whether as northern Europeans or in more specific "Anglo-Saxon" terms, included "every American." Having defined the national community in those terms, an image of a coherent, powerful nation unified against the foreign "enemy" could then be evoked by those who "viewed the conflict as a manifestation of the national future." As the editor of

Scientific American wrote, "Every American must feel a glow of enthusiasm in his [*sic*] heart as he thinks of his country's greatness, her might and her power."[61] Buttressed by the justifications of the Monroe Doctrine and manifest destiny of the United States, popular perceptions of foreign "Others" also fused their races and nationalities. The grounds of the earlier debates on the mixed heritage of Mexico's population seem to have been put aside to some extent in the latter decades of the century as myths of the racial superiority of "Americans"—now reinforced through victory and the social Darwinism of the times—fed the perception of the inferior homogeneous identity of all people of Mexican, and later of Latin American, descent.

The extent to which these images were disseminated in ways that contributed toward erasing the racial and class distinctions among Latin Americans can perhaps best be see in the attitudes of the forty-niners during the gold rush. In 1849 alone, 100,000 newcomers from all over the world arrived in California, including 8,000 Mexicans and 5,000 South Americans. As seen earlier, because of their social class standing as well as their length of residence, the established Mexican elite families had made a point of distancing themselves from more recently arrived lower-class Mexican *cholos* (or "half-breeds," as they were derogatorily called) following Mexico's independence from Spain. But now they suddenly found that the thousands of Yankee Anglo-Saxons pouring into the gold-mining regions made no such social distinctions among the varied Latin American national groups. Instead, as McWilliams notes, "whether from California, Chile, Peru, or Mexico, whether residents of twenty years' standing or immigrants of one week, all the Spanish-speaking were lumped together as interlopers and greasers." Thus unceremoniously and indiscriminately brought together under the "Mexicans" label, Latin Americans—regardless of race, class, or nationality—became the potential and real targets of robberies, murders, rapes, and lynchings, and hence the butt of the often-violent repercussions of the American "glow of enthusiasm."[62]

Similarly, the homogenization of the social and racial differences among Latin American populations is also exemplified in the colonization of Puerto Rico following the Spanish-American War. As in the case of the conquest of Mexico's lands, the 1898 war was largely fueled by the need for external markets. And again, the ideological justifications provided for the economic interests in the society were also to further shape the boundaries of the U.S. imagined community. On the eve of the war, a *Washington Post* editorial, for example, galvanized public support for the war in the following terms:

> A new consciousness seems to have come upon us—the consciousness of strength—and with it a new appetite, the yearning to show our strength. . . . Ambition, interest, land hunger, pride, the mere joy of fighting, whatever it may be, we are animated by a new sensation. We are face to face with a strange destiny. The taste of Empire is in the mouth of the people even as the taste of blood is in the jungle.[63]

But if the American people were being asked to imagine the taste of their "strange destiny," it was the populations of the countries affected by U.S. expansionist actions who were actually to swallow the nation's cultivated self-image as an empire after 1898. The war finally sealed Cuba's century-long struggle for independence, bringing to a close Spanish colonial rule in the hemisphere. In the course of the war, however, U.S. troops had also landed on the nearby Spanish island-colony of Puerto Rico, which, given its location in the Caribbean, was significant in military terms and thus was included, along with the Philippines, as part of the gains of the United States in the Treaty of Paris that ended the war.[64]

The transfer of Puerto Rico to the United States was generally welcomed by the island's population, although the reasons varied according to the social sectors. The propertied classes, for example, were anxious to benefit from both the ideals of democracy and the closer ties with the U.S. economy, while sectors of the poorer classes were convinced that their scores against the corruption of the island's ruling classes would finally be settled and the Spanish colonial castelike hierarchy in which they had for so long been forced to live would be dismantled.[65] These misperceptions were to prove as misinformed as those the U.S. troops held about Puerto Ricans: some Americans found a population that, particularly among the working class and the poor, seemed "patient" and "docile," their very gentleness permitting "the unjust scale of wages they receive to become the custom." Others, however, saw "the natives" as "lazy and dirty, but . . . very sharp and cunning," and found that "the introduction of American ideas disturbs them little, they being indifferent to the advantages offered."[66]

Notwithstanding either the intercultural and political misperceptions on both sides or the island's various social sectors' expectations, Puerto Ricans' sigh of relief at the end of Spanish colonial rule proved to be short-lived. For in contrast to the fate of Mexico's territories, which following annexation were eventually incorporated as states of the union, the case of Puerto Rico, the U.S. Congress adopted a measure largely aimed at exacting tariffs on the island's agricultural products. Known as the Foraker Bill, it also denied, for the first time in U.S. history, both territorial status and constitutional protection and citizenship to a newly acquired territory. This initially provoked heated partisan debate between Democrats and Republicans alike, both of which favored the bill's economic advantages while seeking to avoid blame for what were clearly colonialist implications of the new territorial status created for Puerto Rico. One senator poignantly summarized its potential implications for the nation's identity as well as for the future image of the national community at home and abroad:

> It will end the history of the Republic and open the history of the empire. It
> dethrones the Goddess of liberty and elevates the demon of power. It destroys
> constitutional government and creates a Congressional despotism. It is but
> the forerunner of countless other bills to follow in order to inaugurate the new
> imperialistic regime. It is antagonistic to all the traditions of our country, to
> all the principles of our Government, and will, I believe, be the commence-
> ment of much disgrace and much disaster. (Applause)[67]

Nevertheless, the bill's tariff-related economic advantages were apparently to outweigh its political ramifications, for it was signed into law by President McKinley in 1900. Although, as Benjamin Ringer notes, varied political and economic concerns made it inexpedient for members of either party to raise the issue of race as part of the debate, it was apparently on the minds of at least some of the congressmen, for their concerns about it are also recorded in no uncertain terms:

> I am opposed to increasing the opportunities for the millions of negroes in
> Puerto Rico and the 10,000,000 Asiatics in the Philippines of becoming
> American citizens and swarming into this country and coming in competition
> with our farmers and mechanics and laborers. We are trying to keep out the

Chinese with one hand, and now you are proposing to make Territories of the United States out of Puerto Rico and the Philippine Islands, and thereby open wide the door by which these negroes and Asiatics can pour like the locusts of Egypt into this country.[68]

As the acquisition of both Puerto Rico and of Mexico's territory exemplify, the justifications of expansionism into Latin America had from early on been furthered by racial explanations that, overtly or otherwise, homogenized the complex and heterogeneous class and racial hierarchies that had evolved over more than three hundred years of Spanish colonial rule. The combined effects of the Monroe Doctrine and the idea of the manifest destiny of the United States contributed toward shaping the boundaries of the American community in relation to the Spanish-speaking populations south of the Rio Grande. Moreover, the creation of the *image* of a unified "national community" contributed toward erasing the complex differences in the ways that race, culture, and nationality were understood by the Spanish-speaking people who lived in the United States in the years following the Mexican-American War.

Key to the process of exclusion of people of Latin American descent from the American imagined community was the fact that newly and often violently created customary practices frequently came to define their lack of citizenship rights and to shape their experiences more clearly than the "laws of the land." As Montejano has emphasized, class-based distinctions within the Mexican community were recognized, for example, in Texas. Yet this did not prevent individual Anglos in the Southwest from imputing in their "less dramatic, daily encounters" the same segregationist attitudes they customarily invoked *in relation to blacks*:

> In her first trip to Corpus Christi in 1870, Mrs. Susan Miller of Louisiana stopped at the State Hotel and "was horrified to see Mexicans seated at the tables with Americans. I told my husband I had never eaten with Mexicans or negroes, and refused to do so. He said: '*Mexicans are different to negroes and are recognized as Americans.* However, I will speak to the manager and see if he will not put a small table in one corner of the room for you.' He did so and we enjoyed the meal."[69]

In spite of legal rights, Puerto Ricans and Mexican Americans have remained largely unacknowledged as "fellow citizens" of Americans throughout much of the twentieth century. Denied full citizenship and human rights by the customary practices of exclusion, they could be routinely bounced in and out of the "national community" according to the ever-changing political and economic needs of the nation. This is exemplified in their differentiated incorporation into the U.S. economy. Notwithstanding internal social and racial differentiations, their respective communities have also since been variously affected by the nation's political needs in war and peace, by its employment practices, and by the racial and immigration polices that reflected the nation's economic laws of supply and demand.

The 1917 Jones Act, which imposed U.S. citizenship on Puerto Ricans, for example, allowed for their massive participation in World War I, while simultaneously denying the island's population the right to vote for the presidents who have since sent them to every war. Later, "Operation Bootstrap," and specifically the passage of the 1947 Industrial Incentives Act, combined a massive industrialization program on the island based on long-term tax breaks for U.S. corporations and the export of thousands of displaced workers to the United States. As a result, between 1948 and 1965, Puerto Rico witnessed "the unusual spectacles of a booming economy with a shrinking labor force and . . . shrinking unemployment." During the same period, the number of Puerto Ricans displaced to the United States has been estimated to run from nine hundred thousand to one million, including the children born abroad.[70]

Similarly, U.S. government policies also contributed to the increase in the Mexican American population between the 1940s and the 1960s and determined both the fate of the more established Chicano communities—most of which, by the 1940s, were in urban areas—and their interaction with the thousands of Mexican immigrants in the United States. As a result of labor shortages during the war, for example, the bracero program, begun in 1943, brought 4.8 million Mexican workers across the border between 1943 and 1964. Soon after the war, "Operation Wetback" was begun, ostensibly aimed at tracking down and departing "illegal" Mexican workers. The bracero program was simultaneously extended, however, this time including provision for industrial workers, but also effectively keeping rural wages down and ensuring an ample supply of strike breakers in the fields of the western and southwestern states.[71]

Exclusion from full rights of citizenship has reinforced the *public* perception of Chicanos, like that of Puerto Ricans, as outside of the boundaries of the popular image of the national community. This explains, for example, Mexican Americans' treatment by U.S. officials, who, at various times throughout the twentieth century, felt no qualms in deporting them at will, regardless of their U.S. citizenship and length of time in this country. Ironically, throughout the twentieth century, this same perception often left Mexican Americans with no other recourse than to appeal to the Mexican consulate for protection against discrimination from officials of their own country, namely, the United States. As for the Puerto Ricans, they could not even resort to this option, insofar as they had been declared citizens of the United States in 1917, in the context of the transfer of the island from one colonial power to another.[72]

THE FUSION OF RACE AND NATIONALITY: IMAGINING THE "HISPANIC OTHER" IN THE CUSTOMS AND LAWS OF THE LAND

Rooted in the nineteenth-century search by newly formed nations to define their identities in the hemisphere, the United States relied on a series of ideological assumptions rather than birthplace in forging its population's self-definition as a nation. As a result, the American self-image developed largely from ideological beliefs of superiority and inferiority and hence from the denial of what Todorov in a different context called "the existence of a human substance truly other" in its relations to foreign Others in the hemisphere.[73] To a large extent, these assumptions have since ensured the exclusion from the memory of mainstream U.S. society of knowledge about the lives and diverse historical experiences of Chicanos, Puerto Ricans, and the descendants of Latin Americans in the United States. They have thus served to perpetuate homogenizing popular perceptions of these populations as foreign to the way the national community of Americans is imagined.

The differentiated experiences and responses to the conquest of the Southwest, for example, reduced both rich and poor to a homogeneous image of all Latin American populations as "Mexicans," who were "idle," "shiftless," "fatalistic," and "resigned." Nineteenth-century politicians described native New Mexicans as "a hybrid race of Spanish and Indian origin, ignorant, degraded, demoralized, and priest-ridden,"[74] an image that, as

McWilliams suggested, was projected nationwide, as indicated in letters, journalistic accounts, and travelers' reports:

> Essentially this same impression was formed by a wide variety of observers: men and women; officers, miners, surveyors, trappers, mountainmen, sea captains, and journalists. Passed along to those who were about to leave for the borderlands, repeated by all observers, *these stereotyped impressions were national currency during the Mexican-American war and the patriotic sanction long continued.*[75]

Moreover, these portrayals were extended to include all Spanish-speaking people in the hemisphere and continued to shape both the direction of U.S. policy and popular prejudices toward people with ties to Latin America well into the twentieth century.[76] One hundred years after the conquest, the conflation of race and nationality still underlay the public exclusion of Mexican-American War veterans from celebrations of the imagined community of the United States. Although by this time Mexicans were officially classified as "white" by the U.S. Census during Fourth of July Celebrations in two Texan towns in 1943, for example, local newspapers reported:

> Several hundred citizens of the United States of Mexican extraction were told over the loudspeaker that they should go home because the dance being held in a public square was for white people only. Among the persons ejected were many wearing United States soldiers' uniforms. At still another place, again on the Fourth of July, at an American Legion dance, Spanish-name veterans of World War I were asked to leave because the dance was for "whites" only.[77]

And in the late 1960s, the conflation of nationality and race still exemplified the ways that the gap between the laws and customs of the land continued to shape the style in which public officials "imagined" the national community, such that Mexican Americans were excluded as foreigners in U.S. society:

> It was the quiet discontent and the foreboding of an electoral revolt in the barrios that led to the formation by President Johnson in 1967 of the Inner-Agency Committee on Mexican American Affairs. The "benign neglect" of the Chicanos has since progressed from the vulgar to the sardonic. In the autumn of 1969, a bill, introduced by Senator Montoya to extend the life of the President's committee (rechristened the Cabinet Committee on Opportunity for the Spanish Speaking), passed the Senate and was sent to the House. It was "lost" for four months. Embarrassed by this denouement, its Senate sponsors instituted a hectic search for the missing bill. It was found in the House Foreign Affairs committee. *Someone had assumed that "Mexican-American Affairs" was a "foreign problem."*[78]

The marginalization and invisibility of Chicanos and Puerto Ricans has distorted the ways in which U.S. history is presented to schoolchildren, and thus also affects the way they are taught to imagine their "national community." This was noted as recently as 1970 in a study of the treatment of minorities in 45 junior and senior high school social studies textbooks, which concluded:

A significant number of texts . . . continue to present a principally white, Protestant Anglo-Saxon view of America's past and present, while the nature and problems of minority groups are largely neglected. . . . Even less attention is paid to America's increasingly significant minority groups of Spanish-speaking peoples. In social studies textbooks the Mexican American has replaced the black man as the "invisible American." Puerto Ricans fare only sightly better.[79]

And even in the 1980s, Frank Bonilla could still point to the extent to which invisibility and negative stereotypes about Puerto Ricans have persisted. Reviewing some of the early statements made by U.S. military observers about the Puerto Rican people in 1898, cited earlier, he asks:

What are we to make of the fact that 70 years of increasingly elaborate social science research on Puerto Rico and its mainland offshoots have added practically nothing to the imagery of the Puerto Rican current among our U.S. overseers that could not readily be inferred or extrapolated from the 1900 impressions?[80]

Drawn from the dominant definitions of the manifest destiny of the Anglo-American peoples, the nineteenth-century "laws of custom" thus do not seem to have disappeared in the late twentieth century. Instead, the early fusion of race and nationality had ensured that Chicanos and Puerto Ricans—regardless of race, class, birthplace, or citizenship—were explicitly excluded *as foreigners* from the style in which the white Anglo-Saxon public opinion was encouraged to imagine the national community of the United States.[81] Insofar as the public dominant image of "Americans" was forged in white Protestant Anglo-Saxon terms against the created image of people of Latin American descent as "foreign Others," it is not surprising to find that throughout the twentieth century the latter's images continued to be reinforced in the popular mind as foreign to the style in which the American national community is imagined.[82]

Finally, it is important to note that since the nineteenth century, the public "racial" style of imagining the nation in relation to foreign others was also reinforced by a civil war, which ultimately led to establishing the national community's domestic boundaries in strictly black and white terms. Thus, as in the case of African Americans, the relationship between the American imagined community and Mexican Americans/Chicanos and Puerto Ricans (subsequently extended to embrace Latin Americans as a whole) stems from the historical lack of recognition of the latter groups' membership as citizens of the nation. But, unlike African Americans, it is also based on continually denying their native-born presence and participation in setting the boundaries and constructing the image of the "national community" of the United States.[83]

The boundaries of the national community were "imagined" in white Anglo-Saxon Protestant terms. Yet it is important to note that once "imagined" in those terms and institutionalized through segregationist laws and customs, the reality of the boundaries of inclusion and exclusion were to long affect, albeit in different ways, every aspect of the daily lives of Mexican Americans, Puerto Ricans, African Americans, and other racialized minorities in the United States.

The effects of the nineteenth-century fusion of nationality and race were still strongly visible in the 1960s. They became manifest in the particular forms of mobilization adopted in the struggle against the differentiated exclusion that long determined the lives of various groups in the United States. As the following two chapters suggest, in the process of shaping the respective struggles of Mexican Americans and Puerto Ricans for political inclusion in the late 1960s and early 1970s, they also established the terms of the recent debates to clarify the meaning and social value of *both* "being American" and its corollary, "being Hispanic," in U.S. society today.

NOTES

1. Discussing the confusion raised by the definition of *Hispanic*, Carl Mora remarks: "What do our statisticians and government officials do? They refer to all these people as being 'of Spanish origin' (except the Brazilians) when it is obvious that a great many Spanish-speaking Latin Americans have no ancestral connection at all to Spain (but some Portuguese-speaking Brazilians do). . . . The term 'non-Hispanic white' is . . . used to denote one of European origin; but where then, did the 'Hispanic whites' originate if not also in Europe?" Carl J. Mora, "Americans of Hispanic Origin."

2. Simón Bolívar, *Para nosotros la patria es América;* José Martí, *Páginas escogidas,* ed. Roberto Fernandez Retamar; J. Giordano and D. Torres, eds., *La identidad cultural de Hispanoamerica: Discusión actual;* Angel Rama, *Transculturación narrativa en América Latína;* Gabriel García Márquez, *El general en su laberinto;* Julio Cortázar, *Rayuela;* and Leopoldo Zea, ed., *América Latína en sus ideas.*

3. See chapter 4 in Oboler, *Ethnic Labels, Latino Lives: Identity and the Politics of (Re)Presentation.*

4. See Robert Berkhofer's discussion of the exclusion of Native Americans in *The White Man's Indian: Images of the American Indian from Columbus to the Present* for an analogous argument, and for overviews of the histories of racial minorities in the United States, see, for example, Ronald Takaki, *A Different Mirror: A History of Multicultural America;* Takaki, *Iron Cages: Race and Culture in Nineteenth Century America;* and B. Ringer, *"We the People" and Others: Duality and America's Treatment of Its Racial Minorities.*

5. For accounts of the Spanish colonial heritage in Latin America, see, for example, S. J. Stein and B. H. Stein, *The Colonial Heritage of Latin America: Essays on Economic Dependence in Perspective;* Mark Burkholder and Lyman Johnson, *Colonial Latin America;* and Richard Morse, "The Heritage of Latin America," in *The Founding of New Societies,* ed. L. Hartz, 123-77.

6. Morner, *Race Mixture in the History of Latin America;* and Carlos Fuentes, *Latin America at War with the Past.*

7. Fuentes, *Latin America at War with the Past,* 27.

8. Ibid., 28.

9. New Mexico is perhaps the clearest example of the coexistence of differentiated land and social structural arrangements present elsewhere in colonial Spanish America. By the early nineteenth century, the bulk of what was to become the Mexican population was concentrated in the northernmost region of the Spanish Empire, known today as northern New Mexico. As in other parts of Mexico and the Andean region of South America, "communal villages" were organized in northern New Mexico on the basis of collective land grants given to communities as a whole. But, as Richard Morse notes, while small private farmers were few and far between in most of Spanish America, in northern Mexico they did coexist with the hacienda and *ejidos* (or communal land ownership). In this case, most of the acquired land was equally divided for private farming, but a part of the land grant remained commonly owned, and grazing and water were shared communally (Mario Barrera, *Race and Class in the Southwest*).

Unlike the case in northern New Mexico, the sheepherding industry of the rest of the area (today known as the "ovine nursery of the nation") was organized on the basis of "a traditional social structure and a well-defined division of labor." Two or three *pastores* or sheepherders were under the command of a mounted rider (*vaquero*), who in turn was supervised by a range boss (*caporal*). The superintendent or *majordomo* was over the *caporal.* At the top of the pyramid was the owner or patron, a member of the small but wealthy "Hispano" elite that, in New Mexico, became known as the *ricos* (see Carey McWilliams, "Heritage of the Southwest," in *Chicano: The Evolution of a People,* ed. Renato Rosaldo, Robert Calvert, and Gustav Seligman, 5). These regional patterns of land ownership and of social and racial organization and status, exemplified by the variations found in New Mexico, extended from the southern reaches of the Spanish empire to sparsely populated California. See Stanley J. Stein and Barbara H. Stein, *The Colonial Heritage of Latin America.*

10. Morner, *Race Mixture,* 6.

11. Verena Stolke, "Conquered Women," 23-28; and Ramón Gutiérrez, *When Jesus Came, the Corn Mothers Went Away: Marriage, Sexuality, and Power in New Mexico, 1500-1846.*

12. Morse, "The Heritage of Latin America."

13. This, too, enhanced the social status of both the "white" Latin American-born Spaniards (criollos) and the mestizos born in wedlock to either "pure"

Spaniards or criollo families, while the consequent disdain for the large numbers of illegitimate mestizos and mulattoes in colonial society simultaneously became increasingly entrenched in the laws and customs of Spain's New World colonies. See Morner, *Race Mixture*.

14. Alejandro Lipschütz, *El indoamericanismo y el problema racial en las Américas* (Santiago, 1944), 75.

15. Gutiérrez, *When Jesus came, the Corn Mothers Went Away*, 198-99.

16. Morner, *Race Mixture*, 36-40.

17. See Gutiérrez, *When Jesus came, the Corn Mothers Went Away*, chaps. 5 and 6. Griswold del Castillo notes that "Spanish laws . . . frequently described the relationship between husband and wife in monarchical terms: 'the husband is, as it were, the Lord and Head of his wife.'" Richard Griswold del Castillo, *La Familia: Chicano Families in the Urban Southwest, 1848 to the Present*, 28.

18. See Morse, "Heritage of Latin America"; and Roberto R. Da Matta, "Do You Know Who You're Talking To?" in *Carnivals, Rogues and Heroes: An Anthropology of the Brazilian Dilemma*, 429-42.

19. F. González del Cossío, quoted in Morner, *Race Mixture*, 109; see also Richard Graham, ed., *The Idea of Race in Latin America, 1870-1940*.

20. "Entre el zar de Rusia y un mujik creo que habría menos distancia que entre un comunero de Andahuaylas (mi pueblo natal) y cualquinera de los presidentes del Perú." Quoted in William Rowe, ed., *José María Arguedas: Los ríos profundos*, xvii; my translation.

21. Juan A. Oddone, "Regionalismo y Nacionalismo," in *América Latina en sus ideas*, ed. Leopoldo Zea, 236.

22. Peter Wade, "Race and Class: The Case of South American Blacks," 233. Indeed the very existence of the notion of "continuum," with its attending hierarchical status at each point along the way, points to the entrenched racial prejudices inherited from colonial Spanish society. This continuum "allows mulattoes to dissociate themselves from blacks and be accepted as socially distinct and . . . permits some of them to 'marry up' racially." Ibid.

23. Richard Griswold del Castillo, *The Treaty of Guadalupe Hidalgo: A Legacy of Conflict*. For general overviews of the consequences of the Mexican-American War for the Spanish-speaking populations of the Southwest and California, see, for example, Carey McWilliams, *North from Mexico*; Barrera, *Race and Class in the Southwest*; and Acuña, *Occupied America*. On the complexity and diversity of the effects of the Mexican-American War upon different Mexican populations in specific regions, see, for example, Sarah Deutsch, *No Separate Refuge: Culture, Class, and Gender on an Anglo Hispanic Frontier in the American Southwest, 1880-1940*; David Montejano, *Anglos and Mexicans in the Making of Texas, 1836-1986*; Mario T.

Garcia, *Desert Immigrants: The Mexicans of El Paso*; Leonard Pitt, *The Decline of the Californios: A Social History of the Spanish-Speaking Californians, 1846-1980*; and Arnoldo de León, *They Called Them Greasers: Anglo Attitudes toward Mexicans in Texas, 1821-1900*.

24. Takaki, *Iron Cages*, 161.

25. Barrera, *Race and Class in the Southwest*, 26. See also Pitt, *Decline of the Californios*.

26. Griswold del Castillo, *Treaty of Guadalupe Hidalgo*; Manuel G. Gonzles, *The Hispanic Elite of the Southwest*; Acuña, *Occupied America*; and Barrera, *Race and Class in the Southwest*.

27. The *pobres'* forms of resistance to the disruptive encroaching penetration of Anglo-Americans into their communities and communally owned lands took a different form, graphically described by Rosenbaum: "On the morning of April 27, 1889, the owners of a ranch near San Geronimo, twelve miles west of Las Vegas, awoke to find their four miles of new barbed wire fence cut. Cut is a mild word. It was destroyed, the fence posts chopped to kindling and the wire strewn in glittering fragments. The partners—two English adventurers trying their luck at Wild West ranching—were the first victims of a civil war that raced across San Miguel County for the next eighteen months. Wearing white masks or caps—*gorras blancas*—bands of native New Mexicans—*mexicanos*—struck at night, leveling fences, destroying crops, burning buildings, and not infrequently, shooting people. By the summer of 1890, according to one English language newspaper, *Las Gorras Blancas* had brought business in Las Vegas to a standstill." Robert J. Rosenbaum, "Las Gorras Blancas of San Miguel County, 1884-1890," in *Chicano: The Evolution of a People*, ed. Renato Rosaldo, Robert Calvert, and Gustav Seligman, 129. See also Rosenbaum's *Mexicano Resistance in the Southwest: The Sacred Right of Self-Preservation* for a fuller treatment of the Mexicano resistance strategies.

28. Deutsch, *No Separate Refuge*; and Rosenbaum, *Mexicano Resistance*. Many of the efforts to resist the Anglos have been recorded in the Mexican *Corridos*, or ballads, about the period. The classic text on this question is Américo Paredes, *With His Pistol in His Hand: A Border Ballad and Its Hero*. See also José Limón, *Mexican Ballads, Chicano Poems: History and Influence in Mexican-American Social Poetry*.

29. Montejano, *Anglos and Mexicans*, 84; and Barrera, *Race and Class*.

30. Montejano, *Anglos and Mexicans*, 84. Not surprisingly, this statement rings true beyond the border region to include the Southwest as a whole. See de León, *They Called Them Greasers*; Acuña, *Occupied America*; and Barrera, *Race and Class*.

31. Acuña, *Occupied America*, 55.

32. McWilliams, *North from Mexico*, chap. 2, as quoted by Acuña, *Occupied America*, 55.

33. Nancie Gonzalez, *The Spanish Americans of New Mexico*, 205, quoted in Acuña, *Occupied America*, 56. Similarly, although the numbers of Puerto Ricans in the United States did not reach 1,600 in the census of 1910, Bernardo Vega notes that the rampant racism and discrimination against "everything foreign" and particularly against Puerto Ricans in New York led many of the elite to prefer to pass as Spaniards or to not speak Spanish and to deny their origins in the early twentieth-century Latino community in New York. Bernardo Vega, *Memoirs of Bernardo Vega: A Contribution to the History of the Puerto Rican Community in New York*, ed. César Andreu Iglesias, 97.

34. Quoted in Montejano, *Anglos and Mexicans*, 115; my emphasis.

35. Pitt, *Decline of the Californios*, 14.

36. Wade, *Race and Class*, 233.

37. Benedict Anderson, *Imagined Communities: Reflections on the Origin and Spread of Nationalism*, 14-15.

38. Stephan Thernstrom, "Ethnic Groups in American History," in *Ethnic Relations in America*, ed. American Assembly, 3-27.

39. Gordon, *Assimilation in American Life*, 115.

40. Thernstrom, "Ethnic Groups in American History," 3.

41. Joshua Fishman, *Language Loyalty in the United States*, 32.

42. In some ways, the Dred Scott case of 1857 exemplifies this difference. The Supreme Court did not address the issue raised by Scott of whether he, a freed slave, could be sold into slavery again. Instead it focused on the larger question of whether blacks had the legal right to recourse to the U.S. system of justice at all. In the court's decision, the 84-year-old chief justice, Roger Brook Taney, recognized that "the words 'people of the United States' and 'citizens' are synonymous terms and mean the same thing." Yet arguing that the writers of the Constitution did not intend to recognize blacks and "people" of the United States or to recognize them as citizens of this country, the majority ruling concluded that Dred Scott did not have the right to appeal to the U.S. system of justice in the first place. Hence he was denied legal recognition of his freedom from slavery. In denying the humanity of African Americans, the Dred Scott case thus served to confirm that they were in fact not "citizens" and therefore not entitled to other American's right to constitutional protection. As I discuss in the following pages, the case of the Mexican Americans who were granted citizenship through the Treaty of Guadalupe Hidalgo following the Mexican-American War is very different. On the Dred Scott case, see Ringer, "*We the People*," 103-107, 1110-14; National Advisory Commission on Civil Disorders, *The Kerner Report*, 1968, 211; and, for a fuller discussion of the arguments presented in this case, Vincent C. Hopkins, S. J., *Dred Scott's Case*.

43. Robert F. Foerster, *The Racial Problems Involved in Immigration from Latin America and the West Indies to the United States*, A Report Submitted to the Secretary of Labor, 55.

44. Quoted in E. Fiske, "One Language or Two?" *New York Times*, fall survey on education, Nov. 10, 1985, 1. For an overview of bilingual education in the United States, see Gary Keller and K. S. Van Hooft. "Chronology of Bilingualism and Bilingual Education"; Guadalupe San Miguel Jr., "*Let All of Them Take Heed*": *Mexican-Americans and the Campaign for Educational Equity in Texas, 1910-1981*; R. Padilla, *Bilingual Education and Public Policy in the United States*, vol. 1; and Guadalupe San Miguel Jr., "Conflict and Controversy in the Evolution of Bilingual Education in the United States—An Interpretation," in *The Mexican-American Experience*, ed. R. O. de la Garza et al., 267-79. For debates on the language question in the United States, see, for example, Ana Celia Zentella, "Language Politics in the U.S.A.: The English Only Movement," in *Literature, Language and Politics*, ed. B. J. Craige, 39-51; Fishman, "'English Only'"; J. Crawford, ed., *Language Loyalties: A Source Book on the Official English Controversy*; and C. Cazden and C. E. Snow, *English Plus: Issues in Bilingual Education*.

45. Eric Hobsbawm, "Mass-Producing Traditions."

46. Thus, although referring to the 1870-1914 period, Hobsbawm's explanation of the roots of national identity of Americans continued to be confirmed in the hearings of the "House Committee on *Un-American Activities*" of the 1950s; see Marty Jezer, *The Dark Ages: Life in the United States, 1945-1960*, 77-106.

47. Hannah Arendt, "Lawlessness Is Inherent in the Uprooted," *New York Times Magazine*, Apr. 28, 1968, 24; my emphasis. Benedict Anderson's distinction between the nature of nationalism and racism is helpful: "The fact of the matter is that nationalism thinks in terms of historical destinies, while racism dreams of eternal contaminations, transmitted from the origins of time through an endless sequence of loathsome copulations: outside history." Anderson, *Imagined Communities*, 136.

48. Even late-eighteenth-century appeals by white Americans such as Thomas Jefferson that African Americans should be deported from the newly created nation of the United States were often grounded on a perceived racial incompatibility rather than on their birthplace. See Ronald Takaki, "Reflections on Racial Patterns in America: An Historical Perspective," in *Ethnicity and Public Policy*, ed. W. Van Horne, 1-24.

49. National Advisory Commission on Civil Disorders, *Kerner Report*, 215; my emphasis.

50. Quoted in Ringer, "*We the People*," 220-24. See also Richard Kluger, *Simple Justice: The History of Brown v. Board of Education and Black America's Struggle for Education*. I thank Anani Dzidzienyo for bringing to my attention some of the nuanced implications of the location of the case in Louisiana.

51. As early as 1826, Senator John Randolph, for example, emphasized in a U.S. Senate speech "that his countrymen ought not to associate as equals with the people of Latin America, some of whom had descended from Africans." Quoted in the Mexican newspaper *El Sol*, cited in Brack, 1973, 64. De León makes a similar case in *They Called Them Greasers*.

52. Tomás Almaguer, "Ideological Distortions in Recent Chicano Historiography: The Internal Model and Chicano Historical Interpretations," 7-28.

53. Acuña, *Occupied America*, 38.

54. Ibid.

55. Victor M. Valenzuela, "The Monroe Doctrine," in *Anti-United States Sentiment in Latin American Literature*, 11; see also Reginald Horseman, *Race and Manifest Destiny: The Origins of American Racial Anglo-Saxonism*.

56. According to Jefferson's advice to James Monroe in a letter on the Monroe Doctrine: "[Independence] made us a nation, [the Monroe Doctrine] sets our compass and points the course which we are to steer through the ocean of time opening on us." Quoted in Sculley Bradley et al. eds., *The American Tradition in Literature* 1:330. By February 15, 1905, Roosevelt had clearly shown the unilateral nature of the Monroe Doctrine and his corollary: "The United States determines when and if the principles of the Doctrine are violated and when and if violation is threatened. We alone determine what measures if any shall be taken to vindicate the principles of the Doctrine, and we of necessity determine when the principles have been vindicated. . . . It is our Doctrine to be by us invoked and sustained, held in abeyance or abandoned, as our high international policy or vital national interests shall seem to us, and to us alone to demand." Quoted in Valenzuela, "The Monroe Doctrine," 11-12.

57. "Away, away with all these cobweb tissues of rights of discovery, exploitation, settlement, contiguity, etc. [The American claim] is by the right of our manifest destiny to overspread and to possess the whole of the continent which providence has given us for the development of the great experiment of liberty and federative self-government entrusted to us." Quoted in Gutiérrez, *When Jesus Came, the Corn Mothers Went Away*, 340. In this sense, the Mexican-American War followed a tradition of expansionism first set in motion by early generations of Americans who had encroached on Native Americans' lands; see, for example, Horseman, *Race and Manifest Destiny*, 103-15.

58. Ronald Takaki, for example, summarizes the nationalist and racist justifications for the Mexican-American War put forth by the editor of the *Southern Quarterly Review* in his discussion of the significance of the "Conquest of California": "The Mexican-American War had clarified the national purpose, [the editor] declared. . . . United States troops had chastised arrogant and 'fraudulent' Mexicans. . . . 'There are

some nations that have a doom upon them. . . . The nation that makes no onward progress . . . that wastes its treasures wantonly—that cherishes not its resources—such a nation will burn out . . . will become the easy prey of the more adventurous enemy.'" Takaki, *Iron Cages*, 161.

59. Barrera, *Race and Class*, 13.

60. See Horseman, *Race and Manifest Destiny*, 229-71. Thus, when the question of further expansion into Mexico was again raised for debate in the early 1850s, Senator John Clayton could remind his colleagues that this would involve dealing with the dangers of including Mexico's people as citizens: "Yes! Aztecs, Creoles, Half-breeds, Quadroons, Samboes, and I know not what else—'ring-streaked and speckled'—all will come in, and, instead of our governing them, they by their votes, will govern *us*." Quoted in ibid., 246.

61. Takaki, *Iron Cages*, 162.

62. Pitt, *The Decline of the Californios*, 59; and Acuña, *Occupied America*, 119ff.

63. Quoted in Zinn, *A People's History*, 292. "We want a foreign market for our surplus products," stated McKinley years before his presidency. In 1897 Senator Albert Beveridge declared: "American factories are making more than the American people can use; American soil is producing more than they can consume. Fate has written our policy for us; the trade of the world must and shall be ours." Ibid.

64. Alfred López, *Doña Licha's Island: Modern Colonialism in Puerto Rico*. As Zinn notes, Cuba's full sovereignty was to be marred, however, by the U.S. Army, which refused to leave Cuba until it reluctantly agreed to incorporate the Platt Amendment into its constitution (1902), effectively bringing Cuba into the American sphere of influence. Zinn, *A People's History*, 305.

65. José Luis González, *Puerto Rico: The Four Storeyed Country*, 1-31; and Adalberto López, ed., *The Puerto Ricans*, 25-28.

66. Frank Bonilla, "Beyond Survival: Por quéseguiremos siendo Puertorriqueños," in Adalberto López, *The Puerto Ricans*, 453-54.

67. U.S. Congressional Record 1900, 56, 1:2011, as quoted in Ringer, "We the People,' 974. For a discussion of the status of Puerto Rico since 1898, see Ringer, "We the People," 945-1097; Alfredo López, *Doña Licha's Island*; Edwin Meléndez and Edgardo Meléndez, *Colonial Dilemma: Critical Perspectives on Contemporary Puerto Rico*; History Task Force, *Labor Migration under Capitalism*; and Gordon K. Lewis, *Notes on the Puerto Rican Revolution: An Essay on American Dominance and Caribbean Resistance*.

68. U.S. Congressional Record 1900, 56, 1: 2172; quoted in Ringer, "We the People," 973.

69. Quoted in Montejano, *Anglos and Mexicans*, 84; my emphasis.

70. History Task Force, Centro de Estudios Puertorriqueños, *Labor Migration under Capitalism: The Puerto Rican Experience*, 127, 124 ff.

71. James Cockcroft, *Outlaws in the Promised Land: Mexican Immigrant Workers and America's Future*, chap. 3. Félix Padilla discusses the effects of the bracero program in Chicago in *Latino Ethnic Consciousness*.

72. This comparison was first made by Bernardo Vega in the 1920s. Vega, *Memoirs of Bernardo Vega*, 120.

73. Tzvelan Todorov, *The Conquest of America: The Question of the Other*, 42-43.

74. Senator Thaddeus Stevens, quoted in Octavio I. Romano-V., "The Anthropology and Sociology of the Mexican-Americans," in *Voices: Readings from El Grito*, ed. Romano-V., 37.

75. McWilliams, quoted in ibid.; my emphasis.

76. See Foerster, *Racial Problems Involved in Immigration.*

77. Quoted in George I. Sánchez, "Pachucos in the Making," in *Chicano: The Evolution of a People*, ed. Renato Rosaldo, Robert Calvert, and Gustav Seligman, 208.

78. Stan Steiner, "Chicano Power: Militance among the Mexican-Americans," in *Pain and Promise: The Chicano Today*, ed. Edward Simmen, 130; my emphasis.

79. Michael B. Kane, *Minorities in Textbooks*, 138-42.

80. Bonilla, "Por qué seguiremos siendo," 454.

81. See de León, *They Called Them Greasers.*

82. For historical descriptions and analyses of the portrayals of people of Latin American descent (regardless of nationality) as exotic lovers or violent *bandidos* in Hollywood Westerns and romantic films, see, for example, Gary Kellner, ed., *Chicano Cinema: Research, Reviews and Resources;* Allen Woll, "Bandits and Lovers: Hispanic Images in American Film," in *The Kaleidoscopic Lens: How Hollywood Views Ethnic Groups*, ed. Randall M. Miller, 54-71; Cortés, "'Greaser's Revenge'"; and Noriega, *Chicanos and Film.*

83. For a similar statement on Anglo views of Mexicans at the turn of the century in Texas, see de León, *They Called Them Greasers*, 104.

3

THE INVENTION OF ETHNIC ORIGINS AND THE NEGOTIATION OF LATINO IDENTITY, 1969–1981

J. Jorge Klor de Alva

Introduction

Challenged by Edward Said's (1979) polemic against Orientalist essentialism, in the 1980s a significant sector of the academic community in the United States wisely set itself to the task of expunging interpretations of culture and identity founded on assumed immutable and unique essences. Without our comfortable reliance on national characters and fixed cultural traits, we—anthropologists in particular (see Clifford 1988:273)—were left with the serious problem of how to distinguish between (and within) cultures when neither unity nor continuity could be assumed. A post-Orientalist answer to this difficult quandary has come to be framed by three approaches: a focus on identities (1) as relational, rather than essential; (2) as continually being reconstructed piecemeal as a result of ongoing a historical processes, rather than being articulated as a unified totality; and (3) as subject to constant negotiation and reinvention, thus remaining contingent and unstable rather than ever becoming autonomous and fixed (see Prakash 1990:399). It is this theoretical issue, along with the related problems surrounding the invention of *difference*, and the very practical need to rethink pluralism in a multiethnic community like the United States that motivate this brief contribution to the study of ethnicity in the contemporary New World.

Using textual examples from the 1970s, complemented by ethnographic observations recorded in 1979-81 among young urban Latinos in the United States and Puerto Rico, I point to the need to historicize the collective self-identities Latinos fashioned as they sought to distance themselves, in the early 1970s, from the culture of their national state of origin. Limiting myself to two of the most dramatic moments of Latino self-creation, I explore the ways in which these differentiating moves were undertaken in order to invent new forms of regional identity which I label "nationalist ethnicity" (see Table 3.1). These self-consciously constructed identities were framed within a sociocultural matrix whose axes were made up of (what we commonly think of as) voluntary (internal) and imposed (external) reformulations, constraints, and negotiations. Therefore, I employ an interpretive analysis of ethnicity that stresses the tensions between what are perceived as subjective beliefs and what we understand as objective perceptions, particularly as these encounter each other in the social, economic, and political junctures that make up the sites where ethnic images of self and other are not only forged but contested.

Put another way, although I cannot attempt to wrestle directly with them here, I employ the following broad questions as a background to this study: To what extent are Chicano or Puerto Rican "Latino" identities a result of the subordinate status of the community (i.e., determined by "structural processes") and to what extent are the identities evidence of the vitality of cultural negotiation in a complex multiethnic society (i.e., the result of self-conscious agency)? More precisely, to what extent are the markers of ethnic distinction the effects of what I have named "colonial" forces (Box 3.1), especially as these have been reshaped by the subjects in question in their struggle to contest them or accommodate themselves to them? I raise these somewhat tiresome and primarily rhetorical questions because they help to clarify the following key assumption informing this study: Ethnicity, in the case of United States Latinos, has been the continually changing product of the interplay between (1) "colonially" created cultural images with their accompanying assumptions about the biological basis of ethnicity (e.g., the racialist ideologies behind the "hypodescent" rule [see Harris 1974]); (2) highly restrictive economic and social configurations (e.g., the constant play of exclusions, marginalizations, limitations, and selective opportunities); (3) exclusionary political processes (from indifference to petitions for change to electoral manipulations); and (4) a multiplicity of creative contestations, including the appropriation of markers of ethnic distinction as weapons in the never-ending battles for socioeconomic security and cultural survival. This last point, on the nature of their creative responses, is the specific subject of my inquiry into the Latino invention of ethnic origins.

As is well known, some Latino activists in the late 60s and 70s set out to challenge the dominant "cultural narratives" (see Bruner 1986) on Chicanos and Puerto Ricans. For over a century these narratives, by appropriating for themselves the power to define Latino identities for the mainstream communities, had successfully characterized them as (for example) backward, inferior, and lazy (e.g., Robinson 1977). As with many Mayas today (e.g., Warren 1989) or among the Akwesasne Mohawk of the Northeast of the United States (e.g., Ciborski 1990), Chicanos and Puerto Ricans "invented"—that is, creatively constructed and comprehended (see Wagner 1981; Hobsbawm and Ranger 1984)—new ethnic origins for themselves as a self-conscious maneuver aimed at propagating symbolic forms of separatist nationalism. Specifically, Chicanos sought to make credible a precontact "Aztec" (more precisely, Mexica) ancestry, while Puerto Ricans, equally concerned to found their nationalist claims on a precolonial past, turned to the Taino inhabitants of the ancient Borinquen (the island of Puerto Rico) to legitimate their claim to being a nation rather than an "ethnic minority" (see Klor de Alva 1989).

WHY THE USE OF PRE-COLUMBIAN ICONS AS THE KEY EMBLEMS OF LATINO IDENTITY?

Beginning with Columbus's second voyage, when Fray Ramón Pané wrote his account of Taino religion (Pané 1974), to Gabriel García Márquez's *Love in the Time of Cholera* (1988), anthropological discourse has made up the master narratives of the telluric tales of Latin America. Therefore, it is not surprising that anthropological themes would be used to articulate the metaphors of ethnicity as Latinos attempted to paint an image of collective selfhood that could contrast with both the heritage of their national homeland and that of the dominant culture. Many of the young urban Latinos I interviewed had sought to support a revitalization movement of ethnic pride by identifying themselves with either the well-known civilizations of ancient Mexico or with the peaceful and "wise" Arawak-speaking Taino. Others, using a more encompassing form of social analysis, groped for pre-contact images as they searched for a symbolic nexus which, by being free of gender, class, or geographic specificity, could link together all members of the various regional communities.

The icons were also seen as serving as symbolic weapons with which to mount attacks against the values, practices, and beliefs of "Anglo"-American (white, non-Hispanic) society. That is, they were used to fashion a fetish believed to be capable of defeating the enemy and protecting oneself from its malevolence (see Klor de Alva 1986). Lastly, precontact themes and symbols were believed capable of serving as a moral and political call to resist domination. This last strategy included various tactics that are of particular relevance to this study.

First, those who sought to exchange their "micro-ethnic" (or local) identity for a "nationalist" (or regional) one (see Table 1) commonly believed in the symbolic importance of narrating a new founding myth. In the case of the Chicanos an explicit narrative reflected this belief: the *Plan Espiritual de Aztlán* (1972). Aztlán was the legendary point of origin of the Aztecs, the Nahuatl-speaking Mexicas of Mexico-Tenochtitlan. In some documents these indigenes are said to have claimed that their ancient homeland was located somewhere to the north of their urban center (later Mexico City) (see Kirchhoff 1961:59-73; Klor de Alva 1981; Anaya and Lomeli 1989). The "Plan Espiritual de Aztlán," adopted by thousands of young Chicanos and Chicanas during the 1969 Chicano Liberation Youth Conference in Denver, Colorado, responded to the political conditions of the time by outlining a program for the "liberation" of the Chicanos as a "national minority." In particular, the *Plan* made use of the following set of relations.

Drawing inspiration from Aztec history—wherein Tlacaelel, the power behind the Aztec throne, articulated a new social pact that permitted him to successfully lead the Aztecs and their allies to a victory over their oppressors and, as a result, made possible the establishment in 1427 of an autonomous Aztec state—the Chicanos made of their *Plan* a charter by which to found an independent corporate identity. This new style of self-affirmation, adhering to the "mystico-militaristic" form of Aztec activism said to have been pioneered by Tlacaelel (see León-Portilla 1963), was prescribed to all Chicanos as the personal and communal model of correct behavior. Meanwhile, in a brilliant metonymic maneuver, the ancient Aztlán was identified with the Southwest of the United States. It followed, therefore, that Mexico's loss of the latter sacred territory, following their defeat in the Mexican-American War of 1847-48, was spiritually interpreted as the result of a supernatural transgression. As a consequence, activist Chicanos asserted that there was a need to civilize and humanize the now polluted space through politico-magical efforts, which only a "people of the sun" (a popular label for the Aztecs) responding to "the call of [their] blood and . . . destiny" could effect. In short, the call went out for ethnic boundaries to be shored by personal and communal acts of spiritual renewal and self-defense.

Many young Chicanos, especially the most activist sectors in California schools, identified themselves as a people with a "cosmic" mission of liberation, in opposition to the "Anglos," who were seen as an "occupying force" of "European strangers." Against the back-

ground of this provocative act of defiance, the Chicanos, by portraying themselves in contrast to the "European interlopers," attempted, at least among the sympathetic sectors of
their communities, not only to seize control of the definition of "American," but also to
identify themselves ontologically as the primordial Americans. In effect, through the
appropriation of the Mexica origin myth, some Chicanos came to assert, with a gesture of
dramatic irony, that they were the true Aztecs and, therefore, as descendants of the original
inhabitants of Aztlán they were the only authentic Americans! This reading, of course,
made Anglo-Americans the fundamental other in the United States.

Second, this creative substitution in the cultural narrative called for a redemptive bifur-
cation of cultural traits. Those considered helpful became symbolic weapons in the war
against Anglo domination, and those that were believed to endanger the community were
interpreted as antithetical, antagonistic forces. For instance, the *Plan* proclaims that "our
cultural values of life, family, and home will serve as a powerful weapon to defeat the gringo
[Anglo] dollar value system and encourage the process of love and brotherhood." This
position reflected a then popular messianic application of the law of the excluded middle:
"todo por la Raza, afuera de la Raza nada" ("everything for the 'Race,' outside of the 'Race'
nothing"). In the case of the use of pre-Columbian tropes, the following binary oppositions, which can be interpreted as a shift from Orientalist readings of Chicano culture to
nationalist responses (see Prakash 1990), are representative of the phenomenon:

a. Materialism	v.	Humanism
b. Private property	v.	Communal property
c. Seductive capitalism focused on the self as a destructive force	v.	A life of sacrifice focused on others as a creative force
d. Alienation	v.	Community, integration, and centralization

Third, although they used the term "race" in an ambiguous manner, many Chicanos,
influenced by the political use of skin color in the Black civil rights movement, emphasized
"brown power" in a non-metaphoric effort at reconstituting their corporate identity as a
racially founded nationalism. That is, the authentic inhabitants of Aztlán were said to be
characterized by specific physical features, especially a bronze or brown color. While Puerto
Rican ideas of race are significantly different from those held by Chicanos, most of the
activist Latinos I studied accepted the racialist categories—used by the dominant community to fix the status of the "colonized" ethnic other—as both a strategy for unification
(through the creation of an irreducible difference) and as a way to explain the source of
their oppressed condition. As a result of this, these Latinos tended to interpret the negative
socioeconomic and cultural effects of their micro-ethnicity as primarily the consequence
of their presumed physically marked racial distinctions. Thus, in yet one more ironic reversal, they sought to contest the oppressive logic of racial discrimination and domination by
an unquestioning acceptance of its basic premise: that status can (or should) be solely
determined by empirically observable traits, especially color. At the same time, by conflat-
ing the Anglo-American concept of race with the Spanish-language term *raza*, whose connotations concern spiritual and, ultimately, national unity, rather than physical
distinctiveness, the term "race," particularly in the case of my Chicano informants, went far

outside the popular idea of the existence of demeaning physical characteristics that mark someone for specific, generally ill, treatment.

Nonetheless, perceived and imagined racism, with its emphasis on differences, its exclusionary effects that hinder or prohibit assimilation, and its morally indefensible victimization of the innocent created the space for a new discourse that fused ethnicity, race, and nationality into one narrative of corporate identity. Among Chicanos this narrative was emplotted as a redemptive myth of paradise lost (the Southwest), exile in the desert (as poor agricultural laborers), atonement through suffering, and subsequent and inevitable salvation as a chosen people (coupled with utopic vision of ultimate Chicano hegemony).

This epic quest for the appropriate form of viable nationalism, what I call "regional ethnicity" (i.e., focused on Chicanos as a whole, rather than on any of the local communities), led many of the cultural innovators to experiment extensibly with a mixed set of provocative symbols and inflammatory rhetoric. These oppositional moves include the manipulation of the details of the noble tale of Chicano liberation so as to include within it the most generous dose possible of precontact native motifs, heroes from the Mexican Revolution of 1910-17 (Pancho Villa, Emiliano Zapata, the *soldaderas* [female soldiers], etc.), and emblems of Chicano resistance (e.g., the [Aztec] eagle of the United Farm Workers Union led by César Chávez). All these symbolic strands were meant to be woven into a founding charter of ancient origins that could unite all the heterogeneous components found in the various Chicano communities. But why was race, rather than ethnicity, used to pursue this goal? Two reasons seem evident.

On the one hand, the polemic on self-identification during the heady days of the late 60s and early 70s had already developed around what were considered two opposing poles: racial minorities and white ethnic groups. Not surprisingly, regional or (better) nationalist notions of ethnicity among Latinos, already popularly identified as "minorities" rather than an "ethnics," focused primarily on race. Assuming that a nation (as in "a people") lay hidden within an oppressed race (as in "ethnic minority"), some of the most radical activists argued that unassimilated racial minorities are nations that have not been allowed to become states only because of the oppressive domination of the United States government (e.g., August 29th Movement 1976; Puerto Rican Socialist Party 1974). Therefore, they advocated separatism or at least self-determination, in a manner similar to that then being pursued by Native Americans or other peoples "of color." Still, most Latinos I interviewed, following a more moderate political line, believed that non-white ethnic groups were not nations but rather oppressed "national minorities," each forming apart of the multinational state that is the United States. For the latter, pluralism (adaptive coexistence between races and ethnicities), rather than separatism, was the goal, unlike the assimilationist goals of white European immigrants at the end of the nineteenth and first half of the twentieth centuries.

On the other hand, the label "racial minority," as used by Latinos, followed the logic of race in the United States, which characterized racial groups by the following: Their many non-Anglo-American cultural traits; their frequent and widespread alienation from state institutions (especially those that wield political power); their disproportionate representation in the poorest sectors, sharing with others in the same status the cultural traits of the working class; and their location at a substantial social distance from the dominant community. Therefore, the very real experience of segregation, discrimination, and oppression, along with the cultural reinforcement provided by the constant immigration of compatriots, all fostered a sense of racially unified, regional nationalism, whether expressed as a resistance to assimilation (a form of separatism), or as a claim to exclusive rights and privileges within a multinational state (pluralism).

All this suggests the extent to which Latino nationalism could be conceived as a response both to perceived social, cultural, and economic inequalities, *and* to actual experiences of racial discrimination. Clearly, collective awareness of socioeconomic disparities and racial discrimination slowed to a significant degree the processes of acculturation (cultural adaptation) and assimilation (social, political, and economic integration), thereby helping to maintain the boundaries between regional ethnicities and white ethnic groups. These separations in turn promoted and made "natural" the development of the concept and practice of political "nationalism" that came to the fore when the critical conjunctures of the 60s and 70s made space for it. Put another way, the social and political apertures of the five years prior to the recession of 1973 permitted the Latinos to integrate their ethnic and national narratives within the Third World liberation discourses that held sway among radicalized youth, particularly students, of the first and third worlds.

However, rather than internationalist solidarity, what the Latinos I studied sought was the construction of new identities through novel strategies of interethnic and intraethnic negotiation. These innovative maneuvers included the consolidation of the distinct genealogies of the many Chicano or Puerto Rican micro-ethnicities through their recoding within a master nationalist narrative. I propose that the conditions and parameters for the negotiation process that was (and to a great extent is) taking place can be found within the logic informing Table 3.1.

AZTLÁN: REGIONAL ETHNIC IDENTITY AS NATIONALIST SELF-IMAGE

The central semiotic move employed by activist Chicanos to effect the desired shift from a local micro-ethnicity to a regional nationalism bears repeating to underline its dramatic appeal. In summary, the identification of the mythical geography of Aztlán, the birthplace of the so-called Aztecs, with the historical geography of the Chicano community, the United States Southwest, implied a new genealogy for the Chicanos, one in which their ancestors, commonly considered the descendants of the Aztecs, were transformed into the latters' forebears. In effect, not only were the Chicanos redefining themselves as the primordial Americans, but also as the original Mexicans!

The context, popularity, and dissemination of this creative recreation of lineage can be understood as follows. The determining circumstances were primarily the political apertures of the moment, which gave rise to the necessity to affirm ethnic identities in order to create corporate groupings willing to act in unison on behalf of common agendas. This highly charged field consisted of the anti-Vietnam War, civil rights, New Left, radical feminist, and counter-cultural movements, along with the War on Poverty initiatives of the Johnson administration, which were fueled, in part, by the economic expansion brought on by the war economy of the '60s and early '70s. In addition, there was a strongly felt need to explicitly legitimate and justify regional, radical political programs through their identification with international movements such as the then current wars of liberation, international student uprisings, and widespread nationalist anti-Americanism.

The quick popularity of the new founding myth also owed much to the lack of appropriate competing symbols, particularly in the vacuum left when Chicanos sought to distance themselves from Mexican cultural markers while seeking to identify similarities

Table 3.1 Levels of Corporate Identification

LEVEL	LOCAL	REGIONAL	NATIONAL	GLOBAL
E.g.	Mexica ("Aztec")	Nahua	Indian	Mexican
E.g.	Tejano	Chicano	Latino/Hispanic	American
Type	Local Ethnicity	Regional Ethnicity	National Ethnicity	Global Ethnicity
Form	"Micro-ethnicity"	"Nationalist Ethnicity"	"Macro-ethnicity"	"Meta-ethnicity"
Source of Identity	Identification with the local corporate group is through the nation state of origin	The tension between the identity derived from the nation state of origin and the (distinct) identity resulting from the experience of life in the new country. Ethnicity here requires the invention of a more inclusive type of nationalism.	The identification (invention) of ethnicity depends primarily on the dominant sectors (imposed ethnic identification that disregards ethnic nationalist claims).	The state; therefore, the negation of ethnicity as such (seen as gratuitously divisive by the dominant sectors).
Goal and Category of Interethnic Relations	What nationalists sought to supersede	Sought by nationalist activists.	What is taking place today in U.S. wherever no Latino regional ethnicity predominates, and what is sought by the dominant sectors who want to treat all Latino ethnic groups as one.	Sought by dominant Anglo-American sectors threatened by ethnic-specific demands for social and political space.
	Characterized by ethnic relations	Characterized by racial relations	Characterized by "colonial" relations (see Table 2)	Characterized by class relations

*Table 3.1 and Box 3.1 owe much to the insights and the language of my colleague Kay B. Warren (see Warren 1989, 1992).

Box 3.1 Interethnic Relations by Level of Corporate Identification:
Local/Ethnic <——-> Regional/"Racial" <——-> National/"Colonial" <——-> Global/Class

A. Local "Ethnic" Relations

Within the loosely linked context of the multinational state, each Latino micro-ethnic group generally has a separate sphere of activity (social, economic, cultural), which is con-nected to but distinct from those of the Anglo sectors. Consequently, even if economic lev-els are equal across the diverse groups, local ethnic values determine the hierarchy. Beyond this valuation, however, many distinctive markers of ethnic identity, although seemingly chosen as "cultural" preferences, reflect the subordinate position of the micro-ethnic com-munities not only in quality but also in type (e.g., a "Chevy" versus a Volvo). Nonetheless, unless, as is the case primarily with Puerto Ricans, they are fixed by phenotypic traits iden-tified with the African-American community, ethnic differences are not static. Instead, they are subject to redefinition by insiders and outsiders, therefore "passing," the publicly suc-cessful re-fashioning of ethnic identity, is a frequent phenomenon. It follows that local resis-tance to the values of others can take place either along with (and through) an adaptation to the lifestyles and emblems of the culture/identity of the dominant sectors, or by selec-tively rejecting these. Overall, while some sense of identification characterizes most Latino intra-ethnic relations, inter-ethnic relations tend to be "highly segmental, functionally spe-cific and instrumental, and are circumscribed by well-defined roles" (Colby and Van de Berghe 1969:157).

B. Regional "Racial" Relations

I have in mind primarily the relations between non-Latino communities and the Latino micro-ethnic groups who, in their attempt to unite into a regional ethnicity, assert credi-ble nationalist claims that the members of the group share membership in the same "race" and that that race constitutes a single nation. Here, where "race" is a critical factor because some distinguishing somatic characteristics are in play, the social spheres are understood to be separated by the phenotypic traits. When the phenotypic type is clearly in evidence, it becomes the primary determinant of socioeconomic and occupational status and it delimits the cultural values and options available, thus functioning as an external con-straint. Whether real, as in the case of most African-Americans—Latin or not—or primarily putative, as in the case of less "Indian-looking" Chicanos, little social and cultural flexibili-ty is either possible or thought to be possible given the limited options available (or thought to be available) to choose or exchange identity. Therefore, racially defined identi-ty, as opposed to ethnic, is less voluntary/symbolic and logically the ethnic boundaries are (or are believed to be) extremely impermeable; as a consequence, racial relations are even more circumscribed than are ethnic ones.

C. National "Colonial" Relations

Because of the emphasis on efficiency of effort and economy of communication, govern-ment agencies, the national media, and other public and private state and national insti-tutions continually search for the most seemingly neutral and inclusive categories of ethnic identification. The power exercised by all these is reflected in their capacity to impose eth-nic categories on everyday discourse which disregard not only the troublesome multiplic-ity of micro-ethnicities, but also the regional, nationalist ethnicities that separate Chicanos from Puerto Ricans. It is also the case that in inter-ethnic colonial situations, where rela-tionships are characterized by "ethnic discrimination, political dependence, social inferior-ity, residential segregation, economic subjection, juridical incapacity" (Stavenhagen 1970:269) and institutional subordination, the ethnic group is defined as a monolithic unit, independent of internal social, economic, or cultural variations. Given this similarity of dis-cursive practices, and the fact that this description generally applies to the macro-ethnic relations in the United States, which themselves are a legacy of the ethnic queuing that dates to the colonial and immediate post-colonial periods, I use the concept "colonial rela-tions" to identify macro-ethnic relations.

Although colonial relations are characterized by great contrasts in values and resources, the status and prestige systems of the subjected macro-ethnicity can serve as defensive mech-anisms, permitting the members to create their own internal strategies for the mainte-nance of rank, honor, and respect (e.g., through religious or oratorical virtuosity, or through the maintenance of locally admired occupational, wage, and consumption pat-terns). Macro-ethnic relations between Latinos ("Hispanics") and "Anglos," however, do not fully replicate colonial relations in that despite the insistence on the importance of rit-ualized and dichotomous interaction, the latter encourage rather than minimize the accul-turation of the former to their values. Nonetheless, even when economic levels are shared, cultural values and ethnic attitudes are frequently distinct enough to intervene to make relations hierarchical.

D. Global Class Relations

By "global" I mean both most encompassing and outward-looking (in the sense that an international rather than national context is the frame of reference). While sharing some of the same concerns with the proliferation of ethnic categories that characterize "colonial" bureaucracies, difference, in the case of global relations, is primarily conceived as economic rather than ethnic or "colonial." However, cultural ("ethnic") factors are unavoidable for, as E. P. Thompson has wisely observed, class is culture: "it is experience (often class expe-rience) which gives a coloration to culture, to values, and to thought" (1978:98). Still, in the global context dominant sectors promote acculturation *and* circumscribe assimilation (i.e., the dissolution of ethnic identity along with differential integration into social and economic structures). The stress, therefore, is on class rather than "colonial"-based rela-tions. It follows that the categorizing of social types is primarily along the lines of wealth, on the one hand, and vocation as producers, managers, or consumers, on the other, rather than along ethnic or racial boundaries. Consequently, the boundaries between ethnic groups may become porous in some contexts (e.g., an urban factory), while remaining impermeable in others (e.g., a rural farm, local church, or civic club).

among the micro-ethnicities as the bases of a regional identity. Most importantly, however, its widespread dissemination must be attributed to the symbol's capacity to translate effectively and economically the presumed essence of a sectoral movement into the language of a nationalist project.

As was already noted, its specific narrative was self-consciously shaped in 1969 during the "Chicano Liberation Youth Conference" in Denver. The "national question" raised at that time by Chicanos assumed that nationalism (i.e., regional ethnicity) was more important than local affiliation or class consciousness and was thus the most inclusive corporate form of identification either possible or desired. The *Plan Espiritual de Aztlán* (with all the magical connotations that written "plans" have had for Mexicans), expressed this assessment in these words: "We are a Nation, We are a union of free pueblos, We are Aztlán," advocating "social, economic, cultural, and political independence" as "the only road to total liberation from oppression, exploitation, and racism." Thus what was desired was control of lands "rightfully" theirs, economic autonomy, community control of education (as practiced in the Crystal City, Texas, political revolt and in the formation of the La Raza Unida Party), self-defense (as expressed in the para-military organization known as the Brown Berets), cultural affirmation, and political power through electoral strength.

THE OPPOSITION TO NATIONALISM

Why did the magical power of the symbols that framed the idea of "Aztlán" wane? Or, better, why did a racially-based nationalist identity fail to provide a foundation for a new regional sense of corporate identification among Chicanos?

First, the idea was proposed, promoted, and accepted primarily by students, who for the most part were distanced from the endogamous creative forces that affected most deeply the formation of self-images within the working-class and recent immigrant communities. As could be expected, the students were more assimilated and assimilation prone than the Mexican laborers in the fields, restaurants, sweat shops, or factories. Consequently, questions of identity, ethnic affirmation, or radical (and potentially alienating) nationalism were more specifically student problems; therefore, they lacked both the relevance and the credibility to generate a persuasive alternative to local forms of micro-, that is, national-origin-based ethnicity.

Second, beyond this widespread indifference, strong opposition to a racialist-nationalist identity continually eroded the support for a cultural nationalism. For example, many cultural forms of nationalism—including the term "Chicano" and the emphasis on non-permeable boundary formations, around a relatively small set of cultural traits (e.g., language, food preference, religion)—were vehemently criticized by the coalition-minded community and labor leaders, the civic-minded activist bureaucrats, and the orthodox leftist intellectuals I interviewed. This resistance to a nationalist identity was especially vigorous among those who followed a class-based analysis that interpreted ethnicity and race as epiphenomenal or as mere tactics in the class struggle. Lastly, because the symbols of the nationalist thrust were primarily the product of Latino artists, especially poets, they became the prime targets of radical criticism of cultural nationalism. A very studied but representative sample of this criticism, drawn from the Puerto Rican community, is found in the following eloquent critique:

Unfortunately, we frequently [found] among these [nationalist] poets the same dangers that stand as a barrier between the cultural and political life of the whole community: the strained rhetoric of narrow, short-lived cultural rebellion, the anarchistic flair and utopian constructions, and the formalistic and private airs that hover out of reach of the people.

While it started in the cultural forefront of the political struggle, the . . . poetry as a whole [fell] behind . . . [and] suffered from the lack of political direction, which . . . left wide open the road to a modish aestheticism and willful bohemianism [*Centro Taller de Cultura* 1976:146,148].

Other forms of criticism of the nationalist approach could be summarized as follows: It led to chauvinistic divisiveness among the micro-ethnicities and therefore exacerbated intra-class schisms. It placed too great an emphasis on race and racism, thus obscuring the structural inequalities that were believed by some to be the real sources of social and economic exploitation. It fueled what we could call today an "Orientalist" (see Said 1979) tendency to essentialize cultural traits into binary oppositions: e.g., Chicano or Puerto Rican versus Anglo (white) or Black. In turn, this too rigid dichotomy was criticized for implying a static vision of culture and thereby dismissing the search for and the promotion of cultural elements common to other groups, which, if recognized, could be useful for community building toward macro- and multi-ethnic levels. That is, the nationalists were believed to have failed to generate the context for the type of ethnic cross-fertilization that could lead to new shared forms of multi-ethnic identification and resistance.

In effect, some believed this type of nationalism led to an exaggerated focus on romantic efforts aimed at preserving the culture rather than aspiring to transform it into an efficient instrument for overcoming domination. Echoing this, others argued that it erroneously placed too much emphasis on the search for the roots or essence of the culture and personality of the ethnic group, leading to a reduction of the struggle for self-determination to a mere historical and idealist search for cultural identity. This emphasis on "roots" was said to imply a debilitating dependence on the cultural forms of the ruling sectors in the motherland. This, the critics asserted, was due to the fact that given the socioeconomic and political control of those in power, they had made credible the affirmation that only the elite version of culture could have the status of national culture. Meanwhile, this elite lore and the practices of the privileged in the homeland were considered incapable of expressing the realities of an oppressed people (i.e., they unwittingly served to disparage the culture of the working class). Finally, cultural nationalism was believed to limit its demands to mere reforms, stressing primarily cultural autonomy (pluralism), without paying sufficient attention to the economic, political, and social agendas of the oppressors. Thus, despite the separatist claims of the nationalists, their assumptions concerning the autonomy of culture were interpreted by their detractors as supportive of the false idea that the same economic and political structures can serve as a base for dramatically different and contradictory cultural expressions.

By 1973 the sociopolitical apertures that had made nationalist agendas possible had closed. As a consequence, these activists quickly gave way either to a reformist (i.e., accommodationist, pragmatic, electoral-oriented) pluralism, to vocal but highly circumscribed leftist-oriented initiatives (e.g., the Central de Acción Social Autónoma [CASA], the August

29th Movement, etc.), or to more local and even private projects. Indeed, much of the nationalist energy was channeled away from a political direction to a personal one.

Because much that was said in opposition to the Chicano nationalist thrust is true for that of the Puerto Ricans, in this section I have referred to the latter wherever relevant. However, the situation among the two sets of communities was, for obvious reasons, quite different and merits a separate analysis; thus, I now turn to the Puerto Rican case.

BORINQUEN: LOCAL ETHNIC IDENTITY AS NATIONALIST SELF-IMAGE

For my Puerto Rican informants, on and off the island, ethnic identity was closely associated with and in part was constituted through the following enigma: Is Puerto Rico a nation? Put another way, is the question of collective identity the same as the "national question?" For Puerto Ricans the two key determinants of their ethnic identity have been the island's history as a perennial colony and the consequent emigration to the United States of over one third of its population. Given these conditions the status of the island has become something of a fetish: no subject is more passionately discussed, nothing is believed to oppress more or promise more, and nothing is believed to affect more deeply the lives of Puerto Ricans than a change of status. It is the master metaphor by which all social classes from every shade of the political spectrum understand their collective selves. And with the 1990s plebiscite on statehood near, the status question has remained at the top of any political understanding of Puerto Rican culture or identity.

The problematic nature of the Puerto Ricans' image of their corporate self—at least since 1898, the date when the island fell under the sovereignty of the United States—was believed by some of my more critical informants to be the result of the historical absence of a national-oriented dominant sector, whose presence would have made possible the defense of Puerto Rican culture from the aggressive Americanization policies of the colonial agents. More specifically, they claimed—echoing the literature on the subject (e.g., *Centro Taller de Cultura* 1976; Campos and Flores 1979; *Taller de Formación Política* 1982)—that as a consequence of a very ambivalent political and educational policy, which sought to convince Puerto Ricans that there was no such thing as a Puerto Rican culture while at the same time putting great pressure on them to replace the supposedly nonexistent traits with Anglo-American ones, generations of Puerto Ricans on the island have had to face a difficult task when attempting to define their identity. It follows that for Puerto Ricans on the mainland, especially those in the first and second generations, personal and collective identity has always been a far greater and more critical preoccupation, at all social levels, than was ever the case for second or more generation Chicanos, particularly those who saw themselves as Mexicans.

Nonetheless, by the end of the '60s and beginning of the '70s, the nationalist Puerto Ricans I studied in the United States had turned to the idea of "Borinquen" (the Arawak/Taino name for the island of Puerto Rico) as a tactic by which to gain support for their nation-building project. First, along with many other young Puerto Ricans, they had set out to transform the then tarnished image of the island into one that reflected a promised land rich with hope. Through a romantic equation, which identified Borinquen as a lost tropical paradise, the island was made the repository of all cherished values, the well-spring of all inspiration, the source of the strength to resist acculturation and oppression, and the object of nostalgic remembrances. Following on the footsteps of the late nineteenth- and early twentieth-century nationalist writers, who like Luis Lloréns Torres (see Diaz Quiñones 1986) mythologized the *jíbaro* as the authentic Puerto Rican, they articulated what I call a Jíbaro primitivism, with a sentimental longing for the idealized, spiritually rich, tranquil but productive life, and socially harmonious world of the bygone peasants. This utopic image went beyond the mere improvisation of a fanciful contemporary island to the devising of a perfect Borinquen, formerly graced by peaceful Tainos living an idyllic, Edenic precontact existence, who were in turn replaced by the hard-working jívaros. And in sharp contrast to the dominant ideology on the island, which has long sought to de-emphasize the role of slavery in Puerto Rican history and the presence of African somatic traits and cultural elements, the nationalists underlined their debt to Africa, particularly through music, as found in the lyrics of the *salsa* songs that enjoyed great popularity at the time.

Such lyrical and shocking innovations, which drew from the deep well of Puerto Rican affection for their homeland and a recognition of the complex cultural debts of the island, encouraged an obligatory pilgrimage to Borinquen. Many of my informants, particularly in the second generation, felt the need to return to the home of their ancestors, and their visits became a ritual part of their personal and collective search for cultural shield with which to protect their (to them) precarious identity. However, many of those who were able to make the trip and who highlighted their Africanness, in dress, speech, or music, or separatist ideology through the public veneration of, for instance, the nationalist leader Pedro Albizu Campos, were disappointed by the cold and sometimes hostile greeting they had received. Disillusioned, some nationalists returned to New York and elsewhere with the resolve to carry on at home what they identified as the "class" struggle and the battle for the independence of Puerto Rico.

This change of mind brought with it some important hermeneutical revisions. For instance, the political interpretations of the most radical sector shifted from a focus on what I have been calling nationalist conceptions of ethnicity, with their emphasis on racial distinctions, to what I term a "global" focus on class. This was reflected in the way in which the cultural nationalism of the Young Lords Party was replaced by the Marxist politics of the newly formed Puerto Rican Revolutionary Workers Organization (see PRRWO 1974; Estades 1978:50; Flores et al. 1981). At the semiotic level the exegetic move was from sign to symbol, as the real Borinquen, the island, gave way to the emblematic Borinquen as "un estado deánimo," that is, as a "state of mind" (Barradas 1979:54). Ultimately, this turning to the self gave way to the failure of the symbol altogether. First, its referent went from Edenic island to spiritual state (as was the case with Anaya's *Heart of Aztlán*). This was followed by a replacement of the ancient mythical geography by an internal, psychological one, in turn, the social meanings became primarily personal, and, finally, Borinquen as the sign of a nation collapsed into the mere symbol of a notion.

However, the cultural innovators, who had earlier put forward the idea of Borinquen as an utopic island, put a new trope in the service of regional nationalism: the independence of Borinquen. I call this a "trope" because thy meant for independence to serve primarily as a symbol by which to unify mainland Puerto Ricans rather than as a call for political action on behalf of the island. Furthermore, as many mainlanders made evident, this independence was no longer seen as a panacea guaranteed to cure all the ills suffered by all Puerto Ricans, nor was it imagined as making it possible for all Puerto Ricans to unite once more on the island. Instead, by providing a common discourse of nationalist identity, independence by the mid-70s was conceived by many first and second generation Puerto Ricans as a magical symbol capable of protecting them from the centrifugal forces unchained by the diaspora.

From this it is evident that Puerto Rican nationalists encoded their discourse in a very different register than the one used by Chicanos. While some of the reasons for this are apparent, many are not. In order to attempt to clarify them a somewhat extended conclusion is in order.

CONCLUSION

The relations between mainlanders and islanders and between Puerto Ricans and Anglo-Americans are quite different from those that characterize Chicano-Mexican or Chicano-"Anglo" interactions. Although there are some tensions between the two communities, primarily political and class-related, Puerto Ricans on the mainland, particularly of the first and second generation, have always had intense contacts with their counterparts on the island and, given the close family ties that span the ocean, each side has experienced an ongoing and broad interest in the other's social, economic, and political welfare. Indeed, apart from the separatist sentiments already noted, I have frequently heard in the United States that "what happens in Puerto Rico affects the barrio." However, the desire on the part of mainlanders to participate in the island's plebiscite in the 90s, and the resistance to this request, at least officially, on the part of the islanders may attest to the differential nature of the claims to connection made by each side. Whatever the case may be, connections to the island have served as extremely important sources for the mainlanders' academic, artistic, and political inspirations. It follows that Puerto Rican nationalists in the United States were able to use the island's colonial status to generate a political discourse that could serve as the basis of their narrative on identity. By way of a representative example of the effects of this last point, it bears mentioning that, given the attention to the political situation of the island and, thus, to an international context for political identity, the Young Lords labeled themselves socialists and anti-imperialists before these terms were adopted by politically radicalized Chicano nationalists.

In contrast, prior to the 1970s, second and more generation Chicanos paid relatively little attention to Mexican politics. And the cultural distance between Chicanos and Mexicans (in terms of cultural knowledge and ethnic loyalty) was (and continues to be) much greater than that between island and mainland Puerto Ricans. Indeed, Chicano-Mexican relations are frequently antagonistic, not only among gangs composed of opposing groups of immigrant and resident youths (as I personally experienced while growing up in East San Jose, California, and, later, in the course of my comparative research on Latino gang warfare in Watsonville, California, and Levittown, Puerto Rico), but also, for instance, among highly educated university professors who oppose the hiring of Mexicans in Chicano Studies departments and who prefer to keep Mexican studies separate from the study of Chicanos. It follows that when Chicano nationalists turned to Mexico in the late 60s and early 70s it was primarily to search for cultural symbols and ethnic inspiration, not to look for political answers to their problems. And, consequently, Chicanos themselves were the quintessential object of their investigations, not Mexicans.

Furthermore, Puerto Rican communities in the United States were not transformed by the nationalists into a symbolic Borinquen; in fact, before it lost its political force, the concept remained anchored to the real island. Conversely, many young Chicanos identified

Aztlán literally with the Southwest. This contributed not only to their detachment from the politics of Mexico, but (as is frequently the case today) to the sentiment among some of an opposition to Mexico and "Mexican things" ("lo mexicano"), at least to the extent these were considered foreign (not "Chicano"). As a consequence, the search for a corporate identity openly contested not only Anglo-American but frequently   Mexican options. Therefore, the emphasis in the course of the nationalist search for identity remained on the creation of something completely new.

Although it is difficult to show, I believe that, at first, the diffusion of the novel self-image, negotiated between and beyond United States and Mexican cultural elements, owed its speed to the '60s' spread of working-class social and cultural traits across the full Chicano class spectrum. But later, whatever the reason for this success—and the demographic preponderance of the working class is one—the new collective identity came to contribute to the privileging of working-class cultural traits over those of the upper and middle class. Given this and the cultural distance from Mexico, through mimetic processes of ethnic identification the middle and upper sectors, since the '70s, especially among the second or more generations, when expressing what they consider to be the basic cultural and normative traits of Chicanos imitate those common among the lower strata. This dissemination throughout Chicano society of cultural elements identified primarily with one class has resulted in a continuous creative thrust characterized by an urban exoticism ("lo rasquachi" [Ybarra-Frausto 1989]), which is easily recognizable as Chicano rather than Mexican or Anglo.

Meanwhile, the identification of "Borinquen" solely with the island facilitated the transference of its symbolic power to the ideal of Independence. The magic of Borinquen was thereby replaced by the fetish of pro-Independent symbolism and activism. And despite the disillusionment suffered by the nationalists who traveled to the island in the early 70s, by remaining linked to the politics of the island through the independence movement they managed to maintain a significant public forum. This permitted them to use political discourse to focus their search on new forms of *mainland* cultural identification, even while underlining the common destiny of mainlanders and islanders. However, this hesitation (or unwillingness) to articulate a clearly autonomous mainland self-image may have contributed to, rather than helped to resolve, the frequently expressed problem of United States Puerto Rican identity.

With hesitations of my own, I close with some broad observations concerning the post-Orientalist study of culture and the categories found in Table 3.1, Box 3.1, and Box 3.2. As this essay suggests, I am persuaded that identity and culture can be understood best through the post-structuralist forms most closely identified with Michel Foucault (see 1977, 1979, 1980a, 1980b, 1985). I have found the following power/knowledge assumptions particularly useful and persuasive: (1) His description of power as diffused throughout a multiplicity of sites, including those places where benevolence, intimacy, or familiarity rein. (2) His related understanding of the multivectorial distribution of power (instead of, for instance, the assumed top-down directionality common among Marxists or the idealized bottom-up perspective of Enlightenment political liberalism). And (3) his analyses of the ways in which those with power (at home, in a hospital, in state capitals, or wherever) strategically deploy discourses that, to the extent they become hegemonic, can constitute knowledges, which, in turn, can condition the circulation of power itself.

Like Foucault, I am no longer sure that our nineteenth-century use of culture as an analytic category is still either useful or appropriate. Therefore, rather than to unchanging essences or unified and continuous traits, it is to discursive practices, embedded in constantly shifting networks of power/knowledge, that I turn to in my search for a way to understand *difference*. Corporate groups can be distinguished by the content of and the ways in which they participate in distinct discourses, each with its own rules for the generation of true statements. Recognizable cultural wholes, then, are in a real sense effects of power, complex narratives and related empirical traces produced by the differential knowledges that power, in the Foucaultian sense, can constitute. Obviously, different discourses, the product of variable external constraints and shifting personal understandings, have not only dissimilar content, but produce distinct effects, especially as they are expressive of incompatible, disparate, or conflicting concerns. Corporate identity is in this sense necessarily relational rather than essential. It is carved out of a series of everyday life contingencies, understood through the dominant discourses that at the moment have the power to compel assent, and negotiated as strategies of domination, resistance, or—more typically—accommodation. Thus, in culture-contact conditions, as is the case with Latinos in the

---

Box 3.2 Characteristics of Corporate Identification

I. The Condition of Ethnicity

    A. Geography

        1. geographic origin, migratory status, place of settlement

    B. Social class

        1. employment options, level of education

    C. External perception of distinctiveness

        1. phylogenetic traits (race)

        2. knowledge of a foreign language, use of a dialect, accent

        3. public adherence to or celebration of traditions, values, key symbols, holidays, religious practices

        4. public production and consumption of ethnic food, literature, folklore, or music

        5. participation in ethnic institutions or ethnic politics

II. The Experience of Ethnicity

    A. The subjective experience of an unavoidable distinctiveness maintained by at least some of the following:

        1. a seemingly involuntary identification with the corporate group

            (a) including actual or assumed descent from common ancestors

            (b) a different (perhaps easier) form of communication between members than with outsiders

            (c) a distance from or a possible hostility toward outsiders

        2. a voluntary behavioral conformance to the practices of the group

        3. use of the markers of distinction common to the group (see C.2-5 above)

        4. given the option, a preference for these markers

        5. actual or putative knowledge of their use and the group's history

        6. a pride in and a loyalty to the markers and the group

        7. a belief in the values of the markers and the group

United States, competing discourses generate conflicting truths, any of which can survive only to the extent that its claims can satisfy the needs of its adherents and its adherents have the power to make the claims socially viable facts. In short, truths have a social construction and therefor have a history, what Foucault, following Nietzsche, calls a genealogy.

Based on the above, I suggest that Latino identity in the United States is a constant process of negotiation between the conditions of ethnicity (see Box 3.2), constituted by the dominant discourses on, say, race, economics, cultural tastes, etc., and the experience of ethnicity. I understand the latter as the effect of the seemingly autonomous, but socially constructed sense of individual subjectivity that, in constituting the ("ethnic") self, delimits the acceptable preferences, the right beliefs, the sound practices, an the epistemologically possible truths. This negotiation is how I interpret, at the theoretical level, the relations between socioeconomic and cultural changes and the reconfigurations of ethnic identity commonly used as adaptive responses to these shifts. This, then, is the analytical context within which I understand the brief outline of interethnic relations by level of corporate identification found in Box 3.1. The details must be left for another time, but the examples of the invention of ethnic origins by way of Aztlán and Borinquen should be suggestive.

Although many important questions have been left unanswered, I will end with two very practical ones: Given what I have written, what interests are served in the pluralist, multi-ethnic/multinational United States by the maintenance of systematic inequalities that weaken the competitiveness of the labor force? And how can pluralism function as a viable tactic for generating and maintaining salutary differences that promote self-esteem, interethnic cooperation, and the reduction of the most oppressive aspects of the colonial legacy of ethnic queuing?

REFERENCES

Anaya, Rudolfo A. 1976. *Heart of Aztlán*. Berkeley: Editorial Justa.

_____ and Francisco A. Lomeli (eds.). 1989. *Aztlán: Essays on the Chicano Homeland*. Albuquerque: Academia/El Norte Publications. (Distributed by University of New Mexico Press.)

August Twenty-Ninth Movement. 1976. *Fan the Flames: A Revolutionary Position on the Chicano National Question*. unpublished.

Barradas, Efrain. 1979. "De lejos en sueños verla..." Visión mitica de Puerto Rico en la Poesia neoyorrican. *Revista Chicano-Riqueña* 7: 46-56.

Bruner, Edward M. 1986. Ethnography as Narrative. In *The Anthropology of Experience*. Edited by Victor W. Turner and Edward M. Bruner. Urbana and Chicago: University of Illinois.

Campos, Ricardo and Juan Flores. 1979. Migración y cultura nacional puertorriqueñas: perspectivas proletarias. In *Puerto Rico: Identidad nacional y clases sociales (Coloquio de Princeton)*. Edited by Angel G. Quintero Rivera, et al. Río Piedras, Puerto Rico: Ediciones Huracán.

Centro Taller de Cultura. 1976. *Centro Taller de Cultura*. Centro de Estudios Puertorriqueños. New York: CUNY.

Ciborski, Sara. 1990. *Culture and Power: The Emergence and Politics of Akwesasne-Mohawk Traditionalism*. Ph.D. dissertation, Albany: State University of New York.

Clifford, James. 1988. *The Predicament of Culture: Twentieth-Century Ethnography, Literature, and Art*. Cambridge: Harvard University.

Colby, Benjamin N. and Pierre L. Van den Berghe. 1969. *Ixil Country: A Plural Society in Highland Guatemala*. Berkeley: University of California.

Díaz Quiñones, Arcadio (ed.). 1986. *Luis Lloréns Torres: Antología, verso y prosa*. Rio Piedras, Puerto Rico: Ediciones Huracán.

Estades, Rosa. 1978. *Patterns of Political Participation of Puerto Ricans in New York City*. Hato Rey, Puerto Rico: Editorial Univeritaria.

Flores, Juan, et al. 1981. La Carreta Made a U-Turn: Puerto Rican Language and Culture in the United States. *Daedalus* 110:193-217.

Foucault, Michel. 1977. *Language, Counter-memory, Practice: Selected Essays and Interviews*. Edited by Donald F. Bouchard, translated by Donald F. Bouchard and Sherry Simon. Ithaca, New York: Cornell University.

_____. 1979. *Discipline and Punish: The Birth of the Prison*. Translation by Alan Sheridan. New York: Vintage Books.

_____. 1980a. *The History of Sexuality: Volume 1: An Introduction*. Translated by Robert Hurley. New York: Vintage Books.

_____. 1980b. *Power/Knowledge: Selected Interviews & Other Writings, 1972-1977*. Edited by Colin Gordon. New York: Pantheon Books.

_____ 1985. *The Use of Pleasure: The History of Sexuality: Volume 2*. Translated by Robert Hurley. New York: Pantheon Books.

García Márquez Gabriel. 1988. *Love in the Time of Cholera* Translated by Edith Grossman. New York: Alfred A. Knopf.

Harris, Marvin. 1974. *Patterns of Race in the Americas.* New York: W.W. Norton & Company.

Hobsbawm, Eric and Terence Ranger (eds.). 1984. *The Invention of Tradition.* New York: Cambridge University.

Kirchhoff, Paul. 1961. Se puede localizar Aztlán? *Anuario de Historia* 1:59-73.

Kor de Alva, J. Jorge. 1981. Aztlán. In *Dictionary of Mexican American History,* edited by Matt S. Meier and Feliciano Rivera. Westport, Connecticut: Greenwood Press.

_____. 1986. California Chicano Literature and Pre-columbian Motifs: Foil and Fetish. *Confluencia* 1:18-26.

_____. 1989. Aztlán, Borinquen and Hispanic Nationalism in the United States. In *Aztlán: Essays on the Chicano Homeland.* Edited by Rudolfo A. Anaya and Francisco A. Lomeli. Albuquerque: Academia/El Norte Publications.

León-Portilla, Miguel. 1963. *Aztec Thought and Culture: A Study of the Ancient Nahuatl Mind.* Translated by Jack Emory Davis. Norman, OK: University of Oklahoma.

Pané, Ramón. 1974. *Relación acerca de las antigüedades de los indios.* Edited by José Juan Arrom. Mexico: Siglo Veintiuno.

Plan Espiritual de Aztlán. 1972. Plan Espiritual de Aztlán. In *Aztlán: An Anthology of Mexican American Literature.* Edited by Luis Valdez and Stan Steiner. New York: Vintage Books.

Prakash, Gyan. 1990. Writing Post-Orientalist Histories of the Third World: Perspectives from Indian Historiography. *Comparative Study of Society and History* 32:383-408.

PRRWO (Puerto Rican Revolutionary Workers Organization). 1974. National Liberation of Puerto Rico and the Responsibilities of the U.S. Proletariat. *The Rican: Journal of Contemporary Puerto Rican Thought* 2:70-80.

Puerto Rican Socialist Party. 1974. The National Question. *The Rican: Journal of Contemporary Puerto Rican Thought* 2:47-48.

Robinson, Cecil. 1977. *Mexico and the Hispanic Southwest in American Literature.* Tucson: University of Arizona.

Said, Edward W. 1979. *Orientalism.* New York: Vintage Books.

Stavenhagen, Rodolfo. 1970. Classes, Colonialism and Acculturation. In *Masses in Latin America,* edited by Irving Louis Horowitz. New York: Oxford University.

Taller de Formación Politica. 1982. *La cuestión nacional: El Partido Nacionalista y el movimiento obrero Puertorriqueño.* Rio Piedras, Puerto Rico: Ediciones Huracán.

Thompson, E.P. 1978. *The Poverty of Theory and Other Essays.* New York: Monthly Review Press.

Wagner, Roy. 1981. *The Invention of Culture.* Chicago: University of Chicago.

Warren, Kay B. 1989. *The Symbolism of Subordination: Indian Identity in a Guatemalan Town.* Austin: University of Texas.

_____. 1992. Identidad indigena en Guatemala: Una critica de modelos norteamericanos. *Mesoamerica.*

Ybarra-Frausto, Tomás. 1989. Rasquachismo. In *Le demon des anges: 16 artistes chicanos autour de Los Angeles.* Edited by Pascal Letellier et al. Barcelona, Spain: Centre de Recherche pour le Developpement Culturel, Nantes, and Departament de Cultura de la Generalitat de Catalunya.

PART TWO

IMMIGRATION: COMING FROM THE AMERICAS

INTRODUCTION ❦

Pierrette Hondagneu-Sotelo and Mary Romero

MEDIA REPRESENTATIONS OF LATINO IMMIGRATION play on two main images: "good" immigrants seeking political asylum versus "bad" immigrants flooding across the border for economic reasons. One type of evening news story sympathetically describes events like the Mariel boatlift, Nicaraguan exiles fleeing the Sandinistas, or Salvadorans and Guatemalans escaping the death squads. Here the focus is on repressive political regimes and the hardships of the journey; the immigrants are celebrated as heroic and valiant, and families are shown and interviewed. Quite different news stories report on the "economic" migrants, where Mexicans in search of a living wage are almost universally represented by single males. Their activities are "criminalized" as they are shown racing across the border, spotlighted by helicopters, fleeing raids, or rounded up and "arrested" while awaiting deportation. When so called "in-depth" stories are done, they usually consist of documenting dependence on social services and charity. In each case we are regaled with stories of individual struggles for a new life in America rather than an analysis of distinct peoples responding to specific social, political, and economic circumstances.

The personal account of immigration conveniently supports and strongly reinforces the orthodox view of migration. Rooted in neoclassical economics, the orthodox view explains migration as an individual "rational" or "cost-benefit" response to negative "push" factors in the country of origin and positive "pull" factors in the U.S. This approach searches for explanations in the actions of individual migrants and ignores the economic, political and historical factors that shape immigration. Political debates are shown, but they are carefully framed around local issues: fence building; increasing the patrol of the Mexico border and the Florida coastline; the denial of education, health, and welfare services to the undocumented and to non-citizens; the English only movement, etc. In media productions, U.S. citizens are typically depicted as victims, paying taxes for additional border patrols and social services and being forced to compete with immigrants willing to accept much lower wages.

The articles in this section challenge explanations of Latino immigration implicit in the popular individualistic "immigrant story." The circumstances of Puerto Rican, Mexican, Central American, and Nicaraguan immigration are examined from the perspective and within the context of particular historical and macrostructural circumstances. While mass media images of Latino immigrants depict illiterate peasants fleeing traditional, backwards economies for "modern" jobs in Los Angeles, Miami, or New York City, these articles suggest that migration is more likely to originate in societies already disrupted by rapid-paced political and economic change. Furthermore, U.S. government and private capital play decisive roles in stimulating U.S.-bound migration from Mexico, Puerto Rico, Cuba, Central America, and the Dominican Republic. Activities including U.S. military intervention, American foreign policy, private foreign investment, and direct labor recruitment sponsored by government and particular industries have been and continue to be critical factors stimulating immigration to this country.

The section begins with an overview and critique of U.S. theoretical approaches to the study of immigration. In "Central American Migration: A Framework for Analysis," Nora Hamilton and Norma Stoltz Chinchilla outline a theoretical approach that considers historical and contemporary circumstances, economic and political motivations, and domestic and international structures. They argue that the migration of Central Americans to the U.S. is not only produced by foreign policy and civil war, but also by particular patterns of capitalist development. According to this view, the Central American refugee movement is generated by both political crisis and economic contradictions. Foreign capital investment generated indirect labor recruitment, and once migration began, social networks gained their own self-generating momentum. Thus, Hamilton and Chinchilla demonstrate the relationship between U.S. foreign policy and immigration to the U.S., as well as immigration policy. They argue that Central American immigration in the 1980s was different from prior Latino migrations. This article provides a strong point of reference for reevaluating the extensive immigration of Puerto Ricans and Mexicans, and discussing the more recent experiences of Nicaraguan immigrants.

In the next article, "A Summary of Puerto Rican Migration to the United States," Clara Rodríguez argues that understanding the economic and political history of Puerto Rico and the U.S. is essential to explaining the large numbers of Puerto Ricans on the mainland. She notes that U.S. colonization and annexation at the end of the nineteenth century marked the end of a diversified subsistence economy and inaugurated Puerto Rico's dependency on sugar. The decline in this industry prompted the first wave of Puerto Rican migration in the 1920s. By the mid- twentieth century "Operation Bootstrap," a U.S.-dominated industrialization program emphasizing capital intensive businesses, stimulated further migration to New York City and other Northeast cities. Rodriquez argues that the concentration of Puerto Ricans in decaying urban areas of the Northeast may account for the high poverty rates. Puerto Rican migration patterns differ somewhat from other Latino groups because of their unique political relationship. Since they are U.S. citizens, migration to the island from the mainland and back is a right of citizenship and consequently, does not become an exclusive privilege of the upper class.

In the third article in this section, "The History of Mexican Undocumented Settlement in the United States," Pierrette Hondagneu-Sotelo discusses economic and political transformations in the U.S. and Mexico that shaped contemporary Mexican immigration, namely the large numbers of undocumented immigrants. After the establishment of the U.S.-Mexico border in 1848, most Mexicans who came to the U.S. did so through a "revolving door," as temporary sojourners who worked in railroads, agriculture, and mining. Recent decades have witnessed the multiplication of Mexican immigrant settlement communities and the integration of Mexican immigrant workers into many sectors of the U.S. economy. The emergence of contemporary settlement patterns is explained through an examination of historical patterns of capitalist development in Mexico and the U.S. Southwest, direct labor recruitment such as the Bracero Program (1942-64), and more recently, an increasingly diversified labor demand in the U.S. Political and economic transformations in Mexico's agricultural and industrial structure are also central to the analysis. Hondagneu-Sotelo makes a strong argument for linking immigration to broader global processes.

The final selection in "Coming from the Americas," highlights the importance of the political context in understanding the immigration experiences of Latinos. In their article, "A Repeat Performance? The Nicaraguan Exodus," Alejandro Portes and Alex Stepick examine parallels and differences between Cubans and Nicaraguans in Miami. Here, the focus is on the political context of reception. Both Cubans and Nicaraguans arrived in different phases, and within each group, immigrants were distinguished by a particular class composition. While both Cuban and Nicaraguan immigration to the U.S. is the result of U.S. "cold war" foreign policy, Cubans were greeted with open arms, granted permanent residence and support for resettlement. Nicaraguans did not get the same accommodating political reception that awaited Cubans, and while their right-wing political sentiments have helped them to find alliances in Miami's established Cuban enclave, it seems unlikely that they will follow the same trajectory or upward mobility as Cubans.

DISCUSSION QUESTIONS:

1. Discuss how historical transformations in the economies of the U.S. and Mexico have shaped Mexican undocumented immigration.
2. How does Puerto Rico's unique political and economic relationship with the U.S. shape migration to the mainland? What role did Operation Bootstrap play in stimulating migration?
3. Discuss some of the factors that are likely to preclude Nicaraguans from following the same trajectory of Cubans who have settled in Miami.
4. Explain why the migration of Central Americans to the U.S. has occurred for economic, as well as political reasons.

SUGGESTED READINGS:

Chavez, Leo R. 1992. *Shadowed Lives: Undocumented Immigrants in American Society.* Fort Worth, TX: Harcourt Brace College Publishers.

Grasmuck, Sherri and Patricia R. Pessar. 1995. *Between Two Islands: Dominican International Migration.* Berkeley: University of California Press.

Hagan, Jacqueline Maria. 1994. *Deciding to be Legal: A Mayan Community in Houston.* Philadelphia: Temple University Press.

History Task Force, Centro de Estudios Puertorriqueños. 1979. *Labor Migration Under Capitalism: The Puerto Rican Experience.* New York: Monthly Review Press.

Hondagneu-Sotelo, Pierrette. 1994. *Gendered Transitions: Mexican Experiences of Immigration.* Berkeley: University of California Press.

Massey, Douglas, Rafael Alarcon, Jorge Durand, and Humberto Gonzalez. 1987. *Return to Aztlán: The Social Process of International Migration from Western Mexico.* Berkeley: University of California Press.

Pedraza-Bailey, Silvia. 1985. *Political and Economic Migrants in America: Cubans and Mexicans.* Austin: University of Texas Press.

Portes, Alejandro and Robert L. Bach. 1985. *Latin Journey: Cuban and Mexican Immigrants in the United States.* Berkeley: University of California Press.

Repak, Terry A. 1995. *Waiting on Washington: Central American Workers in the Nation's Capital.* Philadelphia: Temple University Press.

Special Issue: Puerto Rican Migration and Poverty, *Latino Studies Journal,* Vol. 4, No.2, 1993.

Suarez-Orozco, Carola and Marcelo Suarez-Orozco.1995. *Transformations: Immigration, Family Life, and Achievement Motivation Among Latino Adolescents.* Stanford: Stanford University Press.

4

CENTRAL AMERICAN MIGRATION:
A FRAMEWORK FOR ANALYSIS

Nora Hamilton and Norma Stoltz Chinchilla

CENTRAL AMERICANS HAVE MIGRATED for both economic and political reasons, and preliminary research on Central Americans who have come to the United States in recent years suggests that in many cases it is difficult to separate the two (Schoultz 1987, 11-13). Generally, some combination of "push" and "pull" factors influence the decision to migrate, and individual decisions occur within a framework of internal and international structures that condition individual needs and the choices available (Papademetriou 1983, 472-78; Portes and Bach 1985; Zolberg, Suhrke, and Aguayo 1986; Cohen 1987). Temporary moves may become permanent if reasons for leaving continue or are aggravated or the rationale for remaining is increased, as happens when families of labor migrants join them in the host country (Zolberg 1983, 36). Even cyclical migration may establish patterns and networks that become the basis for long-term or permanent migration (Portes 1983, 74-75; Kearney 1986, 353).

Indeed, current migration patterns often have a historical dimension. Although the recent escalation of Central American migration (within the region and to the United States) is in many respects a new phenomenon (Schoultz 1987, 9-10; Aguayo 1985, 21), the long historical tradition of migration within and between the countries of the region has undoubtedly affected current patterns of migration.

The purpose of this article is to develop a framework for analyzing Central American migration that takes into account historical and contemporary dimensions, economic and political motivations, and domestic and international structures. We will begin by briefly discussing some factors already identified in the theoretical literature on characteristics and causes of migration, focusing on structural approaches as a basis for establishing a framework for examining Central American migration. The subsequent section draws on existing studies and statistical data to discuss the historical and contemporary patterns of Central American migration in the context of this framework. In the conclusion, we analyze the appropriateness of the framework for explaining Central American migration through a series of propositions that can serve as the basis for future studies.

THEORETICAL ISSUES

Many proponents of a structural approach identify migration as resulting from the logic of capitalist development, its penetration into peripheral areas (those at a precapitalist or relatively low level of capitalist development), and the incorporation of these areas into the world economy. One major outcome of capital penetration is the direct recruitment of labor from the peripheral area, whether coerced (as in importing seven and a half million Africans to work as slaves in Europe and its colonies from the fifteenth through the eighteenth centuries) or contracted (as in contracting Eastern European peasants to work in U.S. manufacturing industries in the nineteenth century). The latter process has continued in various forms well into the twentieth century (Portes 1983; Cohen 1987; Zolberg 1983).

Exporting capital from core countries (those having a dominant position within the world economy) to peripheral regions may also produce economic distortions and dislocations that result in emigration by uprooted groups who can no longer find work in their own countries. To the extent that these groups emigrate to the relevant core areas, capital penetration becomes an element in indirect labor recruitment (Cheng and Bonacich 1984; Cornelius 1980). These processes have been accentuated as peripheral areas and countries become incorporated into an increasingly integrated but highly asymmetrical world economic system. These areas become even more vulnerable to external economic conditions ranging from fluctuations in commodity prices to global recession, again leading to emigration to core areas by uprooted populations.

Exporting capital from core countries has often been accompanied and supported by political penetration and control by the government of the advanced capitalist country, which reinforces the bilateral dominant-dependent relationship between the core country and the peripheral society. This relationship helps to explain the direction of international migration flows (such as Algerians migrating to France and Mexicans to the United States). Once established, patterns of migration continue to operate, partly because of transnational social networks (Bach 1985, 28; Kearney 1986),[1] even when efforts are made to close off opportunities for migration into the dominant country. A prominent example of the persistence of such patterns is demonstrated by the ineffectiveness of U.S. refugee and asylum policies and related efforts to block immigration via more restrictive laws and sanctions (Cheng and Bonacich 1984; Cornelius 1980, 71-72; 1988; Cue and Bach 1980, 257-59; Portes and Bach 1985).[2]

The penetration of capital into peripheral economies occurs on national as well as international levels, with comparable implications for political or economic dislocation, labor recruitment, and other inducements to migrate. At the same time, the peripheral state may play a pivotal role in facilitating conditions for foreign or national capital or both and in managing contradictions that arise from capitalist development. It may directly or indirectly affect emigration if its development policies deemphasize satisfying internal demands, particularly in a context where cultural penetration creates attraction to actual or perceived opportunities for a higher standards of living in the core (Bach 1985, 25; Portes 1983, 79-81).

While refugee movements tend to be generated by political conflicts what can include political repression, revolutionary movements, and international war, such conflicts result in many cases from economic contradictions—indeed, the same dislocations that lead some to migrate may lead others to revolt. Here the role of the domestic state is again important because state efforts to control such conflicts often lead to political repression.

In short, the dislocations produced by foreign (or domestic) capital penetration and changes in the world economy are not only a direct economic cause of migration but may also be an indirect political cause when they result in revolution or other forms of political conflict. This effect becomes direct when external states intervene politically or militarily and thus share responsibility for generating refugee flows resulting from these conflicts and for determining their course (Zolberg, Suhrke, and Aguayo 1986, 151-52, 156-58).

Finally, foreign states intervene in migration and refugee flows in their "gate-keeping" function, that is, in their immigration and refugee policies. Immigration policy in receiving countries is related to larger domestic and foreign policy concerns, and changes in policy reflect conflicts between domestic groups who benefit from migration flows (in the form of cheap labor, for example) and those who do not (Bach 1985, iii, 24). Refugee policy in prospective receiving countries may also help determine refugee immigration and is often tied to foreign policy, as is evident in the U.S. policy of accepting and even encouraging refugees from communist countries while denying refugee status to individuals fleeing countries friendly to the United States (Zolberg, Suhrke, and Aguayo 1986, 154-56; see also Teitlebaum 1984; Schoultz 1987, 67-69). As noted above, however, the effectiveness of these laws may be partly neutralized by strong migratory networks.

To summarize, migration can be explained as the effect—or one effect—of contradictions, dislocations, and opportunities resulting from the penetration of capitalism (domestic or foreign) into nations or regions at a lower level of development.[3] These processes affect and are affected by the preexisting productive structures and the state's role in maintaining those structures, which requires managing the contradictions resulting from class divisions and from the articulation of different structures of production. In concrete terms, this role ranges from promoting specific development models to repressing groups or forces that oppose the dominant economic structure. Penetration by foreign capital is often accompanied and facilitated by political penetration by the external (core) capitalist state, which takes various forms ranging from diplomatic influence to military intervention in political conflicts. The core state also performs a gate-keeping function through its immigration and refugee policy, which in turn reflects foreign and domestic policy concerns.

The above discussion suggests a framework for our analysis of Central American migration in the following section. We shall be specifically concerned with five issues: first, the relationship between capitalist penetration into less-developed or precapitalist areas and migration (how such penetration affects or is a factor in migration); second, the ways and extent to which developed capitalist or "core" economies (and regions) function as "poles of attraction" for immigration directly through labor recruitment or indirectly through cultural, economic, and social influences; third, the implications for migration of state policies on economic development and the role of the state in mitigating, managing, or aggravating contradictions and conflicts emanating from these policies or from the process of development itself; fourth, the ways and extent to which developed capitalist or core states directly or indirectly encourage or discourage migration through political or military intervention as well as through immigration and asylum policy; and finally, the role of migratory networks in reinforcing preestablished patterns of migration even when the initial conditions accounting for them have been modified or no longer exist.

The following analysis of Central American migration patterns relies on existing studies and statistical data on Central American migration. It includes an extensive study undertaken by CSUCA (the Consejo Superior Universitaria Centroamericana) in the 1970s based on census information from the 1950s, 1960s, and 1970s as well as our preliminary findings on Central American migration to the United States. Although migration within the Central American region predates the colonial period, our analysis will begin with the nineteenth century, the first important period of capitalist development in Central America, and will emphasize the postwar period, one of rapid development of capitalist market and relations of production. El Salvador was chosen for in-depth examination because it typifies the more general patterns of capitalist development and displacement and also because it is the source of the largest Central American immigrant population in the United States.

HISTORICAL PATTERNS: THE CASE OF EL SALVADOR

The dynamics of migration processes can be better understood by examining in greater detail historical developments in one country. As the smallest and most densely populated country in the region and source of the largest number of Central American immigrants to the United States, El Salvador exemplifies how capitalist penetration has resulted in extensive population movement within a limited space.[4]

In the second half of the nineteenth century, coffee displaced indigo as El Salvador's chief export, and elements of capitalist production began to displace subsistence production and previous production relations. Although indigo production had coexisted with subsistence production, expanding coffee production involved dispossessing small subsistence producers, particularly communities in the western highlands of Santa Ana, Sonsonate, and Ahuachapán.

These processes were expedited by control of the state by the emerging coffee oligarchy. It enacted a series of liberal measures that eliminated flexible conditions of land tenure and usage, including communal forms of production, and instituted individual ownership of private property as the dominant form of tenure. Where legislation failed to dislodge the communities, force was used. The state role in establishing capitalism in El Salvador thus included constructing infrastructure to facilitate commercialization, passing legislation reinforcing private property in the means of production, eliminating communal property, and repressing those who resisted this restructuring (Browning 1971, 155ff.).

Although the shift to capitalist forms of property ownership was rapid, elements of pre-capitalist relations of production remained in El Salvador. To insure a permanent labor force, the coffee landowners often established nucleated villages for workers, who also received food in partial payment for their labor. But the landowners continued to depend on the subsistence sector for seasonal labor, provided by migrants from other regions of the country.

As noted above, at least two patterns of population movement resulted from the expansion of coffee production. First, the expulsion of subsistence peasants from their communal lands in the western departments forced many to migrate to other parts of the country, often to marginal rural areas for subsistence farming. Many went to the northern departments of Chalatenango, Cabañas, and Morazán, areas that were to become strongholds of guerrilla activity in the 1970s and 1980s. Second, a pattern of cyclical migration was reinforced as subsistence peasants from other parts of the country (including the northern departments) migrated temporarily to the coffee regions during the harvest season. Also reinforced was the pattern whereby migratory peasant families formed squatter settlements wherever they found unused land—on the fringes of private estates, on government land, along the roads and highways, and eventually even in the riverbeds that intersect the capital city of San Salvador. Partly a result of population pressures, squatting also constitutes a form of resistance to the concept of private ownership of land, an idea alien to the traditional concept of possession based on living on and working the land (Browning 1971, 219-21, 259-64; Pearce 1986, 45-46).

A drop in world coffee prices in the 1920s pushed many of the smaller coffee producers off the land when they defaulted on loans, leading to further concentration. This outcome was followed by a more dramatic drop in coffee exports in 1931 during the world depression, which led to massive unemployment of rural workers in the western zones of the country. This development proved to be central to the peasant uprising in this region in 1932, which was brutally repressed by the military government of General Maximiliano Hernández Martínez. Land concentration in the 1920s, unemployment resulting from the depression in the early 1930s, and particularly the 1932 massacre (in which an estimated thirty thousand peasants were killed) caused a major migratory flow from the western and central region of El Salvador toward the eastern provinces, especially Usulután, San Miguel, Morazán, and La Unión. Migrants also went to neighboring countries, especially Honduras, where they provided labor for banana plantations on the Caribbean coast (Durham 1979, 431; CSUCA 1978a, 141).

In the period following World War II, expanding production of cotton (particularly in the southeastern coastal zones of La Paz, Usulután, and San Miguel) and sugar (chiefly in the central and southwestern departments of San Salvador, Cuscatlán, San Vicente, La Libertad, and Sonsonate) increased land pressures and migration internally and to Honduras. According to the CSUCA study, by 1950 zones of capitalist penetration had encompassed the agro-export departments of the west (Santa Ana, Ahuachapán, and Sonsonate), the more urbanized west-central areas (especially San Salvador) and La Libertad, and the southern coastal departments (especially La Paz). The northern, central, and eastern states (Chalatenango, Cuscutlán Cabañas, San Vicente, Morazán, and La Unión) made up a subsistence region devoted chiefly to grain production with relatively low productivity. San Miguel had elements of both (CSUCA 1978a, 144-45). Prior to 1950, the subsistence areas were the main zones of in-migration (particularly Cabañas, Chalatenango, Morazán, and La Unión), which may be explained by the expulsion of rural workers and peasants from the western regions as a result of unemployment and repression in the 1930s combined with the expulsion of tenant farmers and smallholders from La Paz and other cotton-growing areas in the postwar period.

Beginning in 1950, industrial modernization was also stimulated under the governments of Colonels Oscar Osorio (1950-1956) and José María Lemus (1956-1960). Taking advantage of high world prices for coffee, the government began building infrastructure: completing the Pan American and coastal highways, starting construction of the Acajulta port (in Sonsonate), expanding hydroelectric plants, and extending housing construction. With infrastructure expanding and new legislation promoting industry (including the tariff-free import of capital goods and raw materials as well as tax exemptions), profits from coffee and cotton exports that had been deposited abroad began to be invested in industry. Foreign investment in manufacturing also grew rapidly, and when world coffee prices dropped at the end of the 1950s, foreign loans began to displace export earnings as a major source of financing (CSUCA 1978a, 147-50).

The 1950s brought a marked change in the pattern of migration flows in El Salvador. One explanation for this shift in migration patterns is that it was primarily a rural-urban flow, particularly to San Salvador, which grew by more than fifty-five thousand inhabits. Between 1950 and 1961, 73 percent of all migrants moved to the cities, and 41 percent to the department of San Salvador. Other departments with major urban centers (Santa Ana, San Miguel, and La Libertad) recorded net urban migration gains ranging from three to six thousand (CSUCA 1978b, 73-85). Because the economy was expanding in the 1950s, one may surmise that the growth of industry and urban services enhanced the attractiveness of urban areas of these departments. At the same time, net rural gains occurred in the western coffee-producing departments of Ahuachapán and Sonsonate and the southern cotton department of La Paz. In the coffee regions, limited possibilities for expanding into new areas suitable for growing coffee resulted in intensive use of labor and technology to increase output and thus take advantage of the coffee boom. Finally, the decline in productivity in basic grains suggests that the poorer lands of the northern and eastern zones were becoming less productive, another possible explanation for out-migration from these areas.

Emigration to Honduras continued to increase, with Salvadorans finding work on banana plantations in the northern coastal area of Honduras or establishing their own farms closer to the Salvadoran-Honduran border. Estimates of Salvadorans in Honduras increased from twenty-five to thirty thousand in the late 1930s, to one hundred thousand in 1949, to three hundred and fifty thousand by the 1960s (Durham 1979, 59, 124-25). As Durham points out, striking parallels between internal migration and migration to Honduras suggest similar causation (see Durham 1979, t. 2.6, p. 61).

Finally, increased labor demands during the harvest resulted in large seasonal migrations to work in the coffee, sugar, and cotton harvests between October and April, particularly in November and December. During the rest of the year, migrants returned to their homes to survive on savings, farm subsistence plots, or work in the urban informal sector. By 1970 an estimated five hundred thousand temporary workers were making this annual pilgrimage (Achaerandio 1983, 4).

Thus in El Salvador, internal migration, international migration, and seasonal migration represent three responses to capitalist penetration and its consequences for subsistence production and government initiatives to insure conditions for production, whether through repression, legislation, or incentives to investment. The shift from subsistence to commercial agriculture for export meant expanding commercial estates at the expense of smallholdings and driving small peasant producers to more remote areas of the country, to Honduras, and to new squatter settlements on the fringes of private agricultural estates or on unused rural or urban land. Labor-saving technological innovations resulted in rural workers being expelled into subsistence rural areas or urban centers, which became poles of attraction due to expanding industry and urban services. Finally, declining productivity in subsistence areas in the north and east turned these regions into zones of permanent emigration to urban areas of El Salvador or to Honduras. They also provided seasonal migrants to work on coffee, sugar, and cotton estates.

MIGRATION IN THE 1960S AND 1970S

Quantitative and qualitative changes in Central American migration flows beginning in the 1970s, particularly in international migration, can be explained largely by events of the 1960s and 1970s. These decades were characterized by contradictions built into rapid modernization based on foreign investment in a context where traditional socioeconomic structures remained intact, as in Nicaragua, Guatemala, and El Salvador. Demands for change resulting from modernization and its effects were resisted by traditional political structures, which responded with increased repression that intensified opposition.

As indicated, the period following World War II brought agricultural modernization based on expanding export agriculture into cotton and sugar production, and in El Salvador and Guatemala, limited industrialization. By the end of the 1950s, however, economists, business groups, and government officials in these societies had recognized the limitations of depending on commodity exports and were seeking to promote import-substitution industrialization by creating a regional market (reducing or eliminating tariffs between the Central American countries) and by attracting foreign investment. Regional integration succeeded in obtaining foreign investment (primarily from the United States and later from Western Europe and Japan), chiefly in processing and assembly industries and in nontraditional export crops. Creation of the Central American Common Market and consequent foreign investment fostered impressive rates of growth, which averaged 7.7 percent in the region as a whole during the 1960s. But like previous modernization projects, this one led to numerous dislocations that affected rural and urban areas.

Modernization's impact on the rural areas where most Central Americans lived and worked varied according to country and situation. In some cases, it meant the takeover of peasant lands or Indian communities when members of the landowning oligarchy expanded their estates or government officials seized control of areas where new industrial projects had raised land values (as in the northern Transversal strip of Guatemala). In other cases, modernization caused a shift from subsistence farming to growing cash crops destined for U.S. supermarkets (like cauliflower and snow peas). In still other cases, it meant a reduction in the work force due to mechanized agriculture and the shift in production from agriculture to livestock in response to the market for beef created by rapid growth in hamburger and fast-food chains in the United States. Thus several patterns emerged: the proletarianization or semiproletarianization of the peasantry, a shift from subsistence to market-oriented production, and in some cases, reduced availability of agricultural jobs (Chinchilla and Hamilton 1984b, 240-42).

The precarious economic conditions in which many Central Americans lived were aggravated by increasing inflation in the 1970s, due largely to the increased prices of imports (particularly petroleum), which in turn affected prices of agricultural and manufactured products. Prices of imported inputs for manufacturing industry increased by 11.4 percent annually between 1970 and 1978, and the overall inflation rate increased by 12.8 percent annually between 1970 and 1977 (Weeks 1985, 68-71, 148-49). As a result of changes in the previous two decades, substantial sectors of the population that had previously depended wholly or partly on subsistence farming now depended on cash income and were therefore hit hard by price increases. Even in the sectors that benefitted from minimum-wage laws and wage adjustments, wage increases could not keep up with price increases.

In addition to the economic dislocations accompanying modernization, the 1960s and 1970s witnessed an increased U.S. presence in El Salvador, particularly in the form of multinational corporations investing in manufacturing. In contrast with Guatemala, Honduras, and Costa Rica, where U.S. banana companies had operated for decades, and Nicaragua, which had a long history of U.S. military, political, and financial intervention, direct U.S. penetration in El Salvador was relatively new. In all five countries, however,

increased contract with U.S. manufacturing, commercial, and financial interests undoubtedly expanded information about the United States, including work and educational
opportunities. Employment in U.S. companies may also have made migration to the
United States more accessible: a worker in a Texas Instruments plant in San Salvador could,
at least hypothetically, transfer his or her skills to an electronics assembly plant in the
United States. Or a domestic servant working for an American family in Nicaragua could
work for a similar family (or in some cases, the same family) in the United States. The
growth of a low-wage, semi-informal economy in the United States during the 1970s, based
on services or subcontracting, took advantage of an increasing undocumented labor force
and provided work for immigrants from Central America and other areas.

Finally, a factor generally discussed in studies of refugee populations, rather than in
migration studies, was increasing governmental and extragovernmental repression, which
targeted groups seeking to organize around issues and problems resulting from economic
dislocations: peasant organizations set up to contest land takeovers, labor unions demanding increased wages and improved working conditions, protests by Indian communities who
had lost their land in Guatemala, and demonstrations against increases in food prices and
bus fares in the major cities. Death squads made up of members of the landowning oligarchy
and security and military forces in Guatemala and El Salvador targeted peasant leaders,
union militants, and political activists. In El Salvador in 1969, the military formed a para-
military organization among peasants known as ORDEN (short for the Organización
Democrática Nacionalista) to carry out surveillance and even assassinations of selected leaders and militants (Black, Jamail, and Chinchilla 1984, 83-97; Montgomery 1982, 88-89).

All these factors significantly affected migration during the 1960s and 1970s. Migration
flows increased substantially, and new patterns emerged. For the period from 1950 to 1973,
the CSUCA study of Central American migration suggests three trends. First, mobility
increased in these years: the number of internal migrants doubled in Guatemala, tripled in
Nicaragua, and quintupled in Honduras (comparable figures for El Salvador were not
available). Second, regions with agricultural modernization tended to expel population
except in areas that also contained frontier or new colonization zones (such as Izabal in
Guatemala). Third, new subsistence areas and urban centers became zones of attraction
(CSUCA 1978a, 322-27).

Deteriorating conditions in the countryside, as indicated by increasing numbers of
landless rural families, and the attraction of the urban centers as a result of industrialization (especially San Salvador) undoubtedly contributed to migration trends in this period.
But as noted, the growth of industry and related services were able to absorb only part of
the growing work force because of the capital-intensive nature of new industry. While the
manufacturing sector grew by 24 percent between 1961 and 1971, employees in industry
increased by only 6 percent. Growth in urban and industry-related services could not
absorb the difference between the numbers of rural-urban migrants and jobs available in
manufacturing. By the early 1970s, 40 per cent of the nonagricultural labor force was working in the informal sector, and unemployment in San Salvador had reached 10 percent
(Armstrong and Shenk 1982, 47; Deere and Diskin 1984, 32).

As indicated above, the number of Guatemalans migrating to southern Mexico
increased from an annual average of ten to fifteen thousand in the 1950s to an estimated
sixty thousand per year in the 1970s. The expulsion of Salvadorans from Honduras during
the 1969 war also augmented Salvadoran migration to Guatemala, which has been esti-

mated between 1973 and 1984 at seventy thousand, most going to the frontier and central-south departments or to Mexico (Torres Rivas 1985, 28).

This period also saw dramatic changes in patterns of migration to the United States. As noted, prior to the mid-1960s, a small but growing number of immigrants migrated from Central America. During the following decade, the number of legally admitted Central American immigrants more than doubled, from forty-five thousand between 1951 and 1960 to more than one hundred thousand between 1961 and 1970, and exceeded one hundred and thirty-four thousand during the 1970s (U.S. INS 1978, tt. 55. 13, 14; U.S. INS 1984, t. IMM1.2). The number of illegal immigrants increased even more dramatically, as indicated by the number deported, most of them for having "entered without inspection or with false documents." Moreover, the U.S. Immigration and Naturalization Service (INS) estimates that for every undocumented person apprehended, another three to five remain in the United States undetected. Between 1969 and 1978, the number of Guatemalans deported increased from one hundred to twelve hundred and the number of Salvadorans from one hundred to thirty-four hundred (U.S. INS 1978, t. 27).

Growth in the number of Central Americans coming to the United States in the 1970s has been documented in a study of Central Americans and Mexicans in California based primarily on the 1980 census. This count found that 40 percent of Central American immigrants living in California in 1980 had entered during the previous five years and that 63 percent of these lived in Los Angeles. More than half of the Central American immigrants were women, 45 percent of those over twenty-five had completed high school, about 25 percent had attended college, and some 30 percent had worked in white-collar occupations. Thus in California, at least, Central American immigrants came disproportionately from the upper educational and occupational segments of the population in a region where only one-eighth of the economically active population had completed more than six years of school (Wallace 1986, 659-64). Most Central American migrants who arrived in the United States before 1975 presumably came from economic reasons, but by the second half of the 1970s, many were escaping violence, repression, or persecution at home, which began to accelerate in the mid-1970s.

This immigration coincided with a period of economic restructuring in the United States that involved a decline in traditional manufacturing industries accompanied by growth in high-technology industries and high- and low-skilled services (Sassen 1988). Once in the United States, many of the Central Americans were employed in low-paying jobs in the rapidly growing service sectors, in manufacturing sectors that rely on low-cost foreign labor (like the garment industry), or in agriculture.

Thus the dramatic increase in internal migration, intraregional migration, and the number of Salvadorans and Guatemalans coming to the United States during the 1970s can be correlated with deteriorating economic conditions, increased repression in their own countries in the late-1970s, and perceived opportunities and "indirect" labor recruitment in the United States. Conditions in Central America worsened further in the late 1970s and the 1980s, when the economic situation deteriorated into a region wide crisis while political polarization and conflict deepened in Guatemala, El Salvador, and Nicaragua.

POPULATION MOVEMENTS SINCE THE LATE 1970S

In the last fifteen years or so, war and political upheaval in Nicaragua, El Salvador, and Guatemala compounded by rapidly deteriorating economic conditions have resulted in massive dislocations in all three countries. In Nicaragua, the Somoza regime countered the Sandinista campaign with massive repression, including extensive bombing of rural areas and finally the major cities, prior to the Sandinista victory in July 1979. In El Salvador, revolutionary movements that had developed throughout the 1970s coordinated forces and began a military offensive in the early 1980s. During the same period in Guatemala, a revolutionary movement emerged incorporating Indian and non-Indian (*ladino*) populations.

These revolutionary offensives resulted in escalating violence by military and security forces as well as by death squads. In Guatemala, government-instigated terrorism against opposition leaders in urban areas combined with a brutal counterinsurgency campaign against the Indian population that killed thousands and displaced hundreds of thousands. Nicaragua had not yet recovered from the effects of the revolution against Somoza when the new Sandinista government was confronted by counterrevolution, organized and financed by the U.S. Central Intelligence Agency. In El Salvador, the war against the guerrilla forces often involved attacks against civilian populations in rural areas, including the massacre of the entire population of villages believed to be sympathetic to the guerrillas. Beginning in 1979, the United States became more and more enmeshed in these conflicts, resulting in an exponential increase in the militarization of the region as well as in the technological level of conflict, particularly in El Salvador (Leach, Miller, and Hatfield 1985).

Political repression and war have also aggravated the region's economic stagnation, an additional factor in displacement and migration. In El Salvador, national production declined 33 percent between 1978 and 1983, and by the mid-1980s, gross national product per capita had fallen to the level of the 1950s. The causes include massive capital flight and economic distortions resulting from U.S. financing of balance of payments, which has sustained the commercial sector while production declined (Weeks 1985, 191). Salvadoran unemployment is estimated at 33 percent, and estimates of combined unemployment and underemployment range from 50 to 75 percent (*Coyuntura Económica* 1989).[5]

The combined effects of political crisis, war, and the economic crisis aggravated by political conditions have transformed a normal migration flow into massive displacement and exodus. In terms of internal displacement, it has been estimated that by 1987 up to a million Central Americans (including a quarter-million Nicaraguans, one hundred thousand to a quarter-million Guatemalans, and half a million Salvadorans) had been displaced within their own countries (Fagen 1988, 75).

Various studies of the displaced population in El Salvador indicate that it consists of the most destitute sectors of the Salvadoran population, whose situation has been made even more desperate as a result of their circumstances. Of the displaced, the vast majority (80 to 90 percent) come from rural areas, more than half are under fifteen years of age, and half are illiterate. The mortality rate is high (24.4 per thousand according to one study, 67 percent of the deaths claiming children under five). Already low levels of employment have decreased as a result of displacement: unemployment increased from 58 to 74 percent of the economically active population after forced migration, according to one study (Alens 1984).[6]

Overall, emigration to other countries also increased substantially. Between 1971 and 1978, the annual rate of Salvadoran emigration was 5.1 per thousand inhabitants; by 1978-1980, it rose to 16.2 per thousand (Torres Rivas and Jiménez 1985, 28). Refugees seemed to follow patterns established during previous migration: Nicaraguans went to Honduras, to Costa Rica, and more recently to the United States; Salvadorans went to refugee camps in Honduras and in smaller numbers to Nicaragua and Costa Rica as well as to Guatemala,

Mexico, and the United States; Guatemalans usually went to Mexico and the United States and sometimes to other Central American countries. Much migration within Central America consisted of rural populations moving to border regions: Nicaraguans into Costa Rica and Honduras, Salvadorans into Honduras, and Guatemalans into southern Mexico.

By 1987, some 85 percent of the Central Americans who had left their countries were living in Mexico and the United States. Most of them passed through the Soconusco zone of Mexico, a narrow fertile plane along the Pacific coast that has become the traditional entering point for Central American emigrants. Although many Guatemalans and most Salvadorans continue on to Mexico City and in some cases to the United States, the Mexican states near the Guatemalan border, especially Chiapas, have become major centers for Central Americans. Nearly all of these migrants belong to indigenous populations from the northern and western highland states of Guatemala. Being of Mayan descent, they have a heritage similar to the population of Chiapas, to which they are also linked by trade and by social and kinship ties.

Finally, the number of Salvadorans and Guatemalans coming to the United States since 1979 has continued to grow. Since 1988 the number of Nicaraguans has also increased rapidly, motivated by opposition to the Sandinista government or disintegrating economic conditions. Because most of these migrants are undocumented, exact figures are not available. Salvadorans continue to represent the second-largest number of nonlegal immigrants apprehended by the INS (after Mexicans). The number of undocumented Salvadorans apprehended doubled between 1977 and 1981 from eight to sixteen thousand and reached seventeen thousand in 1985 (data from the INS). Most observers, noting the increased number of Salvadorans and Guatemalans in Los Angeles and other major U.S. cities, believe that the rate of increase has actually been much greater. One recent study estimates that three-quarters of a million to 1.3 million Central American migrants are living in the United States, two-thirds of them Salvadorans, and up to one-fifth Guatemalans (Ruggles and Fix 1985, 45-47). The U.S. General Accounting Office estimates the number of undocumented Salvadorans in the United States at six to eight hundred thousand (U.S. GAO 1989).

The majority of Central Americans (up to a half million) live in Los Angeles, with substantial numbers in San Francisco, Texas (especially Houston), Washington, New York, Chicago, New Orleans, and Miami. Many have been able to take advantage of existing migration networks through Mexico, and some have obtained help from family, friends, or even communities already established in the United States (Rodríguez 1987; Ruggles and Fix 1985; Schoultz 1987, 30-33; Montes Mozo and García Vázquez 1988, 28-29). Those lacking such networks have tended to come to areas with established Latino populations that have cultural and sometimes political affinities (like the Mexicans in Los Angeles or Cubans in Miami). While Salvadorans constitute the majority of Central Americans in most cities (followed by Guatemalans), Nicaraguans predominate in Miami and Hondurans in New Orleans (Ruggles, Manson, Trutko, and Thomas 1985; Ruggles, Fix, and Thomas 1985).

The large number of undocumented Salvadorans and Guatemalans coming to the United States in the 1970s and 1980s indicates that U.S. immigration restrictions have had little impact on the number of Central Americans arriving, although they undeniably affect the process of migration (for example, in forcing migrants to depend on expensive and often unreliable coyotes as "guides"). They also affect the experience of immigrants once they arrive. Similarly, while U.S. refugee and asylum policies tend to reflect foreign policy concerns and thus have tended to discriminate against Central Americans with the partial exception of Nicaraguans, little evidence suggests that they have deterred immigrants from coming or from returning if deported. It is still early to evaluate the consequences of the Immigration Reform and Control Act (IRCA), which grants amnesty to undocumented immigrants who can prove they arrived prior to 1982 but penalizes employers for hiring workers who cannot prove they are here legally. Most preliminary studies indicate, however, that IRCA has had little effect in deterring immigrants from coming to the United States, although the law has made it more difficult for them to obtain employment (Espenshade et al. 1988).[7]

To what extent does the influx of Central Americans since 1979 represent a continuation of previous immigration patterns rather than a qualitatively new phenomenon? Because of the recent arrival and undocumented status of most Central Americans in the United States, information on this population is fragmentary and even contradictory. Compared with the Salvadorans displaced within El Salvador or in refugee camps in Honduras or with the Guatemalans in Mexico refugee camps, the majority coming to the United States appear to have higher levels of education and income, similar to those in Mexico City (Ruggles and Fix 1985; Montes Mozo and García Vázquez 1988, 14-24). But Salvadorans' educational and income levels are undoubtedly lower on average than those of earlier migrants to the United States, and a larger proportion come from rural areas.

It would thus be a mistake to assume that Central Americans migrating to Mexico and the United States during the 1980s represent a simple continuation of previous migration flows. Aside from the greater numbers and socioeconomic differences, many of those coming after 1979 have directly experienced violence or repression, including the assassination of family members, or have themselves been targets of detention, interrogation, and even torture. Many Central Americans living in Mexico and the United States assert that survival and personal safety are their primary motivation for emigrating. Although rural communities in Guatemala and El Salvador have been the major victims of military violence, persons targeted for repression by death squads and security forces tend to be urban-dwellers who are relatively well-educated, including labor and party leaders, students, and professionals (Aguayo and Fagen 1988, 30; Chinchilla and Hamilton 1984a, 11-17; Montes Mozo and García Vázquez 1988, 13; Aguayo 1985, 43, 146, 154). Some young men from El Salvador flee recruitment by the armed forces or the guerrillas. (Montes Mozo and Garcia Vásquez 1988, 31). In short those immigrating since 1979 appear to represent a broader socioeconomic spectrum than past immigrants to the United States, and a large proportion are coming for reasons related to the war.

Many who have not been affected directly by violence and conflict have been affected indirectly, like the factory workers who have lost their jobs because the conflict has prevented production from continuing (Rodríguez 1987, 22). Thus the situation is complex because individuals and families often immigrate to another country for a combination of economic, social, and political reasons and also because the economic difficulties of the Central American countries have been prolonged and aggravated by political conflict (Stanley 1987, 146).

Current migration flows exhibit elements of both continuity and change. War, increased levels of violence, and conditions of economic crisis generated or aggravated by the political situation have become key factors in migration to the United States, to other Central American countries, and to Mexico. At the same time, like regional migrants, recent migrants to the United States for whatever reasons are taking advantage of previously established patterns of migration and networks of family, friends, or other Latino communities already in the country.

SUMMARY AND CONCLUSIONS

The foregoing analysis confirms that national and international capital penetration, resulting structural changes, and foreign intervention are central to explaining Central American migration. This review of the Central American migration experience also demonstrates that causal processes are complex and that careful analysis of each situation is necessary to determine precisely how they will affect migration.

EFFECTS OF CAPITALIST PENETRATION ON MIGRATION

Capitalist expansion in its various forms has resulted in migration between capitalist and precapitalist sectors in each country, while constantly reducing the size of precapitalist sectors and the capacity of capitalist sectors to absorb new workers. But while our earlier discussion suggests that capitalist penetration results in migration from less-developed to more-developed areas, the Central American experience indicates that the direction and patterns of migration vary according to conditions and structures within the peripheral economy or region.

Virtually all major instances of capitalist penetration have led to internal or international migration: the introduction and expansion of the coffee export economy in the nineteenth century; the creation of U.S. banana enclaves at the turn of the century; agricultural modernization by introducing technological innovations in existing crops and introducing or expanding estates that produce new export crops (especially cotton and sugar) in the postwar period; and industrial modernization in the 1960s and 1970s via creation of the Central American Common Market and increased foreign investment.

In addition to the direct effects of capital penetration, the changing dynamic of world capitalisms has affected Central American economies in at least two respects. First, it has directly or indirectly affected penetration of foreign capital in the region. Thus the expansion of U.S. capitalism at the turn of the century was manifested in its growing economic and political hegemony in the Caribbean region, evidenced in Central America in the expansion of United Fruit (and later Standard Fruit) and in U.S. political, military, and financial intervention in Nicaragua. Second, economic cycles, booms, and depressions directly affect economies tied into the world market, whether through depressed (or increased) commodity prices, the opening of new export markets or closing of existing ones, or the transfer of inflated costs through the import of raw materials, machinery, or other agricultural and industrial inputs.

One response to changes and dislocations resulting from these global trends has been migration. Massive unemployment among Salvadoran coffee workers caused by depression-generated production cutbacks in the 1930s was one factor (along with the *matanza* of 1932) in the migration from the western coffee regions to central and eastern sectors of the country and into Honduras. Inflation produced by the oil crisis of the 1970s was passed along to consumers in Central America through higher costs of imported consumer goods or inputs to production and contributed to the dislocations of the 1970s that led many Central Americans to emigrate north. Currently, cotton workers in El Salvador are being driven from the southeastern regions of the country by production cutbacks while world cotton prices remain well below the costs of production.

Although a relationship can be established between capital penetration and migration in Central America, the extent and direction of this migration vary according to a number of factors. If the affected region is sparsely populated or relatively uninhabited, then little or no migration may result, or the region may even become a zone of attraction, as occurred with the development of banana enclaves along the northern coast of Honduras in the early twentieth century and the agricultural expansion following World War II. In some cases, migration to these areas may be reversed, as occurred with the opening of certain areas for cotton cultivation in the postwar period. In such cases, peasants are drawn to clear forested areas, then expelled as cotton plantations take over areas they have cleared and planted in corn; or a labor force attracted to the region to work on cotton plantations in return for small plots of land is subsequently expelled as cotton becomes increasingly mechanized.

In more densely populated areas, where precapitalist structures of production exist, peasants are pushed from their land when it is taken over for capitalist production. In some instances, they may migrate to more developed urban centers, but in other cases, they migrate to more marginal areas to reestablish a subsistence economy. This pattern has recurred in several Central American countries: in El Salvador and parts of Guatemala with the introduction of coffee production in the nineteenth century; in El Salvador and Nicaragua with the expansion of cotton production in the postwar period; in Costa Rica with the transfer of agricultural land to livestock production in the 1960s and 1970s; and in Guatemala with the shift from subsistence to cash-crop production in the highlands and more dramatically with the expulsion of indigenous population from communal lands during the development of the northern Franja Transversal in the 1970s. As opportunities for subsistence agriculture contract, migration takes the form of emigration to neighboring countries, as exemplified by Salvadorans moving to Honduras.

Capitalist penetration has also resulted in migration to the core economy itself, once a relationship is established between the core and peripheral economies. Thus factors determining the direction of migratory flows of uprooted populations include the existence of unincorporated areas in the home or neighboring countries where peasant agriculture can be resumed (an increasingly limited option in Central America), the existence and nature of opportunities in the capitalist sector of the economy, and the existence of structural and institutional ties between the peripheral economy and that of the core.

CAPITALIST OR CORE ECONOMIES AS "POLES OF ATTRACTION" FOR LABOR THROUGH ECONOMIC, SOCIAL, AND CULTURAL INFLUENCES

The same process of capital penetration that pushes peasant cultivators off the land often results in cyclical migration due to seasonal labor recruitment as peasants migrate to work in coffee, cotton, and sugar harvests—a process evident in virtually every country in Central America. Also, areas of capitalist penetration may become poles of attraction with the opening of new lands for settlement (as in Honduras) or in response to actual or perceived opportunities for jobs, education, and other services resulting from urbanization and industrialization. Such opportunity has been at least one factor in rural-urban migration during the postwar industrialization in several countries. The fact that in many cases these opportunities did not materialize is evidenced by the large percentages of urban populations found in the informal sector (particularly in El Salvador), even before the political conflicts and economic crisis of the 1980s. The cultural and economic penetration accompanying the expansion of foreign investment during the 1960s and 1970s undoubtedly became a factor of attraction operating in conjunction with factors of expulsion (the dislocations accompanying modernization) to account for increased migration to the United States during this period. Immigration to the United States also followed a pattern of "indirect" labor recruitment as new Central American immigrants were absorbed into low-paying jobs in agriculture, industry, and the rapidly expanding service sectors in the 1970s and early 1980s.

THE ROLE OF THE PERIPHERAL STATE
IN THE DEVELOPMENT PROCESS
AND IN MANAGING RESULTING CONTRADICTIONS

The role of the state in capital accumulation has affected migration significantly. One example is the legislation enacted by liberal governments to insure land and labor for coffee production during the nineteenth century. It eliminated forms of communal property and forced smallholders off their land in El Salvador and forced indigenous communities in the Guatemalan highlands to supply labor during the harvest season. Another example is the creation of development poles by providing infrastructure and incentives to encourage investment. Other state policies have also affected migration, such as military recruitment in El Salvador and Nicaragua, which has led to an exodus of young men of draft age to neighboring countries, Mexico, and the United States.

Efforts to manage contradictions arising from the development process or resulting dislocations have been most successful in Costa Rica. In general, however, and particularly in Guatemala, El Salvador, and Nicaragua, the state has leaned heavily, if not exclusively, toward repression, which has led to politically motivated emigration. Examples are numerous: the matanza in El Salvador in 1932, which drove Salvadoran peasants from the western departments eastward and into Honduras; the destruction of indigenous villages in Guatemala and repression in other parts of the country in the early 1980s, which has driven hundreds of thousands of Guatemalans into Mexico and the United States; and the combination of persecution and war that has led to the exodus of a substantial proportion of the Salvadoran population. It can be argued that the failure or inability of these states in the past to successfully manage the contradictions resulting from capitalist production and its articulation with precapitalist modes accounts for the current political crises in these countries.

FOREIGN INTERVENTION AND MIGRATION

Intervention by foreign states in internal conflicts may intensify or prolong these conflicts, in turn aggravating conditions that lead to displacement or emigration, but no clear relationship exists between migration and policies on immigration, asylum, and refugees. Foreign (particularly U.S.) intervention has been a factor in intensifying and prolonging the current conflict in El Salvador and in resulting population dislocations. The bombing and strafing of rural areas utilizing bombers, helicopters, and other equipment supplied by the United States since 1984 has directly caused population flight from these areas.[8] Moreover, the Reagan administration's emphasis on a military solution was an important factor in prolonging the war, aggravating the economic crisis, and stimulating the continued flow of migration from El Salvador to other countries. U.S. financing of the Contra war was directly and indirectly responsible for population dislocations and economic crisis in Nicaragua and the flow of refugees and migrants into neighboring countries and to the United States. In Guatemala, where U.S. intervention is less obvious today, a long history exists of foreign military and political intervention, including the U.S.-directed counterinsurgency programs of the 1960s, foreign training of military personnel, and assistance by foreign advisors in the antiguerrilla campaign of the early 1980s.

Overall, U.S. foreign policy appears to have been more effective in generating refugees than U.S. immigration and refugee policies have been in preventing their entry. The latter policies have primarily made migration and the sojourn in the United States more difficult. This situation has been aggravated by IRCA (for all but those eligible for amnesty), although it is too soon to evaluate the effectiveness of the new law in stemming the flow of migrants.

THE ROLE OF MIGRATORY PATTERNS AND NETWORKS

Patterns of migration established in earlier periods may continue to operate even when the original conditions for migration no longer exist or when new causes of migration are introduced, due in part to networking among families or community members at the points of immigration and emigration. This tendency has been particularly evident in the movement of migrants and refugees across borders during the past decade,which appears to follow previous patterns of migration where possible (Nicaraguans into Honduras and Costa Rica, Salvadorans into Honduras and Guatemala, Guatemalans into southern Mexico). In some cases, such migration takes advantage of relationships established in the receiving country through prior migration. Some Central Americans entering the United States have followed migratory networks established by earlier Latino immigrants to communities with cultural and perhaps political similarities. By the mid-1980s, however, a large proportion of the Central American migrants had relatives or friends in the United States, many of them in major urban centers where entire networks from the sending communities may have been established. These social networks reinforce the structural and institutional ties between core and periphery in determining the direction of migratory and refugee flows.

In conclusion, while Central American migration in the 1980s is a quantitatively and qualitatively new phenomenon, the factors identified in our analytical framework help to explain it. What distinguishes the massive population movements in Central America today from those of the past is the conjuncture of several factors: an economic crisis, a consequence of the changes in the capitalist world economy and their specific forms in each Central American country, combined with political conflict arising from the growing contradictions between capitalist modernization and the backward socioeconomic structures maintained over time by the repressive state apparatus. U.S. involvement in these conflicts has prolonged and intensified them without resolving the structural contradictions from which they emerged. Prolonging the conflicts has in turn aggravated the economic crisis, which cannot be expected to disappear once the conflicts ended. Thus one effect that can be anticipated is the continued dislocation, displacement, and migration of substantial sectors of the Central American populations.

NOTES

The authors would like to thank the reviewers and editors of *Latin American Research Review* for their very helpful comments and suggestions.

1. Kearney develops the concept of an articulatory migrant network linking the sending communities with daughter communities in the receiving country or region (1986, 353-55).

2. Wayne A. Cornelius, "Migrants from Mexico Still Coming and Staying," *Los Angeles Times*, 3 July 1988, Metro section.

3. We are not contending that capitalist penetration necessarily leads to migration or that migration necessarily results from capitalist penetration. The relationship between the two depends on the nature of capitalist penetration and the characteristics of the peripheral area, among other factors. But capitalism is a major factor in historical and contemporary patterns of migration, including many cases where this relationship is not immediately obvious.

4. Although it might be expected that population-density pressures would exacerbate dislocations resulting from structural rigidities and capitalist penetration, comparison of internal migration in Guatemala and El Salvador during the 1960s shows that the rate of migration (the proportion of migrants to the total population) is roughly the same in both countries (approximately 15 percent). This finding suggests that El Salvador's greater population density has not affected rates of migration (CSUCA 1978b, 83). Durham points out that while geographic population density in El Salvador is seven times greater than in Honduras, the difference in arable density (agriculturally active population divided by land in cultivation) is less than 1.5 times that in Honduras (Durham 1979, 109-10). Thus population density alone cannot be taken as explaining Salvadoran migration, although it is undoubtedly a contributing factor.

5. See also "Informal Economy Cushions Unemployment," *Central America Report* (27 May 1988: 159-60).

6. Since 1986 some efforts have been made to repopulate rural areas, including the Salvadoran government program United to Reconstruct and efforts by the affected population themselves aided by church or other nongovernmental organizations. Conditions in repopulated zones continue to be insecure, however, and many in the repopulated communities confront the danger of military attack as well as the difficulties of reconstruction (Americas Watch 1987, 155ff).

7. Although the INS has reported a decline in the number of arrests of undocumented migrants attempting to cross the U.S.-Mexican border since 1986, this decline may be partly attributed to a reduction of INS agents in the San Diego area. See Patrick McConnell, "Too Few for So Many," *Los Angeles Times*, 5 Nov. 1989, pp. A3, A48. By the beginning of 1990, however, it was widely agreed that the number of undocumented migrants had increased dramatically, and INS arrests in the period from October 1989 through March 1990 were up 50 percent from the same period in the previous year. See Patrick McConnell, "Illegal Border Crossings Rise after Three-Year Fall," *Los Angeles Times*, 22 Apr. 1990, pp. A1, A34-35. Refugee associations in Los Angeles reported an increase in the number of Salvadorans coming to the area following the November 1989 FMLN offensive. The growth in the number of undocumented immigrants is also apparent in the growing number of street vendors and in the increase in day laborers congregating at street corners in the Los Angeles area. See Cornelius, "Migrants from Mexico Still Coming," *Los Angeles Times*, 3 July 1988, Metro section.

8. As this example demonstrates, when analyzing the role of state, it is difficult to separate the role of domestic regimes from that of the U.S. government, partly because the influence of the latter is often overwhelming and partly because they are generally aligned. Two notable exceptions to alignment are the Arbenz government in Guatemala (1950-1954), whose program for developing national capitalism in Guatemala conflicted with the interests of U.S. capital as epitomized by the United Fruit Company, and the Sandinistas in Nicaragua, whose efforts to extricate themselves from dependence on the United States clashed with the drive from continued hegemony in the region by the U.S. government or the factions that currently control it. More often, differences arise over means rather than goals, such as the occasional disagreements between the U.S. government and the Salvadoran military regarding the internationally permissible level of repression.

REFERENCES

Achaerandio, Luis. 1983. "Introducción al problema de los desplazados en El Salvador (1980-1983)." *Boletín de Psicología* (San Salvador) 2 (July-September).

Aguayo, Sergio. 1985. *El éxodo centroamericano: consecuencias de un conflicto.* Mexico City: Secretaría de Educación Pública.

_____, and Patricia Weiss Fagen. 1988. *Central Americans in Mexico and the United States.* Washington, D.C.: Hemispheric Migration Project, CIPRA, Georgetown University.

Alens, Alex. 1984. *Socio-Demographic and Economic Characteristics of Displaced Persons in El Salvador.* Washington, D.C.: Intergovernmental Committee for Migration, Hemispheric Migration Project.

Armstrong, Robert, and Janet Shenk. 1982. *El Salvador: The Face of Revolution.* Boston: South End Press.

Bach, Robert L. 1985. *Western Hemispheric Immigration to the United States: A Review of Selected Research Trends.* Washington, D.C.: Center for Immigration Policy and Refugee Assistance, Georgetown University.

Black, George, Milton Jamail, and Norma Stoltz Chinchilla. 1984. *Garrison Guatemala.* New York: Monthly Review Press.

Browning, David. 1971. *El Salvador: Landscape and Society.* Oxford: Clarendon Press.

Cheng, Lucie, and Edna Bonacich, eds. 1984. *Labor Immigration under Capitalism: Asian Workers in the United States before World War II.* Berkeley and Los Angeles: University of California Press.

Chinchilla, Norma Stolz, and Nora Hamilton. 1984a. "Characteristics of Central American Migration to Southern California." Paper presented at the Illinois Conference of Latin Americanists, University of Illinois, Chicago, 15-17 November.

_____. 1984b. "Prelude to Revolution: U.S. Investment in Central America." In *The Politics of Intervention*, edited by Roger Burbach and Patricia Flynn. New York: Monthly Review.

Cohen, Robin. 1987. *The New Helots: Migrants in the International Division of Labor.* Brookfield, Vt.: Gower.

Cornelius, Wayne A. 1980. "Mexican Immigration: Causes and Consequences for Mexico." In *Sourcebook on the New Immigration: Implications for the United States and the International Community*, edited by Roy Simon Bryce-Laporte. New Brunswick, N.J.: Transaction.

Coyuntura Economica. 1989. "Condiciones de vida y fuerzas socialis." *Coyuntura Económica* 4, no. 24 (Mar.-Apr.):34-38. Published by the Instituto de Investigaciones Económicas, Universidad de El Salvador.

CSUCA (Consejo Superior Universitaria Centroamericana). 1978a. *Estructura agraria, dinámica de población y desarrollo capitalista en Centroamérica.* San José: Editorial Universitaria Centroamericana.

_____. 1978b. *Estructura demográfica y migraciones internas en Centroamérica.* San José: Editorial Universitaria Centroamericana.

Cue, Reynaldo A., and Robert L. Bach. 1980. "The Return of the Clandestine Worker and the End of the Golden Exile: Recent Mexican and Cuban Immigrants in the United States." In *Sourcebook on the New Immigration: Implications for the United States and the International Community*, edited by Roy Simon Bryce-Laporte. New Brunswick, N.J.: Transaction.

Deere, Carmen Diana, and Peter Marchetti. 1981. "The Worker-Peasant Alliance in the First Year of the Nicaraguan Agrarian Reform." *Latin American Perspectives* 8, no. 2 (Spring): 40-73.

Durham, William H. 1979. *Scarcity and Survival in Central America: Ecological Origins of the Soccer War.* Stanford, Calif: Stanford University Press.

Espenshade, Thomas J., Frank D. Bean, Tracy Ann Goodis, and Michael J. White. 1988. *Immigration Policy in the United States: Future Prospects for the Immigration Reform and Control Act of 1986.* Washington, D.C.: Urban Institute.

Fagen, Patricia Weiss. 1988. "Central American Refugees and U.S. Policy." In *Crisis in Central America: Regional Dynamics and U.S. Policy in the 1980s*, edited by Nora Hamilton, Jeffry A. Frieden, Linda Fuller, and Manuel Pastor, Jr., Boulder, Colo.: Westview.

Kearney, Michael. 1986. "From the Invisible Hand to Visible Feet: Anthropological Studies of Migration and Development." *American Review of Anthropology* 15:331-61.

Leach, Jim, George Miller, and Mark O. Hatfield. 1985. *U.S. Aid to El Salvador: An Evaluation of the Past, A Prospect for the Future.* Report to the Arms Control and Foreign Policy Caucus, U.S. Congress. Washington, D.C.

Montes Mozo, Segundo, and Juan Jose Garcia Vasquez. 1988. *Salvadoran Migration to the United States: An Exploratory Study.* Washington, D.C.: Hemispheric Migration Project, Center for Immigration Policy and Refugee Assistance, Georgetown University.

Montgomery, Tommie Sue. 1982. *Revolution in El Salvador.* Boulder, Colo.: Westview.

Papademetriou, Demetrios G. 1983. "Rethinking International Migration: A Review and a Critique." *Comparative Political Studies* 15, no. 4 (Jan.): 469-98.

Pearce, Jenny. 1986. *Promised Land: Peasant Rebellion in Chalatenango, El Salvador.* London: Latin American Bureau.

Portes, Alejandro. 1983. "International Labor Migration and National Development." In *U.S. Immigration and Refugee Policy*, edited by Mary Kritz. Lexington, KY: Lexington Books.

_____, and Robert L. Bach. 1985. *Latin Journey: Cuban and Mexican Immigrants in the United States.* Berkeley and Los Angeles: University of California Press.

Rodriguez, Nestor P. 1987. "Undocumented Central Americans in Houston: Diverse Populations." *International Migration Review* 21, no. 1 (Spring):4-26.

Ruggles, Patricia, and Michael Fix. 1985. "Impacts and Potential Impacts of Central American Migrants on HHS and Related Programs of Assistance: Final Report." Washington, D.C.: Urban Institute.

_____, Michael Fix, and Kathleen M. Thomas. 1985. "Profile of the Central American Population in the United States." Washington, D.C.: Urban Institute.

_____, Donald Manson, John Trutko, and Kathleen M. Thomas. 1985. "Refugees and Displaced Persons of the Central American Region." Washington, D.C.: Urban Institute.

Sassen, Saskia. 1988. *The Mobility of Labor and Capital: A Study in International Investment and Labor Flow.* Cambridge: Cambridge University Press.

Schoultz, Lars. 1987. "Central America." Manuscript prepared for New York University Research Project, Immigration Policy and U.S. Foreign Relations with Latin America.

Stanley, William Deane. 1987. "Economic Migrants or Refugees from Violence? A Time-Series Analysis of Salvadoran Migration to the United States." *LARR* 22, no. 1:132-54.

Teitlebaum, Michael S. 1984. "Immigration, Refugees, and Foreign Policy." *International Organization* 38, no. 3 (Summer).

Torres Rivas, Edelberto. 1985. *Report on the Condition of Central American Refugees and Migrants.* Hemisphere Migration Project Occasional Paper Series. Washington, D.C.: Center for Immigration Policy and Refugee Assistance, Georgetown University.

_____, and Dina Jimenez. 1985. "Informe sobre el estado de las migraciones en Centroamérica." *Annuario de Estudios Centroamericanos* 11, no. 2:25-66.

U.S. GAO (General Accounting Office). 1989. *Central America: Conditions of Refugees and Displaced Persons.* Washington, D.C.: Government Printing Office.

U.S. INS (Immigration and Naturalization Service). 1978. *Annual Report.* Washington, D.C.: U.S. GPO.

_____. 1984. *1984 Statistical Yearbook of the Immigration and Naturalization Service.* Washington, D.C.: U.S. GPO.

Wallace, Steven P. 1986. "Central American and Mexican Immigrant Characteristics and Economic Incorporation in California." *International Migration Review* 20, no. 3 (Fall):657-71.

Weeks, John. 1985. *The Economics of Central America.* New York: Holmes and Meier.

Zolberg, Aristide R. 1983. "Contemporary Transnational Migration in Historical Perspective: Patterns and Dilemmas." In KRITZ 1983.

_____, Astri Suhrke, and Sergio Aguayo. 1986. "International Factors in the Formation of Refugee Movements." *International Migration Review* 20, no. 2 (Summer):151-69.

5

A SUMMARY OF PUERTO RICAN
MIGRATION TO THE UNITED STATES

Clara E. Rodríguez

THE HISTORICAL CONTEXT

THE MOST IMPORTANT ELEMENT in understanding Puerto Rican migration is perhaps the least visible one: the historical context. In the nineteenth century, Puerto Rico had been receiving people, rather than exporting them. Yet by the middle of the twentieth century, Puerto Rico began to experience a concentrated exodus of people (see Figure 5.1). Although this migration has fluctuated, the flow has continued. In net terms, it has been so significant that it has been referred to as the "Puerto Rican diaspora."[1] The net result of this unprecedented migration is that by 1980 over 40 percent of Puerto Ricans lived outside Puerto Rico, primarily on the U.S. mainland.[2] Aldorondo (1990) projects that by the year 2000, 38.8 percent of Puerto Rico's population will have migrated to the mainland.[3]

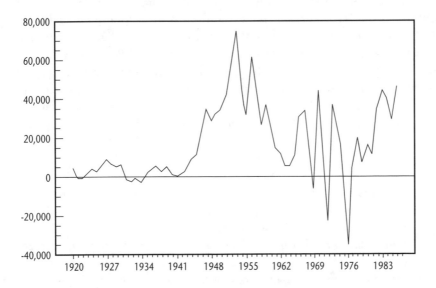

Figure 5.1. Net migration of Puerto Ricans, 1920-1986

CAUSES OF TWENTIETH-CENTURY OUT-MIGRATION

Why have so many Puerto Ricans left the island during the twentieth century? Early theorists like Chenault and Handlin argued that overpopulation in Puerto Rico was the major factor inducing migration.[4,5] Others have argued that this overpopulation had come about as a result of health and medical improvements made under U.S. mainland policies. Senior and Watkins,[6] Mills et al.,[7] and Perloff[8] have posited that job opportunities elsewhere were the major factor motivating migration.[6-8]

More recently, researchers have tended to see migration in more macro terms, i.e., as the response of surplus labor to the economic transformations occurring in Puerto Rico. Influenced by the larger context of economic and political dependence on the mainland, these transformations are seen to have yielded increasingly larger numbers of displaced and surplus workers who were forced to migrate elsewhere for jobs.[2,9-13]

Microlevel analyses have focused on economic push and pull factors.[9,14-19] For example, when the mainland national income goes up and unemployment goes down, Puerto Rican migration increases. Relative wages and unemployment rates in Puerto Rico and the mainland have also been found to affect migration to the mainland and back to Puerto Rico.[15,20] In essence, Puerto Ricans migrate when job opportunities look better on the mainland and/or when they look worse in Puerto Rico. It has also been found that Puerto Ricans do not migrate to secure greater welfare benefits.[20]

Other scholars have emphasized the role of mainland companies in recruiting Puerto Rican labor to work on the mainland.[2,12,21-23] A 1944 issue of *Business Week* confirms this recruitment.[24] In an article entitled "Labor Recruited" it noted that three large mainland firms were recruiting skilled Puerto Rican workers for jobs on the mainland in cooperation with the War Manpower Commission. It also noted that the Commission expected that more workers would be recruited by other firms.

According to Morales, Puerto Rican labor was attractive to employers on the mainland because Puerto Ricans were citizens and because of their agricultural background.[12] He notes that Puerto Ricans were "greatly valued" by their employers and they were seen to be "excellent workers." The low wage rates paid to these workers also produced "substantial profits" for these employers and enhanced the attractiveness of Puerto Rican laborers.

Other scholars have cited the role of the government of Puerto Rico in encouraging migration.[6,13,21,23] Although the official position of the government during Operation Bootstrap was that it did not encourage or discourage migration, some authors dispute this. Padilla[13] maintains that the Puerto Rican government requested that the Federal Aviation Administration (FAA) set low rates for air transportation between Puerto Rico and the mainland, while Lapp argues that the government's Migration Division Office in New York facilitated migration.[23]

Undoubtedly, migration has resulted from a combination of these factors. There are additional factors that have received less attention. Sanchez-Korrol points out that the mainland's 1921 legislation restricting immigration and the conferring of citizenship status on Puerto Ricans in 1917 induced Puerto Ricans to migrate.[19] After the Second World War, there may also have been era-specific factors that contributed to the migration, such as greater participation in the armed forces; pent-up travel demand; surplus aircraft and pilots making for cheaper and more accessible air travel; and greater opportunities on the mainland. What is perhaps the most important factor in propelling the Puerto Rican migration, however, is what is perhaps least visible to the migrants. This is the political and economic relationships between Puerto Rico and the mainland.

THE POLITICAL AND ECONOMIC RELATIONSHIP

The political relationship between Puerto Rico and the mainland resulted not just in political dependence, but also in economic dependence. Changes in the Puerto Rican economy after the mainland invasion were dramatic. The economy went from a diversified subsistence economy around the turn of the century with four basic crops produced for export (tobacco, cattle, coffee, and sugar) to a sugar-crop economy with 60 percent of the sugar industry controlled by absentee owners from the mainland.[25,26] The decline of the sugar cane-based industry (combined with no reinvestment and continued population growth) in the twenties resulted in high unemployment, poverty, and desperate conditions in Puerto Rico. These factors propelled the first waves of Puerto Ricans to the mainland in search of a better life. The thirties saw more migration as workers sought to deal with the then stagnant economic situation on the island.

In the forties, the Second World War boosted the flagging economy somewhat. The Puerto Rican government initiated a series of reforms and entered into what has been variously called its "state capitalist development phase," or its "socialist" venture.[1] A series of government-owned enterprises were established and run by the Puerto Rican Development corporation. These included glass, pulp and paper, shoe leather, and clay products corporations as well as a hotel and a textile mill that were financed but not run by the government. Influenced by the New Deal philosophy, this program stressed both "social justice and economic growth" goals. In these regards, the program was "ahead of its time."[27] Had this program succeeded, greater economic independence would have been achieved. These efforts were frustrated, however, by a combination of technical problems, ideological opposition from conservatives in the U.S. Congress, the local press, business interests both in Puerto Rico and on the mainland, and government bureaucrats.[27,28]

Between 1947 and 1951 there was a changeover from government development of industry to promotion of private investment. The new approach, which was firmly established by 1951, was called "Operation Bootstrap." A forerunner of the economic development strategies subsequently developed throughout the world, the idea was to industrialize Puerto Rico by luring foreign companies, mainly from the U.S. mainland, to Puerto Rico with the promise of low wage and tax incentives. The tourism industry was also developed at this time. Puerto Rico began its thrust toward industrialization and its clear incorporation into an emerging global economy.

Much in Puerto Rico improved during this period, e.g., education, housing, drinking water, electrification and sewage systems, road and transportation facilities. To the residents of Puerto Rico there was a clear and present sense of development and progress and, for some, the perception of a more equitable distribution of income.

The industries that were attracted to the island turned out to be increasingly capital intensive, however, to have little commitment to the development of the island, and to be integrated into sourcing and distribution networks on the mainland or other countries, not in Puerto Rico. As a result, these industries had little indirect employment effects and did not provide sufficient jobs. With increased population growth and displacement from traditional labor pursuits, the result was a growing surplus population that could not be accommodated in Puerto Rico's new industrial order. Much of the surplus labor migrated to the mainland.[2,11,12]

Thus, Operation Bootstrap in Puerto Rico foreshadowed what was to happen in numerous former colonies and developing countries, namely the development of off-shore operations by foreign capital or multinational corporations which siphon off profits so that there is little or no economic benefit to the island. Today, the distinctions between colonies and client states have become less clear-cut. In today's world economy we may no longer need a colonial framework to find conjunctions of political and economic dependence that induce migration. Economic and political dependence are no longer so clearly distinguishable when it comes to the flow of labor, capital, or goods.

The political and economic ties between Puerto Rico and the mainland also helped to fan the migration in a number of other ways. For example, without the ties, tax breaks would not have been granted to mainland firms doing business in Puerto Rico; duty-free exports and imports would not have been allowed between Puerto Rico and the mainland; capital could not have flowed without controls; and American factories and American management would not have come to Puerto Rico in such large numbers during the fifties and sixties. In addition, without this context, increases in national income or employment on the mainland would not have provoked emigration as quickly from Puerto Rico; there would not have been open borders, a military experience for Puerto Rican men and women, citizenship status, accessible and frequent air travel, and early communications and education systems that were tied to the U.S. mainland. In the end, this context made Puerto Ricans "colonial immigrants," i.e., similar to Algerians, Tunisians, Moroccans, and West or East Indians who have immigrated to English, French, and Dutch "fatherlands" over the past two decades.

Thus, within this larger structure, we see that economic push and pull factors were involved in the decision to migrate, and they still are. The most recent analysis of migrants leaving Puerto Rico found that the majority (69 percent) were not employed, and this was especially the case for women.[29] As the Junta de Planificacion points out, however, employment was not the decisive factor for all those leaving because 52 percent of those with 16+ years of education had jobs before they left.[34]

But pull factors have also always been important. Puerto Ricans were (and are) pulled by the promise (or hope) of a better life, a life like the one they perceived Americans to have—a life to which they, as American citizens, were also entitled. They were also undoubtedly pulled by connections to family that were already living on the mainland. These connections expanded into networks that became self-reinforcing pulls; these pulls grew as the migration continued. Finally Puerto Ricans were pulled by an adventurous perspective—one that proposed they try their luck in a new land, that they strive for something better.

PATTERNS OF SETTLEMENT

There have been Puerto Ricans, and even Puerto Rican organizations, in New York since the nineteenth century.[19,35] However, it was only after 1900 that significant numbers of Puerto Ricans came to the city, while the bulk of the migration occurred in the fifties and sixties (see Figure 5.1). The migration of Puerto Ricans after the U.S. takeover in 1898 has been classified into three major periods.[36] During the first period, 1900-1945, the pioneers arrived. The majority of these "pioneros" settled in New York City, in the Atlantic

Avenue area of Brooklyn, El Barrio in East Harlem, and other sections of Manhattan such as the Lower East Side, the Upper West Side, Chelsea, and the Lincoln Center area, while some began to populate sections of the South Bronx. During this period, industrial and agricultural labor under contract also arrived and "provided the base from which sprang many of the Puerto Rican communities" outside of New York City.[21]

The second phase of the migration, 1946-1964, is known as "the great migration" because the largest numbers of Puerto Ricans arrived. During this period the already established Puerto Rican communities of East Harlem, the South Bronx, and the Lower East Side increased their numbers as well as their borders. Settlements in new areas of New York, New Jersey, Connecticut, Chicago, and other areas of the country appeared and grew, but the bulk of the Puerto Rican population continued to reside in New York.

The last period, from 1965 to the present, is termed "the revolving door migration," and involves a fluctuating pattern of net migration as well as greater dispersion to other parts of the mainland. As Figure 5.1 illustrates, the last few years have shown net outflows from Puerto Rico that begin to rival those experienced in the early fifties. By 1980, the majority of Puerto Ricans on the mainland were living outside of New York State.[37]

Contract laborers have been another stream in the Puerto Rican migration. They have generally received less attention in the literature because many returned to Puerto Rico after their contracts were completed, while others moved quickly out of agricultural contract labor and settled in more urban settings. Initially recruited by companies and then by family members and word-of-mouth, these migrants formed the nucleus of Puerto Rican communities that would subsequently develop in less urban areas or in areas outside of the New York metropolitan area. The communities in Hawaii, Arizona, and other southwestern states, San Francisco, Gary, Indiana, and Lorain, Cleveland, and Youngstown, Ohio began in this way.[6] Contract labor migration began soon after 1898 and continued throughout the twentieth century. Indeed, the very first wave of migration after the 1989 takeover of Puerto Rico by the United States was a contract labor group that went to Hawaii.

The class composition of the Puerto Rican communities has changed over time, but the communities have always retained a distinctive diversity. The late nineteenth century Puerto Rican community on the mainland was made up of generally well-to-do merchants, political activists closely allied with the Cuban Revolutionary movement, and skilled workers, many of whom were "tabaqueros" (skilled tobacco workers).[19,35] By the first quarter of the twentieth century the Puerto Rican community is described by a number of scholars as consisting of people who were employed in predominantly working-class occupations.[4,5,38] It was in the post-World War II period that migration from Puerto Rico to the mainland accelerated, causing the communities to grow rapidly. The composition of these communities continued to reflect diversity but with a strong working-class base.

PUERTO RICANS' SOCIOECONOMIC STATUS: A PERSISTENT DISADVANTAGE

For quite some time now, Puerto Ricans on the mainland have been in a most difficult and highly vulnerable economic situation. Soon after the "great migration" of Puerto Ricans to the mainland in the fifties, government and scholarly reports began to highlight the economic adversities Puerto Ricans were experiencing on the mainland. Despite these early warnings, little was done and the situation of Puerto Ricans received little attention by policy-makers.

More recently, however, there has been an emerging interest in the "persisting disad-vantage" of Puerto Ricans. Much of the current interest in Puerto Ricans derives from the results of new studies that have found them to be uniquely disadvantaged relative to other groups in mainland society. That is to say, while other minorities experienced a period of socioeconomic advancement during the 1960s, followed by a phase of limited gains during the 1970s, the Puerto Rican experience is one of continuously growing disadvantage since 1960. During the 1980s, government data and research reports provided growing evidence of the uniquely disadvantaged position of Puerto Ricans within postwar U.S. society.[39,40]

The deteriorating relative position of Puerto Ricans is reflected in the variety of indica-tors. In 1960, Puerto Rican median family income was lower than that of African-Americans, other Hispanics, and Native Americans. Puerto Ricans were the only Hispanic group not to have narrowed the family income gap relative to Caucasians during the sev-enties.[39] By 1980 the difference had widened. In 1987, median family income for Puerto Ricans was less than half that of Caucasians.[40]

Moreover, during the late eighties, the incidence of poverty among Puerto Ricans con-tinued to be higher than for any other group, remaining similar to the poverty rate of a decade earlier.[40] Data on labor force participation present the same story of relative disad-vantage. Puerto Ricans (in 1980) exhibited participation rates lower than that of other groups, and those employed worked fewer hours on the average.[41] Analysis of trends by gen-der indicates that participation rates for Puerto Rican males steadily declined between 1960 and 1980, while that of women improved modestly during the same period.[39] The disad-vantaged situation of Puerto Ricans, relative to other groups, has been so severe that it has led some to speculate about whether Puerto Ricans are becoming a Hispanic underclass.[42]

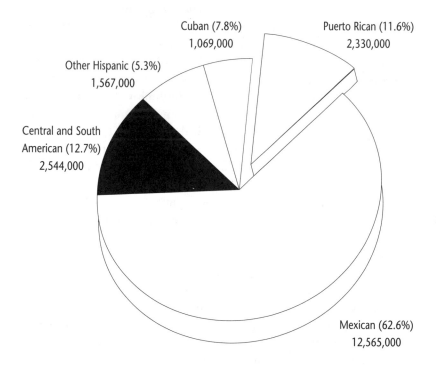

Figure 5.2 Hispanics on the U.S. mainland, by origin, 1989.

Figures 5.2 through 5.9, based on data published by the U.S. Bureau of the Census, present selected aspects of the current situation of Puerto Ricans relative to non-Hispanics and other Hispanic groups on the U.S. mainland. Figure 5.2 shows the number and percentage distribution by origin of Hispanics on the mainland. Figure 5.3 presents similar information with Puerto Ricans living in Puerto Rico added to the mainland total. As may be see in Figures 5.2 and 5.3, the Puerto Rican share of the total mainland Hispanic population rises from 11.6 to 24.7 percent if those living in Puerto Rico are included. Given that government programs and other funding activities often extend to Puerto Rico, it would seem important to include Puerto Ricans in Puerto Rico as part of the total U.S. Hispanic population.

Figure 5.4 presents the poverty rate (percentage of families below the poverty level) for the various Hispanic groups residing on the mainland. The poverty rate is a widely used indicator of socioeconomic disadvantage, and Puerto Ricans have the highest rate. Figure 5.5 shows the median household income for Hispanics, which is another indicator of relative disadvantage. On this indicator, Puerto Ricans score the lowest. Associated with poverty, as cause or consequence, is a low participation rate in the labor force. Figure 5.6 indicates that Puerto Rican women have the lowest labor force participation rate of all Hispanic groups. Figure 5.7 shows another distinguishing characteristic of Puerto Ricans residing on the mainland: a high percentage of female-headed households and a low percentage of male-headed households.

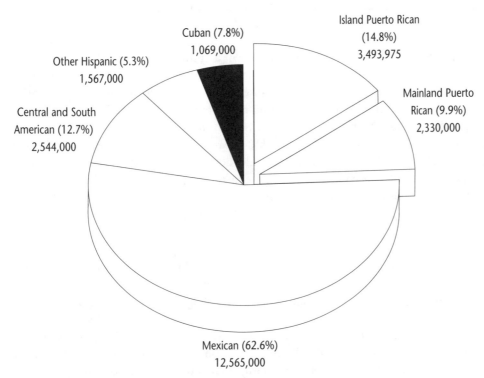

Figure 5.3 Hispanics in the United States (Puerto Rico included), by origin, 1989.

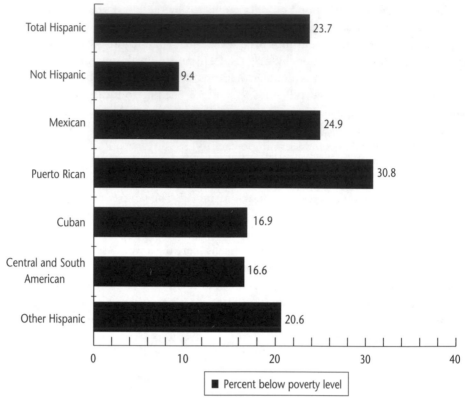

Figure 5.4 Percent of all Hispanic families residing on the U.S. mainland who are below poverty level, by origin, 1989.

Educational attainment is also an indicator of a group's relative socioeconomic advantage/disadvantage. Figure 5.8 shows the percentage of the mainland population that has completed four years of high school or more according to Hispanic/non-Hispanic origin and two broad age groups. In both age groups, Puerto Ricans rank below the total for non-Hispanics; considerably below the total for Hispanics in the 35 years and over age group, but substantially above in the 25 through 34 years of age. While, irrespective of origin, younger adults have more schooling than older adults, the age disparity is wider in Puerto Ricans than in other Hispanic groups, suggesting recent gains for Puerto Ricans (see Figure 5.9). This, in all probability, reflects recent gains achieved by mainland-born Puerto Ricans as well as gains achieved by the Puerto Rico-born migrating to the mainland.

CONCLUSION
It is clear from the scholarly information reviewed that the causes for the migration of Puerto Ricans to the mainland are many, complexly interwoven, and difficult to extricate from the mass of data. Economic and social changes in both the U.S. mainland and Puerto Rico appear to have created a series of pull and push factors that seem to explain the peaks and valleys observed in year to year net migration figures. The most propelling force for the original and the continuing migration, however, is likely to be the unique political relationship existing between Puerto Rico and the mainland. This relationship, relatively speaking, makes movement from the island to the mainland effortless because it

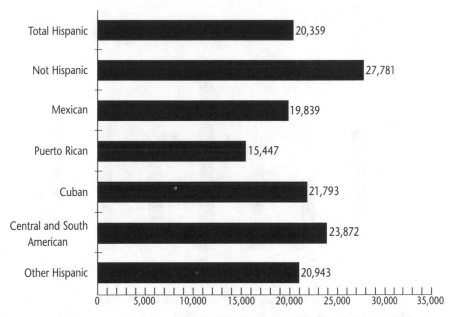

Figure 5.5 Median household income of Hispanic families residing on the U.S. mainland, by origin, 1989.

is a right of citizenship. The right is not any different from the right that residents of the fifty U.S. states have to cross state boundaries either temporarily or permanently. That is not to say that without the unique political relationship, migration would not occur. It is conjectured that it would not be as great, and as in the case of Cubans, politics would play a larger role. In addition, the socioeconomic characteristics of those migrating would be more likely to be skewed toward the upper rather than the lower socioeconomic levels.

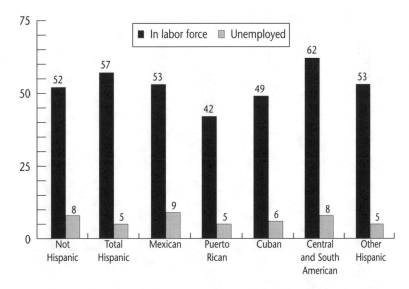

Figure 5.6 Percent of all Hispanic women 16 years and over residing on the U.S. mainland who are in the civilian labor force and unemployed, by origin, 1989.

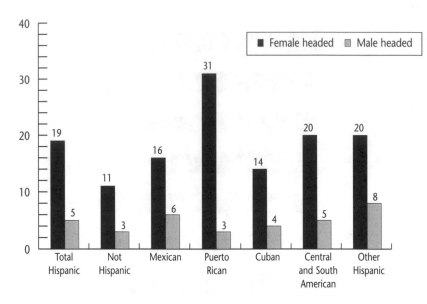

Figure 5.7 Percent of all Hispanic family households on the U.S. mainland headed by a male or a female, by origin, 1989.

This chapter has also reviewed the socioeconomic disadvantage of Puerto Ricans on the mainland over time, as well as in comparison to other Hispanic and non-Hispanic groups at a particular point. The persistence of the disadvantage over the years and the size of the current disadvantage relative to other Hispanic and non-Hispanic groups begs for explanations supported by facts. Unfortunately, only conjectures are possible. One such conjecture is the pattern of settlement which has led to the concentration of Puerto Ricans in the most decaying urban regions of the U.S. mainland. These regions also happen to be experiencing drastic dislocations in their industrial economies and to be suffering from

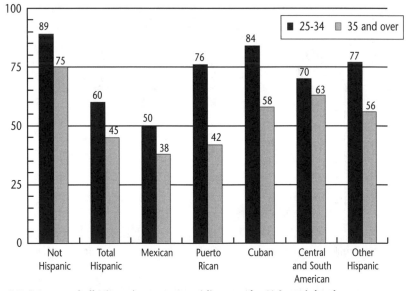

Figure 5.8 Percent of all Hispanic persons residing on the U.S. mainland who have completed four years of high school or more, by origin, 1989.

extremely high levels of unemployment. This, coupled with intractable patterns of job discrimination and residential segregation based on social class and/or imputed racial identity, is creating a situation of persistent poverty for many Puerto Ricans that would be hard for any group to escape.

Indications are that the Puerto Rican population on the mainland may have increased between 18 and 29 percent since 1980, making Puerto Ricans one of the fastest growing ethnic groups on the mainland. Close to 40 percent of all Puerto Ricans currently residing on the mainland are below 20 years of age, with about one-fourth of that 40 percent being five years of age or under. Typically, these are the age groups with the greatest health, education, and social needs, which, in conjunction with the extremely high rates of poverty and female-headed households, translate into a high demand for publicly supported services. Such high demands can only be met to a very limited degree as Puerto Ricans are concentrated in localities with inadequate public services and with economies likely to remain drastically impaired for years to come. A series of well-financed initiatives to improve the situation described is justified. This would require a high level of cooperation between the states where Puerto Ricans are concentrated, the Commonwealth of Puerto Rico, and agencies of the federal government. A joint commission similar to the one operating along the U.S.-Mexico border should be considered.

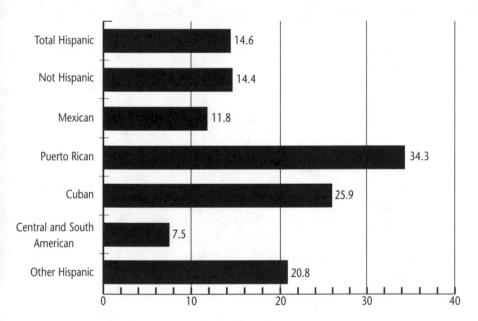

Figure 5.9 Difference in percent completing 4 years of high school or more between U.S. mainland Hispanics aged 25-34 and those 35 years and over (Hispanics, by origin, 1989).

NOTE

1. For analyses of the New Deal period in Puerto Rico see Stahl, 29, Gonzalez, A., 26, Reynolds, 9, Hanson, 30, Goodsell, 3, Lewis, G., 32, Carr, 28, Dietz, 27, and Wells, 33.

REFERENCES

1. Lopez, A., Petras, J.: *Puerto Rico and Puerto Ricans.* Cambridge, MA, Schenkman, 1974.

2. Uriarte-Gaston, M.: *Organizing for Survival: The Emergence of a Puerto Rican Community.* Doctoral dissertation, Boston University, Boston, MA, 1987.

3. Aldorondo, E.: *Perfil de la Comunidad Puertorriqueña en los Estados Unidos.* Departmento de Asuntos de la Comunida Puertorriqueña en los Estados Unidos, 1990.

4. Chenault, L.: *The Puerto Rican Migrant in New York City,* New York, Columbia University Press, 1938, 1970.

5. Handlin, O.: *The Newcomers: Negroes and Puerto Ricans in a Changing Metropolis.* Cambridge, MA, Harvard University Press, 1959.

6. Senior, C., Watkins, D.O.: Toward a balance sheet of Puerto Rican migration, in *Status of Puerto Rico: Selected Background Studies* (prepared for the U.S.-Puerto Rico Commission on the Status of Puerto Rico). Washington, DC: Government Printing Office, 1966.

7. Mills, C.W., Senior, C., Goldsen, R.: *The Puerto Rican Journey: New York's Newest Migrants.* New York, Harper Bros, 1950.

8. Perloff, H.: *Puerto Rico's Economic Future.* Chicago, University of Chicago Press, 1950.

9. Reynolds, I.G. Peter G.: *Wages, Productivity and Industrialization in Puerto Rico.* Chicago, Richard D. Irving, 1965.

10. Maldonado-Denis, M.: *Puerto Rico: A Socio-Historic Interpretation.* New York, Random House, 1972.

11. Bonilla, E., Campos, R.: A wealth of poor: Puerto Ricans in the new economic order. *Daedulus* 110:133-176, 1981.

12. Morales, J.: *Puerto Rican Poverty and Migration: We Just Had to Try Elsewhere.* New York, Praeger, 1986.

13. Padilla, F.: *Puerto Rican Chicago.* Notre Dame, IN, University of Notre Dame Press, 1987.

14. Fleisher, B.H.: *Some Economic Aspects of Puerto Rican Migration to the United States.* Doctoral dissertation, Stanford University, Stanford, CA, 1961.

15. Fleisher, B.H.: Some economic aspects of Puerto Rican migration to the United States. *Rev. Econ. & Statistics* 45:245-253, 1963.

16. Glazer, N., Moynihan, D.P.: *Beyond the Melting Pot,* 2nd ed. Cambridge, MA, MIT Press, 1970.

17. Pantoja, A.: *Puerto Rican Migration.* Preliminary Report to the U.S. Commission on Civil Rights of Puerto Ricans, New York, January 31, 1972.

18. Rodríguez, C.: *The Ethnic Queue: The Case of Puerto Ricans in the U.S.* San Francisco, CA, R&E Research Associates, 1974.

19. Sanchez-Korrol, V.: *From Colonial to Community: The History of Puerto Ricans in New York City, 1917-1948.* Westport, CT, Greenwood Press, 1983.

20. Maldonado, R.: Why Puerto Ricans migrated to the United States in 1947-73. *Monthly Labor Review,* September 1976, pp. 17-18.

21. Maldonado, E.: Contract labor and the origins of Puerto Rican communities in the United States. *International Migration Review,* 13:103-121, 1979.

22. Piore, M.: *Birds of Passage: Migrant Labor and Industrial Societies.* New York: Cambridge University Press, 1979.

23. Lapp, M.: *The Migration Division of Puerto Rico and Puerto Ricans in New York City, 1948-1969.* New York Historical Society, New York, 1986.

24. Labor recruited. *Business Week*, April 29, 1944, p. 114.

25. Steward, J.: *The People of Puerto Rico*. Chicago, University of Illinois Press, 1965.

26. Gonzalez, A.J.: La Economia y el Status Politico. *Revista de Ciencias Sociales* 10:5-50, March, 1966.

27. Dietz, J.L.: *Economic History of Puerto Rico: Institutional Change and Capitalist Development*. Princeton, NJ: Princeton University Press, 1986.

28. Carr, R.: *Puerto Rico: A Colonial Experiment*. New York, New York University Press, 1984.

29. Stahl, J.E.: *Economic Development Through Reform in Puerto Rico*. Doctoral dissertation, Iowa State University, Ames, IA, 1965.

30. Hanson, E.P.: *Land of Wonders*. New York. Alfred Knopf, 1960.

31. Goodsell, C.: *Administration of a Revolution*. Cambridge, MA, Harvard University Press, 1965.

32. Lewis, G.K.: *Puerto Rico: Freedom and Power in the Caribbean*. New York, Monthly Review Press, 1963.

33. Wells, H.: *The Modernization of Puerto Rico: A Political Study of Changing Values and Institutions*. Cambridge, MA, Harvard University Press, 1969.

34. Junta de Planificacion de Puerto Rico: *Characteristics de la Poblacion Migrante de Puerto Rico*. Santurce, P.R., 1986.

35. Iglesias, C.P.: *Memorias de Bernardo Vego: Una Contribucion a la Historica de la Communidad Puertorriqueña en Nueva York*. Rio Piedras, P.R., Ediciones Huracan, 1977, 1980.

36. Stevens-Arroyo, A., Diaz-Stevens, M.: Puerto Ricans in the United States: A struggle for identity, in Dworkin, A.G., Dworkin, R.J. (eds): *The Minority Report: An Introduction to Racial, Ethnic and Gender Relations*, 2nd ed. New York, CBS College Publishing, Holt, Rinehart & Winston, 1982.

37. U.S. Bureau of the Census: *Persons of Spanish Origin by State: 1980*. Supplementary Report PC80-S1-7. August. Washington, DC: Government Printing Office, 1982.

38. Gosnell, Aran P.: *The Puerto Ricans in New York City*. Doctoral dissertation, New York University, New York, 1945.

39. Bean, I.; Tienda, M.: *Hispanic Population in the U.S.* New York, Russell Sage Foundation, 1988.

40. Center on Budget and Policy Priorities: *Shortchanged: Recent Developments in Hispanic Poverty, Income and Employment*, Washington, D.C., 1988.

41. Borjas, G.: Jobs and employment for Hispanics, in San Juan. In Cafferty, P., McCready, W.C. (eds): *Hispanics in the United States*. New Brunswick, NJ, Transaction Books, 1985.

42. Tienda, M.: Puerto Ricans and the underclass debate. *Annals* 501:105-119, January, 1989.

6

THE HISTORY OF MEXICAN UNDOCUMENTED SETTLEMENT IN THE UNITED STATES

Pierrette Hondagneu-Sotelo

"IT'S NOT MEXICANS BUT CALIFORNIA THAT MIGRATED to the United States." This simple statement refers to the fact that prior to 1848, Mexico included what is today the southwestern region of the United States, so that subsequent Mexican immigrants and their descendants found themselves living and working in conquered territory. In fact, one could argue that California migrated north "illegally." Another popular saying refers to contemporary Mexican immigration as *la reconquista* (the reconquest). Although the large Chicano or U.S.-born population of Mexican descent is indeed largely the outcome of post-1848 immigration, the term *reconquista* misrepresents the legacy of labor exploitation and racial subordination that Mexican immigrants and Chicanos have endured in the United States.[1]

Contemporary Mexican undocumented immigration is characterized by a significant presence of women and entire families, increasing integration into permanent settlement communities, and employment in diverse sectors of the economy. This chapter traces the legacy of the bracero program, and economic and political transformations in Mexico and the U.S. as they supported the trend toward long-term settlement of many Mexican undocumented immigrants in the U.S., especially since the late 1960s. These larger structural transformations are best understood by reviewing the historical antecedents of contemporary Mexican immigration.

HISTORICAL ANTECEDENTS

The historical movement of Mexican workers to the U.S. has been characterized by an "ebb and flow" or "revolving door" pattern of labor migration, one often calibrated by seasonal labor demands, economic recessions, and mass deportations.[2] As early as 1911, a report to the U.S. Congress issued by the Dillingham Commission lauded temporary Mexican labor migration and warned of the dangers of permanent Mexican settlement, claiming that although Mexicans "are not easily assimilated, this is of no very great importance as long as most of them return to their native land. In the case of the Mexican, he is less desirable as a citizen than as a laborer" (U.S. Congress, 1911:690-91). Although some employers encouraged the immigration of Mexican women and entire families in order to stabilize and expand an available, exploitable work force, many other employers, assisted at times by government-sponsored "bracero programs," recruited only men for an elastic, temporary labor supply, a reserve army of labor that could be discarded when redundant. Employers did not absolutely command the movement of Mexican workers, but employers' needs constructed a particular structure of opportunities that shaped migration.

Mexicans began migrating to work in U.S. agriculture, mining, and railroading during the late nineteenth century, when post-Civil War U.S. industrial expansion generated new demands for the Southwest's primary products. Previously, a predominantly male Asian immigrant labor force had provided the key to development of the West, but the 1882 Chinese Exclusion Act and the 1907 "gentlemen's agreement" with Japan curtailed this source of labor. As the railroads extended into western Mexico in the late nineteenth century, *enganchistas* (labor recruiters) sought Mexican workers to build and maintain the railroad lines, and then to work in U.S. mines and agriculture (Cardoso, 1980). Mexican migrants in the late nineteenth century were primarily men, but many Mexican women were also working in the Southwest during this period.[3] Most of these migrants appear to have stayed temporarily, as they did not significantly increase the permanent Mexican-origin population in the United States (McLemore and Romo, 1985).

Economic development in the Southwest and the extension of the railways coincided with Mexico's rapid-paced economic development based on foreign investment and export-led growth. The consolidation of the hacienda system under Porfirio Díaz's autocratic regime (1876-1911) displaced a growing peasant population from a communal system of land tenure and transformed them into landless workers who lacked sources of employment.[4] Together with inflation and U.S. labor demands, these conditions accounted for a substantial increase in the U.S. Mexican population from 1900 to 1910. Although Mexicans were concentrated in southwestern agriculture, by 1908 they worked throughout the Midwest and as far north as Chicago in numerous industries. Many of these laborers eventually returned to Mexico, but settlements emerged around isolated railway camps, and along the border in South Texas, where labor recruiters went to seek more workers (Cardoso, 1980).

The period from World War I until the Great Depression marked the first great wave of Mexican immigration, launched when wartime labor shortages in U.S. agriculture prompted a contract-labor program for male Mexican workers.[5] During 1917-21, seventy-two thousand Mexicans registered to work in the fields of the Southwest and the Midwest as temporary contract workers, and countless more migrant workers worked without official contracts or documents. Thousands of Mexicans also found work in factories, packing-houses, and restaurants in eastern and midwestern cities, and in 1918 the contract-labor program officially expanded to include nonagricultural workers (Cardoso, 180:48). Still, until the 1920s, most of these Mexican workers were concentrated in rural areas.

The economic disruption and violence of the Mexican revolution (1910-19), and of the Cristero Rebellion in the central western area of Mexico (1926-29), motivated more northward migration during the 1920s.[6] During this period the booming U.S. economy provided both urban and rural jobs for Mexican workers, and Mexican families settled into the already growing barrios of Los Angeles, El Paso, and San Antonio. These settlement communities also served as labor-distribution centers for Mexican workers who were recruited to rural areas of the Southwest and the Midwest (Romo, 1983).[7]

By the 1920s, many employers sought a more stabilized, steady immigrant labor force. In the sugar-beet fields of Colorado and the midwestern states, growers discovered that they could encourage stabilization by hiring entire families to work (Taylor, 1929; Valdés, 1991).[8] Similarly, in the cotton fields of Texas, growers restricted labor mobility by incorporating Mexican women into a system of family tenant farming. Growers found that they could put women and children to work at lower wages, and that when accompanied by their families, men more willingly endured harsh working conditions (González, 1983).[9] Many of these families performed seasonal farmwork, and lived in cities between harvests. Although the majority remained concentrated in the Southwest, by the 1920s Mexicans were working in many areas of the United States.

In the 1920s, family immigration made up a larger portion of Mexican immigration than it had in prior decades. Although men accounted for 65 to 70 percent of the Mexican immigrants who legally entered the U.S., it is probable that many of them were later joined by their wives and families, who entered "illegally" in order to avoid paying entry fees (Cardoso, 1980:82). During this period, the Mexican anthropologist Manuel Gamino (1971a, first published 1930) chronicled the emergence of segregated settlement communities. Based on numerous sources—including data gathered from postal money orders remitted to families in Mexico—he concluded that most Mexican migrants were intent on staying only temporarily in the United States. Paul Taylor (1929, 1983), an economist who also conducted studies of Mexican immigrant labor in the 1920s and 1930s, argued that the winter decline in remittances reflected seasonal patterns of agricultural work, and that Mexican immigrants were in fact settling permanently in the United States.[10] Other sources concur that Mexican immigration during the 1920s was characterized by family immigration and settlement into urban areas (Romo, 1983).

The Great Depression prompted the deportation to Mexico of as many as half a million people, a group that included Mexican undocumented immigrants, legal permanent residents, and U.S. citizens of Mexican descent (Hoffman, 1976:126). The deportees, reflecting the increase in family migration during the 1920s, included substantial numbers of women and children.[11] Beginning in 1931, local governments and relief agencies threatened to cut Mexican families' public relief, and sometimes paid for the families' return transportation to Mexico. Thousands of Mexican families with their accumulated possessions loaded automobiles and boarded trains bound for the border.[12] By 1940, the Mexican population in the United States had declined to about half of what it had been in 1930 (González, 1983). Deportation campaigns, seasonal agricultural work, and labor-recruitment programs sponsored by the government and employers ensured that a significant proportion of Mexican immigrants during the early twentieth century remained in the United States only temporarily (García y Griego, 1983).[13]

The Second World War brought Mexican workers back to the U.S. when the U.S. government initiated the "bracero program," a contract-labor program designed to meet wartime labor shortages in agriculture; that program continued until December 1964. Between 1942 and 1964, nearly 5 million temporary labor contracts were issued to Mexican citizens, and apprehensions of Mexican workers working without documents numbered over 5 million (Samora, 1971:57; Kiser and Kiser, 1976:67).[14] During the post-Korean War recession in 1954, the Immigration and Naturalization Service launched a deportation campaign, Operation Wetback, which apprehended over 1 million undocumented Mexican workers (Bustamante, 1975; Cornelius, 1978). Yet migration resumed during the late 1950s, when over four hundred thousand Mexican workers each year entered the United States through the bracero program (Cornelius, 1976; Samora, 1971; Galarza, 1964).

Virtually all bracero contracts went to men.[15] This gender-discriminate labor policy mandated an elastic supply of labor, one that could be synchronized with seasonal agricultural fluctuations and that would externalize labor reproduction costs to Mexico. The bracero program legally codified the recommendations made by the Dillingham Commission in the early twentieth century. What the designers of the program had not anticipated, however, was the extent to which the bracero program would stimulate more Mexican immigration, both legal and undocumented. Many of the braceros acquired permanent legal status through labor certification, while others repeatedly migrated without documents or contracts; many of them started social networks that facilitated the future migration of their friends and family. And importantly, the bracero program ultimately germinated large-scale permanent settlement of Mexican immigrants.[16]

THE CONTEMPORARY SETTLEMENT OF MEXICAN UNDOCUMENTED IMMIGRANTS

The end of the contract-labor program heralded a new era of massive legal and undocumented immigration characterized by greater representation of women and entire families, the establishment of permanent settlement communities in geographically dispersed areas, and more diversified uses of Mexican labor (Portes and Bach, 1985; Cornelius, 1992). Between 1960 and 1980, over 1 million Mexicans legally immigrated to the U.S., exceeding earlier numbers. But the biggest increments were shown in records of apprehensions of the undocumented. During the 1960s the INS recorded more than 1 million, and in the 1970s over 7 million, arrests of undocumented Mexican immigrants.[17] INS figures for apprehensions and deportations do not precisely enumerate undocumented immigration because these figures signify events, not persons, who may evade capture altogether or be arrested repeatedly before successfully making one entry. Although the apprehension figures and nativist sentiments led to wildly inaccurate, inflated "guesstimates" (6 million to 12 million) of the size of the Mexican undocumented immigrant population, most observers agree that the proportion of "illegals" in the Mexican immigrant population significantly increased during the late 1960s and the 1970s.

Using census data, demographers estimated that by 1980, approximately 1.7 to 2.2 million Mexican undocumented immigrants lived in the United States (Heer and Passel, 1987; Passel, 1985), 68 percent of them in California (Passel, 1986:191). Based on estimates of annual net flows during the early 1980s, by 1986 the figure had risen to 3.1 million (Passel and Woodrow, 1987), a figure that may be accurately reflected by the 2.3 million Mexican undocumented immigrants who applied for one of the 1986 Immigration Reform and Control Act's legalization programs (Bean et al., 1989; Durand and Massey, 1992).[18]

By the 1970s, both undocumented and legal Mexican immigrants had established a significant number of permanent settlement communities in the United State (Browning and Rodríguez, 1985), and these have been referred to as "settling-out" processes (Cornelius, 1992), as "daughter communities" (Massey et al., 1987), and by the unfortunate, but perhaps illustrative, term "sediment" communities (Portes and Bach, 1985). Women and families played a key part in building these permanent communities (Browning and Rodríguez,

1985), and research conducted during the 1970s and 1980s recorded a significant presence of women in the population of Mexican undocumented immigrants.[19] While women participate in seasonal or sojourner undocumented immigration (Guendelman and Pérez-Itriaga, 1987; Kossoudji and Ranney, 1984), they concentrate in the settler portion of the undocumented population, where they are evenly represented with men (Cárdenas and Flores, 1986; Passel, 1986).

A related development consists of the exit of many Mexican immigrant workers from agriculture and their diversification into various sectors of the economy (Cornelius, 1989b, 1992; North and Houstoun, 1976; Portes and Bach, 1985). Although this trend predates termination of the bracero program, since the late 1960s a greater proportion of Mexican immigrants than ever before have located urban employment. Currently as few as 10 or 15 percent of all legal and undocumented Mexican immigrants work in agriculture in California, Texas, and Arizona (Wallace, 1988:664-65). Undocumented as well as legal Mexican immigrants now work in "plant nurseries, construction firms, foundries, shipyards, cement companies, furniture factories, rubber factories, paper factories, restaurants, hotels and motels, car washes, and butcher shops" (Portes and Bach, 1985:81), in "toy assembly, garment sewing, and electronics production" (Cross and Sandos, 1981:55), and in housecleaning and child care (Cornelius, 1989b; Solórzano-Torres, 1987; Ruiz, 1987; Hogeland and Rosen, 1990).[20]

The late 1960s mark the transition to an increasing volume of documented and undocumented Mexican immigrants, the multiplication of permanent settlement communities, a greater participation of women and entire families in Mexican immigration, and the absorption of Mexican immigrant workers into diverse labor markets. The bracero program and the maturation of social networks certainly played a key role in stimulating these developments, but it is macro-structural transformations in both Mexico and the United States that allowed for their realization. The remainder of this chapter examines these transformations.

STRUCTURAL TRANSFORMATIONS IN THE UNITED STATES

In the United States, the growth of settled-out, urban-based Mexican immigrant communities was fostered by a changing configuration of immigration legislation and labor demand. Although political and economic transformations are intertwined, I look first at legislative measures in U.S. immigration law. In the legislative arena, the termination of the bracero program in 1964 coincided with passage of the Civil Rights Act of 1964, and was immediately followed by the 1965 amendment to the prevailing immigration law. As Bach (1978) points out, antidiscriminatory principles inspired by the civil-rights movement fueled all of these legislative actions.

The 1965 amendments to the Immigration and Nationality Act of 1952, which is still the principal U.S. immigration law, ended racist national-origin quotas, imposed for the first time an annual quota of 120,000 for the Western Hemisphere, and developed a preference system where labor certification and family reunification serve as the primary criteria for obtaining legal immigrant status.[21] Although restrictive in intent, the amendments prompted an increase in immigration and a shift of place of origin from Europe to Asia and Latin America (Keely, 1974; Massey, 1981).[22]

Before the 1965 amendments went into effect, many former braceros and *mojados* (wetbacks) began to legalize their status through their employers' labor certification. Later, the preference system based on family reunification allowed them to legalize their family members. As an attempt to curtail the rise in Mexican immigration, a national quota imposed on all Western Hemisphere countries in 1976 restricted the annual number of Mexicans, excluding close family relatives, who could be granted legal status to twenty thousand. These quota restrictions had the unanticipated effect of stimulating more undocumented immigration.[23]

The most dramatic change in immigration legislation affecting Mexican immigrants after 1965 occurred with passage of the 1986 Immigration Reform and Control Act (IRCA). IRCA, which had been debated in Congress since the 1970s, intended to curb Mexican undocumented immigration by imposing sanctions (civil and criminal penalties) on employers who knowingly hire undocumented immigrant workers. IRCA also included provisions for an amnesty-legalization program for undocumented immigrants who could prove continuous residence in the U.S. since January 1, 1982, and for those who could prove they had worked in U.S. agriculture for ninety days during specific periods.[24]

Although IRCA was restrictionist in intent, 2.3 million Mexican undocumented immigrants applied for legal status under one of IRCA's programs.[25] By granting legal status, the legislation recognized and accelerated the further integration and permanence of long-staying, previously undocumented immigrants in the U.S.[26] And in spite of IRCA's restrictionist provisions, several sources of data gathered after employer sanctions went into effect indicate a noticeable increase in the numbers of Mexican women, children, and first-time migrants crossing the border without legal authorization.[27]

Demographic analyses suggest that after IRCA, women may even compose a majority of the Mexican undocumented immigrant population (Woodrow and Passel, 1990:66). There are several reasons for this. Family members of many newly legalized men came out of fear that the "door was closing," with the hope that they too would qualify for legalization (Cornelius, 1989a, 1992). The increasing number of Mexican women participating in undocumented migration may also reflect the maturation of social networks, as these almost invariably incorporate more women over time (Massey et al., 1987; Durand and Massey, 1992). Once women migrate to the United States from Mexico, they are likely to migrate again (Donato, forthcoming). And IRCA's employer sanctions may have less detrimentally affected Mexican undocumented immigrant women's ability to find jobs, since many of them find employment in domestic work, an occupation situated in private households, which lessens the chance of detection (Bean et al., 1990).[28]

In any case, sanctions on employers who hire undocumented immigrants have had only a modest effect in deterring undocumented migration from Mexico (Bach and Brill, 1990; Donato et al., 1992; Kossoudji, 1992). Most employers comply with the letter of the law by asking for documents before hiring new employees, but employers are not required to check the documents' validity. As one California employer noted: "Blatantly fraudulent documents we don't accept—and we've had some miserable reproductions. Some of the forgeries are absolutely magnificent, however, and we don't question them." And another employer more succinctly stated that "the technology of falsification is far more advanced than the technology of detection" (Cornelius, 1989b:43-44). Employer sanctions exacerbate discrimination, but they do little to curb employers' demand for undocumented immigrant workers, institutionalized in many sectors of the economy since the late 1960s. Due to the imposition of employer sanctions, undocumented immigrants now face an added waiting period while they secure fraudulent documents before seeking employment, a step that may have prolonged the average stay of undocumented immigrants (Bach and Brill, 1990). Some undocumented migrants appear to be staying on longer in the U.S. and returning to Mexico for shorter periods of time between trips in order to compensate for IRCA (Kossoudji, 1992).

I turn now to the processes of economic restructuring that promoted this increasingly diverse labor demand for Mexican immigrants. A large literature focuses on the effects of Mexican undocumented immigrant workers on the labor market, but the discussion here focuses on identifying why there has been a major shift in the concentration of Mexican immigrant labor from seasonal, large-scale agricultural firms toward jobs in year-round, urban-based, relatively small or medium-sized firms in services, construction, and light industry. The explanation involves labor-market segmentation, the global fragmentation of production processes, income polarization, and the expanding role of producer services in the economy.

Relying on a "dual-economy" thesis, Portes and Bach (1985) argue that the diversification of demand for the labor of Mexican immigrants stems from pressures faced by small, competitive, labor-intensive firms. These firms face economic uncertainty, and so, to remain profitable, they create "secondary-sector jobs" characterized by relatively low pay, manual work, lack of benefits, low status, and few opportunities for occupational advancement. Portes and Bach (1985:19) indicate that the competitive sectors' reliance on undocumented immigrant labor, much of it Mexican, "accelerated in the mid-1960s and reached both numerical importance and notoriety during the 1970s." This reliance coincided with the decreasing willingness of citizens with access to protective social welfare—youth and racial-ethnic minority workers—to accept the conditions of secondary-sector jobs (Bach, 1978; Sassen-Koob, 1978; Portes and Bach, 1985). In this context, undocumented immigrant workers' "illegal" status translates into vulnerability in the workplace, a feature that enhances their attractiveness to employers in competitive firms in many industries (Thomas, 1985). Since the late 1960s firms in the construction and service sectors—hotels and restaurants, convalescent homes, and building and landscape maintenance—have met competitive pressures by hiring Mexican undocumented workers in expanding suburban areas and metropolitan centers, especially in California.[29]

Foreign competition prompted the relocation, fragmentation or elimination of many upper-tier manufacturing jobs and their restructuring into a system consisting of millions of globally dispersed, downgraded, de-skilled assembly jobs. By the mid-1970s, firms with large work forces in the garment industry had virtually disappeared, replaced by subcontracting arrangements (Bonacich, 1990; Fernández-Kelly and Garcia, forthcoming); similar patterns emerged in the automobile industry and the electronics industry (Hossfeld, 1990).[30] In order to maintain flexibility, manufacturers in these industries and others now typically contract out labor-intensive tasks to small, nonunion, immigrant-dominated firms, which may in turn subcontract industrial homework (Bonacich, 1990; Cornelius, 1986b; Soldatenko, 1991). It is not the influx of immigrants that has created the concentration of immigrant workers in certain jobs, firms, and industries; rather, processes of national and global restructuring have transformed the occupational structure that sustains and encourages immigration (Cornelius, 1989b; Sassen-Koob, 1984; Sassen, 1988).

Sassen's (1988; 1991) research indicates that trends of economic growth in the 1970s and 1980s favored the expansion of producer services and created an increasingly polarized income and occupational structure in the United States. As manufacturing has become increasingly dispersed, major cities in the U.S. serve as global and national centers of corporate management, finance, and technical and legal services that coordinate geographically scattered production facilities. High-income professional and managers employed in these advanced producer services have generated an entire "reorganization of the consumption structure," creating new labor demands in the informal sector for unique luxury goods, personal services, and residential and commercial gentrification. And it is largely immigrants who fill the void as janitors, gardeners, domestic workers, and producers of custom-made goods (Sassen-Koob, 1984:157).

An important outcome of these processes is the multiplication of domestic work and child-care jobs for immigrant women (Morales and Ong, 1990; Salzinger, 1991). Census and Department of Labor data underestimate the growth of domestic labor because they do not accurately capture occupations where "under the table" pay arrangements and undocumented immigrants are common. Although Mexican immigrant women have prevailed in these jobs in areas of the Southwest for many decades (Romero, 1987, 1992; Ruiz, 1987; Solórzano-Torres, 1987), income polarization and the mass entrance of women into the U.S. labor force have dramatically increased the demand for domestic services. As an elite class of educated women fill business and professional jobs, they and their families increasingly depend on personal household services, especially in areas with concentrated immigrant populations. In fact, the new "spousal egalitarianism" among high-income, dual-career corporate couples, routinely heralded in the popular media, is often predicated on the employment of immigrant women as domestic workers (Hertz, 1981).

STRUCTURAL TRANSFORMATIONS IN MEXICO

Contrary to popular stereotypes, migration originates not in stagnating, "backward" societies, but in those societies undergoing rapid-paced urbanization and industrialization. Mexico provides the classic example of this dictum.[31] A configuration of government economic polices and changing global and national markets stimulated major transformations in Mexico's agricultural and industrial structure after World War II, undermining rural subsistence economies in the mid-1960s and 1970s, and disrupting the livelihood of middle- and working-class sectors in the 1980s. These developments are perhaps best understood by examining the "Mexican miracle" of combined political stability and spectacular economic growth rates, which spans the period between 1940 and 1965; the late 1960s, which witnessed the decline of maize production and the subsequent dependency on food imports; and the period since 1982, during which Mexico has experienced a series of economic and political crises and has pursued neoliberalization policies.

The absence of imported commodities from the U.S. due to the Second World War allowed Mexico to pursue import-substitution industrialization, a development strategy fueled by modernizing agriculture (Alba, 1978).[32] The main source of government investment for the domestic production of previously imported goods came from foreign exchange earned by commercial, export-oriented agriculture.[33]

Government agricultural support became increasingly bifurcated in the 1960s, favoring large-scale, irrigated, commercial agriculture over small-scale, rain-fed, subsistence growing of food crops.[34] With the objective of keeping down food prices for urban consumption, government policies regulated the price of maize, and peasants responded by reducing production to subsistence levels (Grindle, 1986). In search of supplemental income, peasant farmers migrated as seasonal wage earners to the large, irrigated agricultural areas of northwestern and central Mexico, sought work in Mexico's growing urban centers, or worked in the U.S.—an alternative facilitated, until 1964, by the "safety valve" of the bracero program.

Both symbolically and structurally, Mexico's need to import basic foodstuffs after 1965 marks the miracle's demise. The expansion of private and public investment in commercial agriculture continued throughout the late 1960s, while cultivation of basic foodstuffs for domestic consumption declined. By the late 1960s and early 1970s, both market pressures and government incentives encouraged the cultivation of cattle-fodder crops such as sorghum and alfalfa, effectively restructuring production and use of cultivation space, and undermining previous land reforms by exacerbating the already inequitably skewed distribution of land in Mexico (Barkin, 1987).[35] Meanwhile, the "golden age" of plentiful urban jobs in industry and construction in the 1940s and 1950s no longer awaited city-bound migrants in the 1960s, as Mexico experienced the exhaustion of the import-substitution industrialization strategy (Arizpe, 1981).

These developments coincided with the termination of the bracero alternative. In 1965, in an effort to stave off rising unemployment, the Mexican government instituted the Border Industrialization Program (BIP), a program designed to generate the infrastructure and legal conditions to successfully attract foreign manufacturing investment along the border with the United States. Although the BIP was originally intended to occupy primarily male migrant workers, the plants it initiated employed predominantly young, single women. Fernández-Kelly (1983) explains that this was due to employer preferences, and to the growing population of single women without the financial support of husbands or fathers.

The growing rural population faced grim prospects: a declining peasant economy, diminishing urban job growth, *and* the restructuring of agricultural production. By the late 1970s, rural peasant communities were thoroughly integrated into international markets and increasingly unable to achieve food self-sufficiency (Barkin, 1987:292), prompting segments of the rural population to seek migration and what would eventually become permanent settlement in the U.S.

In the 1970s and 1980s, the outcomes of government policies also adversely affected the urban population. The economic crisis initiated by dual agricultural policies, growing trade imbalances and debt, government budget deficits, and the world economic recession of the mid-1970s culminated in 1976 when the International Monetary Fund pressured Mexico to enact a major devaluation of the peso. After years of maintaining a stable currency, the government devalued the peso nearly 100 percent, causing capital flight, decline in private investments, and high unemployment along the border *maquiladoras* and in the interior. Although momentarily mitigated by a brief oil boom (1977-81), the problems associated with the debt crisis were exacerbated by the dramatic increase in the number of people entering the Mexican labor force each year, and by the major population shift from rural to urban areas.[36]

Since 1982, when inflation reached nearly 100 percent, Mexico has undergone one of the world's most severe, prolonged economic crises.[37] Characterized by harsh austerity measures, unemployment, and dramatic inflation, the crisis cut into real wages of urban workers, professionals, government employees, and middle-class entrepreneurs, and so prompted a major shift in the demographic composition of U.S.-bound immigrants—what Cornelius (1988) has called "*los migrantes de la crisis.*" The Mexican population bound for the U.S. became increasingly heterogeneous, drawing from large industrial urban centers without traditions of northbound migration, such as Puebla and the Federal District, and began to include more people from the urban middle and working class (Cornelius, 1988).[38] Women, children, and the elderly also represented a greater proportion of U.S.-bound immigrants, which Cornelius (1988) attributes, in part, to the symptoms of the 1980s economic crisis that has driven more Mexican women into the labor force.

Although women's participation in the Mexican labor force increased approximately 50 percent in the 1970s, when many women assumed formal-sector jobs as teachers and office and factory workers, women's integration into the labor force accelerated in the 1980s, driven by the economic crisis and informal-sector job growth (de Oliveira, 1990; González de la Rocha, 1988). Structural-adjustment policies enacted in the 1980s propelled more women into the labor market and altered the characteristics of women workers. Until the early 1970s, most employed women in Mexico were young, single, and childless; upon marriage or the birth of their first child, they typically withdrew from the labor force. This pattern was substantially modified in the 1970s and 1980s, especially after 1982, when a greater proportion of older women, married women, and mothers entered the labor market. The crisis also modified the traditional positive correlation between schooling and women's employment, as women with little education joined the labor force in greater number (García and de Oliveira, 1991). Since the 1980s, increasing proportions of married and single women have found work in microbusinesses, where they manufacture shoes, clothing, and rubber products (Escobar Latapí and González de la Rocha, 1988); in industrial subcontracting and homework, where they assemble toys and electronic and plastic parts (Benería and Roldán, 1987); in agribusiness, where they pick and pack fruits and vegetables for export (Mummert, 1991); and in various informal-sector activities (de Oliveira, 1990).

Since the 1980s, the Mexican government has pursued monetarist policies—reducing public-sector spending in order to meet foreign debt service requirements—and has liberalized the regulation of trade and investment, much of it oriented to export development. This is exemplified by the Mexican government's strong push to enact the North American Free Trade Agreement.[39] Wages deteriorated throughout the 1980s, while the prices for basic foods rose and nutritional standards declined.[40]

INSIDE THE GLOBAL PARAMETERS

Since the mid-1960s, political and economic transformations in both Mexico and the United States have resulted in the settlement of large numbers of Mexican undocumented immigrants in the United States. While political and economic transformations in the United States and Mexico constantly transform the market for labor needs and opportunities, the effects on Mexican immigrants' lives are mediated by the micro-structural context of family and community. In this regard, I prefer to think of these broader global processes as setting the parameters for Mexican immigration. Global processes define the parameters, but individual lives are situated and animated within families, social networks, specific communities, and local economies. In these specific social contexts, people act in consort and in conflict with friends, family, and kin, and looking at this realm complements the structural portrayal with an acknowledgement of agency.

NOTES

1. The Mexican population living in the Southwest in 1848 numbered between eighty thousand and one hundred thousand people. While the Mexican citizens living in the newly conquered Anglo territories were formally granted civil, language, religious, and land rights under the Treaty of Guadalupe Hidalgo, these rights were rarely and selectively conferred (Acuña, 1981, Barrera, 1979).

2. For analyses of these cyclical migration patterns, see Bustamante (1975), Portes and Bach (1985), and Cockcroft (1986).

3. Chicano historians have chronicled a significant presence of Mexican women working in southern California and Texas during the late nineteenth century, but it is not clear how many of these women came from Mexico and how many were descendants of the original Mexican inhabitants, born in the conquered territories. See, for example, Griswold del Castillo (1984), Barrera (1979), Camarillo (1979), and Garcia (1981). On New Mexico and southern Colorado, see Deutsch (1987).

4. By 1910, communally owned properties were illegal and the majority of Mexico's rural population lived in debt peonage, working as sharecroppers; 97 percent of rural families were landless (Cardoso, 1980:7).

5. In response to pressure from southwestern agricultural growers, the secretary of labor exempted Mexicans from the head tax, and the literacy tax imposed by the Immigration Act of 1917, and instituted special contract-labor provisions for Mexican workers (Kiser and Kiser, 1976:127-31). Labor shortages in agriculture occurred when more than 1 million U.S. citizens were conscripted into the military, drawing poor white and black workers from agriculture to urban jobs (Cardoso, 1980:45-48).

6. The Cristero Rebellion, a popular Christian backlash to the Mexican government's attempt to undermine the powerful hegemony of the Catholic church, consisted of a series of battles and random violence perpetrated in the western area of Mexico.

7. These new urban settlements also drew the attention of "Americanist" groups. Americanization projects targeted Mexican immigrant women with the intention of changing Mexican cultural values and practices (Sánchez, 1990).

8. The recruitment of Mexican family labor in Colorado sugar-beet fields began as early as 1908, and after 1910 the Great Western Sugar Company institutionalized a policy of recruiting only family labor. Many of these Mexican-origin families came from northern New Mexico villages (Deutsch, 1987:34).

9. The lyrics of a popular song from the 1920s, sung from the perspective of a returning migrant worker, suggest men's greater willingness, when accompanied by family, to comply with employer demands. The lyrics tell of a migrant worker who, upon returning to the U.S. with his wife, proclaims:

"What do you say, my contractor? Didn't I tell you I'd be back? Send me wherever you will, because now I bring someone with me." (Gamino, 1971:90).

10. See Durand and Massey (1992) for a discussion of historical and contemporary debates over the number of persons immigrating from Mexico to the U.S., and for debates over the numbers of Mexican immigrants remaining in the U.S.

11. Carreras (1974) reports that between 1931 and 1933, two-thirds of the deportees were women.

12. In Los Angeles, local welfare agencies aggressively promoted the repatriation of men, women, and children (Kiser and Kiser, 1976; Hoffman, 1974). Mexicans did not respond passively to these attacks. Mexican communities organized mutual-aid societies that provided assistance, and that protested the massive raids and the boycotts against hiring Mexicans. And Mexican government officials, under the leadership of President Lazaro Cardenas (1934-40), welcomed the *repatriados* (repatriates) by granting land and tools to help them reestablish themselves (Balderrama, 1982).

13. García Griego reports that U.S. and Mexican government statistics show that more Mexican immigrations returned to Mexico than remained in the U.S. during the first three decades of the century, indicating "a strong component of seasonal labor migration" and "the relative impermanence of Mexican settlement in the United States," especially after the Great Depression (1983:50). As García y Griego (ibid.) and others have noted, however, accurate figures on the number of Mexican immigrants settling in the U.S. are difficult to ascertain because of lax practices in recording border crossings, poor census records, and the undercount of braceros and Mexican workers who migrated illegally.

14. The first bilateral agreement in 1942 allowed U.S. government representatives to recruit in Mexico and assign contract workers to selected employers. In initial negotiations, the Mexican government required that employers pay the cost of the workers' round-trip transportation and subsistence en route, provide adequate housing in the labor camps, and provide minimum standards of wages, working conditions, medical care, and insurance against accidents (McWilliams, 1968). Some growers resented these government interventions, preferring instead a "laissez-faire" open border, and by 1947, employers were allowed to directly recruit workers, which they often did at the border. While provisions for workers' rights were included in the 1947 agreement, government regulation of employer practices decreased, wages declined, and employer abuses rose. During this period, Mexican undocumented immigrants apprehended by the INS were returned to Mexico and then immediately "recruited" under employer contract, a process then crudely known as "wringing out the wetbacks"—that is, authorizing the immigrants for work (Samora, 1971:47). When the Mexican government threatened

to negate these accords because of widespread abuse and the absence of government supervision, the program was formally institutionalized by the U.S. Congress at Public Law 78 in 1951. During this last phase of the bracero program, 1951-65, fewer than 2 percent of commercial farmers received bracero workers (Halwey, 1966:157). See García y Griego (1983) and Samora (1971) for an assessment of the bracero program's operations and legacy.

15. Men accounted for 98 percent of former braceros surveyed in Michoacán and Jalisco by Massey and colleagues (Massey and Liang, 1989:207).

16. For analyses of these outcomes of the bracero program, see Corwin and Cardoso (1978), North and Houstoun (1976), Massey et al. (1987), Massey and Liang (1989), and Mines (1981).

17. From 1961 to 1970, 453,937 Mexicans legally immigrated, 887,635 entered as braceros, and 1,017,719 were apprehended by the INS. While the number of apprehended undocumented Mexican immigrants had decreased between 1957 and 1964 from thirty-eight thousand to twenty-three thousand, in 1966—two years after termination of the bracero program—the number jumped to seventy-one thousand and then steadily increased until 1977, when the INS apprehended over 1 million undocumented Mexican immigrants (Jenkins, 1977). From 1971 to 1980, 640,294 people legally immigrated from Mexico, but more than ten times that number of undocumented Mexicans (7,473,248) were apprehended. See U.S. Immigration and Naturalization Service (1983), and Pedraza-Bailey (1985:77, table 4).

18. Many of the Mexican undocumented immigrants in the U.S. did not qualify for either the legalization-amnesty program, which required proof of continuous illegal residence in the U.S. dating from prior to January 1982 as the major eligibility criterion, or the Special Agricultural Worker (SAW) program, that required proof of having worked a minimum of ninety days in U.S. agriculture from 1985 to 1986. Many other undocumented immigrants feared that the bureaucratic procedure would place them in jeopardy with the authorities, and did not file applications. Using data from the 1988 Current Population Survey, Woodrow and Passel (1990:55) indicate that approximately one-third of the Mexican undocumented immigrants living in the U.S. prior to January 1982 did not apply for amnesty legalization. Hence Durand and Massey (1992) suggest that the 2.3 million Mexican applicants confirms these estimates of the Mexican undocumented immigrant population, accounting for approximately 75 percent of the 3.1 million.

19. See, for example, Cárdenas and Flores (1986), Curry-Rodríguez (1988), Fernández-Kelly and Garcia (1990), Solórzano-Torres (1987), Simon and de Ley (1984), and Villar (1990).

20. See Cornelius (1989b:31) for a list of sixty-six goods and services produced by 177 Mexican immi-

grant-dependent firms studied in metropolitan areas of California. The list includes fish, duck, and chicken processing; electrical machinery; plastic, vinyl, and textile products; and household appliances.

21. From 1921 to 1965 U.S. immigration law mandated the selection of legal immigrants on the basis of national-origin quotas. These racist quotas were designed to exclude Asians and other groups deemed undesirable. For example, the Emergency Quota Act of 1921 established a 3 percent limit on each nationality group already resident in the U.S. when the 1910 U.S. Census was taken, effectively privileging immigration from northwestern Europe. The 1952 McCarran-Walter Act justified quotas on the basis of assimilability. Quotas for the Western Hemisphere were established for the first time with the 1965 amendment, and national-origin quotas were phased out. (Keely and Elwel, 1983:181).

22. While from 1900 to 1965, 75 percent of all legal immigrants to the U.S. came from Europe (Massey, 1981:58), this changed radically after 1968, when the 1965 amendment went into effect. Asia, Latin America, and the Caribbean accounted for approximately 75 percent of all U.S. immigrants during the 1970s, and for 80 percent by the 1980s. (U.S. Immigration and Naturalization Service, 1989).

23. Mexico had previously accounted for approximately forty thousand legal immigrants annually, and with this figure halved in 1976, severe backlogs encouraged many would-be legal migrants with pending applications to come as undocumented immigrants. In 1977, 1978, and 1979, apprehensions of Mexican undocumented immigrants totaled more than 1 million each year (Portes and Bach, 1985:63).

24. IRCA also allowed for a 50 percent increase in budget allocations to the Border Patrol, and provisions to benefit U.S. agriculture, such as a temporary contract-labor program for sugarcane workers.

25. For an evaluation of IRCA, see Bean et al. (1989). One commentator noted that IRCA was a "product of the new restrictionist mentality, in terms of its origins and the symbolic message of control that it transmits to the American public, if not in terms of its actual impact" (Calavita, 1989:162). One can also surmise that even restrictionists recognized that a large proportion of undocumented immigrants were irreversibly established in the United States.

26. Although the acquisition of permanent legal residency facilitates integration into U.S. society, it does not necessarily mandate it. In fact, acquisition of legal status facilitates return trips to Mexico, as crossing the border becomes less problematic with legal papers. Also, many elderly Mexican immigrants retire to Mexico. I am grateful to Maria de Lourdes Villar for this observation.

27. In 1987, an increasing proportion of women were sighted at Zapata Canyon, a popular crossing point in Tijuana for Mexicans illegally migrating into

the United States (Bustamante, 1990), and by 1988 and 1989, the proportion of women and children apprehended by the Border Patrol in California had significantly increased (Bean et al., 1990). Other investigations of undocumented border crossers in Tijuana sponsored by El Colegio de la Frontera Norte also indicate a growing presence of women without prior immigration experience. Daily interviews conducted in Tijuana between September 1987 and July 1989 indicate that more than 80 percent of the women interviewed (N=718) were coming to the United States for the first time. Investigations simultaneously conducted in Ciudad Juárez reveal that the vast majority of Mexican women crossing the border illegally had previous experience in doing so. This is because the majority of the women crossing in Ciudad Juárez are border residents who routinely commute to work in Texas. These women typically do paid domestic work, and may cross the border on a weekly, biweekly, or even daily basis. In Tijuana, the majority of illegal border crossers stem from the interior of Mexico (Woo, 1993).

28. In this regard, Bean et al. (1990) suggest that the labor demand for domestic work and child care may coincide with the end of summer and the start of a new school year. They observe that the peak months of apprehensions for female Mexican undocumented immigrants are July and August, and note that "it would be an ironic twist if IRCA leads to decreased undocumented migration among males, but increased migration of undocumented females" (1990:149). Donato (forthcoming), on the basis of data gathered in ten Mexican communities and in the United States, suggests that during the 1980s Mexican women were more likely to participate in undocumented migration than legal migration, with one exception. The exception is 1988 and 1989, and this is explained by the temporary deterrent effect of IRCA during those years. Donato (ibid.) found that by 1989, Mexican women's likelihood of migrating north "without papers" on a first trip rose back to 1985 levels.

29. For example, until the mid-1960s, U.S.-born workers filled lower-level service jobs in Los Angeles hotels, but by the 1980s, only "the least mobile native-born workers (older minority women and uneducated minority men)" remained in these positions, which are now filled largely by Mexican undocumented immigrations (Cornelius, 1989b:39). See also Rick A. Morales, "The Utilization of Mexican Immigrants in the Restaurant Industry: The Case of San Diego County," and Gary R. Lemons, "Hiring and Employment of Undocumented Workers in the Roofing Industry of Albuquerque, New Mexico," in Wayne A. Cornelius, *The Changing Role of Mexican Labor in the U.S. Economy: Sectoral Perspectives* (La Jolla, Calif.: Center for U.S.-Mexican Studies, University of California at San Diego, forthcoming.)

30. Cornelius's study (1989b) of 177 immigrant-dominated firms in California indicates that foreign competition has also been key to the "Mexicanization" of the work force in rubber and furniture manufacturing, and in food processing.

31. For analyses of how rapid-paced development in Mexico has contributed to U.S.-bound migration, see Alba (1978) and Arizpe (1981). See also Portes (1978).

32. Between 1940 and 1965, the agricultural sector in Mexico boasted an annual growth rate of 5.7 percent (Arizpe, 1981b:629). Agricultural outputs increased over 100 percent between 1940 and 1960, and industrial outputs, stimulated by advertisements promoting "modern" standards of consumption, increased by 120 percent during the same period (Cockcroft, 1983:150).

33. The government invested heavily in a series of *grandes obras de irrigación*—enormous irrigation projects—located primarily in northwestern Mexico, where export crops were cultivated on a large scale (Schumacher, 1981). Investment in irrigation and green-revolution technology supported growth in modernizing commercial agriculture, and this provided the dynamic behind Mexico's postwar growth (Hewitt de Alcántara, 1976).

34. Arizpe (1981:629) cites Banco Nacional de Comercio Exterior data indicating that the proportion of federal investment in irrigated, large-scale agriculture was twice that directed at small-scale, rain-fed agriculture in 1960, but that by 1966 it was seven times greater. For studies on the modernization of commercial agriculture in Mexico, see Hewitt de Alcántara (1976), Esteva (1980), and Grindle (1986).

35. By 1970, the distribution of cultivated land was so highly skewed that 3 percent of all agricultural units accounted for 54 percent of total agricultural production. At the bottom of the hierarchy, one-half of all agricultural units controlled only one-eighth of the land and produced approximately 4 percent of the total value of agricultural production (Esteva, 1980:38-39).

36. From 1970 to 1980, the economically active population in Mexico increased by 62 percent, constituting an "overall absolute surplus of labor" and severely exacerbating unemployment by the early 1980s (Alejo, 1983:87).

37. Many commentators agree that Mexico's economic problems in the 1970s and 1980s grew directly out of the development model pursued in the 1940s and 1950s (Cockcroft, 1983; Hamilton and Harding, 1986). Capital flight, overextension of credit, and wage suppression were familiar problems, yet it was the incremental, quantitative growth and continuity of these trends that resulted in a crisis of qualitatively different proportions. Chant (1991:1983) reports that consumer prices in Mexico rose 981 percent between the second half of 1982 and 1986, while the daily minimum wage rose only 573 percent.

38. The changing class composition is explained by the effects of the economic crisis on different sectors. Employees in the formal sector of the economy

may have suffered these blows more intensely than workers in the unregulated informal sector (Escobar Latapí and González de la Rocha, 1988:554). As far as geographical diversification goes, Cornelius indicates that as late as 1973, 48 percent of undocumented Mexicans apprehended near the Tijuana crossing originated in the traditional immigrant-sending states of Jalisco and Guerrero (Dagodag, 1975), but in a survey conducted in 1987-1988 in southern California with 200 recently arrived undocumented immigrants, the Federal District ranked as the top sending area, followed by Puebla (Cornelius, 1988). Research based on interviews conducted in Laredo, Texas, with 6565 apprehended undocumented immigrants in 1986 found the Federal District to be the third most important state of origin (Fatemi, 1987).

39. Although public-sector spending has been curtailed, the Mexican government's lobbying expenditure for NAFTA constituted one of the most expensive foreign lobbying campaigns waged in the U.S. From 1989 to 1993, the Mexican government spent at least $25 million on NAFTA-related activities. For a report on these lobbying activities, see Charles Lewis and Margaret Ebraham, "Can Mexico and Big Business USA Buy NAFTA?" *The Nation,* June 14, 1993, 826-39.

40. By 1987, the minimum urban wage diminished to 58 percent of what it had been in 1980 (Cordera Campos et al., 1989:114).

REFERENCES

Acuña, Rudolfo. 1981. *Occupied America: A History of Chicanos.* New York: Harper and Row.

Alba, Francisco. 1978. "Mexico's International Migration as a Manifestation of its Development Pattern." *International Migration Review,* 12:502-13.

Alejo, Francisco Javier. 1983. "Demographic Patterns and Labor Market Trends in Mexico." Pp. 79-89 in Donald L. Wyman, editor, *Mexico's Economic Crisis: Challenges and Opportunities.* Monograph Series, no. 12. La Jolla, Calif.: Center for U.S.-Mexican Studies, University of California at San Diego.

Arizpe, Lourdes. 1977. "Women in the Informal Labor Sector: The Case of Mexico City." *Signs: Journal of Women in Culture and Society,* 3:25-37.

_____. 1981a. "Relay Migration and the Survival of the Peasant Household." Pp. 187-210 in Jorge Balán, editor, *Why People Move: Comparative Perspectives on the Dynamics of Internal Migration.* Paris: Unesco Press.

_____. 1981b. "The Rural Exodus in Mexico and Mexican Migration to the U.S." *International Migration Review,* 15:626-49.

Bach, Robert L. 1978. "Mexican Immigration and U.S. Immigration Reforms in the 1960's." *Kapitalistate,* 7:63-80.

_____, and Howard Brill. 1990. "Shifting the Burden: The Impacts of IRCA on U.S. Labor Markets." Interim report to the Division of Immigration Policy and Research, U.S. Department of Labor.

_____, and Lisa A. Schraml. 1982. "Migration Crisis and Theoretical Conflict." *International Migration Review,* 16:320-41.

Balán, Jorge, Harley L. Browning, and Elizabeth Jelin. 1973. *Men in a Developing Society.* Institute for Latin American Studies. Austin: University of Texas Press.

Balderrama, Francisco. 1982. *In Defense of La Raza: The Los Angeles Mexican Consulate and the Mexican Community, 1929-1936.* Tucson: University of Arizona Press.

Barkin, David. 1987. "The End to Food Self-Sufficiency in Mexico," *Latin American Perspectives,* 14:271-97.

Barrera, Mario. 1979. *Race and Class in the Southwest: A Theory of Racial Inequality.* Notre Dame, Ind.: University of Notre Dame Press.

Bean, Frank D., Georges Vernez, and Charles B. Keely. 1989. *Opening and Closing the Doors; Evaluating Immigration Reform and Control.* Santa Monica, Calif., and Washington, D.C.: Rand Corporation and the Urban Institute.

Bean, Frank D., Thomas J. Espenshade, Michael J. White, and Robert F. Dymowski. 1990. "Post-IRCA Changes in the Volume and Composition of Unauthorized Migration to the United States: An Assessment Based on Apprehension Data." Pp. 111-58 in Frank D. Bean, Barry Edmonston, and Jeffrey S. Passel, editors, *Unauthorized Migration to California: IRCA and the Experience of the 1980s.* Washington, D.C.: Urban Institute Press.

Benería, Lourdes, and Martha Roldán. 1987. *The Crossroads of Class and Gender: Industrial Homework, Subcontracting and Household Dynamics in Mexico City.* Chicago and London: University of Chicago Press.

Boagardus, Emory S. 1934. *The Mexican in the United States.* School of Research Studies, no. 5. Los Angeles: University of Southern California Press.

Bonacich, Edna. 1990. *Asian and Latino Immigrants in the Los Angeles Garment Industry: An Exploration of the Relationship between Capitalism and Racial Oppression.* Working Papers in the Social Sciences, vol. 5, no. 13. Los Angeles: Institute for Social Science Research, UCLA.

Bustamante, Jorge A. 1975. *Espaldas mojadas: Materia prima para le expansion del capital norteamericano.* Cuadernos del Centro de Estudios Sociologicos, no. 9. México, D.F.: El Colegio de México.

_____. 1990. "Undocumented Migration from Mexico to the United States: Preliminary Findings of the Zapata Canyon Project." Pp. 211-26 in Frank D. Bean, Barry Edmonston, and Jeffrey S. Passel, editors, *Unauthorized Migration to California: IRCA and the Experience of the 1980s.* Washington, D.C.: Urban Institute Press.

Calavita, Kitty. 1989. "The Immigration Policy Debate: Critical Analyses and Future Options." Pp. 151-77 in Wayne A. Cornelius and Jorge A. Bustamante, editors, *Mexican Migration to the United States.* La Jolla, Calif.: Center for U.S.-Mexican Studies, University of California at San Diego.

Camarillo, Albert. 1979. *Chicanos in a Changing Society.* Cambridge, Mass.: Harvard University Press.

Cárdenas, Gilberto, and Estevan T. Flores. 1986. *The Migration and Settlement of Undocumented Women.* Austin: Center for Mexican American Studies, University of Texas.

Cardoso, Lawrence A. 1980. *Mexican Emigration to the United Sates, 1897-1931.* Tucson: University of Arizona Press.

Carrerras, Mercedes. 1974. *Los Mexicanos que devolvio a la crisis, 1929-1932.* Mexico City: Secretaria de Relaciones Exteriores.

Chant, Sylvia. 1991. *Women and Survival in Mexican Cities: Perspectives on Gender, Labour Markets, and Low-Income Households.* Manchester and New York: Manchester University Press.

Cockcroft, James D. 1983. *Mexico: Class Formations, Capital Accumulation and the State.* New York: Monthly Review Press.

Cordera Campos, Rolando, and Enrique González Tiburcio. 1989. "Percances y damnificados de la crisis economica." In Cordera Campos et al., editors, *México: El reclamo democratico.* México, D.F.: Siglo Veintiuno Editores.

Cornelius, Wayne A. 1976. "Outmigration from Rural Mexican Communities." In *The Dynamics of Migration: International Migration.* Interdisciplinary Communications Program, Occasional Monograph Series, vol. 2, no. 5. Washington, D.C.: Smithsonian Institution.

_____. 1988. "*Los Migrantes de la Crisis*: The Changing Profile of Mexican Labor Migration to California in the 1980s." Paper presented at the conference, Population and Work in Regional Settings. El Colegio de Michoacán, Zamora, Michoacán, Mexico, November 28-30.

_____. 1989a. "Impacts of the 1986 U.S. Immigration Law on Emigration from Rural Mexican Sending Communities." *Population and Development Review,* 15:689-706.

_____. 1989b. "The U.S. Demand for Mexican Labor." Pp. 25-47 in Wayne A. Cornelius and Jorg A. Bustamante, editors, *Mexican Migration to the United States.* La Jolla, Calif.: Center for U.S.-Mexican Studies, University of California at San Diego.

_____. 1992. "From Sojourners to Settlers: The Changing Profile of Mexican Immigration to the United States." Pp. 155-95 in Jorge A. Bustamante, Clark W. Reynolds, and Ratíl A. Hinojosa Ojeda, editors, *U.S.-Mexico Relations: Labor Market Interdependence.* Stanford, Calif.: Stanford University Press.

Corwin, Arthur F., and Lawrence A. Cardoso. 1978. "Vamos al Norte: Causes of Mass Mexican Migration." Pp. 38-66 in Arthur F. Corwin, editor, *Immigrations—and Immigrants: Perspectives on Mexican Labor Migration to the United States.* Westport, Conn.: Greenwood Press, 1978.

Corwin, Arthur F., and Johnny M. McCain. 1978. "Wetbackism Since 1964: A Catalogue of Factors." Pp. 67-107 in Arthur F. Corwin, editor, *Immigrations—and Immigrants: Perspectives on Mexican Labor Migration to the United States.* Westport, Conn.: Greenwood Press, 1978.

Cross, Harry E., and James A. Sandos. 1981. *Across the Border: Rural Development in Mexico and Recent Migration to the United States.* Institute of Governmental Studies, University of California at Berkeley.

Curry-Rodríguez, Julia E. 1988. "Labor Migration and Familial Responsibilities: Experiences of Mexican Women." Pp. 47-63 in Margarita B. Melville, editor, *Mexicanas at Work in the United States.* Mexican American Studies Monograph no. 5. Houston, Tex.: University of Houston.

Dagodag, Tim W. 1975. "Source Regions and Composition of Illegal Mexican Immigration to Canada." *International Migration Review,* 9:499-511.

Deutsch, Sarah. 1987. *No Separate Refuge: Culture, Class and Gender on an Anglo-Hispanic Frontier in the American Southwest, 1880-1940.* New York and Oxford: Oxford University Press.

Donato, Katharine M. Forthcoming. "Current Trends and Patterns of Female Migration: Evidence from Mexico." *International Migration Review.*

Durand, Jorge and Douglas S. Massey. 1992. "Stemming the Tide? Assessing the Deterrent Effects of the Immigration Reform and Control Act." *Demography,* 29:139-57.

Escobar Latapí, Agustín, and Mercedes González de la Rocha. 1988. "Microindustria, informalidad y crisis en Guadalajara, 1982-1988." *Estudios sociológicos,* 6:553-81.

Escobar, Agustín Latapí, Mercedes Gonzálaz de la Rocha, and Bryan Roberts. 1987. "Migration, Labor Markets, and the International Economy: Jalisco, Mexico and the United States." Pp. 42-64 in Jeremy Eades, editor, *Migrants, Workers, and the Social Order*. London: Ravistock.

Esteva, Gustavo. 1980. *La batalla en el México rural*. México, D.F.: Siglo Veintiuno Editores.

Fatemi, Khosrow. 1987. "The Undocumented Immigration: A Socioeconomic Profile," *Journal of Borderlands Studies*, 2:85-99.

Fernández-Kelly, María Patricia, and Anna Garcia. 1990. "Power Surrendered, Power Restored: The Politics of Work and Family among Hispanic Garment Workers in California and Florida." Pp. 130-49 in Louise A. Tilly and Patricia Gurin, editors, *Women, Politics and Change*. New York: Russell Sage Foundation.

Flores, Estevan T. 1984. "Research on Undocumented Immigrants and Public Policy: A Study of the Texas School Case." *International Migration Review*, 18:505-23.

Galarza, Ernesto. 1964. *Merchants of Labor: The Mexican Bracero Story*. Santa Barbara, Calif.: McNally and Loftin.

Gamio, Manuel. 1971a. *The Mexican Immigrant: His Life Story*. New York: Dover Publications (first published 1930 by the University of Chicago Press).

_____. 1971b. *Mexican Immigration to the United States*. New York: Dover Publications (first published 1930 by the University of Chicago Press).

García, Brígida, and Orlandina de Oliveira. 1991. "Economic Recession and Changing Determinants of Women's Work." Paper presented at the Sixteenth International Congress of the Latin American Studies Association, Washington, D.C., April 4-6.

García, Mario. 1981. *Desert Immigrants: The Mexicans of El Paso, 1880-1920*. New Haven, Conn., and London: Yale University Press.

García y Griego, Manuel. 1983. "The Importation of Mexican Contract Laborers to the United States, 1942-1964: Antecedents, Operation, and Legacy." Pp. 49-98 in Peter G. Brown and Henry Shue, editors, *The Border That Joins: Mexican Migrants and U.S. Responsibility*. Totowa, N.J.: Rowman and Littlefield.

González, Rosalinda M. 1983. "Chicanas and Mexican Immigrant Families 1920-1940: Women's Subordination and Family Exploitation." Pp. 59-83 in Lois Scharf and Joan M. Jensen, editors, *Decades of Discontent: The Women's Movement 1920-1940*. Westport, Conn.: Greenwood Press.

González de la Rocha, Mercedes. 1988. "Economic Crisis, Domestic Reorganisation and Women's Work in Guadalajara, Mexico." *Bulletin of Latin American Research*, vol. 7, no. 2.

Grindle, Merilee. 1986. *State and Countryside: Development Policy and Agrarian Politics in Latin America*. Baltimore, Md.: Johns Hopkins University Press.

Griswold del Castillo, Richard. 1984. *La Familia: Chicano Families in the Urban Southwest, 1848 to the Present*. Notre Dame, Ind.: University of Notre Dame Press.

Guendelman, Sylvia, and Auristela Pérez-Itriaga. 1987. "Doubles Lives: The Changing Role of Women in Seasonal Migration." *Women's Studies*, 13:249-71.

Hamilton, Nora, and Timothy F. Harding, editors. 1986. *Modern Mexico, State, Economy, and Social Conflict*. Beverly Hills, Calif.: Sage Publications.

Hawley, Ellis W. 1966. "The Politics of The Mexican Labor Issue, 1950-1965," *Agricultural History*, 40:157-76.

Heer, David M. 1990. *Undocumented Mexicans in the United States*. Cambridge and New York: Cambridge University Press.

Heer, David M., and Jeffrey S. Passel. 1987. "Comparison of Two Methods for computing the Number of Undocumented Mexican Adults in Los Angeles County." *International Migration Review*, 21:1,446-73.

Hertz, Rosanna. 1986. *More Equal Than Others*. Berkeley: University of California Press.

Hewitt de Alcántara, Cynthia. 1976. *Modernizing Mexican Agriculture: Socio-economic Implications of Technological Change, 1940-1970*. Geneva: United Nations Institute for Social Development.

Hoffman, Abraham. 1974. *Unwanted Mexican Americans in the Great Depression: Repatriation Pressures, 1929-1939*. Tucson: University of Arizona Press.

Hogeland, Chris, and Karen Rosen. 1990. *Dreams Lost, Dreams Found: Undocumented Women in the Land of Opportunity*. San Francisco: Coalition for Immigrant and Refugee Rights and Services.

Hossfeld, Karen J. 1990. "'Their Logic Against Them': Contradictions in Sex, Race and Class in Silicon Valley." Pp. 149-78 in Kathryn Ward, editor, *Women and Workers and Global Restructuring*. Cornell University Press.

Keely, Charles B. 1974. "Immigration Composition and Population Policy." *Science*, 185:587-93.

_____, and Patricia J. Elwel. 1983. "International Migration: Canada and the United States." Pp. 181-207 in Mary M. Kritz, Charles B. Keely, and Silvano M. Tomasi, editors, *Global Trends in Migration: Theory and Research on International Population Movements*. Staten Island, N.Y.: Center for Migration Studies.

Kiser, George C., and Martha Woody Kiser, editors. 1976. *Mexican Workers in the United States*. Albuquerque: University of New Mexico Press.

Kossoudiji, Sherrie A., 1992. "Playing Cat and Mouse at the U.S.-Mexican Border," *Demography*, 29:159-77.

_____, and Susan I. Ranney. 1984. "The Labor Market Experience of Female Migrants: The Case of Temporary Mexican Migration to the U.S." *International Migration Review*, 18:1, 120-43.

McLemore, S. Dale, and Ricardo Romo. 1985. "The Origins and Development of the Mexican American People." Pp. 3-32 in Rodolfo O. de la Garza, Frank D. Bean, Charles M. Bonjean, Ricardo Romo, and Rodolof Alvarez, editors, *The Mexican American Experience: An Interdisciplinary Anthology*. Austin: University of Texas Press.

McWilliams, Carey. 1968. *North from Mexico: The Spanish-Speaking People of the United States*. New York: Greenwood Press.

Martin, Philip L., and J. Edward Taylor. 1988. " Harvest of Confusion: SAWs, RAWs, and Farmworkers." Working Paper no. PRIP-U1-4. Program for Research on Immigration Policy. Washington, D.C.: Urban Institute.

Massey, Douglas S. 1981. "Dimensions of the New Immigration to the United States and the Prospects for Assimilation." *Annual Review of Sociology,* 7:57-85.

_____, Rafael Alarcón, Jorge Durand, and Humberto Gonzalez. 1987. *Return to Aztlán: The Social Process of International Migration from Western Mexico.* Berkeley: University of California Press.

_____, Katharine M. Donato, and Zai Liang. 1990. "Effects of the Immigration Reform and Control Act of 1986: Preliminary Data from Mexico.:" Pp. 183-210 in Frank D. Bean, Barry Edmonston, and Jeffrey S. Passel, editors, *Unauthorized Migration to California: IRCA and the Experience of the 1980s.* Washington, D.C.: Urban Institute Press.

Morales, Rebecca, and Paul Ong. 1990. "Immigrant Women in Los Angeles." Working Papers in the Social Sciences, vol. 5. Los Angeles: Institute for Social Science Research, UCLA.

Oliveira, Orlandina de. 1990. "Emplleo feminino en México en tiempos de recesión económica: Tendencia recientes." Pp. 31-54 in Nuema Aguiar, editor, *Mujer y crisis: Respuestas ante la recesión.* Caracas, Venezuela: Editorial Nueva Sociedad.

Passel, Jeffrey S. 1985. "Undocumented Immigrants: How Many?" *Proceedings of the Social Statistics Section, American Statistical Association,* 1985:65-72.

_____. 1987. "Change in the Undocumented Alien Population in the United States, 1979-83." *International Migration Review,* 21:1,304-23.

Pedraza-Bailey, Silvia. 1985. *Political and Economic Migrants in America: Cubans and Mexicans.* Austin: University of Texas Press.

Portes, Alejandro, and Robert L. Bach. 1985. *Latin Journey: Cuban and Mexican Immigrants in the United States.* Berkeley: University of California Press.

Romero, Mary. 1987. "Domestic Service in the Transition from Rural to Urban Life: The Case of La Chicana." *Women's Studies,* 13:199-222.

_____. 1992. *Maid in the U.S.A.* New York and London: Routledge.

Romo, Ricardo. 1983. *East to Los Angeles: History of a Barrio.* University of Texas Press.

Ruiz, Vicki L. 1987. "By the Day or the Week: Mexicana Domestic Workers in El Paso." Pp. 61-76 in Vicki L. Ruiz and Susan Tiano, editors, *Women on the U.S.-Mexico Border: Responses to Change.* Boston: Allen and Unwin.

Salzinger, Leslie. 1991. "A Maid by Any Other Name: The Transformation of 'Dirty Work' by Central American Immigrants." Pp. 139-60 in Michael Burawoy et al. editors, *Ethnography Unbound: Power and Resistance in the Modern Metropolis.* Berkeley: University of California Press.

Samora, Julian. 1971. *Los Mojados: The Wetback Story.* Notre Dame, Ind.: University of Notre Dame Press.

Sánchez, George J. 1990. "'Go After the Women': Americanization and the Mexican Immigrant Woman, 1915-1929." Pp. 250-63 in Ellen Carol DuBois and Vicki L. Ruiz, editors, *Unequal Sister: A Multicultural Reader in U.S. Women's History.* New York and London: Routledge.

Sassen-Koob, Saski. 1984. "The New Labor Demand in Global Cities." Pp. 139-71 in Michael P. Smith, editor, *Cities in Transformation.* Beverly Hills, Calif.: Sage Publications.

_____. 1988. *The Mobility of Labor and Capital: A Study of International Investment and Labor Flow.* Cambridge and New York: Cambridge University Press.

Schumacher, August. 1981. *Agricultural Development and Rural Employment: A Mexican Dilemma.* La Jolla, Calif.: Center for U.S.-Mexican Studies, University of California at San Diego.

Simon, Rita J., and Margo Corona DeLey. 1984. "The Work Experience of Undocumented Mexican Women Migrants in Los Angeles." *International Migration Review,* 18:1,212-29.

Soldatenko, Maria Angelina. 1991. "Who Is Organizing Latina Garment Workers in Los Angeles?" *Aztlán: Journal of Chicano Studies Research,* 20(1 and 2).

Solórzano-Torres, Rosalía. 1987. "Female Mexican Immigrants in San Diego County." Pp. 41-60 in Vicki L. Ruiz and Susan Tiano, editors, *Women on the U.S.-Mexico Border: Responses to Change.* Boston: Allen and Unwin.

Taylor, Paul. 1929. "Mexican Labor in the United States: Migration Statistics." Pp. 237-55 in Carl C. Plehn, Ira B. Cross, and Melvin M. Knight, editors, *University of California Publications in Economics.* Berkeley: University of California Press.

_____. 1983. "Mexicans North of the Rio Grande." Pp. 1-16 in Paul Taylor, *On the Ground in the Thirties.* Salt Lake City: Peregrine Smith Brooks (originally published in 1931).

Thomas, Robert J. 1985. *Citizenship, Gender, and Work: Social Organization of Industrial Agriculture.* Berkeley: University of California Press.

U.S. Congress. Senate. Immigration Commission. 1911. *Immigration Commission Report.* 61st Congress, 3rd session.

U.S. Immigration and Naturalization Service. 1983. *1980 Statistical Yearbook of the Immigration and Naturalization Service.* Washington D.C.: Government Printing Office.

_____. 1989. *Immigration Statistics: Fiscal Year 1988.* Washington, D.C.: Government Printing Office.

_____. 1991. *Statistical Yearbook of the Immigration and Naturalization Service, 1990.* Washington, D.C.: Government Printing Office.

Valdéz, Dennis Nodín. 1991. *Al Norte: Agricultural Workers in the Great Lakes Region, 1917-1970.* Austin: University of Texas Press.

Villar, Maria de Lourdes. 1990. "Rethinking Settlement Processes: The Experience of Mexican Undocumented Migrants in Chicago." *Urban Anthropology,* 19:63-79.

Wallace, Steven P. 1988. "Central American and Mexican Immigrant Characteristics and Economic Incorporation in California." *International Migration Review,* 22:375-93.

Warren, Robert, and Jeffrey S. Passel. 1987. "A Count of the Uncountable: Estimates of Undocumented Aliens Counted in the 1980 United States Census." *Demography,* 24:375-93.

Woo, Ofelia Morales. 1993. "Migración internacional y movilidad transfronteriza: El caso de las mujeres mexicanas que cruzan hacía Estados Unidos." *Mujer y frontera,* 8:115-46. Mexico: El Colegio de la Frontera Norte y Universidad Autónoma de Ciudad Juárez.

Woodrow, Karen A., and Jeffrey S. Passel. 1990. "Post-IRCA Unauthorized Immigration to the United States: An Assessment Based on the June 1988 CPS." Pp. 33-75 in Frank D. Bean, Barry Edmonston, and Jeffrey S. Passel, editors, *Unauthorized Migration to California: IRCA and the Experience of the 1980s.* Washington, D.C.: Urban Institute Press.

7

A REPEAT PERFORMANCE? THE NICARAGUAN EXODUS

Alejandro Portes and Alex Stepick

FOR THOSE RESIDENTS OF SOUTH FLORIDA who still thought of the area as a resort, 1989 began badly, very badly. The worst seemed to be happening all over again. Immigrants, more Spanish-speaking ones, were rolling into the area. At the end of 1988, the U.S.-supported Contra war was winding down, and thousands of Nicaraguans began flowing up through Guatemala and Mexico to Texas and on to Miami. The stream of new immigrants swelled through the last months of 1988 until, at the beginning of 1989, it became a flood. U.S. Immigration and Naturalization Service (INS) officials estimated that as many as three hundred refugees a week had been settling in Dade County since the summer of 1988.[1] At the beginning of 1989, Greyhound assigned special buses to run continuously between the Texas-Mexico border and South Florida. In the second week of January 1989, ten buses arrived in Miami on one day alone.[2]

While the busloads may not have been as dramatic or as numerous as the boatloads arriving in Key West during the 1980 Mariel influx, the Nicaraguan refugees became a concrete part of the public consciousness after INS attempted to intercept and detain them at the Texas-Mexico border. The newly incarcerated Nicaraguans, who had been drifting almost invisibly into Miami for ten years, now appeared on national television, standing behind fences and looking much like the detained Mariel refugees of 1980. They were also saying, again like the Mariel entrants, that they would head for South Florida as soon as they could. Then a federal judge ruled INS's detention policy unconstitutional; the refugees were released, and nearly everyone in Miami braced for "another Mariel."[3]

The Nicaraguan flow did indeed appear similar to that from Cuba. Nicaraguans, like Cubans, were fleeing a radical, left-wing regime. The Nicaraguan exodus, like the Cuban, converged in successive stages on Miami, beginning with the elites, then incorporating the professional and middle classes, and lastly the working class. But there were also important differences from the earlier Cuban exodus. Most notably, Washington did not welcome the Nicaraguans as it had the Cubans. Cubans had their passage from Cuba paid for, were automatically granted permanent residence in the United States, and received numerous other benefits. The federal government classified most Nicaraguans instead as illegal aliens and actively tried to keep them out. The new refugees did have the benefit, however, of coming after the Cuban enclave had been consolidated, and so had in it a powerful ally. "Latin-ness" alone was not the reason for the Cubans' support of the Nicaraguans. Rather, political ideology cemented the alliance—the common circumstances of militant opposition to an extreme-left regime.

PHASES OF NICARAGUAN MIGRATION

The growth and consolidation of Miami's Nicaraguan community roughly followed the pattern established by the Cubans. Both began in response to a major revolutionary upheaval. Both came in successive waves, each distinct in terms of time of arrival, social composition, and geographical concentration in Miami. In both cases, the first to arrive were the ones most immediately and directly affected by the revolutionary government— large landholders, industrialists, and managers of North American enterprises. Many of the Nicaraguan upper-class exiles also had economic roots in the United States and Miami before the upheaval. In both migrations, a second wave of professionals and white-collar workers followed the departure of the upper class. For Nicaraguans, this second wave commenced during the early 1980s. The final wave, consisting primarily of urban blue-collar workers, peaked for Nicaraguans in the dramatic exodus of early 1989, the equivalent of the Cubans' Mariel.

THE WEALTHY

In 1978, Nicaraguan dictator Anastasio Somoza Debayle secretly bought a bayside estate in Miami Beach, paying $575,000 through a Virgin Islands corporation to the owner, Miami's Roman Catholic archdiocese. In 1979, two days before Managua fell, Somoza stepped off a plane at Homestead Air Force Base just south of Miami and was whisked to his sprawling new seven-bedroom house.[4] Even after his 1980 death, his relatives continued their opulent life-style. Hope Somoza, wife of the ousted dictator, and Matilda Debayle, Somoza's aunt by marriage, were among the richest people in Florida. But they maintained a low profile, not attending political rallies and making private visits to the grave of Anastasio Somoza—who, like Cuban presidents Carlos Prío and Gerardo Machado, is buried in Woodlawn Cemetery.[5]

The Somoza family is the most famous Nicaraguan clan living in Miami, but approximately fifteen thousand other rich exiles transferred their assets to Miami banks in the late 1970s, moved their furniture into fashionable residences in Key Biscayne and Brickell Avenue, and invested in condominiums in the suburban western edge of the city.[6]

THE MIDDLE CLASS

The early-arriving elite was soon able to rent and sell those condominiums to other Nicaraguans—the professionals and business people who made up the second wave of the exodus. These refugees established for the first time a visible Nicaraguan presence in Miami, clustering in the western suburb of Sweetwater, right next to the Everglades. Many of these middle-class Nicaraguans arrived on tourist visas, and sometimes they moved back and forth between Managua and Miami, eventually settling in the latter. Like other educated refugees, they initially experienced downward mobility as they retooled for their new environment. A survey conducted in the early eighties estimated that 70 percent of skilled Nicaraguans were working below their training level.[7] Another study found that, of one thousand refugees surveyed, 34 percent were professionals in Nicaragua, but in their adoptive country "many are working outside their fields as laborers because they are so uncertain of their future."[8]

Those professionals who ended up staying did not usually remain laborers for long. Before the revolution, Jorge Savany held a cabinet-level post as the executive secretary of the National Cotton Commission. He fled Managua for Miami in July 1979, just as the Sandinistas ousted Somoza. With a younger brother he started selling hot dogs from a cart and eventually purchased eight such stands. A few years later, however, he was working as a salesman and assistant manager for a Cuban-owned furniture store on Little Havana's Calle Ocho, while his brother went on to become a real estate broker.[9]

Some of these refugees already had some work experience in North America, which they now put to use. The first president of the Nicaraguan-American Bankers Association of Miami, Roberto Arguello, was a Notre Dame graduate who became vice president of a Miami bank within a few years of his arrival in Miami.[10] The first Nicaraguan car dealership in Miami was similarly started by an individual who had attended the University of Miami in the 1970s. To obtain financing, he mobilized the friendships developed in school, especially with Cuban-American students.[11] Still others benefitted from the heavy North American presence in Nicaragua before the Sandinista revolution. Another president of the Nicaraguan-American Bankers Association, Roberto Zamora, was a former trainee at the Citibank office in Managua who quickly made a fortune brokering Latin American loans in debt-equity swaps. And Leo Solorzano had attended the Harvard-affiliated Central American Institute for Business Management; in 1989, he headed the lending division of Miami's Capital Bank.[12]

THE WORKERS

The third wave, comprising Nicaragua's workers and peasants, began in the mid-1980s, when the U.S.-sponsored Contra war disrupted the country's economy.[13] As early as 1984, nearly 20 percent of Nicaraguan migrants came from these modest backgrounds;[14] by the late 1980s, an estimated 50 percent of all Nicaraguans in Miami worked as laborers.[15] Much like Mariel Cubans in 1980, the newly arrived refugees could not afford to live in middle-class suburbs. Instead they occupied the poorest sections of Little Havana—where many Mariel Cubans had previously settled—creating a second Nicaraguan neighborhood.[16] Unlike Sweetwater East Little Havana is poor and deteriorated. Despite its name, it is now mostly an area where Nicaraguans and other Central Americans live.[17]

These new refugees had more difficulty finding jobs than their predecessors. Miami's informal economy of odd jobs and off-the-books employment for minimal pay became the Nicaraguan workers' main means of survival. Flower vendors, a common sight after Mariel, reappeared in every busy intersection. Others took jobs as housepainters, unskilled factory hands, and seamstresses. Lidia Cano, a single mother who fled Nicaragua with two young grandchildren and a draft-dodging son, worked as a seamstress. In Nicaragua she owned a small garment factory. In Miami, she started sewing at home on a machine loaned by a Cuban subcontractor. With her savings, she bought a used Singer and later two other specialized sewing machines. Through expanded homework for Cuban contractors, she was able to earn enough to support her family.[18]

Other Nicaraguan women went to work directly for Miami's numerous apparel factories, replacing the shrinking Cuban labor supply. For Jewish and Cuban factory owners, the arrival of the Nicaraguans was a blessing, as the rapid withdrawal of Cuban women from the garment labor force had already forced the closure of several factories. Ethnic succession in the garment industry neatly reflected the successive immigrant waves shaping the area's economy: from middle-class Cuban women in the sixties and early seventies, to Mariel and Haitian entrants in the early eighties, to poor Central Americans, primarily Nicaraguans, by the end of the decade.[19]

Nicaraguan men had a similar role in Miami's construction industry. The Latin Builders Association—Cuban-owned firms founded in the late sixties and seventies and grouped in a strong guild—confronted a serious labor problem by the mid-eighties. Cuban immigration had virtually stopped after Mariel, and the builders were reluctant to employ union-prone native labor. Again, a few Marielitos and Haitians provided a respite, but it was really the Central Americans who filled the gap. The Nicaraguans' urgent need for work was obvious, as was their ideological affinity with their Cuban employers. Increasingly, Nicaraguans became the preferred workers in the Miami building trades.[20]

Others relied on casual work. Between 6:00 and 7:30 A.M. every weekday from the mid-1980s on, about a hundred men would gather outside a coffee shop on Calle Ocho, downing Cuban coffee, waiting and hoping for a day's work from passing cars and pick-up trucks. Sometimes nearly everyone was hired, but at other times some thirty men were still waiting at 11:00. Job offers ranged from gardening to washing dishes. The normal day's wage was $40, paid in cash at the end of the day when the employer dropped them back at the coffee shop.[21] As one worker stated, "Sometimes the employer is conscientious and pays a decent wage, but sometimes you work eight hours and they pay you $20."[22] In December 1988, the city of Miami employment office began receiving calls from people looking for live-in maids. Pay hovered around $100 a month plus room and board. Although city employees who were helping the Nicaraguans labeled these jobs "slavery," many Nicaraguans willingly accepted the offers.[23]

Nicaraguans also followed the Haitians on the trail toward stoop labor in Florida agriculture. Ana Solis had worked as a cook in a little eatery near Managua's airport, but she left in 1983 when she was summoned to train for the local militia. Married with four children, Solis left her cramped Little Havana apartment at 3:00 A.M. every day for a three-hour bus ride to Immokalee, where she worked for a produce packer for $4 an hour. Her thoughts on surviving in the United States were limited to the immediate concerns of earning an income. "It hurt me to see the tomatoes end, because there was no more work. The lemons are coming, but the contractor can't take more people."[24]

The arrival of the Nicaraguan working class hence had a significant effect on Miami's economy. All employers of unskilled labor benefitted, especially garment contractors, home builders, farmers, and middle-class families in search of domestic help. More specifically, the new immigrants helped the Cuban enclave avert a serious problem. Some local economists had worried that the rapid increase of Latin firms would soon saturate the ethnic market to which they catered. The Nicaraguans, together with other Latin immigrants, expanded that market as well as the labor pool for ethnic firms.

These contributions went unappreciated, however, by other segments of the local population. The Nicaraguans swelled the local informal economy in both low-paying jobs and petty entrepreneurship. The proliferation of street vendors gave to parts of the city a Third World flavor that many natives found distasteful. To overcome this and other consequences of the influx, nativist groups labored mightily to get rid of the new refugees. Like Haitians a few years before, the Nicaraguans found themselves the target of militant hostility by much of the local population. Their weak legal status made them dependent on a few key allies to balance both government hostility and widespread local rejection.

FEDERAL POLICY: NICARAGUANS BELONG IN NICARAGUA

In June 1983, President Reagan asserted that if the United States failed to prevail in Central America it would be invaded by refugees. "The result," Reagan said, "could be a tidal wave of refugees—and this time they'll be feet people and not boat people—swarming into our country seeking a safe haven from Communist repression."[25] In many respects, Reagan was correct. The federal government at the time was primarily preoccupied with the Contra war against the Sandinistas. Because Contra leaders resided in Miami, high-level U.S. policymakers frequented the city. This presence, however, did not help the resettlement of ordinary Nicaraguans. Rather, federal officials appeared to encourage these refugees to go back to Nicaragua to battle the Sandinistas. The Reagan and subsequently the Bush administrations thus focused exclusively on the Contra war, ignoring the concerns of the refugee community.

Nowhere is the contrast between Cuban and Nicaraguan exiles more stark than in the U.S. government's differing responses to each. All arriving Cubans, until the 1980 Mariel flow, were automatically extended the right to remain in the country. As a group, they received one of the most generous benefits packages ever offered to arriving foreigners. Secure in the United States, they could plan and debate their designs for overthrowing the Castro regime. But with respect to the Contra war, a different logic was followed as Washington virtually demanded that the Nicaraguans accept the opportunity to confront the Sandinistas on their own terrain. The rebels' base of operations was to be as close as possible to the Sandinistas—in the neighboring Honduras, not in Miami. In the eyes of the Reagan administration, Nicaraguans in the United States were too far from the action and were not putting enough pressure on the Sandinistas. Federal officials thus did all they could to deter the arrival and settlement of new Nicaraguan refugees.

Through 1985, only about 10 percent of Nicaraguan applicants were granted political asylum—a figure significantly higher than the approximately 3 percent for Salvadorans and Haitians, but far less than the averages for Cubans (almost 100 percent) or for other nationalities such as Iranians (60 percent).[26] Nicaraguans not granted political asylum were declared illegal aliens, and so not entitled to refugee assistance, resettlement aid, welfare, or government loans. In 1981, they were even kicked out of free English classes for Mariel and Haitian entrants.[27]

Until late 1983, when professionals and other middle-class refugees were arriving, Nicaraguan asylum applicants were at least granted work permits that remained valid until their cases were decided. But then this benefit, too, was withdrawn.[28] At that point, would-be refugees were added to the federal government's Operation Save, which attempted to check the immigration status of every alien who applied for state-administered benefits.[29] If an alien was not properly documented, INS was to initiate deportation proceedings.

Unlike Salvadorans—also unsuccessful asylum-seekers—the Nicaraguans found that some aspects of their plight eventually played in their favor. In the mid-1980s, as the Contra war began to prove more intractable than first imagined, State Department officials toured the country to drum up support. One of their most frequent stops was Miami, where they could be assured of a supportive reception. By this time, the initial waves of Nicaraguan business elite and professionals had become established and had cemented their ties with the Cuban-American community. When Elliot Abrams, the top Latin American affairs official in the Reagan administration, journeyed to Miami for a celebration of the 165th anniversary of Nicaragua's independence from Spain, he also met with the Nicaraguan Business Council and attended a dinner for one thousand people sponsored by the Nicaraguan-American Bankers Association.[30]

When a group of Cuban-American businessmen organized a $35-a-plate fund-raiser to lobby for more U.S. support to the Contra rebels, guest speakers included Robert Reilly, the special assistant to President Reagan, whose job it was to travel around the country explaining the administration's policies in Central America. Aside from the money contributed to the Contra cause, Washington had good political reasons to pay attention to such events. The focal point of the dinner was a testimonial to Miami's INS district director, Perry Rivkind, who just before the 1984 presidential election had organized a ceremony in which over nine thousand Cubans received U.S. citizenship—and simultaneously registered as Republicans.[31]

Miami under the Cuban-Americans had become a Republican bastion, and administration officials did not want to alienate it. The strong Washington voice of the Cuban-American National Foundation and similar organizations was now heard in support of the Nicaraguans' cause. This effort helped produce the only significant turn in federal policy during the entire Nicaraguan exodus. In April 1986 Rivkind, still INS district director, announced that he had stopped deporting Nicaraguan aliens from Miami. In stating his reasons he said, "I've always had difficulty viscerally with sending back people to a cowardly Communist government. The Sandinistas are exactly that."[32]

Back in Washington, things moved more slowly. The administration appeared to agree implicitly with Rivkind; in any case, his ruling was neither condemned nor reversed. Nicaraguans in Miami were allowed to stay. But neither did the administration welcome all Nicaraguans. Federal policy became utterly ambivalent, allowing Nicaraguans in Miami to remain but deporting others living elsewhere in the country. Only after more than a year did the Department of Justice officially endorse Miami's new policy. In July 1987, Attorney General Meese declared: "No Nicaraguan who has a well-founded fear of persecution will be deported in the absence of a finding by the Justice Department that the individual has either engaged in serious criminal activity or poses a danger to the national security." He further ruled that every qualified Nicaraguan would be entitled to a work permit and encouraged those who had been denied asylum status to reapply.[33]

This major policy shift was reminiscent of President Jimmy Carter's invitation to Cubans to seek freedom in America during the Mariel episode. The Meese memorandum represented a victory for the Nicaraguan refugee community and its Cuban-American allies even as it directly contradicted the logic of the Contra war. The ruling, after all, encouraged Nicaraguans to flee their country, whereas Contra aid tacitly relied on Nicaraguans staying put to increase popular pressure on the Sandinistas. Not surprisingly, Meese's invitation provoked an unprecedented rush that swamped the Miami INS office, prompting it to establish special weekend hours, outreach centers, and rules that dictated when people could apply on the basis of their birth month. In the course of six weekends more than thirty thousand Nicaraguans applied for asylum in Miami. At approximately the same time, the approval rate for Nicaraguan asylum requests climbed from around 10 percent to over 50 percent.[34]

Nicaraguans were still not treated as favorably as Cubans had been. The United States, in its pursuit of the Contra war, still needed some Nicaraguans to remain in Central America to fight the Sandinistas. Moreover, growing sectors of the South Florida community—including some Cuban-Americans—had become alarmed at the rapidly growing Nicaraguan inflow. Finally, a federal government seeking to reduce a gaping deficit was in no mood to assume the cost for new foreign clients. The first response to these contradictory forces was to process the Nicaraguans' asylum applications but deny them access to any special assistance program, such as that organized for Cubans in the early sixties or even that to which Mariel and Haitian entrants eventually became entitled. The same Miami INS official who had claimed he had "visceral" difficulty sending people back to Nicaragua now asserted that Miami's Nicaraguan students did not deserve scholarships because "they may be looking for something they're not entitled to. Why should the public foot the bill?"[35] Off the record, other officials admitted that they feared that providing benefits to Nicaraguans would attract even more.

Federal policy finally shifted again toward repression in the summer of 1988. In the wake of the congressional freeze on military support for the Contras early that year, the flow of Nicaraguans across the Texas-Mexico border increased notably. Too many were coming—nearly thirty thousand applied for asylum between July and December 1988 alone—and the Justice Department went back to treating Nicaraguans as harshly as other illegal aliens. In the fall, Nicaraguans were stripped of their right to work permits and lumped with Salvadoran asylum-seekers. Washington's INS spokesman, Verne Jervis, claimed that "people who make frivolous applications should not win the right to work here."[36] The strategy adopted by the INS at this point was remarkably similar to its various attempts to expel Haitians during the early eighties. As the 1988-89 Nicaraguan refugee crisis unfolded, immigration authorities speeded up the review of asylum applicants, thereby accelerating the process by which they could be deported.[37]

The Justice Department diverted $28 million toward border enforcement in a detain-and-deport policy for Central Americans that included a veritable south Texas blockade of patrols, detention camps, and immigration courts installed at the border. The policy worked. From a peak of 2,400 Central Americans a week crossing into south Texas in July-December 1988, the number dropped to about 150 in January 1989.[38] A few months later, after the Sandinistas scheduled open elections, President Bush called for Contra directors and other Nicaraguans in Miami to go home and test the democratic opening in their country. The State Department followed with a prod in the pocketbook: it announced that it would cut the Contras' monthly $400,000 administration budget by half, which in turn forced a drastic cutback in staffs in Miami.[39]

Federal policy thus reverted to the logic of Reagan's statement at the beginning of the decade. The Contra war had achieved its goals. The Sandinistas were forced into elections that they lost, and hence all Nicaraguans should return to Nicaragua. As the administration saw things, those who had been living and working in Miami for several years were still not a permanent part of any American community. Instead of a resettlement program like that extended to Cubans and other officially recognized refugee groups, the Nicaraguans got a kick in the pants. This official "unwelcoming" was, of course, heartily approved by those sectors of Miami's population that had sought from the start the refugees' removal.

THE NATIVE RESPONSE:
THE ANGLOS

In 1980, Citizens of Dade United, a grass-roots Anglo organization, placed on the ballot an ordinance that prohibited "the expenditure of any county funds for the purpose of utilizing any language other than English or any culture other than that of the United States."[40] Passage of this ordinance simultaneously galvanized the Cuban community and inaugurated the U.S. English movement nationwide. In 1988, the movement returned to Miami when Citizens of Dade United pushed an English Only amendment to the Florida State constitution. Eighty-four percent of Florida voters approved the amendment in the November election. Support for English Only was not limited to Anglos, but also included much of Dade County's substantial and generally politically liberal Jewish population. In the 1989 Democratic primary to replace Claude Pepper in the U.S. House of Representatives, the Jewish candidate firmly supported English Only, advocating language tests for U.S. citizenship.

By the time of the 1988-89 Nicaraguan refugee crisis, old-time liberal and conservative political positions in Miami seemed to dissolve into either non-Latin anti-immigrant or Latin pro-immigrant views. The first position is illustrated by a letter to the *Miami Herald*:

> Most great civilizations in history were brought down by the "barbarians" of their days, whose military conquest of their wealthy neighbors was preceded by insidious invasion in such numbers that it destroyed the fiber of society of their hosts. This newest wave of immigrants to Miami is just the beginning; there are 400 million Latin Americans who are just as desperate as the Nicaraguans.[41]

For most local public officials, the escalating costs of programs for a rapidly increasing population was the concrete issue behind anti-immigrant sentiment. In the mid-1980s, after the large-scale immigration of working-class Nicaraguans had commenced, public officials began to note the extra strain and cost in public services, especially in health and education, created by the new refugees. In 1987, at the Downtown Clinic run by Dade's Public Health Unit, Nicaraguans became the single largest group of patients, accounting for 60 percent of cases.[42] In the same year, Nicaraguan children overtook Cuban children as the largest foreign minority in Dade County public schools, and articles addressing the problem of lack of resources to meet the new demand began appearing with increasing frequency in the *Herald*.[43]

During the 1989 Nicaraguan exodus, a meeting of Dade County's advisory group on the homeless became an angry forum on the impact of Miami-bound immigrants. "This country should open its doors to receive anybody and everybody who wants to come here from a country under Communist rule or dictatorship," said Metro commissioner Sherman Winn, a member of Dade's Immigration Advisory Committee. "Recall, recall," shouted a half-dozen members of Citizens of Dade United.[44] Sporting a button that stated, "Deport Illegals," Pat Keller, a member of Citizens of Dade, asserted that "illegal aliens are encourage to come here." Another declared that "we cannot afford to take in the Third World excess population."[45] Subsequently, the head of the Immigration Advisory Committee, Commissioner Barbara Carey, urged Dade County to abandon plans to build a trailer-park shelter for Nicaraguan refugees on the grounds that it would only entice more to come.

Most locally elected federal representatives viewed the arriving Nicaraguans in a similar light. Senator Bob Graham, a Miami native who had been governor during the Mariel crisis, sent a letter to U.S. Attorney General Richard Thornburgh on behalf of the local governments. He asserted that America must "regain control of its borders. Those who don't deserve asylum should not be allowed to violate our borders." Florida's other senator, Connie Mack, declared: "We need changes in the law that won't send a message that you can just cross the border, apply for asylum and come to work here."[46]

Congressman Dante Fascell, chair of the House Foreign Affairs Committee and a key figure in obtaining federal funding during the Mariel crisis, stated: "What are we going to do? March six abreast with a gun and shoot the INS commissioner? You're looking at more frustration than can be handled."[47] In the end, they neither had to shoot the commissioner nor open a new trailer park for arriving refugees. The INS's energetic policy at the Texas border deterred new arrivals, and the Nicaraguans already in Miami fended for themselves as well as they could as a new source of cheap labor for the local community.

THE BLACKS

Black Americans did not lead the fight against Nicaraguan migration, but they did repeatedly express their frustration. When the 1988 Nicaraguan refugee crisis hit Miami, Frank Williams, a Miami-born Black worker who had already spent over a year shifting from one day-labor job to another, claimed: "I'll take anything, any job at all. Five dollars an hour? Some people say that's low, but I'll take it." He directly blamed the newly arrived Nicaraguans, usually hired at $5 an hour, for his not being able to find a steady job. "The bosses should be looking out for the people who have lived here for years. They shouldn't allow these foreigners to come here and take our work," he said.[48]

Most Black Americans, however, did not blame the Nicaraguans for the riots that again convulsed Overtown just before the Miami Super Bowl of January 1989. Instead they pointed to the same issues that had always tormented their community: police brutality, a criminal justice system that repeatedly failed them, and a political system in which nobody listened to them.[49] Nicaraguans did not cause all of this; they were merely the latest manifestations and reminders of where Black Americans stood. Miami's Black leaders compared despairingly their own community's situation with that of the Nicaraguans. For despite all the new refugees' suffering and all the forces arrayed against them, they had a significant advantage that allowed them to survive and even prosper in Miami, while Black Americans continued to struggle.

COMRADES-IN-ARMS:
THE ENCLAVE AT WORK

When the Nicaraguan refugee crisis surfaced in late 1988, Cuban-born city of Miami manager Cesar Odio criticized "inhuman" conditions at a private shelter for homeless Nicaraguans, ordered it shut down, and bused more than 150 refugees to Bobby Maduro Stadium—a facility built by wealthy Cubans in the 1950s and the spring training site for the Baltimore Orioles. Odio assured the refugees that they would receive the same consideration given Cuban Mariel refugees in 1980 and told reporters: "Now they understand they have the full support of the city."[50]

The action mobilized squads of city rescue workers, bus drivers, and sanitation employees. Welders fenced off entrances to the baseball field, carpenters built partitions. Cots were placed under the stands, row after row of them along the ramps and the corridors. Outside in center field, the U.S. flag fluttered. In the visitors' on-deck circle, the Nicaraguan flag waved too, from a pole planted by the refugees.[51]

Miami's auxiliary bishop Agustin Román, the same man who had been so decisive during the 1987 Mariel prison riots, dropped by to talk with the new refugees. Doctors from Miami's Pasteur Clinic—run and staffed mostly by Cuban-American doctors—set up an examination room under a stairway. City aides Hiram Gomez and Edgar Sopo raced from a telephone to the parking lot calling names in rapid Spanish: "Centro Vasco, Centro Asturiano, Islas Canarias." They were fielding pledges from restaurants, nearly all Cuban-American, to donate food. Ignacio Martinez, a Cuban exile and retired grocer, showed up with a cigar in his mouth and a sack of clothes in his hand. "We had our time of need, and now it's their turn," he explained. Cuban-American WQBA-AM news director Tomas Garcia Fuste raised $9,000 in one day by calling up local businesses and asking each for a $1,000 donation.[52]

Underneath the stadium seats, two former Cuban political prisoners, Alfredo Menocal and Antonio Candales, manned a green telephone that rang incessantly. As city of Miami employees, they assumed the task of trying to find jobs for the Nicaraguan refugees. A hotel representative inquired about the availability of Nicaraguan maids. A construction foreman asked about refugee day laborers. Some callers, apparently ignorant of the stadium's newest residents, wanted to know when the Baltimore Orioles would be having batting practice.[53]

Two days after Odio promised Miami's "full support" for the homeless Nicaraguans, the Cuban-American manager of Dade County, Joaquin Aviño, unveiled the plan to build a temporary trailer camp to house 350 to 400 new arrivals. Although the plan was eventually shelved, Aviño persisted in demonstrating unwavering support for the refugees: "We're pulling out all the stops. There are a lot of people in this community who are close to the President. I think it's important for those people to be messengers for us."[54]

Those "close to the President" were not the traditional Anglo establishment of Miami, but Cuban community leaders. Within a week, Odio had flown to Washington to meet with INS commissioner Alan Nelson. Odio requested that INS temporarily reverse its policy of denying work permits to the new Nicaraguans. Despite the pleas of Florida senators to "regain control of the borders," Nelson acceded to Odio's request, promising to process the asylum applications of all Nicaraguans in the baseball stadium in three to five days. Those approved were to be issued permanent work permits, and even those rejected were to get temporary work permits while they appealed their cases. Upon returning from Washington, Odio went directly to the stadium to address the escapees, where he was cheered and had bestowed upon him the title "Father of the Nicaraguan Refugees."[55]

This attitude of the city and county governments did not go unresisted. Aside from the usual nativist cries of anguish, the most effective challenge to local refugee policy came from an unexpected quarter. Advocates of the homeless pointed to the obvious paradox that while the city was stretching itself to provide shelter to newly arrived foreigners, native Americans living in the streets of Miami continued to be woefully neglected. The logic of the argument was unimpeachable, and Odio and his aides had to concede. The city's response was remarkably similar to the policy adopted by the Carter administration ten years earlier after being challenged for discriminating in favor of Mariel Cubans and against Haitians. In both cases, the Solomonic official answer was to treat both groups alike, at least on the surface.

Bobby Maduro Stadium became partitioned: the Nicaraguans occupied right field and, quite appropriately, the visitors' dugout; the homeless were housed in the home-team dugout. Upon arriving in Miami and seeing how their spring training camp had been transformed, the Orioles promptly made arrangements to move to Sarasota.[56] One firm building prefabricated houses for recent hurricane victims in Jamaica hired from the stadium some hundred Nicaraguans and another hundred homeless Americans. A month later, about eighty of the Nicaraguans were still working for the company, but few of the homeless remained.[57] City officials used this and similar pieces of evidence to cement their obvious bias in favor of the refugees.

In a matter of weeks, Nicaraguan refugees settling in Miami as part of an apparently uncontrollable flow had secured space on the agendas of local governments that had long argued that the refugees were a federal concern. The refugees achieved this recognition not simply because of the magnitude of the migration problem, but because the Cuban-American community had organized a generous welcome. Miami at the end of 1988 was not the same city it had been just eight years earlier during Mariel. Cuban-Americans, now in positions of political power, saw the Nicaraguans as fellow victims of communism. They extended to the new arrivals what is probably the most unique reception for any immigrant group in recent history: not welcomed by the government and the society at large, the new entrants were still granted access to local resources by dint of political kinship with an established refugee community.

As had happened numerous times in the past, events in Miami were the mirror image of those taking place in Havana. Fidel Castro had hailed the arrival to power of the Sandinistas in 1979 and welcomed them as comrades and allies. In reaction, Cuban-American politicians began referring to the new refugees as "our Nicaraguan brothers."[58] The more the Cuban government came to the aid of the beleaguered Sandinistas, the more the Cuban exile community pumped resources into the Contra struggle. In 1983, Cubans and Nicaraguans in Miami created the Central America Pro-Refugee Commission, whose goal was to assist both Nicaraguan refugees and the Contras fighting in Central America. Within a month they amassed 1,000 boxes of clothes, 475 of food, and 350 of medicine, worth $800,000 altogether. While six Cuban and Nicaraguan physicians volunteered to classify the medicines, air transportation for the goods was arranged by the Cuban-American president of the Hialeah Chamber of Commerce.[59]

Spanish-language radio stations in Miami, in cooperation with community organizations, arranged marathons to raise money for the Contras. One such event, in 1983, mobilized about one thousand Cubans and Nicaraguans to man tables throughout Dade County. The Cuban-managed Republic National Bank and General Federal Savings Association opened their drive-in windows to accept donations.[60] In 1985, when the outspoken critic of the Sandinistas Cardinal Miguel Obando y Bravo visited Miami, Cuban-American radio stations broadcast news of the cardinal's visit for an entire week, exhorting all opponents of communism to attend the mass he would deliver. The day the cardinal spoke, three stations announced another radio marathon to raise funds for the Contras.[61] Speakers on local radio and television repeatedly asserted that "the road to Havana runs through Managua."[62]

Beginning in the mid-1980s, Cuban-American representatives to the state legislature also lobbied for support for the Contras as well as lower tuition for Nicaraguans at state universities. They also succeeded in passing a bill to help Nicaraguan doctors quickly get U.S. licenses. Meanwhile, the city of West Miami, led by its Cuban-American mayor, dissolved ties with its sister city, León, Nicaragua—the first time a U.S. city had broken sister city ties for any reason. Miami-Dade Community College, at the suggestion of its Cuban-American vice president, set aside $100,000 in private donations to pay the tuition costs of some hundred Nicaraguan refugees who were not entitled to U.S. government aid.[63]

The incorporation of Nicaraguans into the exile moral community in turn opened the way for their incorporation into the growing business enclave. In both cases, the larger, more established Cuban-American community extended itself to absorb the Nicaraguans, neutralizing the effects of both federal policy and nativist reaction. The partnership was nevertheless one-sided, for Cubans were in complete control. As the Nicaraguan community diversified and the Contra war dragged on, fractures developed in what had so far been a monolithic alliance. Despite their precarious position, Nicaraguans began to chafe under the all-embracing tutelage of their older cousins. For the new refugees, Cuban-Americans had become *the* mainstream in Miami.

IN SEARCH OF VOICE

The first visible Nicaraguan neighborhood in Miami emerged during the early 1980s when middle-class refugees of the second wave purchased condominiums owned by earlier-arriving members of the elite in the suburb of Sweetwater.[64] Twenty-five years before, Sweetwater had been an enclave of the native white working class—self-styled "rednecks." At that time, one was more likely to hear Greek (from the few Greek immigrants) than Spanish. The Everglades swamps abutted the town on the west, while hundreds of acres of undeveloped land to the east separated it from Miami. During the 1970s, however, metropolitan growth rapidly enveloped Sweetwater as the Cuban-American population spread west along Southwest Eighth Street (Calle Ocho) from its Little Havana hub. The rednecks abandoned Sweetwater, and by the time middle-class Nicaraguans began to arrive in the early 1980s the area was already Latin, with two large Cuban grocery stores, a number of Cuban cafeterias, and assorted other Latin businesses.

As Nicaraguans began to concentrate in Sweetwater, some bought businesses from Cuban-Americans and converted them to the needs of their community. A focal point became Los Ranchos Restaurant, modeled on a Managua favorite. With the Sandinista revolution, the owners of the original had fled and opened a restaurant in Little Havana. As a Nicaraguan neighborhood began to emerge in Sweetwater, co-owner Juan Wong moved the restaurant there and reassumed the name Los Ranchos. He gradually recruited the staff of the old Managua-based establishment, and the restaurant steadily assumed the social importance it had had before the exodus, becoming the most visible gathering place of the refugee community.[65]

The upper- and middle-class Nicaraguans in Miami followed an economic path that closely resembled that of their Cuban brethren. By 1983, when the federal government stopped granting work permits to Nicaraguan asylum applicants, about 100 to 150 Nicaraguan businesses had sprouted in Dade County, including several restaurants, a sprinkling of clothing stores, construction companies, real estate brokers, and florists.[66] Four years later, after the inflow of Nicaraguan working-class immigrants had commenced, the number of Nicaraguan-owned businesses surpassed 600. A shopping center, Centro Commercial Managua, had opened in Sweetwater; there were also markets, pharmacies, bakeries, clothing stores, restaurants, photo studios, insurance agencies, doctors, and dentists. Wealthy exiles gained a majority interest in the Popular Bank. Tractoamerica, a distributor of tractor parts to Latin America, had gross sales estimated at $7 million. Los Ranchos Restaurant had sprouted five branches in Dade County, employing two hundred Nicaraguans and grossing over $5 million annually.[67]

Like Cubans, Nicaraguan business people maintained high ethnic solidarity: "Wherever I go, to a furniture store or a (car) dealership or insurance company, I always ask, 'Where's the Nicaraguan who works here?' I want to give the commission to a countryman," claimed Maria Cerna, a Nicaraguan who worked as a business development representative for a major Miami savings and loan association. The Nicaraguan-American Bankers Association, with four hundred members in 1987, helped about a hundred fellow Nicaraguans find work and vouched for exiles whose good credit was by now only a memory from before the Sandinista revolution.[68]

The Nicaraguan refugee community did not consist, of course, simply of businesses and job assistance networks. It had many cultural components, including ones that had been dormant back home but assumed a new symbolic significance in exile. These symbols served to distinguish the Nicaraguans not only from "Americans" but also from the Cubans. Nicaraguan stores in Sweetwater sold typical Nicaraguan products such as *cotonas* (cotton shirts usually worn only by Indians) to people who never would have bought them back home. As one Nicaraguan store owner put it, "The people who always wore American brands and European clothes now come shopping for a *cotona* to wear to parties."[69]

Other cultural traditions not highly prized at home found new devotees in Miami as well. Auxiliadora Soriano came to Miami from Managua in 1982. Although she had never been a dancer herself, she immediately began recruiting Nicaraguans between the ages of sixteen and twenty-two to form a folkloric ballet troupe. By 1989, what started with only five dancers had grown into the nonprofit Ballet Folklórico Nicaragüense with twenty-four members.[70]

All the signs pointed to a repeat performance of the Cuban experience and the eventual emergence of a strong Nicaraguan-American voice in local affairs. This did not happen, however, for other forces conspired against this plausible outcome. First, the Nicaraguan exodus occurred over a far more compressed period of time than the Cuban. The latter had taken place in several well-spaced waves over two decades, allowing the earlier-arriving entrepreneurs and professionals to consolidate positions in the emerging business enclave. By the time of Mariel—twenty years after the first arrivals—there was an economically affluent and socially well established community to absorb the new working-class refugees. By contrast, the Nicaraguan inflow took less than ten years, with the first working-class waves arriving barely five years after the original elites. In 1988-89, when the movement accelerated to a Mariel-like flood, the middle-class Sweetwater ethnic economy was till too recent and too feeble to absorb all the arrivals. The impoverished new refugees thus had to rely on the charity of the Miami and Dade County governments and on the local informal economy for survival. With the influx of working-class immigrants, the image of Nicaraguan-Americans promptly shifted from a group of well-to-do expatriates to that of another impoverished Third World minority putting pressure on local resources.

Second, the hostility of the federal government toward permanent resettlement of Nicaraguans in the United States weakened the group's voice in local affairs. Federal policy rendered the situation of the working-class arrivals still more precarious, forcing them into minimally paid and informal jobs. The struggle to be allowed to remain in the United States also consumed much of the energy of the community, preventing it from articulating a distinct political discourse. The Nicaraguans were just too busy trying to fend off the INS to develop a coherent local profile.

Third, the Nicaraguan exodus lacked finality, with the option of return remaining open to many, even if that meant joining the Contras. After the Sandinistas announced their willingness to hold elections, the option expanded significantly, especially under the prodding of Bush administration officials. Nicaraguan refugees never had the door firmly and permanently closed behind them; thus they were in effect torn between goals to be pursued either in the United States or in their home country. A mythical Nicaragua could not be constructed in exile, as the Cubans had done with their island, because the real Nicaragua was too accessible.

Despite all these difficulties, Nicaraguan exile organizations struggled gamely to be heard. In 1988, the Casa Comunidad organized a Nicaraguan Community Day that attracted four thousand people. Six months later the same organization sponsored a celebration of Nicaraguan culture in the Dade County Auditorium. Stamped on the back of the program was Comunidad's motto: "Unity is our goal."[71] In December 1986, the Centro Commercial Managua held its first exile *gritería*. Nicaraguans filled the parking lot to pray and sing hymns. Little baskets brimming with candy were passed around, and the faithful yelled the refrains that give the religious celebration its name—"The Shouting."[72] By the late 1980s, Nicaraguan fans packed various public parks each Sunday to watch the Nicaraguan national pastime, baseball. Their league's teams had the same names as those back home—Boer, Esteli, Zelaya—and the fierce allegiances remained the same. "In Nicaragua, first you have bread and then you have baseball," said league organizer Carlos Garcia. "It promotes patriotism and unity."[73]

By this time, Nicaraguan immigration to Miami was dominated by the working classes, who were much more visible than the earlier waves. Miami's informal sector was burgeoning, and the stereotype of Nicaraguans had clearly shifted to a definition focusing on poor and unemployed workers. United Nicaraguan Artists was formed in 1989 specifically to improve the image of Nicaraguans in Miami. As one of its founders stated, "People think we're all uneducated, poor people with work-permit problems."[74]

The Rubén Darío Institute, run by a descendant of Nicaragua's most famous poet, concentrated on garnering public recognition of Nicaragua's contributions to South Florida. He convinced the County Commission to rename part of a street that runs through Sweetwater Rubén Darío Avenue. He then persuaded the Dade County School Board to name a new school in the neighborhood the Rubén Darío Middle School. To embellish the recognition, the institute commissioned a sculptor to produce a bust of the poet and a Nicaraguan artist to donate a life-size oil painting of Darío. It also planned to donate a collection of the works of Darío and other Latin American writers to the school's library.[75]

Despite these efforts, the legal and economic precariousness of the refugee community and its contradictory goals conspired against making a lasting local impression. Among the Nicaraguans, no clear leader or position emerged as multiple agendas arose that mixed exile concerns of ousting the Sandinistas in Nicaragua with immigrant concerns of gaining work permits in the United States. From the Miami-Managua Lions Club to Nicaraguan Democratic Youth, a dozen local groups spoke up, demanding such things as medical supplies for the rebels and legal immigration status.[76] Political issues divide the community more often than immigration problems caused it to coalesce. Roger Blandon, who headed the Ministry of the Economy during the last eighteen months of Anastasio Somoza's regime and then fled to become a car salesman in Miami, declared: "I participated in various groups that were started to unify the exodus but we never arrive at anything. Everybody wants their own ideas to predominate. Some say the Somocistas are to blame. Others say, 'No it's the ones who supported the Sandinistas who are to blame for what happened in Nicaragua.'"[77]

A few months after calling on Senator Connie Mack to allow Nicaraguan refugees to remain in the country, the newly formed Electoral Council of the Nicaraguan exodus asked more than fifty exile groups to nominate candidates and participate in an election scheduled for early 1990, because "it is important for Miami's community to get behind a leader who will address problems like the need for work permits, refugees detained by the Immigration Service, and the future of Contras living in Honduras."[78] In short, no single political voice had emerged, nor could it. The contradictory goals of remaining in the United States and defeating the Sandinistas pulled at each other at the same time that discord divided the anti-Sandinista militants.

As divisive as political differences, but more insidious, were the latent class divisions separating early and late refugees. The flood of working-class arrivals had erased the relatively positive image of elite exiles, and many responded by distancing themselves from the newcomers: "It's not just a language problem anymore," said Lillian Rios, an elementary school teacher. "Many of the students, like their parents, are barely literate." Oscar Mayorga, a U.S.-educated Nicaraguan exile who ran a plastics plant in Pompano Beach, described the contrast between early and later arrivals in blunter terms. "From what I understand, they're people who are twenty years behind in civilization. It's the effect of the environment and a lack of education and religious training. We have been able to identify with Anglo-Saxon culture, where order and dedication to work has made this country great." Despite a shortage of workers at his factory, Mayorga said he would be reluctant to hire refugees from his country until they were schooled in English and had learned American culture.[79]

Caught up by these contradictions—militant exile group versus struggling immigrant minority, freedom fighters in Nicaragua versus informal workers in Miami—the Nicaraguan exodus could not articulate a distinct voice, much less compete with the discourse of their Cuban-American allies. The Cubans' three-decade plight brought about by a firmly entrenched regime in the island and the impossibility of return gave their presence in Miami a finality that helped consolidate their ethnic economy. The Nicaraguans, in contrast, confronted a feebler and less monolithic adversary, and the option of return to their country confused their local priorities. A second distinct Latin voice in Miami did not emerge in the end.

THE "NEW" *HERALD*

As it has done throughout the 1980 Mariel crises, the *Miami Herald* initially opposed the Nicaraguan inflow and castigated the federal government for creating another immigration mess for which Dade County had to pay. During the early 1980s, the newspaper advocated rigid control over the U.S. borders, preventing new refugees from entering and deporting those who did not meet exacting requirements for political asylum.[80] All of this, however, came before the open confrontation between the paper and Cuban-American leaders that culminated in the full-page paid announcement by the Cuban-American National Foundation in October 1987 proclaiming, "The *Herald* Has Failed Us."[81]

Following this and other related events, the *Herald's* position began to change rapidly. Anglos were leaving Miami, and Cubans were not buying the newspaper. Market "penetration"—the percentage of households in greater Miami receiving the *Herald*—was declining continuously, as were advertising revenues. Belatedly, *Herald* editors recognized that their town was not just like any other in the United States. Continuing to spout the old Anglo hegemonic message was a sure way of going out of business.

Nowhere was the change of tack more evident than in the editorial position adopted toward the Nicaraguan exodus in the late 1980s. When, in 1987, Attorney General Meese announced that Nicaraguans would not be deported and that they would receive work permits, the *Herald* endorsed the measure.[82] A year later, it advocated a more stable, permanent status for Nicaraguans.[83] And by late 1988 the newspaper's editorial writers, having apparently forgotten all about their attacks on Mariel, contended that the accelerating Nicaraguan inflow would undoubtedly benefit the community, as had earlier Cuban immigration.[84]

Even more astonishing was the *Herald's* reaction when Bobby Maduro Stadium opened to shelter the new refugees. This action by the Miami city manger would have triggered howls of protest in the newspaper's editorials only a few years before. In late 1988, however, the recently appointed *Herald* editor congratulated manager Cesar Odio, asserting that "the United States has a moral obligation to take these refugees and let them work."[85] In a Christmas Day editorial, the *Herald* drew a parallel between the plight of the homeless Nicaraguans in Miami and that of Mary and Joseph in Bethlehem. It declared that politics, economics, and stingy townspeople had caused both situations and called on everyone—but especially the federal government—to live up to the nation's commitment to life, liberty, and the pursuit of happiness.[86]

Miami was very different in 1989 from what it had been ten years earlier. The 180-degree turn in the *Herald's* position toward supporting the Nicaraguan arrivals signaled no less than a decisive shift in the way local elites thought about their city. Although middle- and working-class Anglo groups continued to embrace the assimilationist discourse and to oppose Latin immigrants as fervently as ever, they had lost their prime channel of expression. Thereafter, Citizens of Dade United and other pronativist groups would be just another minority voice as the Anglo business class distanced itself from them. This singular split came about because corporate leaders realized that the city was not "in transition" to something, but had consolidated a distinct profile, unique in the country. Bilingual Miami was profitable, monolingual Miami was not; as always, the bottom line was what defined corporate policy.

Ironically, the Cuban community was able to do for the Nicaraguans what it had been unable to do for its own co-nationals during the Mariel episode. A decade of investments in U.S.-oriented political organizing made all the difference. Other changes in the *Miami Herald* and its parent Knight-Ridder Corporation, moreover, indicated that the Nicaraguans' sudden welcome was not an isolated event. When the new editor of the newspaper came to Miami in 1990, he took lessons in Spanish and was tutored in the cultural nuances of the Latin community by a Cuban-American professor. Similarly, the same

Herald columnist who had a few years earlier complained that Castro always called the shots in Miami did not suggest sending the new refugees back. Indeed, he declared that it was "insane" that the Nicaraguans were not being treated as well as the Cubans had been.[87]

More important still was the change in the Spanish edition of the newspaper. The original version, *El Herald*, had remained under the complete editorial control of the English-language editor and relied almost exclusively on translated material. Although costly, the effort did not work; circulation rates among Cuban-American households only declined. Then in 1988, Knight-Ridder took an unprecedented step: it created a brand-new Spanish-language newspaper—*El Nuevo Herald*—that was virtually independent of the English edition. It had its own building, its own reporting staff, and, most important, its own editors, overwhelmingly Cuban-Americans. Not surprisingly, *El Nuevo Herald*'s editorial stance came to reflect more closely the conservative discourse of the exile community than the often liberal outlook of its sister English publication. The coexistence of two different versions of the newspaper, each in a different language and with its own editorial line but simultaneously distributed, was a clear evocation of how Miami had been transformed.

The Anglo establishment yielded ground to the Cuban discourse about the city in exchange for social peace and continuing corporate profitability. No matter what the 1980 English Only ordinance and 1988 amendment to the state constitution had mandated, Miami was in fact bilingual and bicultural. The assimilationist discourse receded not only because the business elite toned it down, but also because many of its most fervent native white supporters left the area. Black Americans, on the other hand, stood their ground, and their own interpretation of events became more articulate and urgent. They were well aware that the question of their role and status in this new city, like the role and status of the surging Haitian-American community, remained unresolved.

NOTES

1. Christopher Marquis, "Miami Grapples with Influx of Nicaraguans," *Miami Herald*, December 15, 1988, 1A.

2. Christopher Marquis and Frank Cerabino, "Dade on Edge over Nicaraguans," *Miami Herald*, January 14, 1989, 1A.

3. Dave Von Drehle and Christopher Marquis, "Nicaraguan Stream into Miami; Many Find They Must Fend for Themselves," *Miami Herald*, January 13, 1989, 1A.

4. Christopher Marquis, "Nicaraguan Exile Community Forges New Life in S. Florida," *Miami Herald*, July 16, 1989, 1A.

5. Christopher Marquis, "Refugees Find Exiles Thriving," *Miami Herald*, January 22, 1989, 1B.

6. Ana Veciana-Suarez and Sandra Dibble, "Miami's Nicaraguans: Remaking Their Lives" (pt. 1 of 2 pts.), *Miami Herald*, September 13, 1987, 1G.

7. Marquis, "Nicaraguan Exile Community Forges New Life."

8. Barbara Gutierrez, "We're 'Invisible' Exiles, Nicaraguans Say," *Miami Herald*, February 5, 1984, 1B.

9. Veciana-Suarez and Dibble, "Miami's Nicaraguans."

10. Ibid.

11. Ana Veciana-Suarez, "Nicaraguan Exiles Begin to Climb the Ladder," *Miami Herald*, March 28, 1983, 10BM.

12. "Exiled Nicaraguans Reflect," *Miami Herald*, July 16, 1989, 11A.

13. Carlos Briceno, "Nicaraguan Plea for 'Sanctuary' Doubles in Year," *Miami Herald*, February 5, 1985, 1D.

14. Gutierrez, "We're 'Invisible.'"

15. Jaime Suchlicki and Arturo Cruz, "The Impact of Nicaraguans in Miami: The Nicaraguan Exodus to Miami Under the Sandinistas, and the Future Outlook Following Their Electoral Defeat," Study for the City Manager of Miami prepared by the Institute of Interamerican Studies, University of Miami, March 1990.

16. Sandra Dibble, "Nicaraguan Exiles Find Homes in Little Havana," *Miami Herald*, February 10, 1986, 2B; Gutierrez, "We're 'Invisible.'"

17. Gutierrez, "We're 'Invisible'"; Dibble, "Nicaraguan Exiles Find Homes"; Veciana-Suarez and Dibble, "Miami's Nicaraguans"; Rodrigo Lazo, "There Is So Little Money, but There Is Peace of Mind," *Miami Herald*, December 25, 1989, 2D.

18. Veciana-Suarez and Dibble, "Miami's Nicaraguans."

19. Increased international competition in the 1980s also affected the industry as it began to contract for the first time, lessening demand for workers.

20. Interview with Carpenters' Union organizer, Miami, June 9, 1988.

21. Karen Branch, "Immigrants Jam Street Corner, Hoping for a Job," *Miami Herald*, March 15, 1989, 1B.

22. Rodrigo Lazo, "Without Work Permit, Day Jobs Sustain Him," *Miami Herald*, December 25, 1989, 2D.

23. Rodrigo Lazo, "A Year Later, Panacea Turns to Struggle for Nicaraguans," *Miami Herald*, December 25, 1989, 1D.

24. "Exiled Nicaraguans Reflect."

25. Quoted in Alfonso Chardy, "Much of Blame for Influx Put on Failed Reagan Policy," *Miami Herald*, January 22, 1989, 16A.

26. Sandi Wisenberg, "An Unlikely Champion," *Miami Herald*, April 26, 1985, 1C. At the same time, barely over fifty Nicaraguans were deported and fewer than five hundred who faced deportation left voluntarily; see Briceno, "Nicaraguan Plea for Sanctuary."

27. Fabiola Santiago and Barbara Gutierrez, "Dade's Little Managua: Bastion of Uncertainty," *Miami Herald*, July 19, 1984, 16A.

28. Sandra Dibble, "Nicaraguans in Miami: Living in Limbo, Most Refugees Denied Work Permits, Welfare," *Miami Herald*, December 23, 1985, 1A.

29. Yves Colon, "State-INS Plan Aims to Take Away Alien's Incentives to Stay," *Miami Herald*, December 26, 1984, 1D.

30. "U.S. Official Joins Celebration of Nicaragua's Independence," *Miami Herald*, September 10, 1986, 2B.

31. Fabiola Santiago, "Dinner for INS Chief to Fund Contra Lobby," *Miami Herald*, June 27, 1985, 1A.

32. Sandra Dibble, "INS Halts Deportation of Nicaraguan Aliens," *Miami Herald*, April 11, 1986, 1A.

33. "At Last, Work Permits," *Miami Herald*, July 10, 1987, 24A. Meese's directive was based on a 1986 Supreme Court ruling that loosened standards for granting political asylum, itself based on a provision of the Refugee Act of 1980, which states that a refugee must show a "well-founded fear of persecution" to be granted asylum. Administration officials had interpreted that clause to mean that refugees must prove "a clear probability" of persecution if they returned to their home country. But the Supreme Court ruling relaxed the standard by ruling that asylum claims are valid if "persecu-

tion is a reasonable possibility" (*INS v. Cardoza-Fonseca*). Even though the court decision on asylum applied to all refugees, Meese specifically ordered INS to halt deportation of Nicaraguans from the United States. He made no mention of other groups, however, such as Salvadorans and Haitians. See Tina Montalvo, "Nicaraguans Are Only Immigrants Benefitting from New Asylum Aid," *Miami Herald*, September 11, 1987, 6C.

34. R. A. Zaldívar, "Vague Laws Spur Refugee Movements," *Miami Herald*, January 15, 1989, 1A; Richard Wallace, "Nicaraguans Jam INS Offices for Work Papers," *Miami Herald*, August 23, 1987, 1B; Tina Montalvo, "Job Permits Going Fast at INS Offices; 10,200 Nicaraguans Processed in 4 Days," *Miami Herald*, September 6, 1987, 1B.

35. Rodrigo Lazo, "Lacking Aid, Immigrants Wait to Learn," *Miami Herald*, October 12, 1988, 1B.

36. Christopher Marquis, "In Miami, Confusion Reigns for Applicants," *Miami Herald*, December 17, 1988, 1A.

37. David Hancock, "U.S. Denies Policy Shift on Handling Nicaraguans," *Miami Herald*, December 15, 1988, 1D.

38. Zaldívar, "Vague Laws Spur Refugee Movements"; Chardy, "Much of Blame for Influx Put on Failed Reagan Policy"; Marquis, "Nicaraguan Exile Community Forges New Life."

39. Christopher Marquis, "Many Nicaraguans Reject Call to Go Home," *Miami Herald*, April 3, 1989, 1B.

40. Michael Browning, "Antibilingual Bakers Celebrate Early," *Miami Herald*, November 5, 1980, 1B.

41. "Nicaraguan Refugees: How the Community Feels," *Miami Herald*, January 20, 1989, 24A.

42. Luis Feldstein Soto, "Nicaraguan Influx Strains Schools, Services," *Miami Herald*, July 5, 1987, 2B.

43. Ibid.; Richard J. Feinstein, "Why Public Hospitals Are Ailing," *Miami Herald*, February 10, 1985, 3E; Christopher Marquis, "Dade Unprepared for Refugee Influx," *Miami Herald*, October 23, 1988, 1A; Charles Whited, "Washington Is Guilty of Big, Fat Blunder over Refugees," *Miami Herald*, January 14, 1989, 1B; Marquis, "Nicaraguan Exile Community Forges New Life."

44. Quoted in Sandra Dibble, "Immigration Debate Erupts," *Miami Herald*, December 22, 1988, 1C.

45. Ibid. Of course, there were some who still ignored the newest arrivals in their city. During the 1988-89 Nicaraguan refugee crisis and just before Miami's hosting of the Super Bowl, Tom Ferguson, president of the Beacon Council, a group of businessmen devoted to promoting Miami's image, declared: "I hate to say it, but because of the Super Bowl, people's energies are focused in another direction now."

46. Ibid.

47. "How the Community is Responding," *Miami Herald*, January 13, 1989, 19A.

48. Geoffrey Biddulph, "Blacks Feel Left Out as Refugees Get Jobs," *Miami Herald*, January 20, 1989, 1D.

49. Bea Hines, "Overtown Feels Pain, Frustration," *Miami Herald*, January 18, 1989, 1A.

50. Marquis, "Miami Grapples with Influx."

51. Ibid.

52. Ibid.

53. Joe Starita, "Nicaraguans Stream into Miami Stadium, an Unlikely Refuge," *Miami Herald*, January 13, 1989, 1A.

54. "How the Community is Responding."

55. Rodrigo Lazo, "Mass Offers Ray of Hope for Refugees," *Miami Herald*, December 26, 1988, 1B.

56. Richard Capen, "Hand Is Out to the Tempest-tossed," *Miami Herald*, January 1, 1989, 3; Liz Balmaseda, "The New Nicaragua," *Miami Herald*, February 5, 1989, 1-6G.

57. Biddulph, "Blacks Feel Left Out."

58. Fred Strasser, "Nicaraguans Share Fight for Freedom at Cubans' Rally," *Miami Herald*, May 21, 1984, 1B.

59. Barbara Gutierrez, "Supplies to Be Ferried to Refugees," *Miami Herald*, June 26, 1983, 4B.

60. Barbara Gutierrez, "Cubans Hold Marathon to Raise Money for Nicaraguan Guerrillas," *Miami Herald*, August 1, 1983, 3B. Over four months later the aid, however, was still undelivered; see "Aid for Rebels Undelivered," *Miami Herald*, April 29, 1984, 6B.

61. Sandra Dibble, "Nicaraguan Cardinal Brings Peace Message," *Miami Herald*, June 14, 1985, 1A; Lourdes Melza, "Spanish Radio Marathon to Raise Nicaraguan Aid Funds," *Miami Herald*, June 14, 1985, 2C. The Cuban American radio stations conduct marathons for a variety of causes, most related to the Latin community and a good number concerned specifically with anticommunism; see Sandra Dibble, "Latin Listeners Open Hearts to Airwave Appeals," *Miami Herald*, December 15, 1985, 1A.

62. Strasser, "Nicaraguans Share Fight for Freedom."

63. Fabiola Santiago, "$100,000 Fund to Pay Tuition for 100 Exiles," *Miami Herald*, January 9, 1985, 6B.

64. Veciana-Suarez, "Nicaraguan exiles Begin to Climb the Ladder"; Ben Barber, "Open Three: Enclave for Exiles," *Miami Herald*, "Neighbors S.E." sec., December 29, 1983, 14.

65. Lawrence Josephs, "Ranchos Carries on Tradition," *Miami Herald*, "Neighbors S.E." sec., July 7, 1983, 31.

66. Veciana-Suarez, "Nicaraguan Exiles Begin to Climb the Ladder."

67. Veciana-Suarez and Dibble, "Miami's Nicaraguans."

68. Ibid.

69. Ibid.

70. Karen Branch, "Nicaraguan Culture: Alive and Growing in Dade," *Miami Herald*, "Neighbors" sec., May 25, 1989, 20.

71. Karen Branch, "Nicaraguans Try to Help Their Own," *Miami Herald*, "Neighbors Kendall" sec., June 4, 1989, 10.

72. Veciana-Suarez and Dibble, "Miami's Nicaraguans."

73. Ibid.

74. Branch, "Nicaraguan Culture."

75. Ibid.

76. Santiago and Gutierrez, "Dade's Little Managua," 16A; Sandra Dibble, "Nicaraguans Lobbying to Stay in U.S. Legally, *Miami Herald*, August 15, 1985, 2D; Jay Gayoso, "Nicaraguan Flights for Refugees' Aid," *Miami Herald*, "Neighbors S.E." sec., January 18, 1987, 16; idem, "Battle Unites Nicaraguan Refugees," *Miami Herald*, "Neighbors S.E." sec., February 8, 1987, 3; Karen Branch, "Nicaraguan Exile Groups Unite in Appeal to Mack," *Miami Herald*, July 1, 1989, 3B.

77. Santiago and Gutierrez, "Dade's Little Managua."

78. "Nicaraguan Exiles Seek Overall Leader," *Miami Herald*, September 12, 1989, 3B.

79. Marquis, "Refugees Find Exiles Thriving."

80. "Immigration How to Control It: A Legal Limbo" (5th of a series), *Miami Herald*, December 30, 1983, 28A.

81. "The Cuban-American Community and the Miami Herald," *Miami Herald*, October 19, 1987, 11A.

82. "At Last, Work Permits."

83. "Mercy for Refugees," *Miami Herald*, June 26, 1988, 2C.

84. "Nicaraguan Exodus," *Miami Herald*, October 20, 1988, 24A.

85. "Immoral Policy," *Miami Herald*, December 17, 1988, 34A.

86. "Room at the Infield," *Miami Herald*, December 25, 1988, 2C.

87. Whited, "Washington Is Guilty of Big, Fat Blunder."

PART THREE

RECONSTRUCTING
ETHNIC IDENTITIES

INTRODUCTION 🌿

Mary Romero

Is there any difference, I wonder, between the fights Cubans and Cuban Americans have and the ones Chicanos and Puerto Ricans have with their homeland-based populations? Because of the upper- and middle-class comparison of the mass Cuban migration of the 1960s, and because of the ideological tone of the derogatory terms for exiles, the homeland's image of the immigrant community has a different gloss on it. The problem, however, is fundamentally the same. It's real identity versus fake identity, original versus copy, upper class versus working, good Spanish versus bad Spanish.[1]

THE ARTIST, CURATOR, AND WRITER, Coco Fusco underscored the fundamental questions and issues that Latinos address in reconstructing ethnic identity in the U.S. Borrowing from Shakespeare's *The Tempest*, Fusco's essay "Miranda's Diary" captures the process of self-discovery that searches through the fictions of identity "imparted to us by our symbolic fathers." Miranda's journey takes her to New York City, Havana, Miami, and Mexico City; she encounters Cuban nationals and exiles, Cuban Americans, and Cubans on the island. The journey includes the endless negotiation and reconstruction of ethnic identity that involves generation gaps, as well as political and cultural sensibilities. The articles in this section explore the various negotiations of ethnic identity between groups migrating to the U.S. and those returning to or remaining in their homeland. Ethnic identity includes reconstructing their self-conceptions in the context of the binary White/Black racial paradigm in the U.S., a country that also assumes cultural and historical commonalities among all Latino groups. The following articles investigate the negotiation of cultural identity within specific socio-economic and historical contexts. They share a model of culture-in-process, rather than employing the stagnant structuralism of cultural determinism. These approaches to the study of ethnic identity help us to understand the multitudinous and shifting patterns of identity that have characterized U.S. history. Ethnic labels reflect the polyvalent identities of Latinos in the U.S.: Puerto Ricans, Nuyorican, boricuas, Dominicanyorks, Dominican American, Caribbeans, Central Americans, Peruvian American, Honduran American, Marielitos, Cuban American, Miacubans, Columbian American, including the panethnic identities: Hispanic, Latino and Latina, Latin American, Spanish American, and Raza.

In the first article in the section, "Los Dominicanyorks: The Making of a Binational Society," Luis Guarnizo examines the situation of Dominican immigrants in New York in the late 1980s and early 1990s, highlighting the the way that economic, social, and cultural territory transcends national borders. Similar to the questions Fusco has raised about Cubans and Cuban Americans, Guarnizo explores cultural and national identity of both Dominicans and Dominicanyorks. By focusing on migrants' economic activities, our attention shifts to the dynamics of cultural identity and political participation in both the Dominican Republic and the United States which leads to a creation of a binational society by Dominicanyorks. In addition, the study of Dominicanyorks captures the impact that migration has on returning Dominicans' class identity in their homeland. Too often we have confined our analysis of cultural identity to the U.S. and have failed to observe the ongoing changes of class, race, ethnic, and national identity between the homeland and the new settlements in the U.S.

Juan Flores' essay, "'Qué assimilated, brother, yo soy asimilao': The Structuring of Puerto Rican Identity," challenges the common practice of labeling cultural change as assimilation and demonstrates the ways that popular cultural forms reflect the exchange of Latino cultures in the U.S. By comparing the Chicano experience in the Southwest to the Puerto Rican experience in New York, Flores captures the way that social history, geographical placement, migratory patterns, racial characteristics, and surrounding Latino cultures shape each group's ethnic identity. So while Chicanos and Puerto Ricans find commonalities in claiming a Latino identity, separately Chicanos seek ethnic roots with Native Americans, and Puerto Ricans with Blacks (including African Americans and Caribbeans). Drawing from literary sources of Nuyorican culture, Flores illustrates the cultural energy and creativity present in cultural transformations and challenges the limited characterizations of Nuyorican culture as a process of survival and coping. Addressing the relationship that Nuyoricans have with African Americans and Caribbeans captures the active cultural exchange involved in reconstructing ethnic identities.

Patricia Zavella's essay, "Reflections on Diversity Among Chicanas" is an exploration of the set of questions about terms: What is the difference between Chicano and Hispanic? Why do some prefer the term Chicana and others prefer Mexican American? What do the other terms for this group refer to: like Mexicana, Hispana, Tejana, Manita, India, and Mestiza? Using the notion of social location, Zavella analyzes the cultural, historical, regional, class, gender, generational, sexual, and political distinctions among Chicanas that are represented by various ethnic terms. She demonstrates the possibilities of constructing an ethnic identity among members that is inclusive of their commonalities as well as their differences. Drawing from her personal experiences as an "air force brat," a "scholarship girl," and participant in the Chicano and Chicana movement, she chronicles her "process of self-discovery" that concludes with the identity of a Chicana feminist. Her essay offers a strong argument against cultural determinism, and *for* a view of culture that is fluid and placed within a historical context.

The last article in the section explores the structural constraints of ethnic identity and biculturalism. In her article, "Life as the Maid's Daughter: An Exploration of the Everyday Boundaries of Race, Class, and Gender," Mary Romero analyzes events in the life of a young woman raised in the home of her mother's employer. Teresa, the maid's daughter, describes incidents that reveal how ethnic identity is constructed and the cultural processes leading either to biculturalism or assimilation. Since the maid's daughter has social interaction in both the employer's social world and the working-class Mexicano community in Juarez and Los Angeles, she becomes bilingual and bicultural. Her experiences demonstrate manifold relations between social structure and culture. Without access to communities dominated by Spanish-speaking Mexicans, Teresa would not likely have retained her mother tongue or culture. Her ability to move from one social setting to another involved learning to recognize the social boundaries marking class and culture and to select and employ the appropriate set of norms and values for each. The life story of the maid's daughter exemplifies crucial links between culture and social structure. Issues of assimilation, biculturalism, and ethnic identity are not simply individual decisions, but are linked to the access to social spaces that allow individuals to acquire cultural competence and shape the negotiations of identities.

DISCUSSION QUESTIONS:

1. How do social history, geographical placement, migratory patterns, and racial charac-teristics shape Puerto Rican, Chicano, and Dominicanyork identity?
2. Explain why Nuyorican culture is not assimilation.
3. Discuss the relationship between culture and the social structure in the construction of ethnic identity.

SUGGESTED READINGS:

Flores, Juan. 1993. *Divided Borders: Essays on Puerto Rican Identity.* Houston: Arte Publico Press.

Firmat, Gustavo Perez. 1994. *Life on the Hyphen: The Cuban-American Way.* Austin: University of Texas Press.

Fregoso, Rosa Linda. 1993. *The Bronze Screen: Chicana and Chicano Film Culture.* Minneapolis: University of Minnesota Press.

Gutierrez, David G. 1995. *Walls and Mirrors: Mexican Americans, Mexican Immigrants, and the Politics of Ethnicity.* Berkeley: University of California Press.

Oboler, Suzanne. 1995. *Ethnic Labels, Latino Lives: Identity and the Politics of (Re)Presentation in the United States.* Minneapolis: University of Minnesota Press.

Vasquez, Olga A., Lucinda Pease-Alvarez, Sheila M. Sharon. 1994. *Pushing Boundaries: Language and Culture in a Mexicano Community.* New York: Cambridge University Press.

NOTES

1. Coco Fusco, 1995. *English is Broken Here: Notes on Cultural Fusion in the Americans.* New York: The New Press, p. 15.

8

LOS DOMINICANYORKS: THE MAKING OF A BINATIONAL SOCIETY

Luis E. Guarnizo

The ideal situation is to have a money-making business in the U.S. but live in the Dominican Republic.
—Dominican immigrant in New York City

FOR THE PAST THREE DECADES, emigration from the Dominican Republic, especially to the United States, has grown steadily.[1] At the dawn of the 1990s, international migration has become an intrinsic feature of Dominican society and the Dominican economy. Initially, the politically motivated outburst of U.S.-bound emigration in the 1960s affected just a few Dominican regions and social groups—most particularly, segments of the rural and urban lower-middle classes, as well as left-leaning political activists in the Cibao region and Santo Domingo.[2] To date, however, there is not a single region or segment of Dominican society that has not felt, directly or indirectly, the effects of international migration.

In the United States, immigrant islanders have concentrated mostly in New York City, where, according to the 1990 U.S. census, about seven of every ten Dominicans in the continental United States reside.[3] Moreover, Dominicans have become one of the fastest-growing and most conspicuous immigrant groups in the city. Their prominence stems not only from their sheer numbers and spatial concentration but also from their notable entrepreneurial drive and increasing clout in the local political power structure.

In this article, I will examine the internal dynamics of this social group and its interaction with Dominican and U.S. societies. This analysis builds upon findings from three studies conducted between 1989 and 1991 in the United States and the Dominican Republic. These studies are based on in-depth interviewing with, and face-to-face surveys of, over 500 people.

THE CONVENTIONAL WISDOM AND ITS LIMITATIONS
Existing studies on Dominican migration have produced a wealth of knowledge about the consequences of migration for the societies involved, especially in the economic

realm. However, they have neglected the sociocultural transformations and their implications as experienced by migrants themselves. Such transformations have been especially
accelerated by the rapid global industrial, technological, and sociopolitical changes undergone in the last two decades. Indeed, global restructuring has altered the socioeconomic
contexts in which migrants' actions are embedded. Both in the United States and in the
Dominican Republic, migrants have seen labor markets and other economic conditions
change drastically. New economic opportunities have opened and some old ones shut
down. Existing studies have overlooked the way that the interaction between contextual
changes and the social recomposition of the migrant population has resulted in new social
arrangements and relations in which some of the migrants' old loyalties are being renewed,
and others weakened or lost, while new ones are being forged. Prevailing explanations, thus
far, seem unable to grasp the significance of these emerging social dynamics of migration.

Recent studies informed by economic sociology, which furnish a less totalizing, albeit
more eclectic, perspective on the Dominican migration, provide the basis for an alternative
view of the process. Specifically, the latest evidence suggests that instead of looking at
migrants as a flow of people moving from one nation-state to another, it is better to conceptualize migrants as a distinct social group emerging from the intricate web of political,
economic, social, and cultural forces emanating from the migration experience of U.S.-
bound Dominicans.

In the remainder of this article, I will explore how Dominican migrants are evolving
into a social group whose economic, social, and cultural territory transcends national borders. To do so I will examine some social features of migrants and their economic relationships with both societies, and I will discuss their peculiar cultural identity and political
participation in the two nation-states.

MIGRANTS AND THE NEW DYNAMICS OF
INTERNATIONAL MIGRATION

U.S.-bound Dominican migrants can no longer be considered a homogeneous group
of poor, uneducated people who remain so upon immigration. Nor can they be seen as settlers who stay abroad for good, or as sojourners who return once their initial economic
goals are met, as most existing studies posit.[4] Despite the lack of reliable data on which to
base conclusive comparisons, available census, survey, and ethnographic information
shows the presence of highly educated people among Dominican migrants, at levels higher than among nonmigrants. Although the presence of well-educated people among
Dominicans is not new, their numbers have been growing steadily, especially during the last
decade. According to some estimates, between 1986 and 1991 alone, about 15,000
Dominican professionals entered the United States, some 10,000 of them undocumented
entrants.

Survey data show that even returned migrants, who seem to be the least educated
among the migrant population, are almost twice as likely as the general Dominican population to have some college-level education—11.4 percent versus 6.4 percent, respectively.
Similarly, waged and salaried Dominicans in New York are about three times more likely
than nonmigrants to have had some college education. These differences are even more
pronounced between migrant entrepreneurs and the general population.[5]

Despite the comparative estimate, these data show the presence of a significant and
growing segment of migrants possessing higher levels of formal education than average

Dominicans. In addition to their formal human capital, these migrants have the human capital accumulated through their work and living experiences abroad, which provides them with skills not readily available to the nonmigrant population.

MIGRATION AND CLASS RESTRUCTURING

The mode of economic incorporation of Dominicans in the United States is now much more varied than the singular one traditionally recognized in most existing literature. Thus, instead of social-class homogeneity resulting from a unique mode of labor incorporation, variation in the mode of incorporation has rendered a heterogeneous class recomposition of the migrant population. Although toiling in dead-end, low-paid jobs in the secondary labor market remains the most common path of economic incorporation for Dominicans in the United States, a thriving ethnic economy, particularly in metropolitan New York, yields alternative paths of economic incorporation and, hence, class restructuring.[6]

Yet the rapid development of this ethnic economy has brought about mixed results for the immigrants. It has simultaneously become a vehicle for upward social mobility and a source of class polarization. First, the relative success of many entrepreneurs has become a crucial incentive for nonowners in a process in which the larger the number of entrepreneurs, the greater the possibilities for non-business-owners to become owners themselves. In turn, such business formation is generating a culture of business ownership and self-employment that is permeating important segments of the group as a whole. For many immigrants, becoming one's own boss turns out to be the most sought-after alternative to salaried work.

Still, a drive for business ownership and, more specifically, self-employment by itself does not guarantee economic success. Indeed, in my study of the Dominican ethnic economy in New York, I found that the economy was formed by an amalgam of activities ranging from informal, ethnic-oriented, petty, subsistence activities to formal, open-market-oriented, medium-sized, capitalist enterprises.[7] This distribution of disparate firms underscores the fact that the self-employed are as socially stratified as their firms' economic performance is. Nevertheless, depending on particular historical junctures, these class differences overshadow, but never completely obliterate, the common ground that Dominican entrepreneurs share, namely, national origin and a hostile environment.

As we will see later, such an inauspicious context recurrently bolsters these immigrants' ethnic social capital[8] above and beyond class disparities between the employed and the self-employed, between the affluent entrepreneur and the petty independent operator. Interestingly, in the United States, Dominican immigrants assess their class position and mobility vis-à-vis the Dominican rather than the U.S. class structure.[9] In other words, immigrants form, as it were, a class structure independent from mainstream society.

WEAVING A MESH OF BINATIONAL INTERCONNECTIONS

Besides offering an opportunity for self-employment, Dominican enterprises have generated a demand for conational workers, a demand that produces job opportunities apart from those typically offered to Latin immigrants in the secondary labor market, where harsh working conditions are exacerbated by racial and ethnic discrimination. Such labor demand not only aims at the readily available pool of immigrants in the United States, but stretches across the border to reach relatives, friends, and *paisanos* back on the island. The existence of a binational labor market is not a novelty in itself since it is inherent in the migration process and is also found in other groups. What is new about the Dominican binational labor market, however, is that it is multidirectional: it is fueled not only by labor demands from North American and immigrant Dominican employers in the United States but also by firms linked to migration and Export Processing Zones (EPZs) in the Dominican Republic. This enlarged demand for migrant labor is mostly a result of current global economic and industrial restructuring. In the United States, subcontracting out certain processes and operations, especially in manufacturing and services, has become the most common modus operandi to cut production costs. Immigrant-owned outlets, with ready access to cheap labor from abroad, have become ideal agents in this process, bypassing official labor regulations—particularly after employer sanctions were introduced by the Immigration Reform and Control Act of 1986. Conversely, for Dominican EPZs that export only to the United States, workers with experience in the U.S. labor market are especially attractive. Indeed, the presence of migrants as laborers, supervisors, managers, and even owners in EPZ plants is significant and growing.

This multifarious binational labor market is but one of the many threads in the dense web of relations that migrants have woven between the two countries. The class restructuring that migrants have undergone abroad reflects the types of connections and relationships they build and maintain with their country of origin. So while successful entrepreneurs in the United States become transnational capitalists—investing in formal binational trade, manufacturing, and other economic activities such as finance, real estate, and tourism on the island—the majority of migrants remain modest merchants or proletarians feeding a binational labor pool. Despite these class differences and the reproduction of a pattern in the Untied States similar to that on the island, the traditional Dominican oligarchy and upper-middle classes insist on regarding migrants as a homogeneous social group.

On the island, Dominican migrants gauge their social position in relation to the Dominican local class structure. Upon return, migrants anticipate having their class position adjusted according to their relative economic success abroad. In particular, successful migrant capitalists expect to have a place in the upper strata of Dominican society—with all the privileges traditionally reserved for those strata—regardless of their own class origins. However, because these capitalists are still perceived as belonging to a lower class and are seen as a threat to the upper classes' monopoly of economic and political power, the upper classes try by all means to prevent migrant upstarts from realizing their dreams. Thus successful migrants find themselves in a contradictory class position: they possess the economic power to belong to the upper classes but lack the social status to legitimize such power.[10]

In addition to the rejection migrants experience from the traditionally dominant classes, other factors help reinforce the segregation of migrants as a distinctive social group within Dominican society and thus stimulate the raising of group consciousness and internal solidarity. One of these factors is the relative reduction of migrants' social capital in their society of origin due to the weakening of family-bound solidarity. Specifically, the high cost to island-based relatives of caring for involuntarily returned children—whose behavior appears intolerable by Dominican standards—is overwhelming and, in not a few cases, wears away family support completely. In other cases, migrants find themselves unable to meet the unrealistically high pecuniary expectations of reciprocity from nonmigrant kin, fracturing family-based social capital.

In other words, while social capital furnishes migrant individuals and families with resources beyond their individual reach—creating connections and support for emigrating, returning, and so forth—it also limits their possibilities of success because of obligations and expectations of solidarity that are too demanding. Social capital can thus become negative social capital.[11] One consequence of negative social capital is the strengthening of ingroup social capital among migrants. This social capital cuts across the different educational, social, and occupational backgrounds of migrants. Consequently, Dominican migrants, while on the island, associate and support each other less on the basis of class, regional origin, or long-standing personal connections and more as a fellow returnees or as a result of having common experiences abroad.[12]

SPACIAL MOBILITY:
FROM LABOR STREAM TO A SOCIAL WHIRLPOOL

Another characteristic assigned to contemporary Dominican migration that should also be reevaluated has to do with the prevailing belief that migrants' spatial mobility is definitive and falls into a rigid settler-sojourner dichotomy. From this viewpoint, cyclical mobility is considered marginal rather than the norm. But in fact, continuous mobility between the two countries by long-term emigrants residing abroad as well as by short-term migrants is typical of the complex interconnections migrants build over the years. Such mobility, among other things, has deeply affected family formation and generated the emergence of new domestic units. These units are characterized by the spatial dispersion of their members across the two countries in what we can all multinuclear households—that is, nuclear families living in more than one household, whereas similar domestic units in nonmigration circumstances would live in one.[13]

Furthermore, Dominicans residing in New York travel often to the island for social reasons—such as to visit friends and relatives, to join in traditional festivities, to see family doctors or buy cheaper medicine—or for economic reasons, such as to buy real estate, to invest in a new business, or to tend to an already existing business. According to the Dominican Secretariat of Tourism, Dominicans living abroad accounted for one-fifth of the total number of international visitors to the country and contributed almost one-third of the total revenues from tourism in 1985. Since the tourist industry is officially recognized as the principal source of foreign exchange, the contribution of emigrant visitors makes these figures more relevant.[14] Similarly, returned migrants—those who return to the islands with the idea of remaining there—often travel back to the United States for social and familial reasons, to oversee their own businesses, to work for a salary for short stints, or just to comply with legal requirements in order to keep their U.S. visas from expiring. Finally, others travel constantly between the two countries as informal, small international merchants to supply demands from both sides, or as brokers of Dominican economic interests in either country—such as Dominican Republic-based developers in search of buyers and investors abroad, and immigrant Dominicans abroad looking for market niches in their country of origin.[15]

In addition to people and money, migration-driven nonmonetary resources such as ideas, cultural values, fashion, and so on move daily between the two countries: Dominican newspapers are distributed in the United States on their day of publication, popular

Dominican television series are simultaneously aired in New York and on the island, and Dominican media—print and electronic—regularly cover Dominicans abroad. Similarly, exclusive and not so exclusive boutiques on the island offer the latest fashions imported from New York by small, informal traders, while Dominican stores in New York retail food-stuff and other Dominican-made products. New York-based merengue bands frequently tour the island, while songs about Dominican migration are hits in Latin discos and radio stations in the United States, on the island, and even in Latin America.[16]

In brief, Dominican migrants form neither a one-way nor a two-way stream of poor Third World migrants. Nor are they a group of people who, as some conservative commentators predict of Latin American immigrants, "'have no more intention of shucking the Third World they've lugged across the border than they have of going back after they make their millions. Once here, they're here for good, disrupting our institutions . . . with foreign languages, pagan religions, and oddly spiced foods.'"[17] Instead, Dominican migrants, despite their social, educational, and regional heterogeneity and precisely because of their shared migratory and social experiences in the United States and in the Dominican Republic, have become a group whose territory is a borderless, transnational space. They are here and there and in between. Yet, as we will see later, they are perceived as foreigners in both locations.

FROM FAMILY CASH REMITTERS TO CAPITALIST INVESTORS

Again, although there are no reliable statistics on the economic impact of migration beyond the transfer of family remittances, fragmentary data provide evidence of a signifi-cant presence of migrants in the Dominican national economy. More important for the objective of this article, though, is to untangle the sociology of migrants' economic behav-ior in the Dominican Republic. From sole providers of a free social subsidy to their coun-try—via family remittances—migrants have become determining economic actors in the Dominican economy: as major consumers, producers of goods, and providers of services. Already by 1988, the Dominican Central Bank estimated that migrants' remittances were the country's second most important source of foreign exchange, trailing tourism but sur-passing earnings from sugar and other traditional export commodities.[18] If migrants' par-ticipation in the tourist and housing industries and their investments in other sectors are taken together with family remittances, migrants become not only the primary source of hard currency—well above revenues from tourism and EPZs, the flagships of the country's economic restructuring—but also the single most important social group contributing to the national economy.

The significance of their economic presence is underscored by the fact that nowadays some traditional activities and some new ones are labeled as activities for or of migrants. This labeling signifies that the migrants are the principal consumers of these activities, are the most noticeable operators of them, or have themselves introduced them to the Dominican Republic. Specifically, different industries on the island are targeting migrants as their preferred clients. There are housing projects built exclusively *para ausentes* and *para retornados* (for absent and returned migrants),[19] entertainment establishments—such as discos—catering mainly to them, and educational institutions—such as English-only schools and boarding schools—that have been started to serve solely their children. By 1986, according to the Dominican Chamber of Construction, already some 60 percent of the formal housing industry on the island had been purchased by Dominicans residing abroad. At the dawn of the 1990s, I was told by major urban developers in the two largest Dominican cities that Dominican migrants represented between 80 percent and 90 percent of their clientele.

Similarly, early successful incursions of migrant entrepreneurs into certain types of businesses have encouraged fellow migrants to follow suit. An ensuing overrepresentation of migrants in these activities—and even a redundancy of their establishments—has resulted in their being labeled as *negocios de retornados* or *negocios de domínicans* (migrant businesses). The most visible business niches so labeled are real estate agencies, *financieras* (financial and commercial institutions extremely popular among migrant investors, especially until the late 1980s, when the state regulated them), *remesadoras* (remittance-transferring houses), small supermarkets and corner grocery stores, laundry and dry cleaning stores, car-wash services, car dealers and car rentals, and discos—all of them closely mimicking the physical appearance of Dominican-owned businesses in the United States.[20]

Regardless of their unsophisticated economic and technological makeup, these activities form an economy associated with a social group thus far perceived as different from mainstream Dominican society. In the same way that Dominican ventures overseas have a tinge of Dominicanness, migrant businesses on the island have a streak of Americanness. Whereas businesses in New York are typically named after traditional establishments or locations on the island, in the Dominican Republic, migrant-owned firms are easily identifiable by signs celebrating their owners' endeavors abroad. For example, some of the firms are identified in English, especially using the names of North American cities and neighborhoods where Dominicans concentrate, or are decorated and furnished à la Americana.

MIGRANTS' DOUBLE VISAGE:
DOMINICAN IMMIGRANTS AND *DOMINICANYORKS*

In the United States, Dominicans may well be considered a non-assimilationist, persistently ethnic group. Certainly, significant features of immigrants' Dominicanness are reproduced in their everyday social interactions and are imprinted on the urban space. The colorfulness, blaring music, and liveliness of Dominican neighborhoods in New York City, for example, are a replica of life on the island. Yet by Dominican standards, immigrants' Dominicanness is utterly exaggerated. As one informant, who used to live in Washington Heights while pursuing her graduate studies, put it, "Dominicans in New York want to be more Dominican than the Dominicans themselves." Partly due to their subordinate social position in the city, partly because of their nostalgia for their homeland, partly because of their sheer numbers, their high concentration, and their physical appearance (which may lead to their being misidentified as either African Americans or Puerto Ricans), Dominican immigrants reaffirm and re-create their origins to a degree rarely seen among other Latin American groups.

Interestingly, this sociocultural formation not only encompasses unifying norms, values, and beliefs but also reproduces the divisiveness, particularly along regional, political, and, more recently, social lines, prevailing on the island. Such factionalism, however, has not dissolved migrants' solidarity and unity altogether, but it has postponed them for times when adversity threatens them all. For example, despite all their internal differences, Dominicans have rallied together to demand reforms in the educational system to benefit their children, to protest police brutality, and to overcome quarrels in order to celebrate the Dominican annual parade, the organizing of which is in itself a regular source of dispute.

In stark contrast to their sociocultural reaffirmation while overseas, migrants in the Dominican Republic are perceived as Americanized Dominicans, whose behavior, for the most part, is seen by nonmigrants as an affront to authentic Dominican culture. Migrants' style of living, their tastes, and their manners, especially those of youngsters and the most prosperous (particularly excruciating in the case of those seen as drug traffickers), are judged as tasteless and revolting especially by the upper classes. The epithets minted to refer to migrants, such as *dominicanyork* (seen as the opposite of an authentic Dominican), *cadená* (gold necklace user; the wearing of a gold necklace is associated with drug kingpins and drug peddlers), and *Joe* (an anonymous American-like migrant youngster) are some of the sociolinguistic expressions of such sentiments.

Although many migrants indeed fit these stereotypes, a significant proportion of them do not. However, since the early 1980s, the stigma has become widespread and applied generically to migrants as if they were a homogeneous group. As mentioned before, such stigmatization is grounded not only in cultural differences—migrants' increased individualism, their self-righteousness, and their tastes—but especially in the socioeconomic and political concerns of the upper-middle and upper classes. These latter concerns are driven by the threat that the most prosperous migrants seem to represent for the existing Dominican power structure. Less economically successful migrants, who appear to comply less than nonmigrant workers with existing labor and social conditions on the island, are also regarded as a disturbing force because of their potential influence on the Dominican labor force.

The words of some informants effectively illustrate the opinion of the Dominican elite. A Dominican national business and political leader and owner of one of the most important commodity export houses in the country asserted, "Those who emigrate are the cancer of our society; for that reason, their departure is not that negative for the country. When they return, they bring the vice of drugs; their ostentatious wealth induces others to emigrate too." Another businessman expressed his dismay about the harmful impact of migrants on the discipline of the Dominican workforce, with its disastrous effects on the functioning of the national economy: "Migrants exercise a very damaging influence on workers. Nowadays, employees rebel more easily against employers because, they say, if fired they can always go to New York."

Partly as a result of such unflattering assessments, a blatant wave of social discrimination against migrants has erupted, erecting barriers and exacerbating urban spatial segregation. Today, urban spatial segregation is drawn not only along class lines—a typical feature of Latin American urbanization—but also according to migration status. This generalized aversion to the economic prosperity of migrants has strengthened the cultural identity and solidarity of migrants on the island. Paradoxically, migrants themselves appear more interested in being accepted and legitimized within the existing power structure than in contending with it.[21] Migrants' discourse is one of capitalist development and free-market competition, which coincides with that of the traditional elite. However, class status and cultural differences seem to supersede economic affinities.

One successful returnee, who interprets the economic success of migrants as a contribution to the "economic democratization" of the island thinks that migrants are stigma-

tized and discriminated against only because of their economic power. Moreover, he justi-
fies the pretentiousness of wealthy migrants as follows:

> Migrants show off their power and their wealth precisely because most
> Dominicans don't have either of them. Instead of diminishing, discrimination
> enhances migrants' self-esteem. The *tradicionales* [traditional bourgeoisie]
> criticize their sumptuous consumption, but that consumption generates
> development, creates more businesses.

MIGRANTS' REACTIVE CULTURAL IDENTITY

Although the experience of individual migrants varies—according to their mode of
incorporation, class background, and social capital—and, thus, an unfriendly environment
affects them differently, I argue that migrants in general possess a distinctive migrant culture. While the intensity of their cultural distinctiveness varies according to their social
position, they all retain common cultural patterns and perspectives, precisely because pervasive discrimination and segregation keep them insulated from mainstream power structures in the two societies in which they live.

Hostile contextual forces in their country of origin and overseas have resulted in the
development of a reactive cultural identity. Specifically, migrants cope with adverse structural forces in these two settings by reaffirming some cultural assets that are opposed to
those of mainstream society—namely, they are Dominican immigrants in New York and
Dominicanyorks on the island. This cultural response, however, reinforces the uneven relationship; while it helps them to manage discrimination and hostility, cultural reaffirmation
exacerbates rejection. Their identity, though, is bicultural rather than subcultural. Unlike
subcultures, which are understood as persistent behaviors, values, and norms of socially
homogeneous groups who live in a single society, Dominican migrants are a heterogeneous
social group that lives in two societies and whose behaviors reflect both U.S. and
Dominican cultural influences, elements of which are selectively navigated. Paradoxically,
migrants' transnationalization grows hand-in-hand with their insularity from mainstream
society.

Migrants' relationships with the U.S. and Dominican mainstreams are not static but
dynamic. Changes in both societies, as well as migrants' economic, social, and political
notions, are modifying, and will modify, such relationships. But as long as power relations
remain unfavorable and socioeconomic differences between the two countries persist,
Dominican migrants will continue a process of sociocultural accommodation (rather than
assimilation) and economic articulation (rather than adaptation) in both locations. In
other words, their spatial displacement will continue for the foreseeable future.[22]

BINATIONAL CITIZENS:
POLITICAL PARTICIPATION AT HOME AND ABROAD

Another sphere of struggle is the political, more specifically, migrants' historical relationship with the nation-states involved. The spurt of the U.S.-bound Dominican migration of the 1960s mainly resulted from coordinated efforts of the U.S. and Dominican states
to remove opposition political activists from the island in order to decompress the explo-
sive political crisis following the assassination of the dictator Rafael L. Trujillo.[23] These
efforts involved not only the activists' expatriation but also prevented their prompt return

to their country.[24] In contrast to such pro-emigration policy, three decades and hundreds of thousands of immigrants later, the two governments—most especially the U.S. government—find themselves on the flip side of the predicament, namely, seeking to stop and inhibit—and even how to reverse—the inflow directly at its source.

But as has been documented here, the circumstances of migration have dramatically changed, and the relative autonomy and maturation of the process render those attempts futile and doomed. In effect, Dominican migrants have evolved from a disjointed mass of local political activists and laborers looking for refuge and income in the United States into a complex, heterogeneous social group whose political interests are fragmented between two national states. Dominican migrants profess simultaneously their allegiance to two national states, which implies not only having access to more benefits than other citizens but also a double burden of civil duties. The discussion of how deep such commitment is and how many benefits they are accruing, however, is not within the scope of the present analysis. The point here is to acknowledge the existence of this double loyalty, which exists regardless of migrants' expressed willingness to accept it.[25]

The high cost of maintaining a double national loyalty induces efforts by migrants to dodge burdensome state controls. Migrants' attempts to eliminate or reduce these costs are greatly facilitated, paradoxically, by their simultaneous relationship with two national states. They take advantage of every interstice in the power structure in both societies to gain the best of the two worlds, as it were, by playing out their double-state membership. As multinational corporation do, depending on the particular conditions they are in, migrants—especially documented ones—fluctuate between being more Dominican or more North American. In other words, for practical purposes, most Dominican migrants have a de facto binational citizenship.[26] Although this status is easier to detect among the entrepreneurial elite, it is present in the whole migrant population.[27]

Until the mid-1980s, political relations between migrants and the two national states were disparate. In the United States, migrants were irrelevant to local politics; their political activity, if any, was mostly a matter of individual, token participation. In contrast, since their introduction into the United States, and maybe because of the political origins of their emigration, migrants have remained very much interested in their island's political life. As part of Dominican politics, for example, it became a tradition that any candidate holding serious political aspirations has to come to proselytize in New York and that every Dominican political party has to have a chapter in the city. Migrants' role, however, was until recently reduced to economic support of Dominican political candidates in exchange for lenient regulations for transferring goods to the island.

Changing conditions in New York City, the rapid deterioration of the economic and political conditions in the Dominican Republic, and changes in the social composition of the migrant population have generated a turnaround in Dominicans' political stand vis-à-vis the two societies. From their relative acquiescence in Dominican politics and their dormant political attitude in New York, they have become more active on the island and in the city.

Dominican political participation in New York City is rapidly escalating. Dominicans' struggle to improve their children's school conditions led them to confront and overcome the political forces controlling the education system. Until the late 1970s, a well-established Jewish minority maintained control of the board of education of Washington Heights (School District 6), while Dominicans accounted for the majority of the student population. One of the first victories of Dominicans was gaining some positions on the school board, followed by their entry into the city's broader political arena.[28] These early political triumphs, as well as subsequent ones, were the result not only of the presence of a critical mass of Dominicans in the city but also of an intelligentsia formed by immigrant professionals, former political activists back on the island, and some business leaders.[29]

In the Dominican Republic, on the other hand, migrants' political participation has changed from being followers to becoming activists and leaders. Migrant organizations, especially business organizations, have actively lobbied for legislation favoring migrants. Some migrants have already gained public office, especially in small migration towns, while maintaining their connections with their townspeople overseas. The most important political effort of migrants has been their push for the approval of a unilateral dual citizenship for Dominicans.[30] Under this arrangement, while residing as citizens in the United States, migrants would preserve their Dominican nationality as inactive. Upon return, their Dominican political rights would be reactivated as their U.S. citizenship became inactive. In this sense, they would enjoy the right to live and work in either country, without losing the right to do the same in either. This measure would formalize their current informal access to the two countries' opportunities. Their attempts in this direction, however, has been unsuccessful so far.

U.S. and Dominican official policies sharply contrast with migrants' aspirations for binational citizenship. On the one hand, the U.S. government is mostly interested in stepping up its restrictions on the mobility of labor and migration-driven resources between the two countries. Visa controls and raids by immigration agents on Dominican businesses in New York have been intensified. Under a U.S. initiative, the two governments signed in 1990 the Binational Tax Information Exchange Agreement, aimed at interdicting migrants' monetary transfers that evade U.S. fiscal controls.

On the other hand, the central concern of the Dominican government has been the control not so much of people's mobility but of their monies. In effect, Dominican policies have been directed at securing official access to remittances and other money transfers by migrants. Lately, however, U.S. authorities have increased their pressure on Santo Domingo to improve its border controls in order to prevent illegal departures to Puerto Rico, one of the most common surreptitious pathways to the United States.[31] The resiliency of social networks and people's cunning compelled by their binational social world is rendering these controls useless, however.

CONCLUSION

The historical convergence of contradictory forces has generated the particular conditions for the emergence of a binational society from the Dominican migration process. The continuous struggle of the migrant population against adverse contextual forces, and even forces within itself, has induced the transnationalization of migrants. It seems as though the stronger the attempts in both countries to control migrants' own spatial and social mobility and settlement, the stronger the migrants' resistance and thus the stronger their cohesion and their binationalism. The persistent political and social efforts to dominate and control migrants by the two nation states and the dominant Dominican classes have resulted only in increasing strength and sophistication of this binational group, particularly its entrepreneurial class.

Migrants have acquired a de facto binational citizenship, expressed in their growing struggle for political and social rights and the expansion of their ethnic economy in the

United States and in the maintenance of their social, economic, and political connections with the Dominican Republic. This relatively autonomous society is embedded in a binational setting where territory and social, economic, and cultural actions are all binational. Because of this, traditional frameworks of analysis should be revamped: inquiries that are limited to detecting effects—at either end of the "stream"—and patterns of mobility, and to reaching absolute conclusions encased in totalizing assessments and rigid topologies, are untenable. In addition to the migration process, the migrants themselves should be investigated—as a heterogeneous group embedded in a binational social milieu where they are affected and dominated by, but also affect and resist, the structural forces around them.

Thus any further analysis or policy decision on Dominican migration should have a binational focus. Specifically, instead of espousing doomed policies aimed solely at affecting migrants' mobility and/or their resources, the U.S. and Dominican governments would be better advised to join efforts to foster connections between the linkages, resources, and demands—for goods and services—generated by these binationals, on the one hand, and development efforts in the Dominican Republic and in Dominican settlements in the United States, on the other.

Undoubtedly, these emerging features of the Dominican migration experience are not unique in these times of capitalist globalization. Yet they may shed some light on other contemporary migration processes, especially from Latin America. Our understanding of this new phase of international migration remains limited, however. One of this article's ulterior goals is precisely to spark further research on this subject from a wider vantage point.

NOTES

The author would like to thank Michael Peter Smith, Richard Schauffler, and Krystynn von Henneberg for their helpful comments. The responsibility for the contents is exclusively the author's.

1. During the same period, tens of thousands of Dominicans have also been emigrating to some European and Latin American countries, such as Spain, Holland, Switzerland, and Venezuela.

2. Glenn L. Hendricks, *The Dominican Diaspora: From the Dominican Republic to New York City—Villagers in Transition* (New York: Teachers College Press, 1974); Glauco A. Pérez, "The Legal and Illegal Dominican in New York" (Paper delivered at the Conference on Hispanic Migration to New York City: Global Trends and Neighborhood Change, New York University, New York, 4 Dec. 1981): Sebastián Ravelo and Pedro J. del Rosario, *Impacto de los dominicanos ausentes en el financiamiento rural* (Santiago, Dominican Republic; Centro de Investigaciones, Universidad Católica Madre y Maestra, 1986); Eugenia Georges, "Distribución de los efectos de la migración internacional sobre una comunidad de la Sierra Occidental," in *La inmigración dominicana en los Estados Unidos*, ed. José del Castillo and Christopher Mitchel (Santo Domingo, Dominican Republic: Editorial CENAPEC, 1987); Sherri Grasmuck and Patricia Pessar, *Between Two Islands: Dominican International Migration* (Berkeley: University of California Press, 1991).

3. The 1990 U.S. census reports 520,151 people of Dominican origin, a figure vehemently disputed by Dominican leaders as a gross undercount. The northeastern New Jersey, Miami, and Boston metropolitan areas, respectively, follow New York as the largest concentrations of Dominicans. U.S., Department of Commerce, Bureau of the Census, *Persons of Hispanic Origin in the United States: 1990* (Washington, DC: Department of Commerce, Bureau of the Census, Population Division, 1991).

4. The selection bias of previous studies—which concentrate exclusively on waged and salaried workers—significantly accounts for the persistence of prevailing misconceptions of Dominican migrants.

5. Grasmuck and Pessar, *Between Two Islands*; Nelson Ramirez et al., *Republica Dominicana: Población y desarrollo 1950-1985* (San José, Costa Rica: Centro Latinoamericano de Demografia, 1985); Alejandro Portes and Luis E. Guarnizo, "Tropical Capitalists: U.S.-Bound Immigration and Small-Enterprise Development in the Dominican Republic," in *Migration, Remittances and Small Business Development: Mexico and Caribbean Basin Countries*, ed. Sergio Díaz-Briquets and Sidney Weintraub (Boulder, CO: Westview Press, 1991); Luis E. Guarnizo, "One Country in Two: Dominican-Owned Enterprises in New York and in the Dominican Republic" (Ph.D. diss., Johns Hopkins University, 1992); idem, "Going Home: Class, Gender, and Household Transformation

among Dominican Return Migrants" (Research report, Commission for Hemispheric Migration and Refugee Policy, Georgetown University, 1993).

6. In addition to metropolitan New York, Dominican-owned businesses also flourish in northeastern New Jersey, and in the Boston and Miami metropolitan areas. See Guarnizo, "One Country in Two"; Portes and Guarnizo, "Tropical Capitalists"; Peggy Levitt, "A Todos les Llamo Primo (I Call Everyone Cousin): The Social Basis for Latino Small Business" (Paper, Massachusetts Institute of Technology, 1991).

7. Of 92 Dominican-owned firms surveyed in New York, 28.0 percent reported a net worth of under $30,000, 16.2 percent reported up to $10,000, and 35.9 percent reported a net worth of over $100,000. Nine of the sampled firms were worth $1 million or more. Guarnizo, "One Country in Two," p. 219.

8. The term "social capital" is used here to mean a wealth of intangible social resources—such as information, social support, personal connections, and so forth—indispensable for achieving social, economic, and political goals. "Ethnic social capital" refers to cases where social capital is bound by an ethnic identity. For a detailed discussion of social capital, see Gaurnizo, "One Country in Two," chap. 9; Pierre Bourdieu and Loïe J. D. Waequant, *An Initiation to Reflexive Sociology* (Chicago: University of Chicago Press, 1992); Alejandro Portes and Julia Sensenbrenner, "Embeddedness and Immigration: Notes on the Social Determinants of Economic Action," *American Journal of Sociology*, 98(6): 1320-50 (1993).

9. Grasmuck and Pessar, *Between Two Islands.*

10. The participation of a small proportion of Dominican immigrants in drug-related activities in the United States, with the subsequent capital accumulation by some of them, has sparked the stigmatization of the migrant population. The upper classes' attitude against wealthy migrants is publicly justified by the argument that affluent migrants made their capital in the illicit drug trade. Such justification legitimizes a blatant discrimination against migrants in general, banning them from well-to-do neighborhoods, private schools, social clubs, and even business organizations. See Guarnizo, "Going Home."

11. For a discussion of negative social capital, see Portes and Sensenbrenner, "Embeddedness and Immigration."

12. White found a similar pattern of affinity and solidarity among Japanese who returned home after working overseas for the Japanese government and private multinational corporations. Merry White, *The Japanese Overseas: Can They Go Home Again?* (Princeton, NJ: Princeton University Press, 1992).

13. Contrary to popular wisdom, it is not common to find intact migrant families settled for good in either country. Family arrangements in which one or

both parents live in the United States with none or some of their children, while their other children live on the island, are frequent. Although having more than one household in two different countries might be a source of emotional stress and economic hardship, it also arms family members with special skills to deal with uncertainty and adversity. They become more sophisticated than nonmigrant people in dealing with a rapidly globalizing world. See Guarnizo, "Going Home."

14. Dominican Republic, Secretaría de Estado de Turismo, *Turismo en Cifras-1985* (Santo Domingo, Dominican Republic: Secretaría de Estado de Turismo, 1986).

15. Grasmuck and Pessar, *Between Two Islands*; Guarnizo, "Going Home"; Alejandro Portes and Luis E. Guarnizo, *Capitalistas del trópico: La inmigración en los Estados Unidos y el desarrollo de la pequeña empresa en la República Dominicana* (Santo Domingo, Dominican Republic: FLASCO Dominicana, 1991).

16. In addition, since the second half of the 1970s, a Dominican migration literature has emerged in New York City. Immigrant writers, especially poets, are struggling to create a literary movement that is becoming "the voice of the community." Silvio Torres-Saillant, "La literatura dominicana en los Estados Unidos y la periferia del margen," *Brujula/Compass*, no. 9, pp. 16-19 (1991).

17. *Chronicles: A Magazine of American Culture* (July 1992), quoted in Jack Miles, "The Struggle for the Bottom Rung: Blacks vs. Browns," *Atlantic Monthly* (Oct. 1992).

18. Guarnizo, "One Country in Two," p. 67.

19. *Boletín CADOCON* (Cámara Dominicana de la Construcción) (Sept. 1986).

20. Paralleling the ethnic economy in New York, the migration-linked economy in the Dominican Republic is also made up of a mix of firms located along a continuum running from subsistence to large capitalist ventures. It is worth noting that the presence of migrants is significant in Dominican EPZs, particularly in the garment and leather industries, which, incidentally, are among the most common outlets owned or staffed by Dominicans in New York.

21. See Guarnizo, "Going Home."

22. Of course, as with other migrant groups, there is a residual process through which some migrants settle definitively on either side, cutting any connection with the other side. But these, it seems to me, are still a minority.

23. Grasmuck and Pessar, *Between Two Islands*; John B. Martin, *Overtaken by Events: The Dominican Crisis—From the Fall of Trujillo to the Civil War* (Garden City, NY: Doubleday, 1966).

24. The U.S. government did not confine its role only to granting visas for political opponents of the

regime. The U.S. government also "cooperated, at the [provisional government's] request, by refusing to permit the deportees to leave the United States." Martin, *Overtaken by Events*, p. 347.

25. For the purposes of my analysis, I consider national allegiance to be the individual's compliance—whether willingly or otherwise—with the laws and norms decreed and enforced by the national state apparatus within its territorial jurisdiction.

26. Limitations of space prevent a detailed illustration of the workings of this de facto double citizenship status. An example, however, is provided by Dominicans who, on the island, employ their American status or their Dominican status intermittently, depending on the circumstances, such as participating in politics, dealing with official authorities, or benefiting from rights reserved to Dominican citizens while dodging duties by posing as foreigners.

27. Contrary to popular belief, most migrants possess a rather broad knowledge of the laws that might affect them. Almost every migrant I interviewed knew basic Dominican and North American commercial regulations controlling binational trade and transactions and other regulations, such as those concerning migration, fiscal matters, civil rights, and common police ordinances. Thus one might expect that people with this type of information are in a position to abide by as well as avoid complying with state regulations.

28. Guarnizo, "One Country in Two," pp. 104-105.

29. In November 1991, a former head of the school board, Guillermo Linares, became the first Dominican-born person elected to the New York City Council. Dominicans now have several representatives in visible positions in the city government, as well as in various other agencies controlling local community development.

30. The unilateral acceptance of dual citizenship implies that it would be undertaken only by the Dominican state, with no need for a bilateral agreement with the United States.

31. The crossing of the Mona Passage, separating the Dominican Republic from Puerto Rico, by undocumented Dominicans in small, rickety boats (*yolas*) has grown to such levels that some U.S. authorities in San Juan have proposed imposing a $1000 fine on the Dominican government for the handling of each undocumented person captured. Because of the high volume of illegal crossing since 1987, Aguadilla, P.R., hosts the only border patrol post outside the continental United States.

9

"QUÉ ASSIMILATED, BROTHER, YO SOY ASIMILAO": THE STRUCTURING OF PUERTO RICAN IDENTITY IN THE U.S.

Juan Flores

I carry	mis raices
my roots	las cargo
with me	siempre
all the time	conmigo
rolled up	enrolladas
I use them	me serven
as my pillow	de almohada

—Francisco Alarcón

A YOUNG CHICANO FRIEND, on a recent first visit to New York City, shared with me some interesting impressions of the Puerto Ricans there and made comparisons with his own people in the Southwest. Of course he was reeling with the similarities between the huge Spanish-speaking neighborhoods of New York and Los Angeles where all your senses inform you that you are in Latin America, or that some section of Latin America has been transplanted to the urban United States where it maintains itself energetically, while interacting directly and in intricate ways with the surrounding cultures. Chicanos and Puerto Ricans in the U.S., the present pillars of the so-called "Hispanic" minority, stand at the same juncture, straddling North and South America and embodying the unequal, oppressive relation between them. And Francisco, a sensitive student of Chicano culture, suddenly became even more aware of the remarkable cultural convergence and correspondences that accompany such shared historical experiences. "¡Somos Raza! ¡Somos Latinos!" he would say, thinking of El Barrio and the Lower East Side, and of East Los and La Misión. We are bilingual and bicultural, and for both Chicanos and Nuyoricans those terms signal a complex duality of transcendence and denial, harmony and imposition, solidarity and disadvantage.

Yet, along with this suddenly heightened sense of Hispanic unity and cultural comple-mentarity, Francisco also began to make note of differences, ways in which the Nuyorican position in the U.S. society diverges from that of his fellow Chicanos. The most obvious of these, in his view, was the closeness between Puerto Ricans and Blacks. Of course Chicanos and African Americans have long shared a common cause as victims of racism and exploitation and comprise natural allies in political and social movements. Culturally, too, there has been ample interaction, but nothing resembling the intensity and extent of influ-ence between Black and Puerto Rican cultures in New York. El Barrio flows off impercep-tibly into Harlem, Williamsburgh into Bedford-Stuyvesant, while, by contrast, sharper lines seem to separate East Los Angeles from Watts and other Southwest barrios from their adja-cent black neighborhoods. Wherever he looked and listened, Francisco witnessed young Puerto Ricans and New York Blacks talking and walking in the same manner, singing and dancing with the same style, and often seeming indistinguishable in appearance and action. He heard Nuyorican poetry and salsa and detected more Afro-American language and rhythms than anything familiar to him in Chicano expression. He saw the Guardian Angels in the subways and Black and Puerto Rican families cohabiting the tenements and housing projects. He heard about the Black and Puerto Rican legislative caucus in Albany and the programs in Black and Puerto Rican studies in the colleges. He even took in the movie "Wild Style" and was amazed at the integral participation of both groups in forms of con-temporary street art and performance like graffiti, rap music and break dancing.

You just don't see as much of that out West, he concluded, his fascination at the phe-nomenon betraying both admiration and perplexity. Together we groped for explanations, recognizing that it was important to account for this notable divergence between two groups—Nuyoricans and Chicanos—otherwise so compatible and constituent of a com-mon "Latino" identity. We realized that underlying all the other reasons having to do with factors of social history, geographical placement, migratory patterns, and even racial char-acteristics, the Nuyoricans' relatively closer cultural proximity to U.S. Blacks is based on their Caribbean origins and, even beyond that, with Africa. We couldn't carry the point much fur-ther, but were confident that the Afro-Caribbean traditions borne by Nuyoricans in the new setting, even light-skinned Puerto Ricans and the many who might even look like Chicanos, made for a more fluid, reciprocal relation with the culture of Black Americans. Maybe African Americans are to Puerto Ricans, Francisco suggested, what Native Americans are to Chicanos—a kind of cultural tap root, a latent bond to ethnic sources indigenous to the United States, yet radically challenging to the prevailing cultural hierarchy.

This probing of differences led us back to a sense of the parallels between our two groups, but this time the convergences were of a deeper, more subtle kind than those indi-cated by our common label as "Hispanics." Beneath and beyond that officially promoted category of Spanish language minority, Chicanos and Nuyoricans are caught up in a simi-lar spiritual dynamic, one which, in each case, meshes "outside" and "inside," Latin American background and the internal U.S. cultural context. The close, long-standing interaction between Puerto Ricans and Blacks, and between Chicanos and Native Americans, exposes the superficiality and divisiveness of the term "Hispanic" in its current bureaucratic usage. It became clear that for either group to accept that rubric at face value would mean to agree to relegating and ultimately severing a crucial nexus in its quest for collective identity. This, we felt, was an important lesson to absorb at a time when loudly publicized projections of "Hispanics" as the "fastest growing minority" are setting off waves of Anglo hysteria and some defensive jitters among leaders of the oppressed.

What the Chicano observer could only dimly appreciate on his brief visit, though, was that the striking affinity between Puerto Ricans and Blacks in New York is but one thread in a complex fabric of Third-World cultures cohabitating the inner city neighborhoods and institutions. Emigrants and refugees from many of the Caribbean and Latin American countries are now entering their second and even third generation of presence there, with Dominicans, Jamaicans and Haitians adding most substantially to the Caribbeanization of New York begun by Puerto Ricans and Cubans before them. Add the sizeable numbers of Asian and Arab peoples, and the non-European complexion of the city's multi-ethnic composite becomes still more prominent. As each group and regional culture manifests itself in the new setting, and as they increasingly coalesce and interact in everyday life, New York is visibly becoming the source of a forceful, variegated alternative to mainstream North American culture.

For this crossing and blending of transmitted colonial cultures is not to be confused with the proverbial "melting pot" of Anglo-American fantasy, nor is it a belated example of "cultural pluralism" as that phrase is commonly used in U.S. social science and public discourse. Though characterized by the plurality and integration of diverse cultures, the process here is not headed toward assimilation with the dominant "core" culture, nor even toward respectful coexistence with it. Rather, the individual and interweaving cultures involved are expressions of histories of conquest, enslavement and forced incorporation at the hands of the prevalent surrounding society. As such, the main thrust in each case is toward self-affirmation and association with other cultures caught up in comparable processes of historical recovery and strategic resistance.

The path of "assimilation in American life" has been amply charted in U.S. social science and codified in paradigmatic terms by Milton Gordon.[1] The guiding model rests firmly on analogies to the experiences of European immigrant groups. The attempts at modification, and even rejoinders to this approach pronounced with a view toward cases complicated by racial stigmatization and prolonged economic and social disadvantage, have largely gone to reinforce that familiar image of cultural shedding, adjustment and reincorporation. The theory of "internal colonialism," no doubt the most consistent rejection of the reigning ethnic ideology, nevertheless retains the vision of each minority group forming its sense of identity in its relation to, and self-differentiation from, the dominant Anglo culture. Colonial minority resistance to assimilation is still presented as occurring within the pluralist field of options and with its sight set, however resentfully, on that very ethnic mosaic from which it is being excluded. Each group manifests itself singularly in its own terms and primarily as an effort at cultural maintenance over against that which negates it.[2]

The interaction among popular colonial cultures in New York suggests a markedly different process, one which is indeed pluralist and confluent in nature and perhaps for that reason even more challenging to established thinking on ethnic relations. But if the transformation of Puerto Rican culture in the U.S. setting is something other than assimilation, what is it? How is it to be defined in terms other than loss of the old and acquisition of the new, or as the fateful confrontation between two unequal and mutually exclusive cultural monoliths? The problem is clearly more than a terminological one, for it has to do with detecting a developmental pattern leading neither to eventual accommodation nor to "cultural genocide." Beyond these two options, characteristic respectively of North American and Island-based Puerto Rican commentary on the Nuyorican experience, a more intricate structuring of ethnicity is evident.

In the following I will seek to trace some contours of this alternative dynamic. Though focussing on Nuyorican culture as expressed in its poetry, my observations may be readily generalized to apply to other colonial minorities, with samples of poetic discourse simply serving as distilled representations of other aspects of cultural life. A further qualification is that I have in mind primarily the contemporary generation of Puerto Ricans living in New York City; again it is hoped that my comments also help to clarify, with a minimum of distortion, the cultural experience of earlier generations and of Puerto Ricans in other parts of the U.S. Finally, any interpretation of cultural process presupposes a coherent analysis of the conditioning political and economic reality, in this case colonialism, labor migration, patriarchy and racial inequality. Such an analysis, as it is being advanced by fellow researchers at the Center for Puerto Rican Studies and elsewhere, forms the basis of my present reflections.[3]

One can see four definitive moments in the awakening of Nuyorican cultural consciousness which are linked by three transitional phases from one field to the other. The moments are not necessarily stages in a chronological sense, nor do the transitions follow one another in any set order. I will present them as a sequence for hypothetical purposes, understanding that what I am describing is really more a range of constantly intersecting possibilities and responses arising simultaneously at the individual and collective levels.

The first moment is the here and now, the Puerto Rican's immediate perception of the New York that surrounds the person. Prior to any cultural associations or orientations, there are the abandoned buildings, the welfare lines, the run-down streets, the frigid winter nights with no heat, in short, the conditions of hostility, disadvantage and exclusion that confront the Puerto Rican in day-to-day reality. Corresponding to the absence of economic and political opportunity is the lack of cultural access and direction of any kind: the doors to the prevailing culture are closed. One young writer aptly refers to this sense of emptiness as the "state of abandon,"[4] and another, thinking of his own boyhood, characterizes it in the following lines:

> papote sat on the stoop
> miseducated   misinformed
> a blown-up belly of malnutrition
> papote sat on the stoop
> of an abandoned building
> he decided to go nowhere.[5]

It is this very moment of the Puerto Rican experience in New York that is typically isolated and sensationalized by the dominant culture, as in entertainment packages from "West Side Story" to "Fort Apache" and in social pathologies like Oscar Lewis's *La Vida*.[6] The mass public is made to delight in this drama of sheer desperation and brutality, particularly when it is also comforted with the thought that such "subcultural" misery is, after all, self-inflicted. And, indeed, for many Puerto Ricans themselves the only recourse in the face of this estranging here and now often involves damage and jeopardy and, of course, disproportionate social recrimination.

But for a variety of reasons, often having little to do with the existing educational system, awareness turns in the direction of the second moment: Puerto Rico. The passage from the immediacy of New York to the Puerto Rican cultural background is generally less geographical than spiritual and psychological, its impetus deriving from the intimacy of family life with nostalgic reminiscences of parents and grandparents. It tends to present a romanticized, idealized image of Puerto Rico, and is only rarely informed by any political account of the migration and the colonial conditions that propelled it.[7] A memorable example of this transition from ghetto to garden, from infernal New York to edenic Puerto Rico, may be found in the opening chapters of Piri Thomas's autobiographical novel *Down These Mean Streets*. Piri remembers that as a child during the Depression years, his mother used to warm the frigid winter nights with her soothing words about the "quiet of the greenlands and the golden color of the morning sky, the grass wet from the *lluvia*." And that other Nuyorican "classic," Pedro Pietri's *Puerto Rican Obituary*, illustrates the same type of contrast; the famous title poem, in fact, is structured as a gradual passage from the deathly tedium, hopelessness and "colonial mentality" of Puerto Rican life in New York to a forceful exhortation to rise from the dead and be transported to a "beautiful place," "where beautiful people sing / and dance and work together / where the wind is a stranger / to miserable weather conditions."[8]

If the first moment is the state of abandon, the second is the state of enchantment, an almost dream-like trance at the striking contrast between the cultural barrenness of New York and the imagined luxuriance of the Island culture. This contrast, often expressed in physical terms as one of cold and warmth, darkness and light, grey and bright green, runs through the literature of the migration, one familiar example being the refrain to the popular song: "Mamá, Borinquen me llama, / este país no es el mío, / Puerto Rico es pura flama, / y aquí me muero de frío." This Puerto Rico, of course, cannot be tested for its historical or even geographical authenticity, since it is initially conjured for metaphorical, emblematic reasons.

While making no claim to realism, the evocation of Puerto Rico cannot be dismissed early as mere archaism, for even the opposition of physical environments implies an ecological and esthetic rejection of the imposed New York conditions. The "rediscovery" of Puerto Rico, however utopian, is thus a constituent in the active search for cultural guidance and meaning in a social context bereft of accessible human bearings. Sandra María Esteves, another of the young New York poets, traces this passage from disorientation to dream to reawakening in her poem entitled "Here":

> I am two parts / a person
> boricua / spic
> past and present
> alive and oppressed
> given a cultural beauty
> ... and robbed of a cultural identity
>
> I speak the alien tongue
> in sweet borinqueño thoughts
> know love mixed with pain
> have tasted spit on ghetto stairways
> ... here, it must be changed
> we must change it
>
> I may never overcome
> the theft of my isla heritage
> dulce palmas de coco on Luqillo

> sway in windy recesses I can only imagine
> and remember how it was
>
> But that reality now a dream
> teaches me to see, and will
> bring me back to me.[9]

Clearly, it is not only swaying palm-trees and sunny beaches that the New York Puerto Ricans find in their invoked homeland, as important as that ecological vision may be in the construction of a new identity. It is also "my isla heritage," by which is meant, first of all, a different, more human way of living and relating to people. Beneath the more beautiful landscape the Nuyoricans gain sight of a more appealing culture, one in which they feel included and able to participate. The validation of Spanish is an important initial impetus, even if that means, as in the phrase "my isla heritage," the inclusion of a Spanish word in an English-language context.

More than language, however, the main content of this second moment is the recovered African and indigenous foundation of Puerto Rican culture. Along with increased political awareness comes a more critical relation to the "heritage," and a growing distinction between the official, dominant version of the national culture and its popular base. The racism encountered in the U.S. impels the Nuyorican even more resolutely toward the Taíno and Afro-Caribbean background, which constitutes the major thematic reference point and expressive resource in Puerto Rican culture in the U.S. It is the colonized within the colony whom the Nuyoricans identify as their real forebears in the national tradition, a continuity which is readily evident in much of the music, poetry and art, and in many aspects of daily life.

The continuum is popular culture, the culture of poor and working-class Puerto Ricans spanning the centuries and the process of emigration and resettlement. For at the popular level, the formation of the national culture exemplifies the very transculturation and inter-action of diverse racial and language cultures which is so systematically obstructed and feared in the familiar U.S. setting. It is possible for new cultures to emerge without loss or abandonment of the old, certainly a vital lesson for young Puerto Ricans being pressed into a foreign mold. Recognizing that this so-called "syncretism" has occurred in Puerto Rico under conditions of colonial domination and racial and social inequality further deepens the Nuyoricans' understanding of the social dynamic and points to the class dimension of cultural change.

That which begins as and appears on the surface to be no more than the nostalgic, metaphorical evocation typical of an immigrant sensibility is in the Puerto Rican case an apprenticeship in social consciousness, the reconstructed "patria" serving as the relevant locus of cultural interaction and contention. Identification with the popular traditions within the colonial culture not only exposes the racial and class hierarchy which during the first moment, in the New York here and now, the Nuyorican could only confront at an immediate, experiential level. Popular culture also represents the current of resistance and opposition to that system and, in larger terms, a mode and function of cultural produc-tion different from that of both the dominant elite culture and the commercially packaged mass culture. In this sense, the legacy of oral traditions and artisan craft finds a direct extension in Nuyorican artistic expression. The reliance on improvisation and perfor-mance, and the abiding conception of expressive resources as tools, help counteract the pressure toward standardization and the estrangement of culture from its personal and social origins.

The third moment is located back in New York, but the passage there, the return and reentry, is infused with those new perspectives gathered in the course of cultural recovery. While previously, during the first moment, life was sheer hostility and exclusion, the New York scene now includes the Puerto Ricans, if only by force of their own deliberate self-insertion into the urban landscape. Looking at New York, the Nuyorican sees Puerto Rico, or at least the glimmering imprint of another world to which vital connections have been struck. This transposition of the cultural background finds cogent expression in the poetry of Victor Hernández Cruz, who ends his poem "Los New Yorks" with the stanza, "I am going home now / I am settled there with my fruits / Everything tastes good today / Even the ones that are grown here / Taste like they're from outer space / Walk y suena / Do it strange / Los New Yorks." And in a short poem entitled "BronxOmania," the poet discovers Puerto Rico while riding in the subway:

> snake horse stops at bronx clouds
> end of lines and tall windowed cement
> comes to unpaved roads and wilderness
> where the city is far
> and spanish bakeries sell hot bread
> the roar of the iron snake
> plunges at closing doorways
> down fifty blocks
> is the island of Puerto Rico.[10]

This atmospheric, visionary presence of the homeland, so pervasive in the literature of the migration, is again the outward indication of an awakened cultural consciousness. The spiritual orientation gained through recapturing the Puerto Rican background conditions this renewed encounter with New York, lending meaning and historical perspective to what had been a scene of sheer abandonment and disorientation. The predicament of bilingualism, for example, which confronted the Nuyorican in the first moment as a confining and prejudicial dilemma with no visible resolution, now becomes an issue of social contention and beyond that, a sign of potential enrichment and advantage. Though not a socially recognized asset, bilingual discourse and continued access to Spanish have been a major element in the reinforcement of Puerto Rican cultural identity and in the self-definition of a group demonstrating the full range of Spanish-English language contact.

The racial situation is also altered as a result of the imaginative passage to and from the site of cultural origins. The divisions, confusions and inescapable degradations suffered by Puerto Ricans because of the Black versus White polarities of U.S. racial classification give way to a proud identification with Afro-Caribbean cultural traditions. The influence of the Civil Rights and Black Power movements were, of course, of direct importance to the Nuyorican revival of the late 1960s, but recognizing a similar thrust in the re-interpretation of their own cultural heritage contributed greatly to this active affirmation of African roots. Furthermore, the multi-racial composition of the Puerto Rican people and the elaborate process of mixing evident in the formation of the national culture suggest a more dynamic, historically differentiated relation between race and culture than was conceivable to the Puerto Ricans in their direct, unreflected subjection to U.S. racism.

The Nuyorican also reenters New York with a heightened sense of the duality of cultural life and expression, the differences and interrelationships between official and commercially produced culture on the one hand and popular culture on the other. Thus, in addition to the cultivation of indigenous and Afro-Puerto Rican sources such as *la bomba* and *la plena* in the music and the Afro-Antillean rhythm and language of Luis Palés Matos in the poetry, Nuyorican expression responds to and articulates the creative experience of the people. Instead of the cultural vacuum characteristic of the state of abandon, the feeling that there is and can be no culture where the only concern is survival and coping, there is now a recognition that the life of poor people is a legitimate and abundant source of cultural energy. This validation of popular culture is present in the conversational and colloquial qualities of Nuyorican poetic language and in the common emphasis on public performance and delivery. Exposure to traditional Puerto Rican forms like the *décima, controversia* and *plena* makes clear to the Nuyorican that the cultural life of his people is one of improvisation, communal participation and commentary on topical local events.

All of these horizons of the re-encounter with New York through Puerto Rican eyes comprise what can most aptly be considered an awakened national consciousness, or consciousness of nationality. For taken together and brought to bear on the U.S. context, such new and otherwise concealed perspectives on language, race and cultural dynamics constitute an assertion of national origins. "En el fondo del nuyorican hay un Puertorriqueño," one of the poets has said, paraphrasing the title of a well-known short story by José Luis González.[11] Despite the endless endeavor to reduce Puerto Rican cultural identity to more manageable terms of language group, race or ethnicity, and thus to insert it into some larger aggregate, the third moment of Nuyorican awareness actually involves an introduction of the national dimension to U.S. ethnic relations. For it is on that basis, as a lingually, racially and culturally distinctive national group, that Nuyoricans define their identity in the U.S. And it is on that basis that they constitute their position in the society and their relation to other cultures.

The fourth moment is this branching-out, the selective connection to and interaction with the surrounding North American society. Generally, of course, this experience is considered in isolation, with the overriding concern being the issue of Puerto Rican assimilation. The advantage of tracing the various moments surrounding and conditioning that controversial point of intersection is to suggest that there is a complex process involved, which is by no means unreflected, unidirectional or limited to the options of incorporation or self-exclusion. When account is taken of the fully trajectory and shifting geography of Nuyorican identification, it becomes clear that something other than assimilation or cultural separation is at work.

The first path of Puerto Rican interaction with North American culture is toward those groups to whom they stand in closest proximity, not only spatially but also because of congruent cultural experience. For Puerto Ricans in New York, this means, first of all, Black Americans and other migrants from the Caribbean and Latin America. With such groups, a strong process of cultural convergence and fusion occurs, what one commentator, J.M. Blaut, has called "the partial growing-together of the cultures of ghettoized communities."[12] This "growing-together" is often mistaken for assimilation, but the difference is obvious in that it is not directed toward incorporation into the dominant culture. For that reason, the "pluralism" that results does not involve the dissolution of national backgrounds and cultural histories but their continued affirmation and enforcement even as they are transformed. Given the basis of social parity among groups with a common cultural trajectory, the very relation between unity and diversity contrasts with that operative in the established scheme of ethnic pluralism.

It is from the vantage of this coalescence with the cultures of other colonial minorities that Puerto Ricans assume collective interaction with the Anglo-American society at large. The branching-out is selective, with a gravitation toward other popular cultures with a background of social disadvantage: the Chinese, the Arabs and, more cautiously, the Irish, Italians and Jews. It is a fusion, significantly, at the popular level of shared working-class reality, and one expressive of recognized marginalization and exclusion. And because it involves the retention and extension of the inherited cultures rather than their abandonment, the process has remarkable cultural consequences, described by Blaut as "the healthy interfertilization of cultures, the efflorescence of new creative forms in painting, poetry, music, and the like, and the linking up of struggles."[13]

Even at that point, as Nuyorican modes of expression come to intermingle with others and thus distinguish themselves from those of the Island legacy, it is not accurate to speak of assimilation. Rather than being subsumed and repressed, Puerto Rican culture contributes, on its own terms and as an extension of its own traditions, to a new amalgam of human expression. It is the existing racial, national and class divisions in U.S. society which allow for, indeed necessitate, this alternative course of cultural change.[14]

Such, then, are four moments of Nuyorican cultural interaction with U.S. society, briefly summarized as the here-and-now, Puerto Rican background, reentry and branching out. Again, they are not necessarily to be taken as sequential stages in the manner in which I have presented them but as fields of experience joined by transitional phases of cultural awareness. How and to what extent these moments of sensibility relate to the advance of political consciousness is even another, more complicated matter. It is clear, in any case, that Puerto Rico not only serves as an imaginary realm of cultural self-discovery, but must also be recognized as a nation whose political status looms large on the agenda of international relations. The quest for Puerto Rican identity in the United States thus remains integrally tied to the prospects of national independence or continued colonial subordination to or, as the official euphemism would have it, "association" with the United States. Generally speaking, the gathering of cultural consciousness on the part of the Nuyoricans inclines them toward the first of these options.

It will also be necessary, with further study, to elaborate the correspondences between the cultural geography outlined here and the multiple spatial directions of the Puerto Rican migration. I would only suggest that the spiritual movement back and forth between New York and Puerto Rico bears some significant correlation to the migratory circulation of Puerto Ricans in the ongoing exchange of workers for capital under colonial conditions. In the Puerto Rican case, neither the migration itself nor the cultural encounter with U.S. society is a one-way, either/or, monolithic event. Rather, it is one marked by further movement and the constant interplay of two familiar yet contrasting zones of collective experience.[15]

I would conclude by acknowledging that the structure of the Puerto Rican's coming-to-consciousness which I present here as my own invention actually dawned on me as I read the work of another poet friend, Tato Laviera. For Laviera's three books of poems to date, when read in succession, take us through the entire journey, each volume giving voice to one of the passages from one moment to the next. The first, *La Carreta Made a U-Turn* focuses on the contrast between the New York here-and-now and the Puerto Rico of enchantment and cultural richness. The second book, entitled *En Clave* or *Enclave*,[16] transports that meaning gathered from the national culture and establishes a distinctive place for it in the reencountered New York setting. And the third, most recent volume, *AmeRícan*, is the branching out, the striking of sympathetic chords with other cultural groups on the basis of expansive Puerto Rican sounds and rhythms. The poet ranges widely in his "ethnic tributes," as he entitles a substantial part of the book, addressing and embracing many of the adjacent peoples in the crowded New York environs. One of the heartiest of these embraces is called "jamaican":

> reaches their guts into the Caribbean
> the second africa, divided by yemaya
>
> reaches their guts into the third world,
> marley-manley emerging people
>
> reaches their guts into urban america,
> reggae-reggae, modern english,
>
> reaches their guts into ethiopia,
> rastafarian celebrated deities.
>
> reaches their guts into washington sq. park,
> jamaican english, folkloric blackness,
> reaches their guts into puerto ricans,
> where we shared everything for free,
> yeah, brother, very good, very, very
> good, yeah, real good![17]

Here is the young Puerto Rican refashioning New York City along Caribbean, Third World lines, or voicing resonantly his awareness that history is doing so.

Yet as is clear from the neologistic title "AmeRícan," Laviera is intent on reaching beyond the New York enclave. He seeks to stake a claim for Puerto Rican recognition before the whole U.S. society, especially as Puerto Ricans are by now clustered in many cities other than New York. He is goading the society to come to terms with the "Rican" in its midst, arguing thorough puns and ironic challenges that he will not be an American until he can say "Am-e-Rícan" ("I'm a Rican") and be proud of it. He even diagnoses, in similar playful terms, the problem of assimilation. "Assimilated?" he begins one poem, "qué assimilated, brother, yo so asimilao," and ends with a confident reference to the Black base of Puerto Rican popular culture, "delen gracias a los prietos / que cambiaron asimilado al popular asimilao."

And in reaching across the U.S., not assimilating but growing together with neighboring and concordant cultures, how could the Nuyorican poet fail to embrace the Chicano? Getting to Chicago, Houston and Los Angeles, Tato Laviera surely sensed what Francisco felt during his days in New York. Chicanos and Nuyoricans, concentrated at opposite ends of the country, branching out in different cultural directions, still exemplify a close cultural affinity.

As a final note, listen to Tato Laviera, the Nuyorican, rapping to his Chicano brothers. Here again, in "Vaya carnal," it is the poet affirming a new language mix, "Chicano-riqueño," and at the same time forging those deeper cultural links which unite Mexicans and Puerto Ricans beneath the "Hispanic" surface:

Vaya, carnal
sabes, pinche, que me visto
estilo zoot suit marca de
pachuco royal chicano air
force montoyado en rojo
azul verde marrón nuevo
callejero chicano carnales
eseándome como si el ese ese
echón que se lanza en las
avenidas del inglés con
treinta millones de batos
locos hablando en secreto
con el chale-ese-no-la chingues
vacilón a los gringos americanos,
¿sabes?, simón, el sonido del este
el vaya, clave, por la maceta
que forma parte de un fuerto
lingüismo, raza, pana, borinquen,
azteca, macho, hombre, pulmones
de taíno, de indios, somos
chicano-riqueños, que curado.
simón, qué quemada mi pana,
la esperanza de un futuro
totalmente nuesto,
tú sabes, tú hueles,
el sabor, el fervor del
vaya, carnal.[18]

NOTES

First published in *The Journal of Ethnic Studies* 13/3 (Fall 1985): 1-16. A Spanish translation appeared in *Casa de las Américas* 26/152 (Sept-Oct 1985): 54-63.

1. Milton M. Gordon, *Assimilation in American Life* (Oxford, 1964).

2. See, for example, Robert Blauner, *Racial Oppression in America* (New York: Harper and Row, 1972); Tomás Almaguer, "Class, Race and Chicano Oppression," *Socialist Revolution*, 5 (1975), 71-99; J.M. Blaut, "The Ghetto as an Internal Neo-colony," *Antipode*, 6/1 (1974), 37-42.

3. See Frank Bonilla and Ricardo Campos, "A Wealth of Poor: Puerto Ricans in the New Economic Order," *Daedalus*, 110/2 (1981), 133-176; and "Imperialist Initiatives and the Puerto Rican Worker," *Contemporary Marxism*, 5 (1982), 1-18.

4. José Rodríguez, "Abre el Ojo: A Study of the Current State of Abandon and the Role of the Artist," Unpublished Project Report, 1981.

5. Tato Laviera, *La Carreta Made a U-Turn* (Houston: Arte Público Press, 1979).

6. Oscar Lewis, *La Vida: A Puerto Rican Family in the Culture of Poverty* (New York: Random House, 1965.)

7. A discussion of this mythical imagery in Nuyorican poetry may be found in: Efraín Barradas, "'De lejos en sueños vería . . .'; Visión mística de Puerto Rico en la poesía neoyorrican," *Revista Chicano-Riqueña*, 7 (1979), 46-56. For a more critical approach, see Felix Cortés, Joe Falcón and Juan Flores, "The Cultural Expression of Puerto Ricans in New York," *Latin American Perspectives*, 3 (1976), 117-150.

8. Piri Thomas, *Down These Mean Streets* (New York: Knopf, 1967); Pedro Pietri, *Puerto Rican Obituary* (New York: Monthly Review, 1973).

9. Sandra María Esteves, *Yerba Buena* (New York: Greenfield Review, 1980).

10. Victor Hernández Cruz, *Mainland* (New York: Random House, 1973). See also his *Snaps* (New York: Random House, 1969).

11. Tato Laviera, *AmeRícan* (Arte Público Press, 1985). The González story is entitled "En el fondo del caño hay un negrito."

12. J. M. Blaut, "Assimilation vs. Ghettoization," *Antipode*, 15/1 (1983), 35-41.

13. *Ibid.*

14. Though the argument presented here concurs in general with that in Blaut, 1983, I would object to the term "ghettoization" as a way of characterizing the alternative to assimilation. Blaut's account of the convergence of Black and Puerto Rican cultures tends to reduce that process to impinging socioeconomic and geographical factors, with no emphasis on cultural historical compatibilities and parallels.

15. For a valuable recent discussion of cultural geography, see Denis E. Cosgrove, "Towards a Radical Cultural Geography," *Antipode*, 15/1 (1983), 1-11. An initial consideration of Puerto Rican migration in terms of cultural geography may be found in Frank Bonilla, "Ethnic Orbits: The Circulation of Capitals and Peoples." Conference paper: "Ethnicity and Race in the Last Quarter of the 20th Century" (SUNY-Albany, 1984).

16. *Enclave* (Houston: Arte Público Press, 1981).

17. Laviera, *AmeRícan* (Houston: Arte Público Press, 1985).

18. *Ibid.*

10

REFLECTIONS ON DIVERSITY AMONG CHICANAS

Patricia Zavella

THE DIVERSITY AMONG CHICANAS can initially be seen by the terms of ethnic identification we have claimed for ourselves. When referring to ourselves within a white context, we often prefer more generic terms, like Las Mujeres or the combination Chicana/Latina, in opposition to Hispanic, which is often seen as inappropriate because of its conservative political connotations. When speaking among ourselves, we highlight and celebrate all the nuances of identity—we are Chicanas, Mexicanas, Mexican Americans, Spanish Americans, Tejanas, Hispanas, Mestizas, Indias, or Latinas, and the terms of identification vary according to the context. This complexity of identification reflects the conundrum many Chicanas experience: on the one hand, together we are seen by others as a single social category, often Hispanic women. Yet the term *Hispanic*, imposed by the Census Bureau, is seen as inappropriate by many women who prefer to identify themselves in oppositional political terms. As Chicanas, we have common issues and experiences with other women of color in the United States, and we therefore often feel a strong sense of affinity with their struggles. On the other hand, we are a very diverse group of women, with diverse histories, regional settlement patterns, particular cultural practices, sexual preferences, and occasionally radically dissimilar political outlooks, and our solidarity as Chicanas can be undermined by these differences among us.

My purpose here is to contextualize the notion of diversity among Chicanas and sketch out a conceptual framework for making sense of the commonalities and differences among us. My discussion has two parts: in the first I concentrate on the structural commonalities among Chicanas, based on the subordination engendered by the intersection of race, class, and gender but that are different for particular groups of women; later, I discuss how we Chicanas have constructed our lives, our sense of selves in opposition to the many forms of subordination. We must also examine how Chicano culture is socially constructed in ways that are misogynist, homophobic, or internalize racism and class prejudices.

I suggest that our understanding of difference among Chicanas will be enhanced through close attention to women's social location within the social structure, that is, in looking at the social spaces created by the intersection of class, race, gender, and culture.[1] The term *social location* differs from and complements that of Renato Rosaldo's useful concept of "positioned subject," where the observer/writer/ethnographer is self-reflective of her own social status and takes responsibility for uncovering the power relations within the culture—including her own participation within changing cultural processes. Rosaldo cautions us that cultural analyses by positioned subjects are always provisional.[2] My use also differs slightly from the notion of "crossing borders" suggested by Gloria Anzaldúa, who emphasizes how Chicanas construct a sense of self, a liberating critical consciousness, in oppositional terms.[3] Instead, I am emphasizing the dialectical process in which historical conditions, including cultural traditions, and the social construction of self occurs. That is, I am emphasizing the processes that constrain Chicanas' sense of self, the structures of oppression that make being a "positioned subject" or "crossing borders" problematic.

DECONSTRUCTING DIVERSITY

To begin formulating a framework on diversity among Chicanas, it is important to first deconstruct the stereotypic thinking that comes from outsiders. Stereotypes often have a grain of truth but mask gross generalizations or ignorance of the diversity not only among different groups of women of color but within groups. Some of these stereotypes include the assumption that all Chicanas speak Spanish or that we have such a rich culture—when our culture has been repressed. Other assumptions that I've heard include that Chicanas have such loving, big families; in fact, like other groups, Chicanas experience familial breakdown or abuse toward women.

Probably one of the most insidious stereotypes regarding Chicanas is the notion that culture is determinant of behavior. Because Chicanas are racially distinct and have Spanish language as an ethnic signifier, we seem obviously culturally different than white North Americans. This often leads to the assumption that there is a coherent Chicano cultural heritage: that the values, norms, customs, rituals, symbols, material items (such as women's religious altars) form part of a "tradition" that all Chicanos are socialized into. Moreover, this thinking goes, Chicanos mechanistically base their behavior and decisions on these traditional norms. This stereotype was given new life with Oscar Lewis's notion of a "culture of poverty" based on fieldwork with Puerto Rican and Mexican families, in which people were said to have a whole host of maladaptive cultural traits.[4] This equation of racial status and poverty conditions with culture has been critiqued for being static, ahistorical, and simplistic. More importantly, this view of culture as determinant is really a different version of "blaming the victim," where Chicanas' own cultural heritage is seen as limiting their educational, social, or political aspirations. It is unfortunate that this view has cropped up in feminist thinking as well.

RECONSTRUCTING COMMONALITY

A way to move beyond stereotypic views and reconstructing how Chicanas have common experiences is through a historical perspective. History helps us to understand how particular stereotypes became hegemonic, and how Chicanas have become marginalized and invisible in the popular, political, and scholarly discourses. Although I cannot go into historical detail here, I would like to sketch out a framework that helps us to understand the similarities among Chicanas and helps clarify the sources of diversity among us, based on class, race, gender, and culture.

Some initial historical reorientations are important to point out: Spanish colonizers "discovered" America and the civilizations of indigenous peoples, and Spanish soldiers settled in what is now northern New Mexico in the early sixteenth century, long before the so-called original settlers landed on Plymouth Rock. The history of the Americas, then, is of Spanish, not English origin. Second, the conquest and racial mixtures with indigenous peoples set in motion the "colonized" status of Chicanos today. An important conceptual point is that Chicanas did not enter this country the same way that many white immigrant groups did. European immigrants were pushed out of their countries of origin for important economic and political reasons and then, depending on where they settled and the historical period, found more or less receptive communities in which to settle. As nonracialized peoples, they were able to choose the ethnic signifiers that were important to retain.

Chicanas have been integrated into American society through involuntary means, and internal class, racial, ethnic, and gender divisions within Spain and then within the colonies have been reconstituted through industrial development.[5] Mexican women became U.S. citizens by default after the U.S.-Mexican war, during which the border literally migrated to them—imposing on them a foreign language and sociolegal system. Through a variety of legal and informal mechanisms, Mexicans were displaced from their land and propelled into the bottom of the working class, were disenfranchised and segregated into barrios. Their language and customs were denigrated or even outlawed.[6] Many of the mechanisms that institutionalized racism, sexism, and working-class status that incorporated Chicanos into North American society continue today. This common historical legacy is a powerful basis of solidarity among Chicanas.

DIVERSITY COMPOUNDED

Attention to history, though it does point out the sources of common experiences, also begins our exploration of diversity among Chicanas. History helps us understand the regional settlement patterns of different groups of Chicanas that were then replenished through waves of migration: Women of Mexican descent originally settled in South Texas, northern New Mexico and California in the Southwest, and later migrant streams created settlements in the Midwest, Northwest Coast, and, more recently, on the East Coast. Other recent Latin-American immigrant women have settled in large cities—San Francisco; Los Angeles; New York; Washington, D.C.; Miami—so that Chicano communities are becoming more heterogeneous. Settlement and migration history also helps us to understand the interethnic relations—both conflictual and cooperative—between groups of Chicanos. For example, in California researchers have found that Mexican immigrants who settled here in previous waves of migration have established economic "niches," in particular industries or occupations, and then felt threatened by compatriots who migrated more recently.[7]

Closely related to settlement patterns is the notion of culture-region, a geographic and sociopolitical area where historical processes—including isolation, waves of industrialization, urbanization, and discrimination toward racialized others—have segregated racial/ethnic groups and enabled historical actors to construct particular terms of ethnic identification in opposition to the dominant society.[8] The notion of culture-region helps highlight the particular racial mixtures that occurred—the mestizas from the unions of Spanish men and Indian women in the Southwest, the African and Spanish mixtures near the Caribbean—and helps us to understand the contours of cultural syncretism: Women from the gulf region show Puerto Rican, Cuban, and African influences whereas Chicanas from desert regions demonstrate more indigenous influences. There are also regional differences regarding the preferred terms of ethnic identification among women: *Chicana* in

California, *Mexican American* or *Mexicana* in Texas, *Spanish American* in New Mexico, although there is a good deal of mixing of terms as well.[9]

One implication of culture-region is that generation is important: whether women are of the first generation (that is, born in Mexico) or of subsequent generations born in the United States or are recent immigrants has implications for language use, cultural knowledge, and the process of identification. A Chicana's generation affects whether she feels a sense of identification and solidarity with other Chicanas, whether she feels marginalized, or whether she feels as if she is more "American" than Chicana.

Beyond historical settlement patterns, this framework attends to important internal differences within Chicano populations. Class is clearly an important demarcation: The overwhelming majority of Chicanos are of working-class origins, although with the recent economic crisis in Mexico, a few more middle-class and professional women are migrating to the United States. These women often have higher median incomes and higher education levels, in contrast to those women who have migrated from rural, underdeveloped areas of Mexico. The class status of Chicanas can take on insidious overtones: Foreign-born Chicanas from elite, upper-class backgrounds clearly have very different life chances than those from the working class yet are often categorized as Hispanic and inflate the Affirmative Action statistics about the presence of underrepresented minorities. Class is often a source of tension among Chicanas, coinciding with political disagreements.

Racial physical features are also important: Whether women have fair or dark skin and hair; Indian, African, or European features or some combination thereof bears upon how Chicanas are treated and how they reflect upon their racial / ethnic status. Although some change is occurring regarding the preferred body image, our society still values images of women who are white—and blond in particular—and who have European features. Research shows that women who have dark skin, especially with indigenous features, face the worst treatment from society at large. Individuals within Chicano communities may reflect this devaluation, or even internalize it, so that physical features are often noted and evaluated: Skin color in particular is commented on, with *las güeras* (light-skinned ones) being appreciated and *las prietas* (dark-skinned ones) being admonished and devalued. In contrast to white ethnic women, it is impossible for most Mexican women to "blend in," to opt out of their racial/ethnic status and pass for white. Thus we see examples all the time of U.S. citizens being mistaken for undocumented immigrants and being deported because of the color of their skin.

Sexuality is also a significant demarcation of social location. Whether women establish lesbian, heterosexual, or bisexual relationships is central to their identity and experience. Within our heterosexist society, Chicana lesbians and bisexuals, particularly those of working-class origin, face extreme marginalization from both the dominant and Chicano society. Paraphrasing Cherríe Moraga, being queer and of color is "as rude as women can get."[10] Sexuality, then, forms the basis of, and identity in which, community building is necessary against physical assaults and for survival. Sexual preference has generated political disagreements and conflict among lesbians, bisexual, and heterosexual Chicanas, and some lesbians are creating what Emma Perez calls a lesbian "uninvited discourse" with a separate "lengua y sitio" (language and space.)[11]

These aspects of social location—class, gender, race/ethnicity, and sexual preference— all are indications of social inequality and reflect power relations in which Chicanas are often relatively powerless. Yet specifying women's social locations also means taking into consideration various ethnic or cultural attributes that create "borders" over which women cross in their daily lives. These attributes include nativity—whether Chicanas were born in the United States (and, if so, what generation) or in Mexico, and whether immigrants arrived as children and were socialized in the United States or received their education, socialization, and sense of identity in rural villages or urban centers of Mexico. Language use is critical and closely related to nativity. If Chicanas are born in the United States, particularly if they are reared in integrated communities, they are more likely to speak mainly English and without a Spanish accent, whereas Chicanas reared in Mexico or in segregated barrios in the United States are likely to be bilingual, predominantly Spanish speakers, or have Spanish heavy accents when speaking English. Whether one was reared in the barrios or grew up isolated from other Chicanos has great implications for cultural knowledge and sense of self. Religion is also significant. The majority of Chicanas come from a Roman Catholic heritage in which religious rituals and practices are often the center of women's social activities and are forms of social control of women's sexuality. Finally, women's sexuality, in particular, but other activities as well are controlled through Chicano cultural forms involving the polar opposites of macho male, aggressive sexual license and passive female chastity.

To understand how culture has placed constraints on the experiences of Chicanas, we need to distinguish between "traditional culture"—cultural knowledge as ideology—and culture in process. Cultural ideologies, as Rosaldo points out, are often forms of social control that seem most brittle when under attack.[12] When "culture" is evoked to remind recalcitrant women to be proprietous (for example, when working mothers are reminded of the importance of familism), Chicanos are orchestrating cultural ideology as cultural determinism.[13]

In contrast to a view of culture as determinant, Chicana and Chicano scholars have formulated a view of culture that is much more fluid and is embedded in an American historical context in which differential power relations between classes, Anglos and Chicanos, men and women, or heterosexuals and homosexuals are taken into consideration. This perspective also critiques the ways in which Chicano culture is exoticized and devalued. Further, this view sees culture as socially constructed by actors influenced by both "traditional" cultural norms and the audience of cultural "performances," so that culture is always interactive within particular situations.[14] This perspective focuses on cultural variation and the nuances of culture in process, particularly in daily life by "ordinary" Chicanas. In other words, I'm calling for a perspective that sees the dialectics of how the social structure and culture provide a context for the ways that Chicanas construct their identities. The implications are that ethnographic work should focus on particular subcultural groups and communities among Chicanos. Some of the more recent Chicano ethnographic work has had this focus—on lesbians and gay Chicanos who contest heterosexist traditions, on the elderly of northern New Mexican villages who construct oppositional discourse, on gangs and low-riders in southern California who form alternative support systems, on high school youth in south Texas who resist authority, on south Texas men who resist ethnographic characterizations, or on middle-aged women workers in northern California who consider alternative work and family-based culture.[15] Comparisons between Chicanos within these different social locations reveal important variations of experience. More ethnographies of various communities of Chicanas would heighten our sense of diversity.

I am suggesting that in addition to class, race, and sexual preference, "traditional" culture provides a context in which Chicanas are in positions or situations in relation to other women and men that allow greater or lesser autonomy. Further, these women strategize within this context to construct a sense of self and try to live their lives in opposition to these constraints. Although the limitations on Chicanas' lives can delineate "borders" by which women construct a sense of self in their lives, I am emphasizing that there are "locations" created by the intersection of class, race, gender, sexuality, and culture and that women sometimes cannot "cross" some "borders" that constrain their lives.

I believe that we should construct feminist studies that reflect the myriad of social locations among Chicanas, which specify relationships—both personal and structural—that sustain them. I believe that this is the starting point for understanding the social and cultural symbolic representations and consciousness that women express through literature, art, and daily activity.

It might be helpful to use my own experience to illustrate how culture-region and culture in process is integral to social location: I have been repeatedly told, "You're so different from other Mexicans"—a puzzling, objectifying idea, especially to a child. I am fourth generation, born in the United States in a working-class, predominantly English-speaking family. My cultural heritage is from the northern New Mexico culture-region, my family descended from peasant farmers who migrated from Tierra Amarilla, New Mexico, to Trujillo Creek in southern Colorado. My grandparents were coal miners and farmers. I remember that when I was a child my grandmother used to say we were "Spanish American" (often used synonymously with "Hispano"), the term used in the northern New Mexico culture-region to distinguish Mexican Americans from Indians, whites, and Mexicans from Mexico. Although my parents' native language was Spanish, they were punished for speaking Spanish in school, and we used English at home. (Some of us eventually took Spanish classes in an attempt to regain "our" language.) The Spanish language was all around us, but it was mainly the language of adult kin, who used it when speaking of things they wanted hidden from the children—unfortunately a common occurrence under conditions of language repression.

My father joined the air force to escape the racism and lack of economic opportunities in Laredo, Texas, on the border between the United States and Mexico. As an "air force brat" I was born on an air base in Tampa, Florida. My grandmother's home in Colorado Springs was our home base, but we made annual forays to rural Maine and rural South Dakota (twice) before my family migrated to southern California. We were often one of few Mexican families on the base, so I never lived in barrios. With many experiences of racism (particularly in schools, where I heard the refrain that I was so different from other Mexicans), I grew up feeling marginalized from whites and isolated from other Chicanos. Because we moved so much, I was often the new kid in school, and teachers frequently assumed that because I was Mexican I would be a Spanish speaker and would not perform well. My schooling, then, was in contesting the racist and sexist assumptions about my abilities, and I became a "scholarship girl."[16] I was often puzzled at being called Mexican. Although my racial features are clearly Mexican, I had never been to Mexico, nor did I know any relatives who were living there. Yet my grandmother and mother are staunch Catholics, and part of my sense of being Chicana comes from chafing from the misogyny of Catholic rituals and doctrine.

I am part of the limited class mobility occurring among Chicanos: I am of the first generation that received a higher education, the only Ph.D. among my large extended family, the only writer. I was fortunate to take part in the Chicano movement and Chicana movement, which shaped my consciousness and identity as a Chicana feminist. My social location, then, of working-class, English speaking Hispana Catholic background, clearly demarcates my experiences from those of other Chicanas. My experiences in constructing culture in process (feminist parenting, for example) embody the contradictions generated from my now privileged social location.

CHANGING DEMOGRAPHY

If anything, the heterogeneity of Chicanas will only increase in the future. Stepped-up migration from Mexico and some class mobility mean that the class polarization will become more pronounced. More Chicanas are entering higher education and professional occupations; others—women from rural Central American and Latin American countries are entering this country, often without documentation, at the bottom margins of the social structure. In California, but also in other settlement areas like Washington, Miami, and New York, Chicano communities are becoming global cities with polyglot organizations and neighborhoods.

CONCLUSION

Let me conclude by returning to the notion of identity, which captures the heart of the problematic of understanding Chicanas. I have suggested that we pay attention to the history of particular groups of Chicanas, where they settled or migrated to, how their communities were formed, how there are key, structurally based differences among Chicanas. For each woman, this means understanding her social location structurally and culturally. Instead of lumping all Chicanas together into separate sections of a course on women, we might better ask, what purpose does it serve to categorize all of these very disparate groups? Whose interests get served? When is it appropriate to think of these women as Chicanas, and when it is better to specify a particular regional form of identity?

Regarding curriculum development, I have found that "social location" is helpful for white and other students as well. In trying to develop feminist curriculum to include Chicanas, we might think about when it is useful to make comparisons between women with different cultural backgrounds but in similar social locations. In a course on women and work, for example, we might contrast Chicana and Jewish working-class factory workers. At other times, our strategy might be to contrast women from very different social locations: the poetry and novels of Alice Walker and Ana Castillo, both women who searched for their historic roots. More importantly, what identity does a particular Chicana claim, and why? It is obvious that we have much work before us in understanding diversity among all women and in struggling to develop solidarity with women of different social locations. Yet it is exciting to envision a feminist studies in which women "on the margins" are demanding that the "center" be reconstituted.

NOTES

This is a revised version of "Divergent Histories, Common Bonds: Chicanas/Latinas in the United States," keynote talk presented at the Instituto de las Mujeres, Project on Incorporating Feminist Scholarship Concerning Gender and Cultural Diversity into the Curriculum, Metropolitan State University, St. Paul, MN, 19 February 1990. Thanks to Louise Lamphere and the anonymous reviewers of *Frontiers* for their helpful comments.

1. For a discussion of "social location" that compares ethnographic data from two research sites, see my article: "Mujeres in Factories: Race and Class Perspectives on Women, Work and Family," in Leonardo, *Gender at the Crossroads of Knowledge.*

2. Renato Rosaldo, *Culture and Truth: The Remaking of Social Analysis* (Boston: Beacon Press, 1989).

3. Gloria Anzaldúa, *Borderlands/La Frontera: The New Mestiza* (San Francisco: Spinsters/aunt lute foundation, 1987).

4. For a critique of this view, see Leonarda Ybarra, "Empirical and Theoretical Developments in Studies of the Chicano Family," in *The State of Chicano Research on Family, Labor and Migration: Proceedings of the First Stanford Symposium on Chicano Research and Public Policy,* eds. Armando Valdéz, Albert Camarillo, and Tomas Almaguer (Stanford: Stanford Center for Chicano Research, 1983).

5. See Tomas Almaguer, *Contested Racial Frontier: Mexicans, Indians and Asians in Anglo California, 1848-1903* (Berkeley: University of California Press, forthcoming).

6. Mario Barrera, *Race and Class in the Southwest: A Theory of Racial Inequality* (Notre Dame: University of Notre Dame Press, 1979); Albert Camarillo, *Chicanos in a Changing Society* (Cambridge: Harvard University Press, 1979).

7. Wayne A. Cornelius, Richard Mines, Leo R. Chavez, and Jorge G. Castro, *Mexican Immigrants in Southern California: A Summary of Current Knowledge* (San Diego: University of California, Center for U.S.-Mexican Studies, Research Report Series 40, 1982).

8. Ernesto Galarza sketches out some Chicano culture-regions. See "Mexicans in the Southwest: A Culture in Process," in *Plural Society in the Southwest,* eds. Edward H. Spicer and Raymond H. Thompson (New York: Interbook, 1972).

9. For literature on the process of ethnic identification for Chicanos as a whole, see: John A. García. "Yo So Mexicano . . . : Self-Identity and Sociodemographic Correlates," *Social Science Quarterly* 62 (1, 1981), 88-98; Ramón Gutierrez, "Unraveling America's Hispanic Past: Internal Stratification and Class Boundaries," in *Proceedings of the AU-UC Invitational Conference on the Comparative Study of Race, Ethnicity, Gender and Class,* ed. Sucheng Chan (Santa Cruz: University of California, 1987); Susan E. Keefe and Amado M.

Padilla, *Chicano Ethnicity* (Albuquerque: University of New Mexico Press, 1987); José E. Limon, "The Folk Performance of Chicano and the Cultural Limits of Political Ideology," in *"And Other Neighborly Names": Social Process and Cultural Image in Texas Folklore,* eds. Richard Bauman and Roger D. Abrahams (Austin: University of Texas Press, 1981); Joseph V. Metzgar, "The Ethnic Sensitivity of Spanish New Mexicans: A Survey and Analysis," *New Mexico Historical Review* 49 (1, 1974), 49-73. For discussion of how race/ethnicity and gender are intertwined in ethnic identification, see Anzaldúa, *Borderlands/La Frontera*; Cherríe Moraga, *Loving in the War Years, lo que nunca pasó por sus labios* (Boston: South End Press, 1983); Maxine Baca Zinn, "Gender and Ethnic Identity Among Chicanas," *Frontiers* 5 (2, Summer 1981), 18-24.

10. Moraga, *Loving in the War Years.*

11. Emma Perez, "Speaking from the Margin: Uninvited Discourse on Sexuality and Power," in Beatriz Pesquera and Adela De La Torre, eds., *Building with Our Hands: Issues in Chicana Studies* (Berkeley: University of California Press, forthcoming). For other works on Chicana/Latina lesbians, see Norma Alarcón, Ana Castillo, and Cherríe Moraga, eds., *The Sexuality of Latinas,* special issue of *Third Woman* (1989); Juanita Ramos, ed., *Compañeras: Latina Lesbians (An Anthology)* (New York: Latina Lesbian History Project, 1987).

12. Rosaldo, *Culture and Truth.*

13. Beatriz Pesquera, "Work and Family: A Comparative Analysis of Professional, Clerical and Blue-Collar Chicana Workers" (Ph.D. dissertation, University of California, Berkeley, 1986).

14. Américo Paredes, "On Ethnographic Work Among Minority Groups: A Folklorist's Perspective," *New Scholar* 6 (1/2, 1977), 1-32.

15. Tomas Almaguer, "The Cartography of Homosexual Desire and Identity Among Chicano Men," *Differences: A Journal of Feminist Cultural Studies* 3 (Summer 1991); Charles L. Briggs, *Competence in Performance: The Creativity of Tradition in Mexicano Verbal Art* (Philadelphia: University of Pennsylvania Press, 1988); Douglas E. Foley, *Learning Capitalist Culture, Deep in the Heart of Tejas* (Philadelphia: University of Pennsylvania Press, 1990); José Limon, "Carne, Carnales, and the Carnivalesque: Bakhtinian Batos, Disorder and Narrative Discourses," *American Ethnologist* (August 1989); Diego Vigil, *Barrio Gangs: Street Life and Identity in Southern California* (Austin: University of Texas Press, 1988); Patricia Zavella, *Women's Work and Chicano Families: Cannery Workers of the Santa Clara Valley* (Ithaca: Cornell University Press, 1987).

16. Gloria Cuadráz, "The Social Construction of Chicana 'Scholarship Girls' and Their Paths to Higher Education," 1991.

11 ❧

LIFE AS THE MAID'S DAUGHTER: AN EXPLORATION OF THE EVERYDAY BOUNDARIES OF RACE, CLASS, AND GENDER

Mary Romero

INTRODUCTION

THE CALL FOR INCLUSION across disciplines has arrived at a time when the United States is reassessing the gains in the area of race relations, particularly in the face of continued segregation in our schools, communities, churches, and homes. Distinct boundaries dividing men and women of different racial, ethnic, and class backgrounds are exemplified in the data on salary and educational levels, housing markets, rates of unemployment and underemployment, and health care. Differences point to the existing gaps between the social, economic, and political worlds people live in and seriously challenge the assumptions that researchers and politicians have made about society based on groups depicted as "mainstream." While the realities of the persons depicted as mainstream are affirmed and enhanced by a wide range of institutional mechanisms, they are not good informants about the social structure. As members of the status quo, their knowledge is embedded in ideological systems that justify their superior social positions, and, consequently, their experiences are quite limited. Understanding the everyday realities of race, class, and gender requires uncovering the knowledge gained from individuals negotiating between social boundaries and those who are considered "outsiders." Persons of color who move from one social setting dominated by the white middle class to one dominated by an ethnic working class are aware of the different standards of behavior governing each domain.

My current research attempts to expand the sociological understanding of the dynamics of race, class, and gender in the everyday routines of family life and reproductive labor. Again I am lured to the unique setting presented by domestic service; this time, however, my focus is shifted, and I turn to the realities experienced by the children of private household workers. This focus is not entirely voluntary. While presenting my research on Chicana private household workers, I was approached repeatedly by Latina/os and African Americans who wanted to share their knowledge about domestic service—knowledge they obtained as the daughters and sons of household workers. Listening to their accounts about their mothers' employment presents another reality to understanding paid and unpaid reproductive labor and the way in which persons of color are socialized into a class-based, gendered, racist social structure. The following discussion explores issues of stratification in everyday life by analyzing the life story of a maid's daughter. This life story illustrates the potential of the standpoint of the maid's daughter for generating knowledge about race, class, and gender. It is, at the same time, exemplary of the challenge scholarship grounded in the experience of feminist women of color has posed to women's studies scholarship that has presumed to be "universal."

SOCIAL BOUNDARIES PRESENTED IN THE LIFE STORY

The first interview with Teresa,[1] the daughter of a live-in maid, eventually led to a life history project. I am intrigued by Teresa's experiences with her mother's white, upper-middle-class employers while maintaining close ties to her relatives in Juarez, Mexico, and Mexican friends in Los Angeles. While some may view Teresa's life as a freak accident, living a life of "rags to riches," and certainly not a common Chicana/o experience, her story represents a microcosm of power relationships in the larger society. Life as the maid's daughter in an upper-middle-class neighborhood exemplifies many aspects of the Chicano/Mexicano experience as "racial ethnics" in the United States, whereby the boundaries of inclusion and exclusion are constantly changing as we move from one social setting and one social role to another.

Teresa's narrative contains descriptive accounts of negotiating boundaries in the employers' homes and in their community. As the maid's daughter, the old adage "Just like one of the family" is a reality, and Teresa has to learn when she must act like the employer's child and when she must assume the appropriate behavior as the maid's daughter. She has to recognize all the social cues and interpret social settings correctly—when to expect the same rights and privileges as the employer's children and when to fulfill the expectations and obligations as the maid's daughter. Unlike the employers' families, Teresa and her mother rely on different ways of obtaining knowledge. The taken-for-granted reality of the employers' families do not contain conscious experiences of negotiating race and class status, particularly not in the intimate setting of the home. Teresa's status is constantly changing in response to the wide range of social settings she encounters—from employers' dinner parties with movie stars and corporate executives to Sunday dinners with Mexican garment workers in Los Angeles and factory workers in El Paso. Since Teresa remains bilingual and bicultural throughout her life, her story reflects the constant struggle and resistance to maintain her Mexican identity, claiming a reality that is neither rewarded nor acknowledged as valid.

Teresa's account of her life as the maid's daughter is symbolic of the way that racial ethnics participate in the United States; sometimes we are included and other times excluded or ignored. Teresa's story captures the reality of social stratification in the United States, that is, a racist, sexist, and class-structured society upheld by an ideology of equality. I will analyze the experiences of the maid's daughter in an upper-middle-class neighborhood in Los Angeles to investigate the ways that boundaries of race, class, and gender are maintained or diffused in everyday life. I have selected various excerpts from the transcripts that illustrate how knowledge about a class-based and gendered, racist social order is learned, the type of information that is conveyed, and how the boundaries between systems of domination impact everyday life. I begin with a brief history of Teresa and her mother, Carmen.

LEARNING SOCIAL BOUNDARIES:
BACKGROUND

Teresa's mother was born in Piedras Negras, a small town in Aguas Calientes in Mexico. After her father was seriously injured in a railroad accident, the family moved to a small town outside Ciudad Juarez. Teresa's mother soon became involved in a variety of activities to earn money. She sold food and trinkets at the railroad station and during train stops boarded the trains seeking customers. By the time she was fifteen she moved to Juarez and took a job as a domestic, making about eight dollars a week. She soon crossed the border and began working for Anglo families in the country club area in El Paso. Like other domestics in El Paso, Teresa's mother returned to Mexico on weekends and helped support her mother and sisters. In her late twenties she joined several of her friends in their search for better-paying jobs in Los Angeles. The women immediately found jobs in the garment industry. Yet, after six months in the sweatshops, Teresa's mother went to an agency in search of domestic work. She was placed in a very exclusive Los Angeles neighborhood. Several years later Teresa was born. Her friends took care of the baby while Carmen continued working; child care became a burden, however, and she eventually returned to Mexico. At the age of thirty-six Teresa's mother returned to Mexico with her newborn baby. Leaving Teresa with her grandmother and aunts, her mother sought work in the country club area. Three years later Teresa and her mother returned to Los Angeles.

Over the next fifteen years Teresa lived with her mother in the employer's (Smith) home, usually the two sharing the maid's room located off the kitchen. From the age of three until Teresa started school, she accompanied her mother to work. She continued to live in the Smiths' home until she left for college. All of Teresa's live-in years were spent in one employer's household. The Smiths were unable to afford a full-time maid, however, so Teresa's mother began doing day work throughout the neighborhood. After school Teresa went to whatever house her mother was cleaning and waited until her mother finished working, around 4 or 6 P.M., and then returned to the Smiths' home with her mother. Many prominent families in the neighborhood knew Teresa as the maid's daughter and treated her accordingly. While Teresa wanted the relationship with the employers to cease when she went to college and left the neighborhood, her mother continued to work as a live-in maid with no residence other than the room in the employer's home; consequently, Teresa's social status as the maid's daughter continued.

ENTRANCE INTO THE EMPLOYERS' WORLD

Having spent her first three years in a female-dominated and monolingual, Spanish-speaking household in Juarez and in a Mexican immigrant community in Los Angeles, Teresa had a great deal to learn about the foreign environment presented by her mother's working conditions as a live-in maid. As a pre-schooler, Teresa began to learn that her social status reflected her mother's social position. In Mexico her mother was the primary wage earner for her grandmother and aunts. In this Mexican household dominated by women, Teresa received special attention and privileges as Carmen's daughter. Teresa recalled very vivid memories about entering the employers' world and being forced to learn an entirely new set of rules and beliefs of a Euro-American social order that consisted of a white, monolingual, male-dominated, and upper-middle-class family life. Teresa's account of her early years in the employers' homes is clearly from the perspective of the maid's daughter. She was an outsider and had to learn the appropriate behavior for each setting.

Rules were a major theme in Teresa's recollections of growing up in the employers' homes. She was very much aware of different rules operating in each home and of the need to act accordingly. In one of her mother's work sites, she was expected to play with the employer's children, in another she was allowed to play with their toys in specific areas of the house, and in other workplaces she sat quietly and was not allowed to touch the things around her. From the beginning she was socialized by the employers and their children, who emphasized conformity and change to their culture. The employers did not make any attempt to create a bicultural or multicultural environment in their homes or community. Teresa was expected to conform to their linguistic norms and acquiesce to becoming "the other"—the little Spanish-speaking Mexican girl among the English-speaking white children.

In the following excerpt Teresa describes her first encounter with the boundaries she confronted in the employers' homes. The excerpt is typical of her observances and recollections about her daily life, in which she is constantly assessing the practices and routines and reading signs in order to determine her position in each social setting and, thus, select the appropriate behavior. While the demands to conform and change were repeated throughout her experiences, Teresa did not embrace the opportunity to assimilate. Her resistance and struggle against assimilation is evident throughout her account, as indicated by her attempt to leave the employer's home and her refusal to speak English:

> I started to realize that every day I went to somebody else's house. Everybody's house had different rules.... My mother says that she constantly had to watch me, because she tried to get me to sit still and I'd be really depressed and I cried or I wanted to go see things, and my mother was afraid I was going to break something and she told me not to touch anything. The kids wanted to play with me. To them, I was a novelty and they wanted to play with the little Mexican girl... .

> I think I just had an attitude problem as I describe it now. I didn't want to play with them, they were different. My mother would tell me to go play with them, and in a little while later I'd come back and say: "Mama no me quieren aguntar"—obviously it was the communication problem. We couldn't communicate. I got really mad one day at these girls, because "no me quieran aguntar," and they did not understand what I was trying to say. They couldn't, we couldn't play, so I decided that I was going to go home, and that I didn't like this anymore. So I just opened the door and I walked out. I went around the block and I was going to walk home, to the apartment where we lived. I went out of the house, and walked around and went the opposite direction around the block. The little girls came to my mom and said: "Carmen your little daughter she left!" So my mom dropped everything and was hysterical and one of the older daughters drove my mom around and she found me on the corner. My mom was crying and crying, upset, and she asked me where I was going and I said: "Well, I was going to go home, porque no me quieran aguntar," and I didn't want to be there anymore, and I was gonna walk home. So my mother had to really keep an eye on me.

> I would go to the Jones' [employers], and they had kids, and I would just mostly sit and play with their toys, but I wouldn't try to interact with them. Then they tried to teach me English. I really resented that. They had an aquarium and fishes and they would say: "Teresa, can you say Fiishh?" and I would just glare

at them, just really upset. Then I would say "Fish, no, es pescado." You know, like trying to change me, and I did not want to speak their language, or play with their kids, or do anything with them. At the Smiths they tried to teach me English. There were different rules there. I couldn't touch anything. The first things I learned were "No touch, no touch," and "Don't do this, don't do that."

At different houses, I started picking up different things. I remember that my mother used to also work for a Jewish family, when I was about five, the Altman's. We had to walk to their house. Things were different at the Altman's. At the Altman's they were really nice to me. They had this little metal stove that they let me play with. I would play with that. That was like the one thing I could play with, in the house. I immediately—I'd get there and sit down in my designated area that I could be in, and I'd play there. Sometimes, Ms. Altman would take me to the park and I'd play there. She would try to talk to me. Sometimes I would talk and sometimes I would just sit there.

Teresa's account of going to work with her mother as a toddler was not a story of a child running freely and exploring the world around her; instead, her story was shaped by the need to learn the rules set by white, monolingual, English-speaking adults and children. The emphasis in her socialization within employers' homes was quite different than that given to the employers' male children; rather than advocating independence, individuality, and adventure, Teresa was socialized to conform to female sex roles, restricting her movement and playing with gendered toys. Learning the restrictions that limit her behavior— "No touch. Don't do this"—served to educate Teresa about her social status in the employers' homes. She was clearly different form the other children, "a novelty," and was bound by rules regulating her use of social space and linguistic behavior. Teresa's resistance against changing her language points to the strong self-esteem and pride in her culture and Mexican identity that she obtained from her experience in a Mexican household. Teresa's early memories were dominated by pressure to assimilate and to restrain her movement and activity to fit into a white, male-dominated, upper-middle-class household.

The context in which Teresa learned English was very significant in acquiring knowledge about the social order. English was introduced into her life as a means of control and to restrict her movement within employers' homes. The employers' children were involved in teaching Teresa English, and they exerted pressure that she conform to the linguistic norms governing their households. Teresa was not praised or rewarded for her ability to speak Spanish, and her racial and cultural differences were only perceived positively when they served a function for the employer's family, such as a curiosity, entertainment, or a cross-cultural experience. While her mother continued to talk to Teresa in Spanish when they were alone, Carmen was not able to defend her daughter's right to decide which language to speak in the presence of the employers' families. Furthermore, Teresa observed her mother serving and waiting on the employers' families, taking orders, and being treated in a familiar manner. While Teresa referred to the employers formally, by their last names, the employers' children called Teresa's mother by her first name. The circumstances created an environment whereby all monolingual, Spanish-speaking women, including her mother, were in powerless positions. The experiences provided Teresa with knowledge about social stratification—that is, the negative value placed on the Spanish language and Mexican culture—as well as about the social status of Spanish-speaking Mexican immigrant women.

ONE OF THE FAMILY

As Teresa got older, the boundaries between insider and outsider became more complicated, as employers referred to her and Carmen as "one of the family." Entering into an employer's world as the maid's daughter, Teresa was not only subjected to the rules of an outsider but also had to recognize when the rules changed, making her momentarily an insider. While the boundaries dictating Carmen's work became blurred between the obligations of an employee and that of a friend or family member, Teresa was forced into situations in which she was expected to be just like one of the employer's children, and yet she remained the maid's daughter.

The expectations of responsibility and obligation created by the pseudofamily relationships were demonstrated in the incidents related to Mr. and Mrs. Smith's decision to pay Teresa's school tuition rather than pay her mother a salary. While the arrangement served to decommercialize the Smith's relationship with Carmen and allowed her not to pay taxes on the income, the arrangement also created the appearance that the Smiths, rather than Teresa's mother, were paying her tuition, as they did their own children. Teresa attributed the arrangement to blurring the boundaries between the employer and employee families. The employer assumed the right to act on Carmen's behalf and made decisions about Teresa's education. Teresa recalled, for instance, that the decision to take Spanish rather than French class was a decision the employer made:

> I really wanted to learn French. I was really upset that the Smiths had enrolled me in the Spanish course. I said, "How come I have to take Spanish? I already know Spanish." "No, we want you to speak perfect Spanish, we want your Spanish to be like—so you can talk to the queen of Spain." It took me a long time to get over it.

While Teresa asked her mother to support her decision to take French, Carmen submitted to the employer's decision. If Carmen had paid the tuition directly out of her salary, the employer's paternalistic relationship to the worker and her daughter and their power to make parental decisions for Carmen may have been reduced. Instead, the arrangement created a situation in which Mr. and Mrs. Smith could claim a right to make decisions about Teresa's education. Similar paternalistic actions in other employer households shaped their relationship to Teresa and her mother, blurring the boundaries between Teresa and Carmen as a family unit and as separate from the employers' families.

While boundaries between insider and outsider were frequently ignored, Teresa never lost sight of the fact that her mother was the maid and spent long hours cleaning, picking up, and caring for the employers and their families. Unlike the Smith family, Teresa was constantly drawing the distinction between the household tasks Carmen did as her mother and the tasks completed as the maid. Furthermore, she understood that the additional demands on an employer's family made resulted in less time she had to spend with her mother. Teresa forcefully expressed her resentment over an employer's requests for Carmen to work overtime, including weekends and holidays. She wanted her mother to have time and energy to do things with her, as a family, such as visiting friends and relatives in the Mexican barrio. No doubt she also wanted to receive some of the caring and nurturing she observed her mother giving to the employer's children. She was also aware of the physical demands of housecleaning and was concerned about her mother's health.

Living under conditions established by the employers made Teresa and her mother's efforts to maintain a distinction between their family life and an employer's family very difficult. Analyzing incidents in which the boundaries between the worker's family and employer's family were blurred highlights the issues that complicate the mother-daughter relationship. Teresa's account of her mother's hospitalization was the first of numerous conflicts between the two that stemmed form the live-in situation and their relationships with the employer's family. The following excerpt demonstrates the difficulty in interacting as a family unit and the degree of influence and power employers exerted over their daily lives:

> When I was about ten my mother got real sick. That summer, instead of sleeping downstairs in my mother's room when my mother wasn't there, one of the kids was gone away to college, so it was just Rosalyn, David and myself that were home. The other two were gone, so I was gonna sleep upstairs in one of the rooms. I was around eight or nine, ten I guess. I lived in the back room. It was a really neat room because Rosalyn was allowed to paint it. She got her friend who was real good, painted a big tree and clouds and all this stuff on the walls. So I really loved it and I had my own room. I was with the Smiths all the time, as my parents, for about two months. My mother was in the hospital for about a month. Then when she came home, she really couldn't do anything. We would all have dinner, the Smiths were really, really supportive. I went to summer school and I took math and English and stuff like that. I was in this drama class and I did drama and I got to do the leading role. Everybody really liked me and Ms. Smith would come and see my play. So things started to change when I got a lot closer to them and I was with them alone. I would go see my mother everyday, and my cousin was there. I think that my cousin kind of resented all the time that the Smiths spent with me. I think my mother was really afraid that now that she wasn't there that they were going to steal me from her. I went to see her, but I could only stay a couple of hours and it was really weird. I didn't like seeing my mother in pain and she was in a lot of pain. I remember before she came home the Smiths said that they thought it would be a really good idea if I stayed upstairs and I had my own room now that my mother was going to be sick and I couldn't sleep in the same bed 'cause I might hurt her. It was important for my mother to be alone. And how did I feel about that? I was really excited about that [having her own room]—you know. They said, "Your mom she is probably not going to like it and she might get upset about it, but I think that we can convince her that it is ok." When my mom came home, she understood that she couldn't be touched and that she had to be really careful, but she wanted it [having her own room] to be temporary. Then my mother was really upset. She got into it with them and said, "No, I don't want it that way." She would tell me, "No, I want you to be down here. ¿Qué crees que eres hija de ellos? You're gonna be with me all the time, you can't do that." So I would tell Ms. Smith. She would ask me when we would go to the market together, "How does your mom seem, what does she feel, what does she say?" She would get me to relay that. I would say, "I think my mom is really upset about me moving upstairs. She doesn't like it and she

just says no." I wouldn't tell her everything. They would talk to her and final-ly they convinced her, but my mom really, really resented it and was really angry about it. She was just generally afraid. All these times that my mother wasn't there, things happened and they would take me places with them, go out to dinner with them and their friends. So that was a real big change, in that I slept upstairs and had different rules. Everything changed. I was more inde-pendent. I did my own homework; they would open the back door and yell that dinner was ready—you know. Things were just real different.

The account illustrates how assuming the role of insider was an illusion because neither the worker's daughter nor the worker ever became a member of the white, middle-class family. Teresa was only allowed to move out of the maid's quarter, where she shared a bed with her mother, when two of the employer's children were leaving home, vacating two bedrooms. This was not the first time that "space" determined whether Teresa was includ-ed in the employer's family activities. Her description of Thanksgiving dinner illustrates that she did not decide when to be included but, rather, the decision was based on the avail-able space at the table:

I never wanted to eat with them, I wanted to eat with my mom. Like Thanksgiving, it was always an awkward situation, because I never knew, up until dinner time, where I was going to sit, every single time. It depended on how many guests they had, and how much room there was at the table. Sometimes, when they invited all their friends, the Carters and the Richmans, who had kids, the adults would all eat dinner in one room and then the kids would have dinner in another room. Then I could go eat dinner with the kids or sometimes I'd eat with my mom in the kitchen. It really depended.

Since Teresa preferred to eat with her mother, the inclusion was burdensome and unwant-ed. In the case of moving upstairs, however, Teresa wanted to have her "own" bedroom. The conflict arising from Teresa's move upstairs points to the way in which the employer's actions threatened the bonds between mother and daughter.

Teresa and Carmen did not experience the boundaries of insider and outsider in the same way. Teresa was in a position to assume a more active family role when employers' made certain requests. Unlike her mother, she was not an employee and was not expected to clean and serve the employer. Carmen's responsibility for the housework never ceased, however, regardless of the emotional ties existing between employee and employers. She and her employers understood that, whatever family activity she might be participating in, if the situation called for someone to clean, pick up, or serve, that was Carmen's job. When the Smiths requested Teresa to sit at the dinner table with the family, they placed Teresa in a different class position than her mother, who was now expected to serve her daughter alongside her employer. Moving Teresa upstairs in a bedroom alongside the employer and their children was bound to drive a wedge between Teresa and Carmen. There is a long his-tory of spatial deference in domestic service, including separate entrances, staircases, and eating and sleeping arrangements. Carmen's room reflected her position in the household. As the maid's quarter, the room was separated from the rest of the bedrooms and was locat-ed near the maid's central work area, the kitchen. The room was obviously not large enough for two beds because Carmen and Teresa shared a bed. Once Teresa was moved upstairs, she no longer shared the same social space in the employer's home as her mother. Weakening the bonds between the maid and her daughter permitted the employers to broaden their range of relationships and interaction with Teresa.

Carmen's feelings of betrayal and loss underline how threatening the employers' actions were. She understood that the employers were in a position to buy her child's love. They had already attempted to socialize Teresa into Euro-American ideals by planning Teresa's education and deciding what courses she would take. Guided by the importance they placed on European culture, the employers defined the Mexican Spanish spoken by Teresa and her mother as inadequate and classified Castillan Spanish as "proper" Spanish. As a Mexican immigrant woman working as a live-in maid, Carmen was able to experience certain middle-class privileges, but her only access to these privileges was through her relationship with employers. Therefore, without the employers' assistance, she did not have the necessary connections to enroll Teresa in private schools or provide her with upper-middle-class experiences to help her develop the skills needed to survive in elite schools. Carmen only gained these privileges for her daughter at a price; she relinquished many of her parental rights to her employers. To a large degree the Smiths determined Carmen's role as a parent, and the other employers restricted the time she had to attend school functions and the amount of energy left at the end of the day to mother her own child.

Carmen pointed to the myth of "being like one of the family" in her comment, "¿Qué crees que eres hija de ellos? You're gonna be with me all the time, you can't do that." The statement underlines the fact that the bond between mother and daughter is for life, whereas the pseudofamily relationship with employers is temporary and conditional. Carmen wanted her daughter to understand that taking on the role of being one of the employer's family did not relinquish her from the responsibility of fulfilling her "real" family obligations. The resentment Teresa felt from her cousin who was keeping vigil at his aunt's hospital bed indicated that she had not been a dutiful daughter. The outside pressure from an employer did not remove her own family obligations and responsibilities. Teresa's relatives expected a daughter to be at her mother's side providing any assistance possible as a caretaker, even if it was limited to companionship. The employer determined Teresa's activity, however, and shaped her behavior into that of a middle-class child; consequently, she was kept away from the hospital and protected from the realities of her mother's illness. Furthermore, she was submerged into the employer's world, dining at the country club and interacting with their friends.

Her mother's accusation that Teresa wanted to be the Smiths' daughter signifies the feelings of betrayal or loss and the degree to which Carmen was threatened by the employer's power and authority. Yet Teresa also felt betrayal and loss and viewed herself in competition with the employers for her mother's time, attention, and love. In this excerpt Teresa accuses her mother of wanting to be part of employers' families and community:

> I couldn't understand it—you know—until I was about eighteen and then I said, "It is your fault. If I treat the Smiths differently, it is your fault. You chose to have me live in this situation. It was your decision to let me have two parents, and for me to balance things off, so you can't tell me that I said this. You are the one who wanted this." When I was about eighteen we got into a huge fight on Christmas. I hated the holidays because I hated spending them with the Smiths. My mother always worked. She worked on every holiday. She loved to work on the holidays! She would look forward to working. My mother just worked all the

time! I think that part of it was that she wanted to have power and control over this community, and she wanted the network, and she wanted to go to different people's houses.

As employers, Mr. and Mrs. Smith were able to exert an enormous amount of power over the relationship between Teresa and her mother. Carmen was employed in an occupation in which the way to improve working conditions, pay, and benefits was through the manipulation of personal relationships with employers. Carmen obviously tried to take advantage of her relationship with the Smiths in order to provide the best for her daughter. The more intimate and interpersonal the relationship, the more likely employers were to give gifts, do favors, and provide financial assistance. Although speaking in anger and filled with hurt, Teresa accused her mother of choosing to be with employers and their families rather than with her own daughter. Underneath Teresa's accusation was the understanding that the only influence and status her mother had as a domestic was gained through her personal relationships with employers. Although her mother had limited power in rejecting the Smiths' demands, Teresa held her responsible for giving them too much control. Teresa argued that the positive relationship with the Smiths was done out of obedience to her mother and denied any familial feelings toward the employers. The web between employee and employers' families affected both mother and daughter, who were unable to separate the boundaries of work and family.

MAINTAINING CULTURAL IDENTITY

A major theme in Teresa's narrative was her struggle to retain her Mexican culture and her political commitment to social justice. Rather than internalizing meaning attached to Euro-American practices and redefining Mexican culture and bilingualism as negative social traits, Teresa learned to be a competent social actor in both white, upper-middle-class environments and in working- and middle-class Chicano and *Mexicano* environments. To survive as a stranger in so many social settings, Teresa developed an acute skill for assessing the rules governing a particular social setting and acting accordingly. Her ability to be competent in diverse social settings was only possible, however, because her life was never completely submerged in the employers' world. While living and going to school with the employers' children, Teresa and her mother maintained another life—one that was guarded and protected against any employer intrusion. Their other life was Mexican, not white, was Spanish speaking, not English speaking, was female dominated rather than male dominated, and was poor and working-class, not upper-middle-class. During the week Teresa and her mother visited the other Mexican maids in the neighborhoods, on weekends they occasionally took a bus into the Mexican barrio in Los Angeles to have dinner with friends, and every summer they spent a month in Ciudad Juarez with their family. Without the constant emergence in the *Mexicano* community, Teresa's story would simply be another version of Richard Rodriguez's *Hunger of Memory*—a story of assimilation and rejection of bilingualism and biculturalism as a way of life.

Teresa's description of evening activity with the Mexican maids in the neighborhood provides insight into her daily socialization and explains how she learned to live in the employer's home without internalizing all their negative attitudes toward Mexican and working-class culture. Within the white, upper-class neighborhood in which they worked, the Mexican maids got together on a regular basis and cooked Mexican food, listened to

Mexican music, and gossiped in Spanish about their employers. Treated as invisible or as confidants, the maids were frequently exposed to the intimate details of their employers' marriages and family life. The Mexican maids voiced their disapproval of the lenient child-rearing practices and parental decisions, particularly surrounding drug usage and the importance of material possessions:

> Raquel was the only one [maid] in the neighborhood who had her own room and own tv set. So everybody would go over to Raquel's. . . . This was my mother's support system. After hours, they would go to different people's [maids'] rooms depending on what their rooms had. Some of them had kitchens and they would go and cook all together, or do things like play cards and talk all the time. I remember that in those situations they would sit, and my mother would talk about the Smiths, what they were like. When they were going to negotiate for raises, when they didn't like certain things. I would listen and hear all the different discussions about what was going on in different houses. And they would talk, also, about the family relationships. The way they interacted, the kids did this and that. At the time some of the kids were smoking pot and they would talk about who was smoking marijuana. How weird it was that the parents didn't care. They would talk about what they saw as being wrong. The marriage relationship, or how weird it was that they would go off to the beauty shop and spend all this money, go shopping and do all these weird things and the effect that it had on the kids.

The interaction among the maids points to the existence of another culture operating invisibly within a Euro-American and male-dominated community. The workers' support system did not include employers and addressed their concerns as mothers, immigrants, workers, and women. They created a Mexican-dominated domain for themselves. Here they ate Mexican food, spoke Spanish, listened to the Spanish radio station, and watched novellas on TV. Here Teresa was not a cultural artifact but, instead, a member of the Mexican community.

In exchanging gossip and voicing their opinions about the employers' lifestyles, the maids rejected many of the employers' priorities in life. Sharing stories about the employers' families allowed the Mexican immigrant women to be critical of white, upper-middle-class families and to affirm and enhance their own cultural practices and beliefs. The regular evening sessions with other working-class Mexican immigrant women were essential in preserving Teresa and her mother's cultural values and were an important agency of socialization for Teresa. For instance, the maids had a much higher regard for their duties and responsibilities as mothers than as wives or lovers. In comparison to their mistresses, they were not financially dependent on men, nor did they engage in the expensive and time-consuming activity of being an ideal wife, such as dieting, exercising, and maintaining a certain standard of beauty in their dress, makeup, and hairdos. Unlike the employers' daughters, who attended cotillion and were socialized to acquire success through marriage, Teresa was constantly pushed to succeed academically in order to pursue a career. The gender identity cultivated among the maids did not include dependence on men or the learned helplessness that was enforced in the employers' homes but, rather, promoted self-sufficiency. However, both white women employers and Mexican women employees were expected to be nurturing and caring. These traits were further reinforced when employers asked Teresa to babysit for their children or to provide them with companionship during their husbands' absences.

So, while Teresa observed her mother adapting to the employers' standards in her interaction with their children, she learned that her mother did not approve of their lifestyle and understood that she had another set of expectations to adhere to. Teresa attended the same schools as the employers' children, wore similar clothes, and conducted most of her social life within the same socioeconomic class, but she remained the maid's daughter—and learned the limitations of that position. Teresa watched her mother uphold higher standards for her and apply a different set of standards to the employers' children; most of the time, however, it appeared to Teresa as if they had no rules at all.

Sharing stories about the Smiths and other employers in a female, Mexican, and worker-dominated social setting provided Teresa with a clear image of the people she lived with as employers rather than as family members. Seeing the employers through the eyes of the employees forced Teresa to question their kindness and benevolence and to recognize their use of manipulation to obtain additional physical and emotional labor from the employees. She became aware of the workers' struggles and the long list of grievances, including no annual raises, no paid vacations, no social security or health benefits, little if any privacy, and sexual harassment. Teresa was also exposed to the price that working-class immigrant women employed as live-in maids paid in maintaining white, middle-class, patriarchal communities. Employers' careers and lifestyles, particularly the everyday rituals affirming male privilege, were made possible through the labor women provided for men's physical, social, and emotional needs. Female employers depended on the maid's labor to assist in the reproduction of their gendered class status. Household labor was expanded in order to accommodate the male members of the employers' families and to preserve their privilege. Additional work was created by rearranging meals around men's work and recreation schedules and by waiting on them and serving them. Teresa's mother was frequently called upon to provide emotional labor for the wife, husband, mother, and father within an employer's family, thus freeing members to work or increase their leisure time.

DISCUSSION

Teresa's account offers insight into the ways racial ethnic women gain knowledge about the social order and use the knowledge to develop survival strategies. As the college-educated daughter of an immigrant Mexican woman employed as a live-in maid, Teresa's experiences in the employers' homes, neighborhood, and school and her experiences in the homes of working-class *Mexicano* families and barrios provided her with the skills to cross the class and cultural boundaries separating the two worlds. The process of negotiating social boundaries involved an evaluation of Euro-American culture and its belief system in light of an intimate knowledge of white, middle-class families. Being in the position to compare and contrast behavior within different communities, Teresa debunked notions of "American family values" and resisted efforts toward assimilation. Learning to function in the employers' world was accomplished without internalizing its belief system, which defined ethnic culture as inferior. Unlike the employers' families, Teresa's was not able to assume the taken-for-granted reality of her mother's employers because her experiences provided a different kind of knowledge about the social order.

While the employers' children were surrounded by positive images of their race and class status, Teresa faced negative sanctions against her culture and powerless images of her race. Among employers' families she quickly learned that her "mother tongue" was not valued and that her culture was denied. All the Mexican adults in the neighborhood were in subordinate positions to the white adults and were responsible for caring for and nurturing white children. Most of the female employers were full-time homemakers who enjoyed the financial security provided by their husbands, whereas the Mexican immigrant women in the neighborhood all worked as maids and were financially independent; in many cases they were supporting children, husbands, and other family members. By directly observing her mother serve, pick up after, and nurture employers and their families, Teresa learned about white, middle-class privileges. Her experiences with other working-class Mexicans were dominated by women's responsibility for their children and extended families. Here the major responsibility of mothering was financial; caring and nurturing were secondary and were provided by the extended family or children did without. Confronted with a working mother who was too tired to spend time with her, Teresa learned about the racial, class, and gender parameters of parenthood, including its privileges, rights, responsibilities, and obligations. She also learned that the role of a daughter included helping her mother with everyday household tasks and, eventually, with the financial needs of the extended family. Unlike her uncles and male cousins, Teresa was not exempt from cooking and housework, regardless of her financial contributions. Within the extended family Teresa was subjected to standards of beauty strongly weighted by male definitions of women as modest beings, many times restricted in her dress and physical movements. Her social worlds became clearly marked by race, ethnic, class, and gender differences.

Successfully negotiating movement from a white, male, and middle-class setting to one dominated by working-class, immigrant, Mexican women involved a socialization process that provided Teresa with the skills to be bicultural. Since neither setting was bicultural, Teresa had to become that in order to be a competent social actor in each. Being bicultural included having the ability to assess the rules governing each setting and to understand her ethnic, class, and gender position. Her early socialization in the employers' households was not guided by principles of creativity, independence, and leadership but, rather, was based on conformity and accommodation. Teresa's experiences in two different cultural groups allowed her to separate each and to fulfill the employers' expectations without necessarily internalizing the meaning attached to the act. Therefore, she was able to learn English without internalizing the idea that English is superior to Spanish or that monolingualism is normal. The existence of a Mexican community within the employers' neighborhood provided Teresa with a collective experience of class-based racism, and the maids' support system affirmed and enhanced their own belief system and culture. As Philomena Essed (1991, 294) points out, "The problem is not only how knowledge of racism is acquired but also what kind of knowledge is being transmitted."

Teresa's life story lends itself to a complex set of analyses because the pressures to assimilate were challenged by the positive interactions she experienced within her ethnic community. Like other bilingual persons in the United States, Teresa's linguistic abilities were shaped by the linguistic practices of the social settings she had access to. Teresa learned the appropriate behavior for each social setting, each marked by different class and cultural dynamics and in which women's economic roles and relationships to men were distinct. An overview of Teresa's socialization illustrates the process of biculturalism—a process that included different sets of standards and rules governing her actions as a woman, as a Chicana, and as the maid's daughter.

While most racial ethnics do not share intimate social space with individuals of different cultural and social class background, Teresa's experiences living with her mother's employers provided insight into the ways in which a class-based, gendered, racist social order is maintained through a process of inclusion and exclusion. In Teresa's case inclusion occurred under the rubric of being like one of the family. Teresa adjusted her behavior to fit this new role, but she never actually quit being the maid's daughter, and she did not become white, middle-class, or a member of the employer's family. The employer was always in the position of power to decide when Teresa was to behave like one of the family and when she was expected to assume her position as the maid's daughter. The incidents of inclusion were symbolic and did little to change the social order, but the illusion of equality allowed white, middle-class employers to maintain images of themselves as generous, kind, and honest. By distorting the relationship between employer and employee, the Smiths were able to withhold Carmen's salary and claim they were providing Teresa with the same education their own children received. The arrangement affirmed their generosity, allowed them to claim credit for Teresa's successes, and denied Carmen her parental rights. Analysis of Teresa's experiences points to the function of maintaining the current social order through symbolic rituals of inclusion. Only through her relationship with the employers was Teresa able to enjoy certain privileges; thus, mother and daughter were locked into modes of behavior that maintained the social order.

Teresa's narrative of life as the maid's daughter challenges many traditional concepts in sociology. The socialization process of racial ethnics is not simply an either/or proposition resulting in individuals becoming assimilated. Socialization cannot be fully understood without analyzing social structure. Understanding the social order is essential in recognizing the lack of multiculturalism in our society; few, if any, social settings are governed by standards or cultural practices of groups considered to be racial ethnics. Consequently, we live in a society in which only individuals are bicultural or multicultural, not our neighborhoods, schools, communities, or families. Conceptualizing assimilation or biculturalism requires an analysis of the opportunity structure as experienced by groups outside the mainstream who have knowledge of the social order. A class-based, racist social order is maintained through social constraints establishing monolingualism and monoculturalism in social institutions. Providing incidents of inclusion creates the illusion that multiculturalism exists and suggests to conservatives that there has been a transfer of power—to women or to racial ethnics, for example—that threatens the American way of life. Without an analysis of the social order, concepts are based purely on ideology. Placing the experiences of women of color at the center of the discipline uncovers the taken-for-granted reality embedded in sociological assumptions used to develop theory.

Exploring the reproductive labor in white, middle-class households from the standpoint of the Mexican maid's daughter challenges assumptions, embedded in feminist scholarship, about women's universal experiences. When reproductive labor becomes the devalued and underpaid work of ethnic immigrant women, an analysis of housework and child care is incomplete without considering the relationship between the female employer and female employee. The experiences of household workers and child care workers cannot simply be ignored or translated into inappropriate concepts and categories used to describe white, middle-class women as mothers and wives—and we cannot rely on the old adage that "a woman's work is never done." The life story of the maid's daughter exposes the way that white female employers can use their class and race privilege to shift the burden of sexism onto women of color employed as household workers. Mothering is not always unpaid labor, and the family or household unit can be transformed into a workplace in which women sell their physical, mental, and emotional labor. Only by exploring the wide range of gender experiences in society can feminist scholarship address the complexities of sexism in a class-based, racist social order.

NOTES

This essay was originally presented as a paper at the University of Michigan, "Feminist Scholarship: Thinking through the Disciplines," 30 January 1992. I want to thank Abigail J. Stewart and Donna Stanton for their insightful comments and suggestions.

1. The names are pseudonyms.

REFERENCE

Essed, Philomena. 1991. *Understanding Everyday Racism.* Newbury Park, Calif.: Sage Publications.

PART FOUR

PAID AND UNPAID WORK: NEGOTIATING GENDER RELATIONS

Pierrette Hondagneu-Sotelo and Mary Romero

GENDER RELATIONS BETWEEN MEN AND WOMEN are negotiated within specific historical, social, and economic circumstances. All too often when Latinos are under discussion, culturally deterministic models are used to describe gender norms and values. Among Chicanos, Puerto Ricans, Cubans, and other Latinos, inclusive, exclusive, and controlling concepts of "machismo" and "marianismo" are used as descriptors. Although similar behaviors and patriachial characteristics are easily found in other cultures, *machismo* and *marianismo* are treated as exclusive Latino traits. There is a second cultural stereotype concerning Latino family life, that in "traditional" ethnic families women are full-time homemakers and mothers. However, unlike the married life of Lucy and Ricardo depicted in the "I Love Lucy" series in the 1950s, women in Latino households do engage in full-time employment outside the home. Working mothers are the norm rather than the exception. Women's greater participation in the labor force has had significant impacts on gender relations and family life.

The following articles carefully explore gender relations in specific circumstances by exploring paid and unpaid labor in family life. A woman's unpaid labor in the home, the cooking, laundry, cleaning, and childcare, becomes her "second shift" of the day. Her contribution to the financial resources of the family can be an important factor empowering her in the decision-making process, and facilitating a renegotiation of the allocation of household labor between men and women in the family. Furthermore, employability allows the option of divorce or separation to women in oppressive relationships. The articles in the following section are based on qualitative studies that explore gender issues in the family among working Latinos. Each study attempts to relate particular working conditions in the household to more broadly conceived social gender relations. Gender relations in Latino households are complex and require attention to relations of class and race as well as gender, and require an examination of how cultural practices intersect with dramatic shifts in the economy.

In the first article in this section, "Power Surrendered, Power Restored," M. Patricia Fernández-Kelly and Anna M. García compare the household and employment circumstances of Mexican-origin women in southern California with those of Cuban women in south Florida. Both groups of women are employed in the garment industry either in factories or as industrial homeworkers. By taking into account both garment industry imperatives and the household negotiations of women and men, Fernández-Kelly and García contrast distinct notions of household gender relations. For Mexican women, the sparse economic resources brought home by men make women's employment a necessity and make traditional patriarchal subordination difficult to maintain. In contrast, employment for the Cuban women proved to be a temporary means of recovering middle-class status, and they later welcomed their renewed subordination in the home because it signified the return of economic privilege. Here, class appears to condition gender relations in the household.

Scott Coltrane and Elsa Valdez's article, "Reluctant Compliance," explores the relationship between the allocation of household tasks and the provider role in working- and middle-class Chicano families. Interviews were conducted with husbands and wives in twenty dual-earner Chicano families in California. Analyzing the relative economic resources that husbands and wives bring home, Coltrane and Valdez found that Chicano husbands who earn significantly more than their wives do fewer household tasks. However, they also found a perceived incremental change between generations; that is, sons reported doing more household work than their fathers did, particularly tasks related to child care. Couples also reported using a fair and equal decision-making process. Education, occupational achievement, and ideology were identified as important factors in understanding the way couples justify the division of labor within the home.

Terry Repack's article, "New Roles in a New Landscape," examines gender relations between Central American immigrant men and women employed in Washington, D.C. Data collected from extensive interviews with Central American women are used to explore how migration and work experiences have shaped their identities as wage earners and have transformed gender roles and relationships. Focusing on household and employment arrangements of Central Americans in Washington, D.C., Repack argues that women's labor force participation, as well as migration, has contributed to the erosion of patriarchal relations in the household. While Central American women enjoy greater autonomy, household decision-making power, and increasingly share household chores with their men, they also experience numerous costs and strains with their new lives in the U.S., such as working harder in jobs below their skill level. The stories of various immigrants draw important links to the social, economic, and political context that these Central American women negotiate gender relations.

DISCUSSION QUESTIONS:

1. How do the experiences encountered by Mexican and Cuban women in the garment industry lead to radically different household and family arrangements? How do interactions of class, education, and ethnicity yield different outcomes in gender relations for Cuban and Mexican women?
2. Although Central American women living in Washington, D.C., enjoy new freedoms, they also express ambivalences about the costs of these new gains. Explain and discuss these costs.
3. How does the household division of labor among Chicano couples described in the article compare with popular stereotypes? Discuss the reasons for the discrepancies and/or similarities.

SUGGESTED READINGS:

De la Torre, Adela and Beatriz Pesquera. 1993. *Building with Our Hands, New Directions in Chicana Studies.* Berkeley: University of California Press.

Lamphere, Louise, Patricia Zavella, and Felipe Gonzales, with Peter B. Evans. 1993. *Sunbelt Working Mothers: Reconciling Family and Factory.* Ithaca: Cornell University Press.

Repack, Terry A. 1995. *Waiting on Washington: Central American Workers in the Nation's Capital.* Philadelphia: Temple University Press.

Romero, Mary. 1992. *Maid in the U.S.A.* New York: Routledge.

Williams, Norma. 1990. *The Mexican American Family: Tradition and Change.* Dix Hills, NY: General Hall Publishers.

Zambrana, Ruth E. (Ed.) 1995. *Understanding Latino Families: Scholarship, Policy, and Practice.* Thousand Oaks: Sage Publications.

Zavella, Patricia. 1987. *Women's Work and Chicano Families: Cannery Workers of the Santa Clara Valley.* Ithaca: Cornell University Press.

12 ❦

POWER SURRENDERED,
POWER RESTORED:
THE POLITICS OF WORK
AND FAMILY AMONG
HISPANIC GARMENT WORKERS
IN CALIFORNIA AND FLORIDA

M. Patricia Fernández-Kelly and Anna M. García

Iconoclast that I am, I would not abandon the central wisdom of natural history from its inception—that concepts without precepts are empty, and that no scientist can develop an adequate "feel" for nature (that undefinable prerequisite of true understanding) without probing deeply into minute empirical details of some well-chosen group of organisms.

Stephen Jay Gould, *The Flamingo's Smile*

INTRODUCTION

This chapter addresses a dimension of political action neglected in most writings on politics. We examine the manner in which women participate in decision-making processes affecting the access to vital resources within their own households and as part of the larger wage economy. The women in question belong to one ethnic group (Hispanic), but two different national heritages (Cuban and Mexican), and represent at least two distinct class backgrounds (workers and small business owners). All of them have been, or still are, garment workers in Los Angeles and Miami counties. Their experience accounts significantly for the boom of apparel manufacturing in southern Florida during the 1970s and for the survival and gradual expansion of the needle trade industry in southern California in the last two decades.[1] An important aspect in the life history of many of these women is their involvement in home assembly. In other words, they have been or still are part of the informal economy.

The theoretical focus of this chapter is on the intersection of gender, class, and ethnicity as a subject relevant to the study of political behavior.[2] Two questions guide our analysis. The first one centers on exchanges of power and authority between the sexes: To what extent do women act in their own interest as they relate to men in homes and workplaces? The second question opens up an even more elusive inquiry: How do women's personal exchanges with men interact with patterns of collective socioeconomic advancement or disadvantage?

In the case of Mexican women in southern California, employment in garment production tends to be precipitated by long-term financial need. Wives may choose to work outside the home in order to meet the survival requirements of their families in the absence of adequate earnings by their husbands or male companions. In other cases, female heads of household join the labor force after losing male support as a consequence of illness, death, or, more often, abandonment. In many of these instances, women must opt for industrial homework in order to fulfill the contradictory demands of domestic care and wage employment. Theirs is a situation of vulnerability made extreme by the proletarian status of the ethnic group to which they belong.

By contrast, Cuban women who arrived in southern Florida as exiles saw garment jobs as a transitory experience aimed at recovering or attaining middle-class standards of living. The consolidation of an economic enclave in Miami, which accounts for much of the prosperity of Cubans, was largely predicated upon the incorporation of women into the labor force. While they toiled in factories, hotels, and restaurants, their husbands formed their own businesses. Theirs was a condition of vulnerability qualified by shared objectives of upward mobility in a foreign society.

Despite their different national backgrounds, migratory histories, and class affiliations, Mexican and Cuban women share many perceptions and expectations about sexual roles: Patriarchal norms of reciprocity are considered desirable; marriage, motherhood, and dedication to family life are high priorities. Men are expected to hold authority, to be good providers, and to be loyal to their family units. However, Mexicans' and Cubans' divergent economic and social circumstances have had a differential impact upon the possibilities of upholding these values. Thus, Mexican women are often thrust into positions of financial "autonomy" as a result of men's inability to fulfill their socially assigned role, while among Cubans patriarchal mores have served to maintain group cohesion and have allowed women a marginal advantage in the labor market.

Both Cuban and Mexican women face the challenges posed by their subordination as family members and as low-skilled workers in highly competitive industries. Nevertheless, their contrasting class backgrounds and modes of incorporation into local labor markets entail different political and socioeconomic potentials. Individual and collective consciousness is implicated in this process. Our discussion below shows that among Mexican garment workers disillusion about the viability of men as economic actors can translate into greater receptivity to ideals and hopes of personal emancipation, progress, and financial independence. These ideals, however, are often distorted by poverty and the stigma attached to ethnic and gender status.

Cuban women tend to see no contradiction between personal fulfillment and a fierce commitment to patriarchal standards. Both their entrance into, and later withdrawal from, the southern Florida labor force were contingent on their adherence to hierarchical patterns of authority and a conventional division of labor between the sexes. As in the case of Mexicans in southern California, Cuban women's involvement in homework was an option mediating domestic and income-generating objectives. However, it differed in that homework among the latter was brought about by relative prosperity and expanding rather than diminishing options.

HISPANICS AND WAGE EMPLOYMENT

There are almost 20 million persons of Hispanic ancestry living in the United States—that is, 14.6 percent of the total population. With demographic forecasts predicting that they will surpass African-Americans in number by the end of the century, Hispanics already constitute the second largest ethnic minority in this country.

Although there are many studies comparing ethnic minorities and whites in the United States, there have been few attempts to look at variations of experience *within* ethnic groups. This is true for Hispanics in general and for Hispanic women in particular. The few exceptions contrasting the employment and socioeconomic profile of Hispanic women of various national backgrounds show similarities as well as differences. For example, an in-depth examination of the 1976 Survey of Income and Education (U.S. Department of Commerce, 1978) conducted by George Borjas and Marta Tienda (1985) as well as more recent compilations based on the 1980 census (Bean and Tienda, 1987) confirms the view that socioeconomic characteristics vary significantly between Hispanic and non-Hispanic populations. These statistics also show the ample differentiation among Hispanics.

Mexicans constituted more than half of all Hispanics between ages 18 and 64 living in the United States. Of these, approximately 70 percent were born in this country. Average levels of education are quite low, with less than 50 percent having graduated from high school. About 60 percent of working-age Mexicans are under age 35 compared with less than 50 percent of working-age non-Hispanic white workers. Cubans, on the other hand, represent about 7 percent of the Hispanic population. They are mostly foreign-born and have a mean age of 39 years. They also have a higher level of formal education than Mexicans. Fifty-eight percent of Cubans had 12 or more years of formal schooling in 1976.[3]

Cuban and Mexican marital profiles and household compositions are similar; intact marriages predominate in both groups and a low percentage of households are headed by women. Approximately 67 percent of Mexican women and 64 percent of Cuban women are married and living with their spouses. Similarly, 65 percent of Mexican men and 70 percent of Cuban men live in stable marital unions. Finally, about 74 percent of Mexican women have children under age 17 living with them. The equivalent figure for Cuban women is 62 percent.

These figures capture a general profile for comparative purposes. However, other variations are noticeable among workers in specific industries. For instance, in both southern California and southern Florida most direct production workers in the garment industry are Hispanic. Approximately 75 percent and 67 percent, respectively, of operatives in Los Angeles and Miami apparel firms are Mexican and Cuban women. Among Los Angeles garment workers, there is a high incidence of female-headed households: almost 30 percent, a figure almost double that of Mexicans living in the United States in general. By contrast, the incidence of female-headed households among Cuban garment workers is 19 percent, a figure only slightly above that of their group in general.[4]

The labor force participation rates of Mexican and Cuban women dispel the widespread notion that work outside the home is a rare experience for Hispanic women: 54.2 percent of native-born and 47.5 percent of foreign-born Mexican women were employed outside the home in 1980. The equivalent figure for the mostly foreign-born Cuban women was almost 65 percent. These figures approximate or surpass the labor force participation of non-Hispanic white women which in 1980 was 57.9 percent (Bean and Tienda, 1987).

Moreover, our review of the 1970 and 1980 Census Population shows that while other ethnic groups in the United States have diminished their participation in blue-collar employment, Hispanic women have increased their relative share in it. This is particularly so in the production of nondurable goods. Fully 35 percent of all women employed in manufacturing in the New York Metropolitan, Greater Los Angeles, and Greater Miami areas are Hispanic. The contrast between the proportion of Hispanic and non-Hispanic women in manufacturing is striking. In Los Angeles 35.7 percent of all females in that sector are Hispanic while only 19.0 percent are Caucasian. The equivalent figures for New York and Miami are 35.1 and 17.5 percent and 28.6 and 15.4 percent, respectively.[5]

The importance of minority women's employment in assembly is readily apparent in southern California, where 67 percent of working women classified as "operators, fabricators, and laborers" belong to ethnic minority groups. Fifty-one percent of those are Hispanic. These findings run counter to the impression that Hispanic women's participation in the labor force is not significant. Moreover, census figures may underestimate the actual involvement of Hispanic women in wage labor. Many are part of the underground economy—that is, they are found in small unregulated assembly shops or doing piecework and industrial homework.

Census figures for Los Angeles County further confirm the significance of Hispanic women's employment in manufacturing: Almost 74 percent of all female "operators, fabricators, and laborers" (136,937 persons) are members of ethnic minorities. Almost 60 percent of that sub-group (105,621 persons) are Hispanic. Even more revealing is the composition of workers classified as "textile, apparel, and furnishings machine operators." Approximately 46,000 women are employed in that occupation in Los Angeles. Almost 91 percent of those are minorities; 72 percent of them are Hispanic. Equivalent data for New York and Miami (the two other areas with the fastest-growing Hispanic populations) indicate that we are looking at a substantial percentage of the manufacturing labor force.

Garment production has historically provided a locus where immigrant women, including Hispanics of various national backgrounds, have found paid employment. We now consider the features of this type of manufacturing in California and Florida.

CALIFORNIA

The history of the garment industry in southern California is closely related to changes in apparel production in New York. The latter part of the nineteenth century witnessed the preeminence of New York as a garment producer and the emergence of California as a center of manufacture of ready-made wear for mass consumption. In the 1920s the Los Angeles clothing industry expanded, stimulated in part by the arrival of runaway shops evading unionization drives in New York. From the very beginning, Mexican women were employed in nearly all positions of the industry. Accounts of the time describe the work force in the Los Angeles clothing manufacturing sector as formed mainly by Mexican females, three quarters of whom were between the ages of 16 and 23, two thirds of whom were born in the United States, and nine tenths of whom were unmarried.[6]

The Great Depression sent the Los Angeles garment industry into a period of turmoil, but the rise of the cinema in the 1930s established new guidelines for fashion and fresh opportunities for production. Los Angeles began to specialize in inexpensive women's sportswear. By 1944 the number of garment manufacturers in Los Angeles had grown to 900 with a work force of 28,000 people, 75 percent of whom were Mexican women. The value of the product was said to be in excess of $110 million. By 1975 there had been a dramatic increase of plants to an estimated 2,269 with a work force of 66,000 people.[7]

During the late 1970s and the 1980s alarm over the growing employment of undocumented Mexican women, violations of the Labor Code and Tax Law, and the expansion of homework also grew. The recent history of the apparel industry in Los Angeles has been characterized by concerns over unregulated home assembly and the negative impact of foreign imports. Throughout the 1980s there has been continued restructuring of the industry, with decreasing numbers of large firms and the proliferation of small manufacturing shops. Of 2,717 apparel and textile manufacturers in Los Angeles County in 1984, 1,695 (or 62 percent) employed between one and 19 workers. The total work force in the formal sector hovered around 81,400 persons, many of whom were heads of households.

Contrary to a widespread impression, garment production in Los Angeles is growing quickly. This may be due to the expansion of the so-called informal sector. Garment contractors in Los Angeles County generated approximately $3.5 billion in sales 1983. It is estimated that between 30 and 50 percent of that value may have originated in home production and unregulated shops.[8]

FLORIDA

In the early 1960s the Florida garment industry specialized in the manufacture of belts, gloves, and purses and employed fewer than 7,000 persons. This was a highly seasonal industry depending on the periodic arrival of New York entrepreneurs feeding luxury markets in Europe and the United States.

The advent of several waves of refugees as a result of the Cuban Revolution was seen by many as an opportunity for revitalizing industrial activity in southern Florida. Retired manufacturers from New York who had homes in Miami saw the advantage of opening new businesses and hiring large numbers of freshly arrived Cuban women. At the same time, New York was experiencing a resurgence of union drives. The two factors combined to create a boom in apparel manufacturing in southern Florida. By 1973 the industry employed more than 24,000 workers, of whom the vast majority were Cuban women. The same process led to the predominance of Cuban males among contractors catering to New York manufacturers. Thus, from its inception, apparel manufacturing in Miami became an illustration in gender and ethnic stratification, with 70 percent of the manufacturers being Jewish, 90 percent of the subcontractors being Cuban men, and 95 percent of the work force being Cuban women.

In 1984 the Florida apparel industry employed 35,000 workers (in the formal sector), with 716 firms located in Miami. Most of these firms employed fewer than 30 workers, and their quarterly direct payroll amounted to $64 million. The sales volume reaches approximately $1 billion yearly. Government officials estimate that at least one third of that value originates in unregulated shops and homes.

Since the late seventies there have been labor shortages in the Florida apparel industry as a result of several trends, particularly the relatively advanced age of the work force, averaging over 40 years, and the absence of a new labor supply. As we will discuss below, it is the decreasing availability of Cuban women's labor that has contributed to the expansion of industrial homework in Miami.

COMPARATIVE ASPECTS

The contrast of garment manufacture in Los Angeles and Miami raises several issues. First, the two sites differ in the timing of the industry, its evolution, maturity, and restructuring. In Los Angeles, garment production is not only older but also rooted in specific events such as the Great Depression, changing conditions for assembly in New York, emphasis on new definitions of fashion linked to casual wear, and, finally, continued reorganization during the seventies and eighties as a response to the impact of foreign imports. The apparel industry in Miami has had a shorter and more uniform history.

Second, the expansion of the Los Angeles clothing industry resulted from capitalists' ability to rely on continuing waves of Mexican immigrants, many of whom were undocumented. Mexican migration over the last century ensured a steady supply of workers for the apparel industry. By contrast, the expansion of garment production in Miami was owed to an unprecedented influx of exiles ejected by a unique political event. Cubans working in the Florida apparel industry arrived in the United States as refugees under a protected and relatively privileged status. Exile was filled with uncertainty and the possibility of dislocation but not, as in the case of undocumented Mexican aliens, with the probability of harassment, detention, and deportation.

Third, implicit in the previous point is a differentiation, on the basis of social class, between the two cases. For more than a century, the majority of Mexican immigrants have had a markedly proletarian background. Until the 1970s the majority had rural roots, although in more recent times there has been a growing number of urban immigrants.[9] In sharp contrast, Cuban waves of migration have included a larger proportion of professionals, mid-level service providers, and various types of entrepreneurs ranging from those with previous experience in large companies to those qualified to start small family enterprises. Entrepreneurial experience among Cubans and reliance on their own ethnic network accounts, to a large extent, for their success in business formation and appropriation in Miami.[10] Thus, while Mexican migration has been characterized by relative homogeneity regarding class background, Cuban exile resulted in the transposition of an almost intact class structure containing investors and professionals as well as unskilled, semiskilled, and skilled workers.

Fourth, in addition to disparate class compositions, the two groups differ in the degree of their homogeneity by place of birth. Besides the sizable undocumented contingent mentioned earlier, the Los Angeles garment industry also employs U.S.-born citizens of Mexican heritage. Firsthand reports and anecdotal evidence indicate that the fragmentation between "Chicana" and "Mexicana" workers causes an unresolved tension and animosity within the labor force. Cubans, on the other hand, were a highly cohesive population until recently, when the arrival of the so-called Marielitos resulted in a potentially disruptive polarization of the community.

Fifth, perhaps the most important difference between Mexicans in Los Angeles and Cubans in Florida is related to their distinctive labor market insertion patterns. Historically, Mexicans have arrived in the U.S. labor market in a highly individuated and dispersed manner. As a result, they have been extremely dependent on labor market supply-and-demand forces entirely beyond their control. Their working-class background and stigma attached to their frequent undocumented status have accentuated even further their vulnerability vis-à-vis employers. By contrast, Cubans have been able to consolidate an economic enclave containing immigrant businesses that hire workers of a common cultural and national background. According to Alejandro Portes and Robert Bach (1985), the economic enclave is characterized by ". . . first, the growth and visible presence of immigrant enterprises and, second, the fact that the average immigrant does not need to go beyond the physical and social limits of the enclave to carry out many routine activities."[11]

Thus, the economic enclave partly operates as a buffer zone separating and often shielding members of the same ethnic group from the market forces at work in the larger society. The existence of an economic enclave does not preclude exploitation on the basis of class; indeed, it is predicated upon the existence of a highly diversified immigrant class structure. However, the commonalities of culture, national background, and language between immigrant employers and workers can become a mechanism for collective improvements of income levels and standards of living. As a result, differences in labor market insertion patterns among Mexicans and Cubans have led to varying social profiles and a dissimilar potential for socioeconomic attainment.

Finally, the two paths of labor market incorporation are significantly related to household composition and household strategies for gaining access to employment. It is to this point that we now turn.

HOUSEHOLD ORGANIZATION AND THE POLITICS OF HOME AND WORK

Neither proletarian atomization among Mexicans nor participation in an economic enclave among Cubans can be explained without giving attention to the role played by households and families in the allocation of workers to different segments of the labor market. Some conceptual clarification is needed at this point.

First, a distinction between "family" and "household" must be established. Family can be seen as a normative, that is, ideological notion that frequently transcends class barriers. Rayna Rapp (1984) notes the prevalence of a family ideal shared among working- and middle-class people in the United States. Such an ideal includes marriage and fidelity, the role of men as main providers and of women as primary caretakers of children, and, finally, the expectation that families so formed will reside in the same home. In other words, while changes have taken place over time, the patriarchal family as a prescriptive model continues to prevail.

While "family" designates the way things *should be*, "household" refers to the manner in which men, women, and children *actually* come together as part of observable domestic units. Households represent mechanisms for the pooling of time, labor, and other resources in a shared space. The concept of the family appears natural and unchangeable, but households constantly adjust to the pressures of the surrounding environment; they frequently stand in sharp, even painful, contrast to widespread ideals regarding the family.

Second, class accounts largely for the extent to which notions about the family can be upheld or not. Anthropological writings note that the conditions necessary for the maintenance of long-term stable unions where men act as main providers and women as principal caretakers of children have been available among the middle and upper classes but woefully absent among the poor. Nuclear households are destabilized by high levels of unemployment and underemployment or by public policy making it more advantageous for women with children to accept welfare payments than to remain dependent upon an irregularly employed man. Thus, the poor often live in highly flexible households where resources and services flow constantly but where adherence to the norms of the patriarchal family are unattainable.

These differences are apparent in the circumstances surrounding industrial homework. Homework has been an alternative sought by both Mexican and Cuban women to reconcile the responsibilities of domestic care with the need to earn a wage. Homework has also been a means for employers to lower the wage bill, evade government regulations, and maintain competitiveness in the market.

Some of the conditions surrounding Mexican homeworkers in southern California are illustrated by the experience of Amelia Ruíz. She was born into a family of six children in El Cerrito, Los Angeles County. Her mother, a descendant of Native American Indians, married at a young age the son of Mexican immigrants. Among Ruíz's memories are the fragmentary stories of her paternal grandparents working in the fields and, occasionally, in canneries. Her father, on the other hand, was not a stoop laborer but a trained upholsterer. Her mother was always a homemaker. Ruíz grew up with a distinct sense of the contradictions that plague the relationships between men and women:

> All the while I was a child, I had this feeling that my parents weren't happy. My mother was smart but she could never make much of herself. Her parents taught her that the fate of woman is to be a wife and mother; they advised her to find a good man and marry him. And that she did. My father was reliable and I think he was faithful but he was also distant; he lived in his own world. He would come home and expect to be served hand on foot. My mother would wait on him but she was always angry about it. I never took marriage for granted.

After getting her high school diploma, Ruíz found odd jobs in all the predictable places: as a counter clerk in a dress shop, as a cashier in a fast food establishment, and as a waitress in two restaurants. When she was 20, she met Miguel—Mike as he was known outside the barrio. He was a consummate survivor, having worked in the construction field, as a truck driver, and even as an ESL (English as a Second Language) instructor. Despite her misgivings about marriage, she was struck by his penchant for adventure:

> He was different from the men in my family. He loved fun and was said to have had many women. He was a challenge. We were married when I was twenty-one and he twenty-five. For a while I kept my job but when I became pregnant, Miguel didn't want me to work anymore. Two more children followed and then, little by little, Miguel became abusive. He wanted to have total authority over me and the children. He said a man should know how to take care of a family and get respect, but it was hard to take him seriously when he kept changing jobs and when the money he brought home was barely enough to keep ends together.

After the birth of her third child, Ruíz started work at Shirley's, a women's wear factory in the area. Her husband was opposed to the idea. For her, work outside the home was an evident need prompted by financial stress. At first, it was also a means to escape growing disillusion:

> I saw myself turning into my mother and I started thinking that to be free of men was best for women. Maybe if Miguel had had a better job, maybe if he had kept the one he had, things would have been different.... We started drifting apart.

Tension at home mounted over the following months. Ruíz had worked at Shirley's for almost a year when one late afternoon, after collecting the three children from her parents' house, she returned to an empty home. She knew, as soon as she stepped inside, that some-thing was amiss. In muted shock she confirmed the obvious: Her husband had left, taking with him all personal possessions; even the wedding picture in the living room had been removed. No explanations had been left behind. Ruíz was then 28 years of age, alone, and the mother of three small children.

Under these circumstances, employment became even more desirable, but the difficul-ty of reconciling home responsibilities with wage work persisted. Ruíz was well regarded at Shirley's, and her condition struck a sympathetic chord among the other factory women. In a casual conversation, her supervisor described how other women were leasing indus-trial sewing machines from the local Singer distributor and were doing piecework at home. By combining factory work and home assembly, she could earn more money without fur-ther neglecting the children. Mr. Driscoll, Shirley's owner and general manager, made reg-ular use of homeworkers, most of whom were former employees. That had allowed him to retain a stable core of about 20 factory seamstresses and to depend on approximately ten homeworkers during peak seasons.

Between 1979, the year of her desertion, and 1985, when we met her, Ruíz had struggled hard, working most of the time and making some progress. Her combined earnings before taxes fluctuated between $950 and $1,150 a month. Almost half of her income went to rent for the two-bedroom apartment which she shared with the children. She was in debt and used to working at least twelve hours a day. On the other hand, she had bought a double-needle sewing machine and was thinking of leasing another one to share additional sewing with a neighbor. She had high hopes: "Maybe some day I'll have my own business; I'll be a liberated woman.... I won't have to take orders from a man. Maybe Miguel did me a favor when he left after all...."

With understandable variations, Ruíz's life history is shared by many garment workers in southern California. Three aspects are salient in this experience. First, marriage and the stable family life are perceived as desirable objectives which are, nonetheless, fraught with ambivalent feelings and burdensome responsibilities.

Second, tensions surrounding the domestic sphere entail a contradiction between the intent to fulfill sexual roles defined according to a shared ideology and the absence of the economic base necessary for their implementation. The very definition of manhood includes the right to hold authority and power over wives and children, as well as the responsibility of providing adequately for them. Frustrations derived from the impossibil-ity of implementing those goals are felt equally by men and women but expressed differ-ently by each. Bent on restoring their power, men attempt to control women in abusive ways. Women often resist their husbands' arbitrary or unrealistic impositions. Both mani-festations are imminently political phenomena.

Third, personal conflict regarding the proper behavior of men and women is related to the construction of alternative ideological universes and the redefinition of sexual roles. Women may seek personal emancipation, driven partly by economic need and partly by dissatisfaction with men's performance as providers. At the level of the household, eco-nomic and political conflict is experienced as the clash between personal inadequacies while broader structural factors remain obscure.

The absence of economic underpinnings for the implementation of patriarchal stan-dards may bring about more equitable exchanges between men and women, as well as a feminist consciousness fostering individual well-being and personal autonomy. However, in the case at hand, such ideals remain elusive. Mexican garment workers, especially those who are heads of households, face great disadvantages in the labor market. They are targeted as a preferred labor force for jobs that offer the lowest wages paid to industrial workers in the United States; they also have among the lowest unionization rates in the country. Ironically, household atomization, partly caused by proletarianization and the ensuing breakdown of patriarchal norms, has not been followed by the elimination of similar patriarchal standards in the labor market.

Experiences like the ones related above can be found among Cuban and Central American women in Miami. However, a larger proportion have had a different trajectory. Elvira Gómez's life in the United States is a case in point. She was 34 years old when she arrived in Miami with her four children aged three to 12. The year was 1961.

> Leaving Havana was the most painful thing that ever happened to us. We loved our country. We would have never left willingly. Cuba was not like Mexico: we didn't have immigrants in large numbers. But Castro betrayed us and we had to join the exodus. We became exiles. My husband left Cuba three months before I did and there were moments when I doubted I would ever see him again. Then, after we got together, we realized we would have to forge ahead without looking back.

> We lost everything. Even my mother's china had to be left behind. We arrived in this country as they say, "covering our nakedness with our bare hands." My husband had had a good position in a bank. To think that he would have to take any old job in Miami was more than I could take; a man of his stature having to beg for a job in a hotel or in a factory? It wasn't right!

Gómez had worked briefly before her marriage as a secretary. As a middle-class wife and mother she was used to hiring at least one maid. Coming to the United States changed all that:

> Something had to be done to keep the family together. So I looked around and finally found a job in a shirt factory in Hialeah. Manolo [her husband] joined a childhood friend and got a loan to start an export-import business. All the time they were building the firm, I was sewing. There were times when we wouldn't have been able to pay the bills without the money I brought in.

Gómez's experience was shared by thousands of women in Miami. Among the first waves of Cuban refugees there were many who worked tirelessly to raise the standards of living of their families to the same levels or higher than those they have been familiar with in Cuba. The consolidation of an ethnic enclave allowed many Cuban men to become entrepreneurs. While their wives found unskilled and semiskilled jobs, they became businessmen. Eventually, they purchased homes, put their children through school, and achieved comfort. At that point, many Cuban men pressed their wives to stop working outside the home; they had only allowed them to have a job, in the first place, out of economic necessity. In the words of a prominent manufacturer in the area:

> You have to understand that Cuban workers were willing to do anything to survive. When they became prosperous, the women saw the advantage of staying at home and still earn additional income. Because they had the skill, owners couldn't take them for granted. Eventually, owners couldn't get operators

anymore. The most skilled would tell a manager "my husband doesn't let me work out of the home." This was a worker's initiative based on the values of the culture. I would put ads in the paper and forty people would call and everyone would say "I only do homework." That's how we got this problem of the labor shortages. The industry was dying; we wouldn't have survived without the arrival of the Haitians and the Central Americans.

This discussion shows that decisions made at the level of the household can remove workers highly desired by employers from the marketplace, thus endangering certain types of production. In those cases, loyalty to familial values can mitigate against the interests of capitalist firms. Interviews with Cuban women involved in homework confirm the general accuracy of this interpretation. After leaving factory employment, many put their experience to good use by becoming subcontractors and employing neighbors or friends. They also transformed so-called Florida rooms (the covered porches in their houses) into sewing shops. It was in one of them that Elvira Gómez was first interviewed. In her case, working outside the home was justified only as a way to maintain the integrity of her family and as a means to support her husband's early incursions into the business world:

> For long years I worked in the factory but when things got better financially, Manolo asked me to quit the job. He felt bad that I couldn't be at home all the time with the children. But it had to be done. There's no reason for women not to earn a living when it's necessary; they should have as many opportunities and responsibilities as men. But I also tell my daughters that the strength of a family rests on the intelligence and work of women. It is foolish to give up your place as a mother and a wife only to go take orders from men who aren't even part of your family. What's so liberated about that? It is better to see your husband succeed and to know you have supported one another.

As in our earlier example, several points are worth noting in the experience of Cuban garment workers. Perhaps the most obvious is the unambiguous acceptance of patriarchal mores as a legitimate guideline for men's and women's behavior. Exile did not eliminate these values; rather, it extended them in surprising ways. The high labor force participation rates of Cuban women in the United States have been mentioned before. However, it should be remembered at this time that prior to their migration only a small number of Cuban women had worked outside the home for any length of time. It was the need to maintain the integrity of their families and to achieve class-related ambitions that precipitated their entrance into the labor force of a foreign country.

In their descriptions of experience in exile, Cuban women often make clear that part of the motivation in their search for jobs was the preservation of known definitions of manhood and womanhood. Women worked in the name of dedication to their husbands and children and in order to preserve the status and authority of the former. Husbands gave them "permission" to work outside the home, only as a result of necessity and temporary economic strife. In the same vein, it was a ritual yielding to masculine privilege that led women to abandon factory employment. Conversely, men "felt bad" that their wives had to work for a wage and welcomed the opportunity to remove them from the marketplace when economic conditions improved.

As with Mexican women in southern California, Cuban women in Miami earned low wages in low and semiskilled jobs. They, too, worked in environments devoid of the benefits derived from unionization. Nevertheless, the outcome of their experience as well as their perceptions are markedly different. Many Cuban women interpret their subordination at home as part of a viable option ensuring economic and emotional benefits. As a result, they are bewildered by feminist goals of equality and fulfillment in the job market. Yet, the same women have the highest rates of participation in the U.S. labor force.

CONCLUSION

Our purpose in this chapter has been to investigate some dimensions of political action which influence the bargaining capacity of women within their households and in the larger wage economy. What are the lessons derived from this inquiry? Several issues for further consideration and research emerge from our comparison of Cuban and Mexican women's experiences in the garment industry.

First, data regarding Mexicans in southern California and Cubans in southern Florida point in two different directions: In the first case, proletarianization is related to a high number of female-headed households and households where the earnings provided by women are indispensable for maintaining standards of modest subsistence. In the second case, women's employment was a strategy for coping with the receiving environment and raising standards of living. These contrasting experiences involving the relationship between households and labor markets occurred despite shared values regarding the family among Mexicans and Cubans. While both groups share similar mores regarding the roles of men and women, their actual experiences have differed significantly.

Second, the unique and contradictory position that women have had over time forces us to shift the emphasis of political analysis beyond the public world into the household. It is within households that the pressures of gender, class, and ethnicity give rise to political options and limitations. Negotiation, conflict, compromise, and resolution characterize the daily lives of women. To denude these phenomena of political meaning can only be the effect of androcentric theories spun equally, at times, by Marxists and non-Marxists. To include these minute but significant events in the study of "the political" furthers our understanding of the participation of various groups of people in decision-making processes, the sharing of power, and the distribution of resources.

Third, our comparison of Mexican and Cuban experiences also shows that the meaning of women's participation in the labor force remains plagued by paradox. On the one hand, paid employment expands the potential for greater personal autonomy and financial independence. This should have a favorable impact upon women's capacity to negotiate an equitable position within their homes and in the labor market. On the other hand, women's search for paid employment is frequently the consequence of severe economic need; it expresses vulnerability rather than strength within the home and in the marketplace. Under certain conditions, women's entry into the labor force also parallels the collapse of reciprocal exchanges between men and women. Conversely, the "partnership for survival" illustrated by Elvira Gómez's perceptions of her own life is not predicated on the existence of a just social world, but it is made acceptable by an ideological universe entailing different benefits and obligations for the two sexes and shared equally by men and women.

Fourth, our comparison underscores the impact of class on gender. Definitions of manhood and womanhood are implicated in the very process of class formation. At the same time, the norms of reciprocity sanctioned by patriarchal ideologies can operate as a form of social adhesive consolidating class membership. For poor men and women, the issue is not so much the presence of the sexual division of labor or the persistence of patriarchal ideologies but the difficulties of upholding either.

Ultimately, our inquiry is about the factors—imperfect as they may be—that empower or debilitate men and women and about the definition of a pact for collective survival. This is a central political question; it is also a key feminist issue.

NOTES

1. This chapter is based on the research project entitled "A Collaborative Study of Hispanic Women in Garment and Electronics Industries." Data collection took place in the New York Metropolitan Area and in southern California between 1983 and 1986. Preliminary research took place in Miami-Dade County, Florida, during the winters of 1985 and 1986. Funds for research in southern California were provided by the Ford and Tinker Foundations.

2. Relevant definitions and treatments of these terms are contained in the following writings: on gender—Kelly (1984); Benería and Roldán (1987); Scott (1986); on class—Aminzade (1981); Burawoy (1985); Przeworski (1980); Evans, Skocpol, and Rueschemeyer (1985); Wright (1985); on ethnicity—Bach (1986); Nelson and Tienda (1985); Portes and Bach (1985).

3. Borjas and Tienda (1985).

4. See U.S. Bureau of the Census (1980); and Fernández-Kelly and García (1989).

5. Figures abstracted from the U.S. Bureau of Census (1980) and the Census of Manufacturers.

6. Taylor (1980).

7. Taylor (1980).

8. Commission on California State Government, Organization and Economy (1985).

9. Portes and Bach (1985), p. 67.

10. Portes (1987).

11. Portes and Bach (1985), p. 135.

REFERENCES

Aminzade, Ronald. 1981. *Class, Politics and Early Industrial Capitalism.* Albany: State University of New York Press.

Bach, Robert L. 1986. "Immigration: Issues of Ethnicity, Class and Public Policy in the United States." *Annals of the American Academy of Political and Social Sciences* 485:139-151.

Benería, Lourdes, and Martha Roldán. 1987. *The Crossroads of Class and Gender.* Chicago: University of Chicago Press.

Borjas, George J., and Marta Tienda, eds. 1985. *Hispanics in the U.S. Economy.* New York: Academic Press.

Burawoy, Michael. 1985. *The Politics of Production.* London: New Left Books.

Commission on California State Government, Organization and Economy. 1985. *Review of Selected Taxing and Enforcing Agencies' Programs to Control the Underground Economy.* Los Angeles: Commission on California State Government.

Fernández-Kelly, M. Patricia, and Anna M. García 1989. "Informalization at the Core: Hispanic Women, Homework and the Advanced Capitalist State." In Alejandro Portes, Manuel Castells, and Lauren Benton, eds., *The Informal Economy: Comparative Studies in Advanced and Third World Societies.* Baltimore: Johns Hopkins University Press.

Kelly, Joan. 1984. "The Doubled Vision of Feminist Theory." In *The Essays of Joan Kelly: Women, History, and Theory.* Chicago: University of Chicago Press.

Nelson, Candace, and Marta Tienda. 1985. "The Structuring of Hispanic Ethnicity: Historical and Contemporary Perspectives." *Ethnic and Racial Studies* 8:49-74.

Portes, Alejandro. 1987. *Sociological Perspectives* 30:340-372.

_____, and Robert L. Bach. 1985. *Latin Journey: Cuban and Mexican Immigrants in the United States.* Berkeley: University of California Press.

Scott, Joan W. 1986. "Gender: A Useful Category of Historical Analysis." *American Historical Review* 91:1053-1075.

Taylor, Paul S. 1980. "Mexican Women in Los Angeles Industry in 1928." *Aztlán International Journal of Chicano Studies Research* 11:99-129.

U.S. Bureau of Census. 1980. *Census of Population.*

Wright, Erik O. 1985. *Classes.* London: New Left Books.

13 🌿

RELUCTANT COMPLIANCE: WORK-FAMILY ROLE ALLOCATION IN DUAL-EARNER CHICANO FAMILIES

Scott Coltrane and Elsa O. Valdez

ACCORDING TO POPULAR IMAGE AND EARLY RESEARCH, Latino husbands and fathers are authoritarian and uninvolved in the daily routines of family life. Although this stereotypical portrayal has been challenged recently, we still know little about the interplay of Latino men's work and family roles. In this chapter, we draw on interviews with 20 Chicano (Mexican-American) couples to explore how mothers and fathers balance paid and unpaid work. We are especially concerned with whether wives in dual-earner Chicano families assume the role of co-provider and whether women's higher earning power is associated with husbands' assuming more responsibility for child care and housekeeping.

Our everyday experiences, as well as past academic research, show us that housework and child care tend to be divided into separate spheres on the basis of gender. Women usually do most of the indoor tasks, especially cooking, laundry, cleaning house, washing dishes, and caring for young children. Men usually do most of the outdoor tasks such as lawn and car care, performing household repairs, and sometimes playing with older children (Berk, 1985). This inside-outside gender dichotomy appears timeless and natural, although it is inaccurate to assume that such divisions of labor are universal or impervious to change (Coltrane, 1988, 1989). Because most studies of household labor have included few minority families, our impressions of task allocation and work-family linkages, like most findings in social science, reflect a white, middle-class bias. This study attempts to redress this shortcoming by focusing on a group of dual-earner Chicano couples. By analyzing the ways in which these couples divide daily chores, we hope to better understand how work and family influence each other in a specific cultural context.

Most theoretical models assume that paid work and family work are interdependent, but we have not yet identified the processes through which they are linked. "New" home economics theories tend to ignore gender and assume that family members allocate responsibility for various tasks based on "tastes" for certain types of work and the underlying desire to maximize benefits for the entire family unit (Becker, 1981). Materialist and conflict theories assume that all family members' needs are not equally served by conventional task allocation, and that responsibility for housework can be seen as a measure of women's powerlessness (Hartmann, 1981). Contemporary role theories suggest that the boundaries between work and family roles are "asymmetrically permeable," buffering men's paid work from their family obligations, but allowing women's family commitments to intrude on their work roles (Pleck, 1977). Underlying most theoretical models is the assumption that changes in paid work will promote shifts in family work, but specific changes have been difficult to predict.

Hood (1986) calls attention to the importance of accurately measuring the provider role if we are to isolate how and why work roles and family roles interpenetrate. In particular, husbands' and wives' perceived responsibility to provide financially for the family and their sense of duty to care for family members and maintain the home can have important impacts on the division of paid and unpaid labor. Accepting the wife as an essential economic provider may be precursor to the husband partially assuming the parent/home-maker role (Haas, 1981; Hood, 1983).

RESEARCH ON MEXICAN-AMERICAN FAMILIES

In most social scientific research before the late 1970s, Mexican-American families were characterized as rigidly patriarchal. The father was seen as having full authority over mother and children, and wives were described as passive, submissive, and dependent (Zinn, 1980). William Madsen (1973) emphasized the destructive aspects of Mexican-American *machismo* by comparing the men to roosters: "The better man is the one who can drink more, defend himself best, have more sex relations, and have more sons borne by his wife" (p. 22). According to such depictions, Chicano men were aloof and authoritarian, and rarely participated in the everyday business of running a household. In contrast, some contemporary scholars have rejected such stereotypes as misguided. For instance, Mirandé (1988) asserted that *machismo* implies respect, loyalty, responsibility, and generosity and noted that contemporary Chicano fathers are now participating more actively in child care than in the past.

Some recent research on marital interaction in Mexican-American families supports the notion that gender relations are more egalitarian than the traditional model assumes. Studies of marital decision making have found that Chicano couples tend to regard their decision making as relatively shared and equal (V. Cromwell & R. Cromwell, 1978; Hawkes & Taylor, 1975; Ybarra, 1982). Most researchers agree, however, that marital roles are not truly egalitarian in dual-earner Mexican-American households any more than they are in dual-earner Anglo-American households (Hartzler & Franco, 1985; Segura, 1984; Williams, 1988, 1990; Zavella, 1987). Because Mexican cultural ideals require the male to be honored and respected as the head of the family, Zinn (1982) contends that Chicano families maintain a facade of patriarchy even as mothers assume authority over day-to-day household activities. A key factor according to some researchers, is that Mexican-American women, like their Anglo-American counterparts, exercise more marital decision-making power if they are employed outside the home (Ybarra, 1982; Zinn, 1980).

Because research on Latino families is still exploratory, we cannot yet describe the most important social processes, nor make accurate predictions about the causes of the division of labor. For instance, Vega (1990) notes that researchers often aggregate divergent groups of Chicanos, Cubans, and Puerto Ricans, and typically fail to control for socioeconomic status (p. 1019). Although studies of Anglo couples tend to focus on the middle class, past studies of ethnic minority families have tended to include a preponderance of working-class people. We concur with Zinn (1990) that "marriage patterns, gender relations, kinship networks, and other family characteristics result from the social location of families, . . . where they are situated in relation to societal institutions allocating resources" (p. 74). To understand Chicano families' divisions of labor, we need to consider their social context and examine the simultaneous impacts of race, class, and gender. This chapter focuses on the allocation of tasks among a small group of relatively affluent Chicano couples with young children and is part of a larger study of Chicano family life (see Coltrane & Valdez, 1991; Valdez & Coltrane, 1993).

RESEARCH DESIGN

We collected data from a sample of Chicano couples by interviewing husbands and wives separately using a semistructured format. We relied on snowball sampling techniques (Biernacki & Waldorf, 1981) to select 20 couples with one child at least four years old, but without children of high school age or beyond. Interviews were tape-recorded and portions transcribed for coding into emergent categories (Glaser & Strauss, 1967).

SAMPLING STRATEGY

We selected our sample on the basis of several conceptual concerns. Relying on large samples of mostly Anglo couples, other researchers had reported that couples in the "child-less" or "empty nest" stages of the family life cycle share more housework than those living with young children in the home (Rexroat & Shehan, 1987). Past studies also documented the arrival of a first child typically occasioning a shift toward more conventional and gender-based allocations of household tasks (Cowan et al., 1985; R. LaRossa & M. LaRossa, 1981). Because we were primarily interested in exploring how and why Chicano couples might share both child care and housework over the long term, we avoided selecting child-less couples and those in the initial transition to parenthood. Because researchers have also reported that teenage daughters often assume responsibility for significant amounts of housework and child care (Goodnow, 1988), we avoided sampling families with children of high school age. By restricting the age range of the oldest child to four to 14 years, we were able to reduce, somewhat, the impact of life cycle stage on the division of household labor.

To explore the potential impacts of sharing the provider role, we selected only couples in which both spouses were employed at least 20 hours per week. Because most previous studies of upper-middle-class dual-career couples included few ethnic minority families (R. Rapoport & R. Rapoport, 1971), and because many previous studies of Latino families focused on the working class (e.g., Lewis, 1960; Ruiz, 1987; Zavella, 1987), we felt that an exploratory look at role allocation in middle-class Chicano couples would be fruitful. Because the majority of Latino dual-earner families are composed of husbands and wives with service sector jobs (Segura, 1984), we began by interviewing Chicano white-collar workers. Because these clerk and secretary positions offer modest wages, limited autonomy, and few chances for upward mobility, they are more accurately classified as white-collar working class rather than middle class. Other white-collar positions held by our informants, such as teacher or administrator, entail both giving and taking orders and can be appropriately labeled middle-class occupations (Collins, 1988).

We began our interviews with staff employees of a university, but soon obtained referrals to couples far removed from this venue (over three quarters of the final sample were

Table 13.1 Demographic Characteristics of Sample Families

Couple No.	Spouse	Age	Occupation	Hrs/Wk Employed	Annual Income	Yrs Education	Children's Sex and Age	Domestic Labor Index
MAIN/SECONDARY PROVIDER COUPLES								
4	Husband	33	Public Admin.	45	$ 39,000	18	boy 8	1.6
4	Wife	30	Secretary	40	$ 15,000	12	girl 6	
11	Husband	26	Law Clerk	40	$ 19,000	19	boy 4	1.8
11	Wife	25	Bookkeeper	20	$ 7,000	16	boy 1	
12	Husband	36	Mechanic	55	$ 40,000	14	boy 11	1.9
12	Wife	38	Teacher's Aide	30	$ 8,000	13	boy 9	
17	Husband	37	Admin/Tech	45	$ 48,000	22	boy 5	1.8
17	Wife	28	Teacher's Aide	20	$ 6,000	16	girl 4	
19	Husband	36	Law Clerk	45	$ 29,000	19	girl 10	1.7
19	Wife	36	Teacher's Aide	20	$ 4,000	12	boys 6, 3	
MAIN/SECONDARY PROVIDER COUPLES WITH FAILED ASPIRATIONS								
8	Husband	31	House Painter	50	$ 30,000	18	girl 5	2.4
8	Wife	34	Secretary	40	$ 13,000	13		
15	Husband	37	Utility Lineman	40	$ 34,000	13	boys 13, 8, 4, 3	2.0
15	Wife	33	In-Home Day Care	45	$ 10,000	13		
20	Husband	42	Elem. Teacher	50	$ 31,000	17	girl 9	2.3
20	Wife	42	Public Admin.	20	$ 5,000	25		
AMBIVALENT CO-PROVIDER COUPLES								
1	Husband	35	City Planner	40	$ 38,000	17	girls 8, 11	2.0
1	Wife	39	Office Manager	40	$ 23,600	14	boy 4	

#	Role	Age	Occupation	Hours	Income		Children	Rating
2	Husband	33	H.S. Teacher	35	$ 41,000	26	girl 4	1.9
2	Wife	35	Education Admin.	40	$ 38,000	17	boy 3	
16	Husband	38	H.S. Teacher	40	$ 45,000	17	boys 8, 4	1.3
16	Wife	35	Registered Nurse	26	$ 29,000	16	girl 8	

AMBIVALENT CO-PROVIDER COUPLES WITH PAID OUTSIDE HELP

#	Role	Age	Occupation	Hours	Income		Children	Rating
13	Husband	37	Attorney	45	$ 40,000	19	boys 8, 5	1.8
13	Wife	36	Social Worker	40	$ 36,000	18		
14	Husband	35	Const. Laborer	45	$ 30,000	12	boys 14, 9, 2	2.2
14	Wife	34	Social Worker	40	$ 24,000	18		

CO-PROVIDER COUPLES

#	Role	Age	Occupation	Hours	Income		Children	Rating
3	Husband	38	Contractor	40	$ 30,000	16	boy 12	2.6
3	Wife	37	Public. Admin.	50	$ 36,000	16	girl 9	
5	Husband	36	Mail Carrier	40	$ 29,000	12	boys 13, 7	2.4
5	Wife	36	Exec. Secretary	40	$ 19,000			
6	Husband	36	Educ. Outreach	50	$ 29,000	16	girls 12, 10	2.5
6	Wife	34	Exec. Secretary	40	$ 22,000	12	boy 13	
7	Husband	36	Public. Admin.	50	$ 25,000	16	girls 7, 6, 1	2.7
7	Wife	35	Exec. Secretary	45	$ 19,000	15	boy 8	
9	Husband	34	Public. Admin.	55	$ 40,000	16	boy 4	2.5
9	Wife	33	Clerk	40	$ 21,000	14	girl 2	
10	Husband	35	Engin. Technician	40	$ 27,000	14	boy 7	2.6
10	Wife	36	Engin. Technician	40	$ 27,000	15		
18	Husband	43	Public. Admin.	40	$ 34,000	16	boy 6	2.3
18	Wife	40	Preschool Teacher	40	$ 22,000	17		

unconnected to the university). In the initial phase of the study, we were concerned that there might be too little variation in occupational status, so we explicitly included some families in which the men held professional jobs (i.e., lawyer, agency director) or blue-collar jobs (i.e., mechanic, laborer). The resulting sample varied from what might be termed lower middle class (or "comfortable" working class) to upper middle class. These terms, however, are too simple to capture the complexity of the class and status positions of the husbands and wives we interviewed (see Stacey, 1990).

CHARACTERISTICS OF THE SAMPLE

Table 8.1 shows that husbands in the sample ranged in age from 26 to 43 years old, with two thirds between the ages of 35 and 38. Wives tended to be slightly younger, with most between the ages of 33 and 36. Spouses' ages in 14 of 20 couples were within two years of each other, but four husbands were at least three years older than their wife, and one wife was four years older than her husband. At the time of the interviews, couples had been married an average of 13 years, with five couples married less than ten years, and eight couples married for 15 years or more. Thus, the sample is composed of couples with long-standing marriages and tends to represent more stable, and perhaps more "successful," marriages than exist in the population at large.

Four couples had one child, nine couples had two children, five couples had three children, and two had four children. The ages of the children ranged from one to 14 years, with a median age of seven. Two-thirds of the couples had at least one child in the family who was five years old or younger, but only four couples had youngest children under three years old. Thus, the sample consists of couples with multiple children of preschool and school age, with few infants or older teenagers.

Fifteen of the couples lived in suburban communities of southern California, and five in rural communities of the same region. Just one of the husbands and four of the wives spent some time growing up in Mexico; the rest were born and raised in the United States. Although most currently considered themselves to be middle class, the vast majority came from working-class backgrounds. Of the 40 husbands and wives interviewed, none had a parent with more than a high school education, and the average educational attainment of the parents was eighth grade. Most of the informants' fathers worked in menial jobs in agriculture or construction. Roughly half of informants' mothers were employed at least seasonally, most in low-paying agricultural jobs. Over 90 percent of informants identified their current religion as Catholic, and most reported that they went to church at least monthly.

All husbands and 14 wives were employed at least 35 hours per week, and six wives spent 20-30 hours per week on the job. Unlike their own parents and Latinos in general, the informants were relatively well educated: 15 husbands and nine wives had at least a B.A. degree; three husbands and seven wives had attended some college; and just two husbands and four wives had only a high school diploma. In contrast, 78 percent of all U.S. Hispanics in dual-earner couples had a high school education or less at about the time of the interviews (U.S. Bureau of Census, 1989). Annual family incomes for the sample families ranged from $26,000 to $79,000, with a median of $53,400, well above the national median for Hispanic dual-earner families of $32,185 (U.S. Bureau of Census, 1989). Individual incomes also varied widely: from $4,000 to $48,000. Ninety-five percent of the men, but only 25 percent of the women earned at least $25,000 per year. Five husbands were employed in blue-collar jobs such as painter, laborer, and mechanic; 11 in semiprofessional white-collar jobs such as teacher, administrator, or technician; and four in more prestigious professional jobs such as lawyer or agency director. Six wives were employed in low-status, low-paying jobs such as teacher's aide or day care provider; eight worked in skilled female-dominated jobs including secretary, bookkeeper, and clerk; and six wives had a professional or semiprofessional career as a social worker, teacher, administrator, nurse, or technician.

COMPARISON TO PREVIOUS RESEARCH

Our sample and method of data collection differ somewhat from the few previous studies of household labor or conjugal decision making in Chicano couples. We interviewed both husbands and wives in mostly middle-class southern California dual-earner families with children. In contrast, Zavella (1987) interviewed only working-class women cannery workers in northern California. Zinn (1980) and Ybarra (1982) focused primarily on employed and nonemployed wives in both middle-class and working-class Chicano families in New Mexico and central California, respectively. Hartzler and Franco (1985) used structured scales and inventories to study 25 Anglo and 25 Chicano families (class not specified) in New Mexico, and Williams (1990) used interviews to collect information from both husbands and wives in a sample of 75 stable working- and middle-class Texas Chicano couples.

Like Hartzler and Franco (1985), we collected structured data about the performance of specific household chores, but our instrument included three times as many tasks (see below). Others focused on broad issues of "conjugal role patterns" (Ybarra, 1982) or "role making" (Williams, 1988) assessed with just a few global survey items or by coding depth interviews. Like Williams (1988), we collected information from both husbands and wives and focused on relatively privileged working-class and middle-class Chicano couples. We chose not to sample both Anglo and Chicano couples as Hartzler and Franco (1985) did, because we felt that an explicitly comparative research design with a small unrepresentative sample might be misleading. Our decision to focus only on Chicano couples with children, most of whom were broadly middle class, restricted the range of variation within our sample. This research strategy limited the number of potential exogenous variables we could consider and constrained our ability to make conclusions about relative levels of sharing in Chicano versus Anglo or in working-class versus middle-class families. Because making such comparisons based on snowball samples is risky at best, we were content with ensuring that our small sample had enough couples of various emergent "types" to describe some social processes and offer some theoretically informed generalizations. For grander theorizing, our results must be compared to other small studies with diverse samples or used for developing hypotheses to test on larger, more representative, populations.

MEASURING HOUSEHOLD LABOR

We collected detailed data on housework and child care by asking each individual to sort stacks of cards listing various household and child care tasks. Husbands and wives separately indicated who had performed each of 64 tasks during the previous two weeks: (a) wife mostly or always, (b) wife more than husband, (c) husband and wife about equally, (d) husband more than wife, and (e) husband mostly or always. Following Smith and Reid's (1986) "strict criteria" for evaluating the extent of sharing in dual-earner couples (pp. 72-74), we computed a mean husband-wife score for each task and considered scores in the

2.5-3.5 range to be shared. The 64 tasks were grouped into six major areas: (a) house-cleaning (vacuum, mop, sweep, dust, clean bathroom sinks, clean toilets, clean tub/show-ers, make beds, pick up toys, tidy living room, hang up clothes, take out trash, clean porch, wash windows, and spring cleaning), (b) meals (plan menus, shop for food, put food away, make breakfast, make lunch, cook dinner, prepare snacks, bake, wash dishes, put dishes away, and wipe kitchen counters), (c) clothes care (laundry, hand laundry, ironing, shoe care, sewing, and buy clothes), (d) home maintenance (inside repairs, interior painting, exterior painting, redecorate, wash car, maintain car, automotive repairs, maintain yard, water, mow lawns, garden, and external house maintenance), (e) finances and home man-agement (bills, taxes, insurance, investments, major purchases, run errands, plan couple dates, and write/phone relatives and friends), and (f) child care (awaken, help dress, bathe, put to bed, supervise, discipline, drive, take to doctor, care for when sick, arrange baby-sit-ting, play with, and go on outings with).

For the following analysis, we combined the first three areas, housecleaning, meals, and clothes, into an additive 32-item index and refer to these activities as housework. When we discuss the sharing of child care, we refer to scores for the 12-item Child Care Index. In order to focus on the extent to which husbands share in the most time-consuming and repetitive household tasks, which are also conventionally performed by wives, we com-bined all housecleaning items except trash and porch, and all meals, clothes, and child care items to produce a 42-item Domestic Labor Index. Domestic Labor Index scores are listed for each couple in Table 8.1 and discussed below. Scores lower than 1.5 indicate that wives always perform the associated domestic tasks; scores between 1.5 and 2.5 indicate that wives perform the tasks more than husbands; and scores between 2.5 and 3.5 indicate that the tasks are relatively evenly shared.

FINDINGS

The results of the interviews and card sorts showed that wives were primarily respon-sible for housecleaning, clothes, meals, and child care; husbands were primarily responsi-ble for home maintenance; and finances/home management tended to be shared. These results are not surprising. Similar to findings on dual-earner Anglo couples, these dual-earner Chicano couples shared more child care tasks than housework tasks, but divisions of household labor still conformed to conventional expectations.

The families we interviewed did not conceive of themselves as having chosen to become two-job families. Like the dual-earner couples in some previous studies (Hood, 1983), our informants reported that they were simply responding to financial necessity. Although all husbands and almost three-fourths of wives were employed full-time, the couples varied in the extent to which they accepted the wife as a permanent co-provider. By considering the employment and earnings of each spouse, along with each spouse's attitudes toward the provider and homemaker roles, we divided the 20 families into two general groups: main/secondary providers and co-providers (see Hood, 1986). In analyzing the couples' divisions of market and household labor, we further subdivided the two groups. Main/sec-ondary provider couples were isolated for special analysis if the husband's career aspira-tions were unfulfilled. Co-provider households were divided into those who relied on paid household help, those who were ambivalent co-providers, and those who were full co-providers (Table 8.1 lists the sample families according to these five categories). We focus on the division of family labor in each of these groups below.

MAIN/SECONDARY PROVIDERS

In 8 of 20 families (40 percent), husbands made substantially more money than wives and assumed that men should be the primary breadwinner and women should be responsible for home and children. Such families were categorized as main/secondary providers because they generally considered the wife's job to be secondary and treated her income as "extra" money to be earmarked for special purposes (Hood, 1986). The eight main/secondary provider couples included all five wives who were employed part-time and three wives who worked in low-status full-time jobs. Wives in these families made substantially less than their husband, contributing an average of 20 percent to the total family income. In main/secondary provider households, wives typically took pride in the homemaker role and readily accepted responsibility for managing the household. This often meant limiting their employment to a part-time job so that the women could be home when their children were home.

Most wives in main/secondary provider households talked about their husband creating domestic work rather than lessening it. In general, secondary provider wives not only performed virtually all housework and child care, but both spouses accepted this as "natural" or "normal." The wife's commitment to outside employment was generally limited, and her income was considered supplementary rather than primary. Main provider husbands felt that financial support was their main responsibility and often made light of their wife's contribution to the family income. Similarly, secondary provider wives made light of their husband's child care or housework, and both spouses referred to his domestic contributions as "helping out." In their talk about who did what around the house, and in their sorting of the household task cards, main provider husbands took much more credit for their housework than their wife was willing to grant them (Valdez & Coltrane, 1993). Nevertheless, when we averaged husbands' and wives' ratings, we still arrived at scores indicating wives did most of the housework and child care. The first five main/secondary couples listed in Table 8.1 had Domestic Labor scores ranging from 1.6 to 1.9, with an average of 1.7. A score of 1.5 would mean that wives "mostly or always" performed all 42 chores that make up the Household Labor Index. Thus we find that main provider husbands with secondary provider wives in this sample contributed little to housework and child care.

THE IMPACT OF FAILED ASPIRATIONS

Three main provider husbands with unfulfilled career goals tended to share more domestic labor than the others. One, a house painter with six years of college, wished he was doing something more "worthwhile" and was encouraged by his wife to change occupations. Another made good money working as a telephone line worker, but regretted dropping out of school and was told by his wife that he should go to college and make more of himself. The third husband in this category was a successful elementary school teacher, but his real love was art, and he and his wife openly lamented that he was not pursuing his true calling. Like the other main provider husbands, these three husbands earned substantially more money than their wives. Even though the three men earned over $30,000 per year, and their wives contributed an average of just 22 percent to family earnings, the fact that these men had failed career goals altered negotiations over household labor. Whereas other main provider husbands were able to minimize contributions to housework by claiming they were tired from long hours on the job, the three husbands with unfulfilled career goals were not able to use their outside job as an excuse to avoid family work.

Whereas other main provider husbands were able to claim incompetence for tasks like laundry or cooking, the husbands with failed aspirations were pressed by their wives to learn the necessary domestic skills. Because they were not fulfilling their "true potential," the failed aspirations husbands were not able to translate their superior earnings into avoiding mundane household chores.

Whereas the first five main provider couples listed in Table 8.1 had an average Domestic Labor Index score of 1.7, the three main provider husbands with failed career aspirations had an average Domestic Labor score over 2.2 (see Table 8.1). Although wives in failed aspirations couples were more likely than husbands to perform stereotypical "feminine" household tasks, both husbands and wives rated the husbands' contributions as coming much closer to equal sharing.

Most secondary provider wives, regardless of their husband's perceived level of success at fulfilling career goals, reported that they received little help unless they "constantly" reminded their husband to contribute to housework or child care. When main provider husbands assumed some domestic chores in response to "necessity" or "nagging," they clung to the idea that it was not their responsibility. According to their accounts, this seemed to justify their resentment at having to do "her" chores. What generally kept a wife from resenting her husband's reluctance was her acceptance of the homemaker role and appreciation for his substantial financial contributions. When performance of the provider role was deemed to be lacking in some way—for example, failed aspiration or low occupational prestige —wives' resentment appeared closer to the surface and couples reported that she was more persistent in demanding his help.

CO-PROVIDER COUPLES

Based on an evaluation of their employment, earnings, and ideology, we classified the remaining 12 families in our sample as co-providers. Compared to main/secondary provider couples, co-providers tended to have more equal earnings and to value the wife's employment more highly. Among the 12 co-provider couples, wives averaged 44 percent of the family income as compared to 20 percent for the 8 main/secondary provider couples. There was considerable variation among co-provider husbands, however, in terms of their willingness to accept their wife as an equal provider or to assume the role of equal homemaker. Accordingly, we divided these families into ambivalent co-providers (five couples) and co-providers (seven couples). The ambivalent co-provider husbands accepted their wife's job as important and permanent (Hood, 1986), but often used their own job commitments as justifications for doing little at home. We discuss each group in turn, considering variation between subgroups in terms of earnings, job status, ideology, role attachments, and divisions of household labor.

AMBIVALENT CO-PROVIDERS

Compared to their wife, ambivalent co-provider husbands usually held jobs that were roughly equivalent in terms of occupational prestige and worked about the same number of hours per week. All of these husbands earned more than their wife, however, with husbands' average annual earnings of $39,000, compared to the wives' average of $30,000. Although both husbands and wives thus had careers that provided "comfortable" incomes, the husbands, and sometimes the wives, were ambivalent about treating her career as equally important to his. For example, few ambivalent co-provider husbands let their family work intrude on their paid work, whereas wives' family work often interfered with their paid work. Such asymmetrically permeable work-family boundaries (Pleck, 1977) are common in single-earner and main/secondary provider families, but must be supported with subtle ideologies and elaborate justifications when husbands and wives hold similar occupational positions.

Ambivalent co-provider husbands remained in a helper role at home, perceiving their wife to be a more involved parent and assuming that housework was also their wife's responsibility. Husbands used their breadwinner responsibilities to justify their absence, but most lamented not being able to spend more time with their family. For instance, one husband who worked full-time as a city planner was married to a woman who worked an equal number of hours as an office manager. In talking about the time he puts in at his job, he commented, "I wish I had more time to spend with my children, and to spend with my wife too, of course, but it's a fact of life that I have to work." His wife, in contrast, indicated that her paid job, which she had held for 14 years, did not prohibit her from adequately caring for her three children, nor from taking care of "her" household chores. With an average Domestic Labor Index score of 1.8, ambivalent co-provider husbands did not perform significantly more housework and child care than main provider husbands, and generally did fewer household chores than main provider husbands with failed career aspirations (see Table 8.1).

Two of the five ambivalent co-provider couples attempted to alleviate stress on the woman by hiring outside help. For example, a self-employed male attorney making $40,000 per year finally agreed with his social worker wife that they should hire a housekeeper to help with "her" chores. Another couple paid a live-in baby-sitter/housekeeper to watch their three children during the day while he worked full-time in construction and she worked full-time as a psychiatric social worker. Although she labeled the outside help as "essential," she also noted that her husband contributed more mess than he cleaned up. He saw himself as an involved father because he played with his children, and although she acknowledged his role, she also complained that he competed with them in games as if he were a child himself. His participation in routine household labor was considered optional and he tended to select where and when he would contribute, usually focusing on the fun activities. Only one other family—Couple 3—talked about paying for household help. This co-provider couple, as described below, hired a gardener to do some of "his" chores, freeing him to do more child care and housework. This strategy reflects an assumption that the husband "should" share in family work, an assumption that main provider and ambivalent co-provider husbands did not willingly embrace.

CO-PROVIDER COUPLES

Unlike the ambivalent co-providers discussed above, the seven true co-provider couples fully accepted the wife's employment and considered her career to be just as important as his. Like the ambivalent couples, co-provider spouses each worked about the same number of hours, but on the whole, these couples worked more total hours than their more ambivalent counterparts. The mean total amount of time per week that couples spent in paid labor for the ambivalent group was 78 hours and for the co-provider group, 87 hours. Co-providers also tended to have lower incomes. Men's average annual income for this group was $30,000–$9,000 less than for the ambivalent group. Similarly, co-provider wives' incomes averaged $24,000, or $6,000 less than for wives in the more ambivalent co-provider families. Nevertheless, the average percentage income contribution from wives was similar in both groups: 43 vs. 44 percent.

The sharing of housework and child care was substantially greater for co-providers (mean Domestic Labor Index score = 2.5) than for main/secondary providers (mean = 1.7), main providers with failed aspirations (mean = 2.2), or ambivalent co-providers (mean = 1.8) (see Table 8.1). No co-provider couple had a mean Domestic Labor Index score over 3.0—the true midpoint of the index—but five of the seven families had mean husband-wife scores of 2.5 or higher, indicating substantial sharing of these tasks. Because husbands often take more credit for family work than their wives grant them, we also analyzed husbands' contributions to domestic chores using only the wife's ratings (results not shown). Six of seven co-provider wives rated their husband over 2.5 for child care tasks, and two of these wives rated husbands over 2.5 for housework tasks as well. The co-provider families thus represent the most egalitarian families in this sample. On the following pages we investigate how similar or different these families are from the others and discuss some of the factors that the couples identified as reasons for their allocation of household labor.

Like the more ambivalent co-providers, husbands in these families discussed conflicts between work and family and sometimes alluded to their occupational advancement being limited by their commitments to their children. Nevertheless, co-provider husbands were less likely to use paid work as an excuse to avoid child care of housework. Comparable occupational status and earnings, coupled with relatively egalitarian ideals, led to substantial sharing of both child care and housework among the co-providers. Although some co-provider wives complained that husbands wouldn't do certain chores or didn't always notice when thing were dirty, they were generally appreciative of their husband's contributions.

Although co-provider husbands, like the other husbands, tended to take more credit for their involvement than their wife granted them, we observed a difference between their talk and that of the husbands discussed above. When other husbands complained about their wife's high standards, they treated housework, and even parenting, as primarily the wife's duty. Main provider husbands and ambivalent co-providers talked about resenting being "nagged" to do more around the house, and even when they reluctantly complied with their wife's requests, they rarely moved out of a helper role to consider it *their* duty to anticipate, schedule, and take care of family and household needs. In many co-provider households, however, that asymmetric allocation of responsibility was taken less for granted. Because of this, negotiations over housework and parenting were sometimes more frequent than in the other families. Because both held expectations that each would fulfill both provider and caretaker roles, resentments came from both spouses—not just from the wife.

Our data suggest that it might be easier for couples to share both provider and homemaker roles when the wife's earnings and occupational prestige equal or exceed her husband's. For instance, in one of the co-provider couples reporting the most sharing of child care and housework, the wife earned $36,000 annually as a management consultant and director of a nonprofit organization, and her husband earned $30,000 as a self-employed contractor. According to both spouses, they shared most of the housework. What differentiates this couple from most others is that the wife made more money than the husband and had no qualms about demanding help from him. Not yet accepting the idea that interior chores were equally his, he reluctantly performed them. In the card sorts, she ranked his contributions to child care to be equal to hers and rated his contributions to housework only slightly below her own. Even though the husband did not eagerly rush to do the cooking, cleaning, or laundry, he nonetheless complied with her frequent reminders. The power dynamic in this family, coupled with their willingness to pay for outside help to reduce "his" yard work, and the flexibility of his self-employed work schedule, led to substantial sharing of domestic labor. Because she was making more money and working more hours than he was, he was unable to claim priority for his provider activities.

A similar dynamic was evident in other co-provider couples with comparable earnings and career commitments. Even when wives' earnings did not exceed husbands', some co-providers shared the homemaker role. A male college admissions recruiter and his executive secretary wife share substantial housework according to mutual ratings and most child care according to her rating. He made $29,000 per year working an average of 50 hours per week; she made $22,000 working a 40-hour week (see Couple 6 in Table 8.1). Like some other co-providers, this wife was willing to give her husband more credit than he claimed for child care. Like all of the men in this study, however, he was reluctant to perform many housecleaning chores and took more credit for housework than she granted him. Like many of the co-provider husbands, however, he had redefined many routine housework chores as shared responsibilities. When asked what he liked least about housework, he laughingly replied, "Probably those damn toilets, man, and the showers, the bathrooms; gotta scrub 'em, argghh! I wish I didn't have to do any of that, you know, the vacuuming and all that, but it's just a fact of life."

Although secondary provider wives and ambivalent co-provider wives assumed that men were incapable of performing many domestic chores and allowed them to use their job as an excuse for doing less family work, co-provider wives did not accept such excuses. Like the wives of main providers with failed aspirations, co-provider wives rejected the assumption that all the housework was naturally "woman's work," and some refused to do certain chores. Hood (1983) describes this strategy as "going on strike," and suggests that it is most effective when husbands feel the specific task *must* be done (p. 131). As appearing neat and well dressed was a priority for one husband, when his wife stopped ironing his clothes, he started doing it himself. Because he felt it was important for his children to be "presentable" in public, he also began to remind them to iron their own clothes before going visiting or attending church. Ironing has *not* been identified as one of the tasks performed frequently by husbands in other studies. In our study, ironing was one of the only housekeeping tasks that a majority of both wives and husbands indicated was shared. High levels of church attendance among Chicanos and the symbolic importance of being well dressed in public probably makes Chicano men more likely than Anglo men to share the ironing.

Although some co-provider couples reported overt ongoing contentious struggles over housework, other co-providers claimed that their divisions of labor evolved "naturally." Such claims should not be taken to mean that these couples have not "negotiated" a division of household labor. Hood (1983) notes that because family processes involve chains of hundreds of little bargains over long periods of time, family patterns like household task divisions appear to "just happen" when in fact they have been subtly negotiated (p. 176).

Once co-provider spouses assume that household tasks are a shared responsibility, negotiation can become less necessary. For example, a co-provider husband who worked as a mail carrier commented, "I get home early and start dinner, make sure the kids do their homework, feed the dogs, stuff like that." He and his wife, an executive secretary, agreed that they rarely talk about housework. She said, "When I went back to work we agreed that we both needed to share, and so we just do it." Although she still reminded him to perform chores according to her standards or on her schedule, she summed up her appreciation by commenting, "At least he does it without complaining."

Although co-provider husbands were often reluctant contributors to housework, they were very involved with their children and bristled when friends or co-workers character-ized their parenting efforts as "helping" the wife. Although most of the co-provider hus-bands were rated by their wife as performing almost half of the child care tasks, none of the main providers or ambivalent co-providers fell into this category. This is not to suggest that the other husbands did not love their children or interact with them on a regular basis. But there was something different about the way that co-providers characterized what they were doing as a decision to put their children's needs first. Main providers tended to use their job as an excuse for spending little time with their children. Ambivalent co-providers lamented how children sometimes detracted from their careers. Co-provider husbands, on the other hand, even though they were employed at least as many hours as the others, talked about making a definite choice to spend time with and care for their children.

DISCUSSION

Our interviews with dual-earner Chicano couples revealed considerable sharing in several areas. First, as in previous studies of ethnic minority families, wives were employed a substantial number of hours and made significant contributions to household income. Second, like Hawkes and Taylor (1975), V. Cromwell and R. Cromwell (1978), and Ybarra (1982), we found that couples described their decision making as relatively fair and equal. Third, fathers in these families were more involved in child rearing than their own fathers had been, and seven of 20 husbands were rated as sharing most child care tasks. Finally, although no husband performed fully half of the housework, a few made substantial con-tributions in this area as well.

One of the power dynamics that appears to undergird the household division of labor in these families is the relative earning power of each spouse, though this is modified by occupational prestige, provider role status, and personal preference. In 40 percent of the families, the wife earned less than a third of the family income, and in all of these families the husband performed little of the routine housework or child care. In two families, wives earned more than their husband and shared much of the domestic labor with him. Among other couples sharing significant amounts of housework and child care, a preponderance had relatively balanced incomes. In two families with large financial contributions from wives but little household help from husbands, couples hired housekeepers to reduce the total household work load.

Although relative incomes make a difference, we are not suggesting a simple or straight-forward exchange of market resources for domestic services. Other factors like failed career aspirations or occupational status differentials influenced resource/power dynamics and helped us understand why some wives were willing to push a little harder for change in the division of household labor. In most cases, husbands responded reluctantly to requests for help. Only when wives actively demanded help did some of the day-to-day burden of housework begin to shift toward husbands. Even when they shared housework and child care, men tended to do more pleasant tasks like playing with the children or putting clean dishes away. Comparing these men to their fathers and their wives' fathers, we can see that they are sharing more domestic chores than the generation of parents that preceded them.

Even when wives made much less money than their husband, if they expected husbands to "make more" of themselves, pursue "more important" careers, or follow "dream" occupational goals, then they were able to get them to do more around the house. This perception of failed aspirations, if held by both spouses, served as a reminder that husbands had no excuse for not helping out at home. In these families, wives were not at all reluctant to demand assistance with domestic chores, and husbands were rarely able to use their job as excuse for getting out of housework. When husbands accepted wives as co-providers, either because of her earnings and job status, or because of his own failings, the division of household labor was more symmetrical. Similarly, when wives relinquished a portion of the homemaker role by delegating duties to husbands, household labor allocation became more balanced. If wives made lists for their husbands or offered them frequent reminders, they were more successful than if they waited for husbands to take the initiative. Even when they received help, however, remaining responsible for managing home and children was cause for resentment on the part of many wives.

Over a third of the families we interviewed exhibited divisions of household labor that contradicted cultural stereotypes of male-dominated Chicano families. Particularly salient in these families was the lack of fit between their own class position and their parents'. Most of the parents were immigrants with little education and low occupational mobility. The couples we interviewed, in contrast, were well educated and relatively secure in middle-class occupations. Although the couples could have compared themselves to their parents, evaluating themselves to be egalitarian and financially successful, most compared themselves to their Anglo and Chicano friends and co-workers. These social comparisons occasionally motivated both husbands and wives to negotiate further changes in the household division of labor, in part because their referents were perceived as more egalitarian than themselves. Still, there was no absolute or fixed standard against which the couples were making judgments. Rather, implicitly comparing their earnings, occupational commitments, and perceived aptitudes to those of their spouse, these individuals negotiated new patterns of work-family boundaries and developed new justifications for their emerging arrangements. These were not created anew, but emerged out of the popular culture in which they found themselves. Judith Stacey (1990) labels such developments the making of the "postmodern family," because they signal "the contested, ambivalent, and undecided character of contemporary gender and kinship arrangements" (p. 17). Our findings confirm that families are an important site of new struggles over the meaning of gender and the rights and obligations of men and women to each other and over each other's labor (Hartmann, 1981). Overt and covert negotiations over who should do what in the home also suggest that some subtle shifts may be under way.

Because we sampled only parents with school-aged children and used more detailed measures of housework and child care than previous researchers studying Chicano families, it is difficult to compare our results directly to previous findings. The extent of sharing we uncovered, particularly for child care, contradicts monocausal analyses that depict Latino households as patriarchal (e.g., Lewis, 1960; Madsen, 1973) and supports Mirandé's (1988) suggestion that Chicano fathers are relatively involved in their families. Nevertheless, with fathers doing so much less than mothers, our findings also contradict the notion that Chicano families are essentially egalitarian (V. Cromwell & R. Cromwell, 1978; Hawkes & Taylor, 1975; Ybarra, 1982). Like Zinn (1980), Williams (1988), and Zavella (1987), we found that gender is the primary axis of labor allocation in Chicano families, but that Chicanas actively struggle against oppressive assumptions about their duty to perform all domestic labor. Like these researchers, we found that when Chicanas are employed, their bargaining power can increase, but that the simple fact of employment is not sufficient to bring about changes in the cosmetic division of labor. We did find that Chicana wives who had more income, were employed more hours, and whose occupation was comparable in status to that of their husband, were the most likely to be considered coproviders and demand help with domestic chores.

One of our most interesting findings has to do with the class position of Chicano husbands and wives who shared domestic labor. The white-collar working-class families shared more than the upper-middle-class professionals. Contrary to findings from nationwide surveys predicting that higher levels of education for either husbands or wives will be associated with more sharing (Ross, 1987), the most highly educated of our well-educated sample of Chicano couples shared only moderate amounts of child care and little housework. Contrary to predictions from Zavella (1987), Stacey (1990), and others, neither was it the working-class women in this study who achieved the most sharing. It was in the middle group, the executive secretaries, clerks, technicians, teachers, and midlevel administrators who extracted the most help from husbands. Their husbands were similarly in the middle in terms of occupational status for this sample—administrative assistants, a builder, a mail carrier, a technician—and in the middle in income. What this means is that the highest status wives—the program coordinators, nurses, social workers, and office managers—were not able, or chose not to transform salaries or occupational status into more participation from husbands. This was probably because their husbands had even higher incomes and more prestigious occupations. The lawyers, program directors, ranking bureaucrats, and "community leaders" parlayed their status into extra leisure at home, either by paying for housekeepers or ignoring the work. Finally, Chicana wives at the lowest end fared least well. The teacher's aides, entry-level secretaries, day care providers, and part-time employees did the bulk of the work at home whether they were married to mechanics or lawyers. When wives earned considerably less than their husbands, they were only able to enlist husbands' assistance if the men held jobs considered "below" them—a telephone line worker, a painter, an elementary school teacher.

In general, then, our analysis suggests that researchers must consider the education and occupational achievement of both husbands and wives simultaneously. Only by comparing incomes, occupational prestige, and ideology of both spouses can we understand how men and women assume provider role status and justify domestic divisions of labor. Focusing on wives alone, or husbands alone, gives us only half of the picture.

Although we studied only Chicano couples, our results are similar to most in-depth interview studies of Anglo couples (Hochschild, 1989; Hood, 1983). Our interpretation is that the major processes shaping divisions of labor in other middle-class Chicano couples are similar to those shaping divisions of labor in other middle-class couples as well. That is not to say that ethnicity did not make a difference to the people we interviewed. They grew up in recently immigrating working-class families, watched their parents work long hours for minimal wages, and understood firsthand the toll that various forms of racial discrimination can take. Probably because of some of these experiences, and their own more recent ones, our informants looked at job security, fertility decisions, and the division of household labor somewhat differently than their Anglo counterparts. In some cases, this may give Chicano husbands in working-class or professional jobs license to ignore more of the housework and might temper the anger of some working-class or professional Chicanas who are still called on to do most of the domestic chores. If our findings are generalizable, however, it is couples in between the blue-collar working class and the upper-middle-class professionals that might be more likely to share housework and child care.

Assessing whether our findings apply to other dual-earner Chicano couples will require the use of larger, more representative samples. If the limited sharing we observed represents a trend—however slow or reluctant—it could have far-reaching consequences. More and more Chicana mothers are remaining full-time members of the paid labor force. With the "postindustrial" expansion of the service and information sectors of the economy, more and more Chicanos and Chicanas will enter white-collar working-class occupations. As more Chicano families fit the occupational profile of those we studied, we may see more assumption of housework and child care by Chicano husbands.

REFERENCES

Becker, G. (1981). *A treatise on the family*. Cambridge, MA: Harvard University Press.

Berk, S. (1985). *The gender factory*. New York: Plenum.

Biernacki, P., & Waldorf, D. (1981). Snowball sampling. *Sociological Methods and Research, 10*, 141-163.

Collins, R. (1988). Women and men in the class structure. *Journal of Family Issues, 9*, 27-50.

Coltrane, S. (1988). Father-child relationships and the status of women. *American Journal of Sociology, 93*, 1060-1095.

_____. (1989). Household labor and the routine production of gender. *Social Problems, 36*, 473-490.

Coltrane, S., & Valdez, E. (1991, April). *Not seeing is believing*. Paper presented at the Pacific Sociological Association Annual Meetings, Irvine, CA.

Cowan, C., Cowan, P., Heming, G., Garrett, E., Coysh, W., Curtis-Boles, H., & Boles, A. (1985). Transitions to parenthood: His, hers, and theirs. *Journal of Family Issues, 6*, 451-482.

Cromwell, V., & Cromwell, R. (1978). Perceived dominance in decision-making and conflict resolution among Anglo, Black, and Chicano couples. *Journal of Marriage and the Family, 40*, 749-760.

Glaser, B., & Strauss, A. (1967). *The discovery of grounded theory*. New York: Aldine.

Goodnow, J. (1988). Children's household work. *Psychological Bulletin, 103*, 5-26.

Haas, L., (1981). Domestic role-sharing in Sweden. *Journal of Marriage and the Family, 43*, 957-965.

Hartmann, H. (1981). The family as the locus of gender, class, and political struggle. *Signs, 6*, 366-394.

Hartzler, K., & Franco, Jr. (1985). Ethnicity, division of household tasks and equity in marital roles. *Hispanic Journal of Behavioral Sciences, 7*, 333-344.

Hawkes, G., & Taylor, M. (1975). Power structure in Mexican and Mexican-American farm labor families. *Journal of Marriage and the Family, 37*, 807-811.

Hochschild, A. (1989). *The second shift*. New York: Viking.

Hood, J. (1983). *Becoming a two-job family*. New York: Praeger.

_____. (1986). The provider role: Its meaning and measurement. *Journal of Marriage and the Family, 48,* 349-359.

LaRossa, R., & LaRossa, M. (1981). *Transition to parenthood.* Beverly Hills, CA: Sage.

Lewis, O. (1960). *Tepoztlan.* New York: Holt, Rinehart & Winston.

Madsen, W. (1973). *Mexican-Americans of South Texas* (2nd ed.). New York: Holt, Rinehart & Winston. (Originally published 1964)

Mirandé, A. (1988). Chicano fathers: Traditional perceptions and current realities. In P. Bronstein & C. Cowan (Eds.), *Fatherhood today* (pp. 93-106). New York: John Wiley.

Pleck, J. (1977). The work-family role system. *Social Problems, 24,* 417-427.

Rapoport, R., & Rapoport, R. (1971). *Dual career families.* Baltimore: Penguin.

Rexroat, C., & Shehan, C. (1987). The family cycle and spouses' time in housework. *Journal of Marriage and the Family, 49,* 737-750.

Ross, C. (1987). The division of labor at home. *Social Forces, 65,* 816-833.

Ruiz, V. (1987). *Cannery women/cannery lives.* Albuquerque: University of New Mexico Press.

Segura, D. (1984). Labor market stratification: The Chicana experience. *Berkeley Journal of Sociology, 29,* 57-91.

Smith, A., & Reid, W. (1986). *Role-sharing marriage.* New York: Columbia University Press.

Stacey, J. (1990). *Brave new families.* New York: Basic Books.

U.S. Bureau of the Census. (1989) *Current Population Reports* (Series P-20, No. 431). Washington, DC: U.S. Government Printing Office.

Valdez, E., & Coltrane, S. (1993). Work, family, and the Chicana. In J. Frankel (Ed.), *Employed mothers and the family context* (pp. 153-179). New York: Springer.

Vega, W. (1990). Hispanic families in the 1980s. *Journal of Marriage and the Family, 52,* 1015-1024.

Williams, N. (1988). Role making among married Mexican-American women. *Journal of Applied Behavioral Science, 24,* 203-217.

_____. (1990). *The Mexican American family.* New York: General Hall.

Ybarra, L. (1982). When wives work: The impact on the Chicano family. *Journal of Marriage and the Family, 44,* 169-178.

Zavella, P. (1987). *Women's work and Chicano families.* Ithaca, NY: Cornell University Press.

Zinn, M. B. (1980). Employment and education of Mexican-American women. *Harvard Educational Review, 50,* 47-62.

_____. (1982, Summer). Qualitative methods in family research. *California Sociologist,* 58-79.

_____. (1990). Family, feminism, and race in America. *Gender and Society, 4,* 68-82.

14

NEW ROLES
IN A NEW LANDSCAPE

Terry A. Repack

THE ENTIRE PROCESS OF MIGRATION incites dramatic transformations in women's and men's attitudes about their work, their gender roles, and relationships within the family. Wage work in the United States is simply one change-inducing element in a broader social-cultural context where women find themselves transformed through the processes of migration and settlement. In tandem, migration and labor force participation in the United States effectively erode the political and economic basis of patriarchal authority, since men rarely perform as sole heads of households upon settlement in this country. The balance of power between men and women in family structures shifts as women gain greater personal autonomy, independence, and decision-making leverage from their participation in the labor force and in community life. Men, on the other hand, are forced to share authority, decision-making, and sometimes even household responsibilities (albeit unevenly) with women, particularly if women are employed full-time outside the home.[1]

For many Central American women, wage work was already an accepted norm (as well as a matter of economic survival), and they faced fewer cultural sanctions against women in the wage-labor force in their home countries than other women of Latin American origin confronted at home.[2] Political and economic conditions in certain Central American countries that set the stage for migration to the United States had already eroded some of the patriarchal and societal strictures that would have inhibited women from active participation in the wage-labor force or in community activities. As few immigrant households were able to survive in the Washington area without the financial contribution of women's wages, these women became direct actors in the labor market and in their communities immediately upon resettlement.

This chapter documents the ways in which the migration and work experiences that women encounter in the United States foment profound transformations in perceptions about their identities as wage earners, about gender roles in relationships, and about career aspirations.[3] As Conseula Mendez, a divorced mother of two children from El Salvador observed,

> Men need women more here, economically speaking, because they can't get by
> very easily without women working. They need women's wages and they have

to help more in the house, even taking care of the children more because there is not much money for child care. Also, men can't go after other women as easily here because they can't support two families at one time and they have to work too hard. So I think it's better for women here.[4]

Yet many Central American women trade one set of contradictions (such as performing as wage earners and/or single heads of households in traditional Catholic cultures) for an altogether different set of contradictions upon resettlement in the United States. Reverberations from the migration process in the work-family nexus are manifest in the different responses of immigrant women and the immigrant men to the myriad changes that the migration and settlement processes engender.

TRANSFORMING GENDER ROLES AND RELATIONSHIPS

Studies conducted in a variety of racial-ethnic communities have demonstrated that women's paid employment and economic contribution to the family enhance self-esteem and decision-making leverage for immigrant women at the same time as it burdens them with the assumption of double and triple roles.[5] In particular, the literature on women and migration has already described some of the ways in which the migration process enables women to renegotiate their relationships and gender roles with men—in decisions concerning labor force participation, in control over the household budget, and in the division of labor within the household. Once women become aware of the advantages that the migration process may confer on them, this role renegotiation may even provide inducement for migration. A study of Dominican immigrants, for example, found that many women veiled their reasons for migration under such explanations as "I wanted to join my husband" or "We wanted our family to be together in one place."[6] Family reunification was generally a subterfuge for more personal goals as many Dominican women sought to alter circumstances in their country of origin that left them totally dependent on men's earnings within the household. These women sought to attain greater decision-making power and control over their lives through migration and labor force participation in the United States, where fewer sanctions against women in the work force exist. Fernández-Kelly and García (1988:2) observed that many Mexican women entered the labor force in the United States because they could not survive on men's earnings alone or because they had been abandoned by male partners. As a result, when the Mexican women were thrust into positions of financial autonomy, "disillusion about the viability of men as economic actors [could] translate into greater receptivity to ideals and hopes of personal emancipation, progress and financial independence."[7]

Like the Mexican women in the California study, Central American women in Washington often entered the wage-labor force as single heads of households or as essential contributors to the family's economic survival. For those who were married, the traditional ideology that cast men in the role of sole bread-winner had to be jettisoned at the onset of the settlement process in the United States because families were simply unable to survive on one income. The labor force participation rate of Central American women in Washington is extremely high (at 87 percent) because of economic necessity and because many women prefer to earn their own income in order to acquire material goods and to maintain personal autonomy. As typologies of traditional male/female wage-earner roles erode, control over the household budget and the division of duties within households become pivotal points of dispute for many immigrant families. The Dominican women in New York who pooled incomes with their partners, for example, were able to enhance their control over domestic resources and shift toward a relatively egalitarian division of labor inside the home.[8]

All but one of the Central American women who were interviewed in Washington worked outside the home and pooled their incomes with partners (if they were living with a man).[9] Every one of these women felt that their participation in the wage-labor force earned them the right to voice opinions when decisions about expenditures and other household issues arose. Half of the women were single mothers or single women without children and therefore did not encounter conflicts about gender roles within their households. Half of those who were married (or living with a man) met their partners in the United States and formulated or negotiated their roles on their own terms within this "first-world" culture. The women in this group reported that their partners in the United States willingly helped with housework on a regular basis.

In only one household was a man responsible for all of the housecleaning chores, while his wife did most of the cooking and grocery shopping. More commonly, housekeeping and cooking responsibilities were shared equally by both partners—particularly in households where women held full-time white-collar jobs outside the home (e.g., as counselors, teachers, or secretaries). In several households men did most of the cooking, while women were responsible for the cleaning. In the few cases where men held two or more jobs, women said that they did not ask their partners to share the housework. Only two women among all those interviewed retained the belief that home was the woman's domain and that it was their responsibility as women to take care of their husbands. Most women—single, married, or accompanied—believed in principle that men should share household chores if both partners worked full-time outside the home.

Few Central American men had been accustomed to sharing household responsibilities and child care in their countries of origin, and half of the married or accompanied men interviewed in Washington continued to balk at doing so after settling in the United States. Even when women worked full-time outside the home, these men still expected their partners to do most of the cooking, cleaning, and caring for children in the household. One woman (Eva) who worked at a social service agency insisted that men "don't even pick up the dishes when they finish eating! With all my friends and family, the men expect women to do all the work. When they live alone, men learn to do the dishes and laundry themselves but once they get married, they expect women to do everything." Yet Eva herself was able to negotiate an equal sharing of household chores and child care with her U.S.-born husband. She believed that only women who formed new attachments to men after they migrated to the United States might be successful in convincing men to share domestic responsibilities and child care. Teresa Lopez was a prime example of this type of relationship, since she had recently allowed her boyfriend to move into the apartment she shared with her son. She proudly relished her authority within her household as she opined: "Men are very different here. In the United States I can insist that my *compañero* [partner] help me with the housework, and I know many marriages where the women make men do more housework in this country. In El Salvador, all the women have to do whatever men tell them to do, but not in the United States!" Nonetheless, other women complained that men from their countries of origin still displayed patriarchal attitudes toward women even after they migrated and settled in the United States. Such perceptions may be indicative of a sea change in women's expectations and personal goals once they become adjusted to North American culture and work routines. These changes are far more dramatic and prompt than those exhibited by their male compatriots.

One consequence of women's greater financial independence and adoption of new cultural norms in the United States is that they are less likely to tolerate physical abuse from a partner as they gain confidence in their abilities to support themselves. Women also say that men are less likely to abuse them physically (and children as well), because there are more societal sanctions against domestic violence in the United Sates. Carmen Montes, for example, confided that her husband developed an alcohol problem after a long period of unemployment in the United States. When he became intoxicated one night and tried to hit her, she threatened to call the police and actually picked up the phone in order to place the call. Her husband immediately backed off and never physically threatened her after that time. Carmen felt that her life had improved immeasurably since she settled in the United States. She claimed that

> Women in my country are like slaves to their husbands, even when they earn money by working and most women do work. It is much more acceptable for men to abuse women in El Salvador. My *compañero* used to beat me when we lived there but since we came to the United States, I don't allow him to do it anymore. At least women can find protection here.

But Rhina Garcia and Marina Suarez asserted that among the families they counseled, men still treated women badly in the United States if the men had been accustomed to such behavior in their countries of origin. Rhina (the nurse from Guatemala) explained: "men demand more of women than they did at home, where women didn't have to work as hard. Now women have to do many jobs [inside and outside the home]. The men from El Salvador especially are taught to be very macho and there is a lot of domestic violence in these families." Likewise, Marina felt that the potential for domestic violence within Central American families might increase upon settlement in the United States because people, particularly men who were unable to maintain steady employment, found drugs and alcohol more accessible when they became depressed. Althea, a preschool teacher, believed that if men physically abused their wives and children at home, they were unlikely to stop the practice when they moved to the United States. "I often see children coming to our school with bruises on them, and I know many men act violently towards their wives and children here."

Most women asserted that relationships became more complicated and contentious as women tried to relate to men under altered circumstances in their adopted country. Maria Herrera, for example, was raised in El Salvador until she entered high school in the United States, and she observed that "men's behavior changes because they have to learn to follow different cultural rules, to see and accept many things when both partners work and scrape to make a living. Women have very different roles here and the men have to adjust to them." Another young woman lambasted the men from her country as macho traditionalists but later admitted that she had succeeded in convincing her Salvadoran father to allow her to live with her boyfriend in Washington.

When women initiate changes in gender roles within a "first-world" culture—for example, by dressing like North Americans and working away from home all day—the reaction from men is often negative. Several informants claimed that their marriages broke up because husbands became jealous after they began working outside the home. Carmen confessed that her husband was exceedingly jealous of her newfound independence and resented the long hours she spent on her job away from home. "He thinks I'm looking for another man because I like to go to work so much!" Particularly if wives work when their husbands are unemployed, men feel threatened as their wives exhibit greater financial and personal independence. The strain on families occasionally leads to divorce, especially in the early years after migration to the United States. Families in which the husband or wife migrated alone in advance of the partner are particularly vulnerable to the stresses of reset-tlement in the United States. Marina Suarez observed that "if the man comes first and leaves his wife and children at home, he usually finds another woman here. There is this idea that men from El Salvador have that they can't be alone for a long time and they need a woman. A lot of women accept this and think it's okay. Even if the woman comes to the United States first, when the man is left behind he makes another family there." Rhina Garcia, who counseled many pregnant women in her social service agency, noted that most of the women who frequented her agency were separated from their partners and children because the women migrated to the United States first. She related the story of one of her clients, a woman who left six children and her partner in El Salvador to search for work in Washington. When the woman learned that her husband had been killed in the fighting in El Salvador, she grew lonely and despondent. Almost immediately she met another man and became pregnant by him. "Most of the women who come to our agency admit that they got pregnant because they were lonely. They don't speak English when they come here and they don't know about clinics where they can get help with family planning."

Settlement in the United States and the ensuing cultural contradictions and tensions are magnified for the children of recent immigrants. Parents are unable to mediate as children attempt to find their niche in a new society, particularly when the parents are forced to work long hours away form home or are compelled to separate because of domestic prob-lems. Alienation within the family increases with time as children become acculturated more quickly than their parents and lose respect for parental authority. Young people come of age as obvious outsiders seeking to belong in a city known for its high crime rate and drug wars as well as its racial tensions. In the process of becoming "Americanized," trying to be like their peers, or even trying to help the family with extra income, immigrant youths may be sorely tempted by the easy money and fast life of drug dealing. They may also join street gangs, which confer a sense of safety and belonging.[10]

For those who fled their countries because of political persecution or because they were unable to provide a living for their families, migration becomes a Catch 22 situation. Individuals move north in order to help maintain the family back home or to ensure their safety by relocating family members to the United States; but the separations and cultural dis-tances they must traverse enhance the loneliness that causes some to look for new partners, peers, or gangs upon resettlement. Families are torn apart amid the contradictions and strug-gles surrounding them, and unexpected outcomes may be worse than the problems that inspired the migration in the first place. As Rhina wryly observed: "That's the worst part about coming to America and it's the thing that's affecting our societies the most—that fam-ilies break up when someone comes to America. The children never behave as well when they come here and easily get into trouble with drugs because of the disintegration of the family."

FREEDOM OR NOTHING LEFT TO LOSE?

The levels at which women experience personal freedom and autonomy in the United States depend fundamentally on such factors as marital status, urban versus rural origin, education level, and other indicators of class background. The consensus among all the Central American women interviewed in Washington is that women enjoy more independence and freedom in the United States then they had in their countries of origin; but they pay dearly for these rights by having to work harder than they did at home, often at jobs below their skill levels, and by having to juggle full-time work with added family responsibilities. Regardless of class background and marital status, most women insisted that they enjoyed more rights in their marriages after migration to this country, rights that came with full-time jobs, economic independence, and greater control over financial resources. Only one woman in the interview sample was completely financially dependent on her partner, and she was so because he refused to allow her to work outside the home when she came to the United States. After five years of virtual seclusion with her children in their small apartment, Marta ascribed women's freedom in the United States above all to economic independence. "If a man is supporting a woman he still thinks he has more rights over her and she has no freedom or economic security."[11]

Women with lower levels of education emphasized that they had less control over financial resources when they were living in their countries of origin. Teresa Lopez, who grew up in a rural town in El Salvador and only finished three years of formal education, commented: "Since I came here I was able to develop myself because I can work and go to school and make my own decisions about where I go or what I do. In my country many women have to stay home and they can't work or have their own money. I am glad that women don't need men here and they can live better without them."

Many women applaud the fact that hard work in the United States enables them to earn and spend their own money as they please—at stores, in restaurants, or socializing with friends. They appreciate such forms of independence as owning cars and literally wearing pants (trousers) in the family (a practice that is taboo in many settings in Central America). Women's economic independence accompanies widening social and personal opportunities that were lacking in their countries of origin. Patricia, a divorced mother of two children with seven years of education, believed that in the United States "if you want to be somebody you can do it. Even if I am old, if I want to study I can do it. In my country, even if you work, the pay is not that good and you can only manage to buy food and that's it. But here, if you work really hard and you want to buy a new car, you can do it." The ultimate freedom for many of these women is the option of leaving living situations in which partners physically abuse them. Carmen, whose unemployed husband had abused her, was the sole supporter of a family of seven. The fact that she controlled her own money and drove her own car had obviously empowered her, although she complained that life in the United States was difficult and that she often felt beleaguered by pressures that were nonexistent in El Salvador.

Teresa Lopez believed that women were not really "free" in this country, because they had to work longer hours with higher stress levels in the United States. "I wasn't really free until six years ago when I finally had some savings and could buy a new car. For almost ten years I had to live and work in other people's houses and I wasn't free," she lamented. Once they earned their independence and became accustomed to newfound freedoms, women like Teresa expressed profound gratitude for enhanced economic independence and the opportunity it afforded them to control their own destinies. In particular, the women who originated in rural sectors of their countries and had little formal education relished the opportunity to work outside the home in the United States. Many of these women were expected to work in the home or fields in their countries of origin and held little control over personal or financial decisions. For rural women who adapted to life in the United States and exercised the freedom to venture out on their own, the resulting conflicts with men were far more stressful than for their compatriots from urban areas. Immigrant men with little formal education and of rural origin tended to exhibit greater difficulties in adjusting to partners who had achieved financial independence. In the social service agency where she worked, Marina had seen families break apart because "it's not easy to change the minds and habits that people have had for many years, and it causes problems for couples." On the other hand, well-educated women who came from the middle and upper classes in their countries of origin but who experienced downward mobility in their careers upon migration were less enthusiastic about the benefits that migration conferred upon women—particularly if they were forced to migrate for political reasons.

Additionally, marital status influenced women's assessment of the personal gains they had realized upon migration to the United States. Married women said that in the United States they had to work harder to keep up with the physical and emotional needs of their families, which left them little time to enjoy enhanced independence. Consuela, a divorced mother of two, asserted that "women are more free here in every way, especially in being able to work and drive cars. But it's better for single women because married women have so many responsibilities that they don't have much time to enjoy their independence." Married women complained that after they migrated to the United States, their work load doubled if they had to work full-time inside and outside the home without the help of extended family. Carmen lamented: "Only the men are going to be able to better themselves financially in this country. Women can barely make ends meet… it isn't freedom to be isolated and alienated in this culture here."

Several married women vocalized a deep-seated envy of single women, since they held the impression that single women were able to venture out when they pleased, to work for good wages, and then to spend the money on themselves—to a degree unprecedented in their countries of origin. Some of the single women verified that they did indeed enjoy added personal liberties as a consequence of their labor force participation and the acquisition of possessions such as automobiles. Even more so they relished the freedom from community pressures and sanctions that were an integral part of life in small Central American towns. As Isabel noted, "In El Salvador women are rejected for doing 'bad' things. But people can't fire you for your personal behavior here. Women can go out with more than one man and they are free to do what they want … even abortion is an option here, which it isn't in El Salvador." Other women observed that single women had the unprecedented liberty to date different men, to live alone, or to live with a man without being criticized by the surrounding community. "A woman never really has the ability to experience what it is to live on her own in our countries," according to Eva. "Women have more sexual freedom in the United States and they can drink and do anything that men do, which is impossible in our countries."

Several women observed that too much sexual freedom was harmful and that as recent immigrants they were more vulnerable to isolation and loneliness after they settled in the United States. Althea, a college-educated teacher, commented that although many families boasted of improvements in financial status and material acquisitions in the United States, they faced more alienation and greater challenges to the moral fabric of their relationships. "People get confused because they have so many things to divert and entertain themselves with here—the bars and restaurants, for example—and they think that this is freedom."

Compared with what they left behind in their countries of origin, immigrants confront the rigors of life in the United States with less time to unwind and socialize among families and friends. Especially for parents, anxieties are amplified because of the profusion of unfamiliar influences on their children and the underlying racial tensions pervading American society. Without the ameliorating presence of extended families to help diffuse these pressures, parents are expected to be involved in the emotional lives of their children, to visit their schools, and to help children with problems they encounter in the United States. Counseling children and assisting them with complex problems and influences within a foreign culture occupies a great deal of parents' time and resources.

DREAMING NORTH AMERICAN DREAMS

Common themes repeatedly surfaced in the dreams that Central American women from a broad spectrum of backgrounds had formulated for themselves and for their families. They included home ownership, the prospect of better jobs, and furthering their individual development. After they had settled in the United States, most women generally associated the proverbial American dream with higher education. Over half of the women interviewed envisaged college or graduate school for their children, and three-fourths of them resolved to take classes and to acquire new skills themselves in the United States. Many expressed the desire to attend school to learn skills that could put them on more promising career paths. In particular, the women who came to the United States with high school degrees aspired to work as secretaries one day, and they resolved to learn English and word processing in order to surmount the frustrations they experienced in low-status domestic service jobs. An overwhelming majority of the women interviewed contemplated the future with optimism because they believed it was possible to develop themselves and to enable their children to attain high education levels in the United States.

Women with only a moderate level of education (six to ten years) formulated goals in line with the skill levels they brought with them from their countries of origin. Rosaria Lopez, the seamstress and former factory worker, aspired to operate her own dress-making shop someday; and another woman who cooked in a Mexican restaurant hoped to manage her own small restaurant in the future. Many women who held college degrees when they emigrated aspired to regain careers they once held or to assist and counsel people from their countries of origin. Two women voiced a desire to teach again, three social workers intended to pursue graduate degrees, and two counselors hoped to earn more money in order to buy their own homes someday. Whether women had only three years of education or held college degrees, all concurred in their aspirations for their children: they wanted their children to have the opportunity to attend college and to attain professional careers in the United States. Women like Patricia, who had experienced sharp downward mobility upon migration to the United States, intended to remain in this country specifically to further their children's education. "I'm working very hard because I want my children to be somebody. I don't want them to have to work at a Roy Rogers or clean other people's houses."

None of the women spoke of their tenure on jobs outside their homes as temporary. None of them expressed the desire to leave the wage-labor force in order to remain at home or to allow their partners to be sole supporters in the household. All the women said that they preferred to be busy and to work with other people on a job site in order to maintain their financial independence from men. Yet there were disturbing trade-offs for mothers who worked outside the home. Maria Herrera, the Salvadoran woman who earned the highest salary among the women in the interview sample, expressed the conflicts that her ambitions aroused.

> I've already reached many of my goals but at the expense of having to leave my children when they were little to work full-time. I would have preferred to be a full-time mother for awhile . . . . I wasn't able to be with my children enough because my husband and I had to work full-time. Now I want my children to go to college and have some skills so that they can be in command of their job opportunities and not be dependent on anyone.

Few women still harbored intentions of returning to live in their countries of origin someday, although half of them admitted that they had only intended to live and work in the United States for two or three years when they first emigrated. Over time a third of the women had revised their plans and intended to reside permanently in the United States, and another third planned to retire someday in their countries of origin. Only one-fourth of the women still hoped to return to their countries of birth when "the situation improved," meaning peaceful living conditions and job opportunities.[12] Five years after the initial interviews, I spoke with many of these women again, and only two women out of twenty-two had actually returned to their countries of origin. Several women from El Salvador explained that although the government and insurgents had formally signed a peace treaty, conditions there remained tense and the peace tenuous. One of the women who returned to El Salvador did so because her husband had been elected to the new Congress of Deputies. But upon her return she was so alarmed at the extent of the violence in the country that she promptly sent two more sons and a daughter to join her daughters already living in the United States. Eva confessed that she remained in the United States because "the message I hear from everyone is 'do not come back here, because the country is not ready to receive you yet.'" Consuela contended that she must remain in the Washington area for the sake of her children. "It's not war any more in El Salvador, but it's not peace yet either. It's still not easy to live there, and there is too much robbery and violence. We don't have our beautiful country back yet."

Over time and with increasing exposure to North American norms and values, Central American men were also adapting to the transformations in gender roles that settlement in the United States conferred. Few men envisioned a return to their countries of origin as a means for regaining authority and privileges. Yet there were some who did return after agonizing at length over the relative merits of attempting to achieve success in a competitive "first-world" society. Eric Romero and his wife Silvia, for example, returned to Guatemala after spending two difficult years in the United States. Before their original migration Eric and Silvia had been working in relatively high-status jobs at a bank in Guatemala City. But when violence in Guatemala prevented them from living and working in peace, they decided to join Eric's parents and brothers in the United States. During their first year in Washington, Silvia worked as a housekeeper, while Eric worked as a dishwasher in a restaurant. He eventually found a better job as a warehouse manager, but when Silvia had a child and quit her job, they found that they could not survive on one salary. Eric had to take a second job at a commercial cleaning company and was unable to see his family even on weekends or evenings. Silvia became disillusioned with their lives in the United States and decided to return to Guatemala with the child. Eric followed her two months later, when he realized, "In the United States I will always be stuck in low-status jobs and will never be free from worries about making enough money for my family." Although Eric's parents and brothers obtained permanent-residence status, he claimed he never wanted to live in the United States again. "Why should I have to suffer in three jobs with low status just so my children can have some benefits when they grow up? I never could be with my children in the U.S., and parents and children have a different relationship there."

Two women had vowed in the initial interviews that they would return to their countries of origin someday because they believed that life was safer and healthier for children in a drug-free environment and with extensive family support systems surrounding them. Both women had actually left daughters behind to be raised by their grandmothers in Guatemala because, as one explained, "I wanted her to live with the love of God and of brothers and sisters around her without any discrimination. Even though we are poor in our country, it is better for children to grow up in an environment of love and support where life is more modest and sincere." The other woman planned to work hard for two or three years in order to return to El Salvador with money for her daughter's future. But five years later both women had remarried men from their countries of origin who were also living in Washington, and they had started new families in that city. Despite contradictory impulses to return home, newcomers often develop ineradicable ties over time to the communities where they live and work in the United States. Clearly these forces counterbalance those encouraging return to the country of origin, as Leo Chavez observed.[13] Experiences such as maintaining steady employment, learning English, forming a family in the United States, raising children in U.S. schools, adapting to North American culture, and ultimately gaining legal status lead inexorably to immigrant incorporation into U.S. society.

NOTES

1. Grasmuck and Pessar 1991; Hondagneu-Sotelo 1992; Pessar 1986.

2. Grasmuck and Pessar 1991; Pedraza 1991.

3. The lengthy open-ended interviews with women in the sample of fifty Central American individuals were particularly useful in exploring the impact of the migration experience on gender roles and on women's lives and relationships. Thirty women offered detailed responses to questions about their responsibilities in the home, their relationships with partners and family members, how the migration experience had altered these relationships, and what they aspired to be in their adopted country. This chapter's discussion on gender roles and the migration experience is based primarily on the interview sample. The women in the interview sample were representative of the survey sample in that comparable proportions were married or living with a companion and had children living with them (over half the samples) and most women worked full-time outside the home. Like their counterparts in the survey sample, a majority of the women entered the wage-labor force in the United States in domestic service and over half were still working in that capacity at the time of the interviews. For this reason I am confident that many of the women's perceptions about changes in gender roles accurately reflect the perceptions of Central American women in Washington generally.

4. Consuela claims that the sex ratio in Washington is a major element contributing to women's elevated status in the United States. She believes that in Washington there are more single Central American men from her native region than there are single women, which makes it more difficult for men to meet and maintain relationships with other women outside of their established households.

5. Fernández-Kelly and García 1988; Kibria 1990; Pessar 1984, 1986.

6. Grasmuck and Pessar 1991.

7. Fernández-Kelly and García 1988:2.

8. Grasmuck and Pessar 1991.

9. Only one woman among the thirty interviewed in Washington was prevented from working outside the home by a husband who felt that she should remain at home with their children.

10. In response, local governments and private sources have established programs within the social service agencies and churches to deal specifically with substance abuse and other youth-related problems, instituting widely use drug-counseling and education programs for both children and their parents.

11. Several women noted that at the very least they were safe from political persecution and that their

children would not be drafted into the army. As Carmen exclaimed, "Here we don't have to be afraid of fighting or that someone will kill us or take us away in the night."

12. A further 10 percent planned to reside permanently in the United States but wished to relocate to California; 6 percent wanted to live in Mexico or in Europe someday.

13. Chavez 1992:184.

REFERENCES

Chavez, Leo. 1992. *Shadowed Lives: Undocumented Immigrants in American Society.* Philadelphia: Harcourt Brace Jovanovich.

Fernández-Kelly, Maria Patricia, and Anna García. 1988. "Invisible Amidst the Glitter: Hispanic Women in the Southern California Electronics Industry." In *The Worth of Women's Work*, ed. Anne Statham et al. Albany: State University of New York Press.

Hondagneu-Sotelo, Pierrette. 1992. "Overcoming Patriarchal Constraints: The Reconstruction of Gender Relations Among Mexican Immigrant Men and Women." *Gender and Society* 6, no. 3:393-415.

Kibria, Nazli. 1990. "Power, Patriarchy, and Gender Conflict." *Gender and Society* 4:924.

Pedraza, Silvia. 1991. "Women and Migration: The Social Consequences of Gender." *Annual Review of Sociology* 17:303-25.

Pessar, Patricia. 1986. "The Role of Gender in Dominican Settlement in the United States." In *Women and Change in Latin America*, ed. June Nash and Helen Safa. South Hadley, Mass.: Bergin & Garvey.

_____. 1984. "The Role of Households in International Migration and the Case of U.S.-Bound Migration from the Dominican Republic." *International Migration Review* 16:342-64.

PART FIVE

ECONOMIC AND POLITICAL RESTRUCTURING

INTRODUCTION ❧

Mary Romero

TWO MAJOR EVENTS HAVE TAKEN PLACE over the past three decades that have dramatically affected the life chances of Latinos in the labor marketplace. First, the Latino population has increased dramatically to the point where, between 1980 and 1990 Latinos comprised 30 percent of the nation's population gain (see Part II). Second, the U.S. economy underwent a wrenching shift from a manufacturing to a service economy, eliminating huge numbers of high wage blue-collar jobs in manufacturing, mining, and industrial production. Affirmative action programs and other civil rights legislation passed during the 1970s made it possible for larger numbers of Latinos to earn a college education and for some Latino workers to move up to middle-level management positions and other desirable white-collar jobs. However, the latest round of economic restructuring, euphemistically termed "downsizing," is eliminating many middle-management and white collar jobs. The old rules of last hired, first fired mean that hard-won and precarious footholds in the new economy are at high risk. While some of the new service sector jobs have been high-wage, high-tech positions in the information economy, the largest number have been low-wage, temporary, or part-time jobs in industries like tourism and food preparation. Moreover, when some of the traditional positions are eliminated they are replaced with temporary, part-time, or contract labor. These new positions seldom have job stability or benefit packages. Researchers estimate that the weekly wage has dropped from $315 to $258 from 1973 to 1990.[1] Thus, like many other workers, Latinos have experienced the last twenty years of economic restructuring as an increase in economic insecurity, the loss of stable family-wage jobs, a decline in real wages, increasingly unsafe working conditions, and a declining social infrastructure. Signs of economic restructuring in Latino communities in the U.S. include an increase in the number of sweatshops in Miami, Los Angeles, and New York City; Spanish-speaking hotel maids and restaurant workers in Washington, D.C., Boston, San Francisco, Denver, and Chicago; and the elimination of white collar jobs through downsizing at huge companies including AT&T, IBM, and state and local government.

Economic restructuring impacts other areas of society as well. Immigrant and non-immigrant Latinos frequently find themselves side by side, residing in the same neighborhood, seeking employment in the same industry, shopping in the same grocery stores, and directly competing for dwindling resources. Work and community relations must be negotiated across a range of boundary lines, including race, culture, citizenship, gender, age, and education. Racial conflict among Latinos, and between Latinos and Anglos, African Americans, Asians, and other groups complicates social interaction even when they are able to find common interests as workers. Political debates are fueled by images of "aliens" as invading the United States to threaten the American way of life with crime, foreign languages and cultures. Signs of political restructuring dominate the national news; they include English-Only initiatives in Florida, California, and Colorado; Spanish language billboards in Latino communities; Latino presidential appointees; the backlash against affirmative action programs; increased patrolling along the U.S./Mexico border; and urban riots. This section presents a micro perspective of economic and political restructuring. Examining case studies conducted in Miami and Houston, the articles explore the impact that the macro shifts in the economy have had on Latino communities, particularly their social interaction between groups. Each study highlights both the restructuring of the local political economy and addresses issues affecting Latinos in major urban centers throughout the country. The studies illustrate how economic and political restructuring affect not only occupational patterns, but also the politics of language and housing.

The first article in the section, "Brothers in Wood," is a case study of Latino construction workers in the changing economy in Miami. Alex Stepick and Guillermo Grenier examine the construction project that built the Miami Beach Convention Center. The study captures the intra-ethnic work relations between younger bilingual Cubans and older monolingual Spanish-speaking Cubans, and the inter-ethnic relations between Haitians, African Americans, Cubans, Nicaraguans, and Anglos. Descriptions of ethnic dominance and cultural hegemony in the construction industry help make visible the shifting relations between power, culture, and identity. The construction industry had long practiced exclusionary policies established by Anglo-dominated unions. This legacy was apparent in the large number of Latinos among the lower-paid nonunion construction workers and ethnic groups stratified by race within the industry. Cubans used ethnic networks to gain access and eventually to transform the industry. Ethnicity regulated social interaction, particularly in terms of language; however, Stepick and Grenier clearly demonstrate that language in itself did not cause conflict and some coworkers were able to find a common language. However, ethnicity continued to shape interaction between management and co-workers. This study demonstrates the way that ethnic and class interests are negotiated and how they may result in either conflict, alliances, or class solidarity.

In their article "Apartment Restructuring and Latino Immigrant Tenant Struggles: A Case Study of Human Agency," Nestor Rodriquez and Jacqueline Maria Hagan investigate the impact that restructuring of the real-estate industry had on Latinos in Houston. Data collected from a two year ethnographic study conducted in an apartment complex revealed that Latino immigrants were targeted as potential clients during the economic recession in order to fill vacant apartments, and later were targeted for removal when the complex was upgraded to attract higher income (Anglo) tenants. To recruit Latino tenants, apartment managers advertised in Spanish, hired bilingual staff in the office and on the grounds crew, and were less likely to enforce regulations about children, number of people in a household, and informal businesses on the premises. When management began restructuring the complex to attract higher income tenants, Latino immigrant renters were placed in the back apartment buildings where they became invisible to other tenants. Within the political context of the Immigration Reform and Control Act (IRCA) in 1986 and the changing management policies, Rodriguez and Hagan describe a range of ethnic relations between Anglo, African American, Mexican American, and Mexican and Central American immigrants. The case study highlights the undocumented immigrant-survival strategies and the intergroup relations that became sources of individual and collective resistance.

In the case study presented in the article "The Politics of Language in Miami," Max J. Castro chronicles the history of language issues from the first bilingual public school program in 1963 to the English Only Movement of the 1980s. Castro links the occurrence of both events in Miami to the growing number of Cubans and their political empowerment. Castro argues that instead of opposition, Cubans received cultural and linguistic accommodations in the media, schools, and government. They encountered an "enlightened assimilationism" from Miami's elites rather than monolingual and monocultural policies and practices. Examples of the accommodations are Dade County's establishment of bilingual education in 1963 and the *Miami Herald*'s creation of a Spanish edition, *El Herald,* in 1976. Castro points out that, unlike most other Spanish-speaking immigrants, Cubans were urban, middle-class and better educated; thus, Cubans were in a strong bargaining position for the "right to be serviced and heard." The antibilingual referendum, was an organized resistance against the Latinization of Miami by non-elite Whites; while African Americans were divided on the issue. Castro explains the racial division by noting that non-elite Whites were likely to have experienced demographic and economic displacement from 1970 to 1980, and African Americans may have seen the referendum as White racism.

DISCUSSION QUESTIONS:

1. Discuss the economic ascendancy of Cubans in Miami in relation to the campaigns for bilingualism and antibilingualism.

2. Explain how economic restructuring in Houston, and apartment managements' strategies set the context for inter-ethnic group interactions. Did Latino immigrants face closed borders or opening frontiers in their interactions with Anglos and African Americans?

3. Describe how the immigration of Cubans and other Latinos transformed the construction industry and workplace relations in Miami. How does trade segregation relate to racial ethnic segregation?

SUGGESTED READINGS:

Delgado, Hector L. 1993. *New Immigrants, Old Unions: Organizing Undocumented Workers in Los Angeles.* Philadelphia: Temple University Press.

Grenier, Guillermo J., and Alex Stepick III (Eds.)1992. "Immigration, Ethnicity and Social Change." In *Miami Now!* Gainesville: University of Florida Press.

Lamphere, Louise, Alex Stepick, and Guillermo Grenier (Eds.). 1994. *Newcomers in the Workplace.* Philadelphia: Temple University Press

Moore, Joan and Raquel Pinderhughes (Eds.). 1993. *In the Barrios: Latinos and the Underclass Debate.* New York: Russell Sage Foundation.

Morales, Rebecca and Frank Bonilla (Eds.). 1993. *Latinos in a Changing U.S. Economy.* Newbury Park: Sage Publications.

Torres, Andres. 1995. *Between Melting Pot and Mosaic: African Americans and Puerto Ricans in New York Political Economy.* Philadelphia: Temple University Press.

NOTES

1. Rebecca Morales and Frank Bonilla (eds.) 1993. *Latinos in a Changing U.S. Economy.* Newbury Park, CA: Sage Publications.

15 🌿

BROTHERS IN WOOD

Alex Stepick and Guillermo Grenier
with Steve Morris and Debbie Draznin

Yeah, there's always going to be prejudice, but it's not that bad here. Everyone's in the same boat. Everyone gets sweaty, dirty, and smelly.
—A young Cuban American carpenter.

Pretty soon there'll be no whites in this trade. It won't be worth it. You can't make a living. You can't buy shit—a nice house, a new car. Shit, you can't even go on a fucking trip when you get time off. Pretty soon the fucking Cubans and sambos will take it over. They know how to live on less.
—A middle-aged Anglo carpenter.

DURING 1987, the Miami Beach Convention Center was the largest single building being constructed in Dade County. It was being built solely by union labor, an anomaly in Miami's primarily nonunionized construction industry. Thirty years ago, however, before the Cubans took over most of the industry, the convention center would not have been such an aberration. Then, the unions controlled most of the industry, and virtually all the workers were white Anglos, with the exception of African American laborers. Now, things are different. Not only have the unions lost control of most of the industry, but among the workers there are nearly as many Latins and whites, and among the Blacks, many are immigrants from the Caribbean, especially Haiti.

Immigration has assuredly restructured Miami's construction industry. Not only has there been deunionization and the penetration of immigrant workers, but also immigrant-owned firms control a large portion of the industry that has been divided into union, nonunion, and informal firms. Immigrants have penetrated each of these sectors, although unevenly, predominating in nonunion firms. As the two quotes that open this chapter reveal, the immigrants' impact is mixed, with some American workers blaming them for a decline in the industry and others maintaining that solidarity persists regardless of a worker's origins.

This chapter examines these trends based on an analysis of secondary sources and fieldwork. Steve Morris worked for one summer as a carpenter's apprentice at the Miami Beach Convention Center. Debbie Draznin worked out of the Carpenters' Union Hall for two summers. Alex Stepick and Guillermo Grenier conducted interviews of union officials and managers and owners of construction firms. We first describe the transformation of the industry wrought by immigration and then the actual relationships within the workplace, the resistance of workers to management, and the conflicting forces of solidarity and autonomy among workers themselves.

THE BUILDING TRADES IN MIAMI

Between 1940 and 1960, Dade County's population increased by nearly 90 percent every ten years. For the following twenty years, the rate declined but remained a significant 30 percent per decade. Correspondingly, the construction industry boomed. Until the late 1960s, unions controlled 90 percent of all housing construction in Miami. This changed as the first wave of Cubans inundated the local labor market.

The refusal from the 1960s until the mid-1970s of local building trade unions to accept Cuban workers fundamentally transformed, rather than preserved, the construction industry. The false security created from a near-monopoly of the industry combined with nativist sentiments to create an implicit policy of exclusion. One of our Cuban respondents tried to join the Carpenters Union in 1969. He had to pay $25 to take a test in English, a language he did not speak at the time. He failed the test and was denied entrance. A few weeks later, he responded to a newspaper advertisement announcing openings for carpenters through the union. This time he did not take the test or pay any money. They simply refused to allow him in. The third time, he finally got in the union because he had married an Anglo woman whose father was a member of the Carpenters Union. His new father-in-law recommended him, and the union's business agent helped him pass the test. Subsequently, he consciously devoted himself to bringing more Latins into the Carpenters Union and urged them to become involved in union politics.

In short, recruitment patterns did not change; they still relied on personalistic ties. The only difference was that through marriage one Cuban penetrated those networks and then expanded them to include more Cubans. He later became an important officer in the union and explained his role thus: "The way I see it, it is my job to give Latins a chance. If you are no good, you won't stay long, but I will always give a Latin a chance to prove himself."

Unlike many other U.S. minorities, Cubans rejected by the unions did not simply return to low-wage, unskilled work. Instead, Cuban immigrants began creating their own, nonunion firms and competing for housing contracts. Meanwhile, unionized construction workers focused on higher-paid jobs building condominiums in Miami Beach and office buildings in downtown Miami. Then the 1973 recession, which severely depressed the construction industry (see Table 15.1), impelled many Anglo construction workers to abandon Dade County altogether, leaving a void that newer, nonunion Cuban firms began to fill as the recovery began in the late 1970s.

When the unions finally recognized that excluding Cubans was a mistake, it was too late. The number of unionized carpenters declined from a high of ten thousand to a low of three thousand in the late 1970s. The 1980s were especially hard on construction unions. Throughout the United States, construction unions suffered some of the most severe economic conditions since the 1950s. On top of this, mismanagement and corruption in Miami's Carpenters Union forced the International Brotherhood of Carpenters to assume control of the Miami area local Carpenters Union. The union began to recapture some membership, but the influx of more than one hundred twenty thousand Cubans and

Table 15.1. Miami's Construction Industry: Employment, Earnings, and Firms, 1973-1989			
	Number of Employees	Annual Payroll ($1,000)	Number of Firms
1973	44,707		2,544
1974	47,662	482,194	2,694
1975	30,992	331,140	2,362
1976	25,250	309,068	2,486
1977	26,614	330,021	2,675
1978	33,135	402,963	2,702
1979	37,993	486,112	2,854
1980	41,459	612,907	2,967
1981	44,716	701,896	2,950
1982	38,117	642,732	2,770
1983	35,834	640,081	3,220
1984	37,363	668,069	3,234
1985	37,039	645,637	3,328
1986	36,325	654,192	3,428
1987	38,609	708,510	3,689
1988	37,612	755,767	3,606
1989	37,532	783,600	3,581

Source: County Business Patterns (Dade County). Bureau of Economic Research, Gainesville, Florida. Annual Reports 1974-1990.

another twenty thousand Haitians during 1980 provided more workers willing to work for nonunion wages. Then the early 1980s recession reduced the amount of work. The most recently hired were the first to go. As an Anglo leader of the Plumbers Union states:

> We are a pretty red-neck union.... At first, we wanted to keep them out. That was OK with my members. I was one of the few that wanted them in anyway. Then, we decided we had to let them in... so we loosened up and set up some training... so, then the contractors put them on but they are the first ones out when the job gets done.... The contractors are red-necks, too.... to keep working, then they go work non-union. You can't blame them but that's our problem. (Grenier 1992)

In contract negotiations in the mid-1980s, the unions were forced to accept wage cutbacks and relinquish their right to strike. By that time, the Latin Builders' Association, thoroughly nonunion, had emerged as one of the most influential forces in Dade County politics, and Cuban firms, mostly nonunion, controlled more than 50 percent of all Dade County construction and nearly 90 percent of new housing, the fastest-growing sector of the industry.

When Cubans first began penetrating the construction industry in the 1960s, informal practices predominated in Cuban construction firms. Small-scale entrepreneurs operated out of the back of their trucks, accepting cash for payment and paying their workers with cash. As the industry and the number of Cuban firms grew through the 1970s, work relationships became regularized. Larger firms began subcontracting with smaller Cuban firms. By the 1980s, most larger firms paid by check, as did many of the subcontractors, who also generally made all the appropriate deductions. Wages were assuredly lower, approximately by one-third, than union wage scale, but they remained far above the minimum wage. The Cuban construction industry, in short, started informally and then became formalized.

In the wake of the 1980 Mariel influx and then again in the mid-1980s when working-class Nicaraguans began settling in Miami, small-scale subcontractors exploited the unemployed new immigrants by offering lower wages, hovering near the minimum wage, paid in cash without any deductions. Since 1980, many subcontractors, especially smaller ones, have no longer paid time and a half for overtime and have falsified records to conceal the true number of hours worked.

The ethnic composition of the labor force, seen in Figure 15.1, further reflects this transformation. The proportion of Latin construction workers doubled in the 1970s, from 20 percent to nearly 40 percent. Latins achieved this relative growth primarily at the expense of Anglos, many of whom, as mentioned earlier, were packing up and leaving Dade County and whose relative numbers in the construction industry declined from 60 to 44 percent.[1]

Immigrant penetration of the construction industry did not affect all sectors of the industry equally. Nonunion work is obviously more likely to be Latin dominated. But unionized work has also been affected. Different construction trades tend to be dominated by particular ethnic groups. They are also stratified in terms of prestige by race and as a result of previous political gains. The Black tradesmen, Laborers,[2] are exclusively African American and Haitian. At the other end of the scale, workers whose trades require state licensing, for example Electricians and Plumbers, receive the highest wages and have the highest prestige. These trades are not only virtually all white but have also been the slowest to admit Latins. Carpenters fall in the middle of this hierarchy. Latins have significantly increased their percentage in the Carpenters Union, giving it the highest proportion of Latins among the unionized trades.

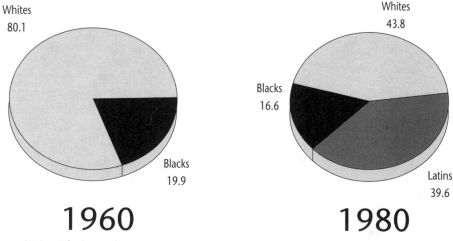

Figure 15.1.   Ethnic employment percentages in Miami's construction industry, 1960 and 1980. From U.S. Bureau of the Census figures, Florida.

Unionized Latin Carpenters do mostly "inside work," that is, cabinet and door shops, where they probably constitute about 70 percent of the overall unionized workforce. In "outside work," Anglos continue to hold on. Nevertheless, even in unionized work, the trend is clear: Latins are increasing, while Anglos are declining.[3]

At the worksite where Steve Morris conducted his fieldwork, Carpenters were more or less evenly balanced between Anglos and Latins, although among all the trade workers at the site, Anglos predominated. Out of a maximum of seventy-five Carpenters working at once, there was only one African American. At the entire site, there were approximately seventy Blacks, nearly all of whom were Laborers. Laborers were further divided informally into African American (about three-quarters) and Haitians (about one-quarter).

Immigration, then, has dramatically affected the ethnic composition of the Miami construction industry, not only through the penetration of immigrant workers, but also and even more significantly through the creation of immigrant, that is, Cuban firms and the establishment of an informal sector of construction work. This resulted from the forces that created the Miami Latin enclave. In the construction industry, the usurpation of the majority of the industry by Cuban firms was greatly advanced by the exclusionary policies of Anglo-dominated unions. Although the unions subsequently reversed their policies, the example cited of a Latin joining the Carpenters Union through his Anglo father-in-law's intercession reveals that discriminatory, Anglo-dominated recruitment patterns persisted. Cubans simply penetrated the networks and used them to incorporate fellow ethnics.

WORKERS' ATTITUDES AND RELATIONSHIPS

The nature of construction work directly affects construction workers' control of their labor, their consciousness, and the perception and nature of class conflict. Unlike most employees in modern industrialized society, construction workers, especially those involved in "outside" work, such as the site where Steve Morris worked, maintain a high level of independence and autonomy. Owning their tools, construction workers are freed from the technological dependence found in occupations alienated from the means of production. In Applebaum's (1981) and LeMasters's (1975) analyses of construction worker autonomy, independence among workers was found to extend through the entire process of construction work, including control over one's managerial supervision, the ability to regulate which partners to work with, and the sovereignty to decide whether or not to work in adverse environmental conditions. In Miami, we found all this to be true. But we also found that ethnic changes wrought by immigration have introduced variation in management-labor relations while complicating and apparently partially eroding solidarity among the workers.

In contrast to the workers in Miami's apparel industry, construction workers are defiant and resistant toward management. A Haitian recalled his experiences constructing the Hyatt Regency in Coral Gables. "They [the owners] wouldn't even let me go through the front door. Once we bust our balls and finish a building, the guys who own it think we are not good enough to walk in the front door. People might see us or something. What bullshit! They even told us we would get fired if we did."

Workers are especially likely to confront and resist management on safety issues. For example, an Anglo supervisor, Mark, wanted an Anglo Carpenter, Willie, to build a soffit (the underside of an enclosure to conceal air-conditioning ductwork) with a two-foot span between the studs that framed it. Willie thought a two-foot span was unsafe and directly told Mark that he would not built it to those dimensions. Mark meekly conceded and indicated that Willie could build it as he saw fit.

Another time, Alberto, a Cuban Carpenter in his fifties, had been working alone, about a hundred feet from the ground, framing the sides where the ceiling met the walls. To reach the third-story scaffolds, he had to carry ten-foot studs in one hand up a ladder. About 2:00 P.M., Steve Morris went to the gang box to get a chop-saw blade. When he arrived, he noticed that Alberto was visibly upset, sweating profusely, red in the face, shaking his head as if it bothered him, and nodding his head as if in disgust. Just then Dan, an Anglo supervisor, walked up, put his arm around Alberto's neck, and asked what was wrong. Alberto responded in English, "Danny, you know I'm a good worker. I do what you tell me. But now, I have to say something. That scaffolding is dangerous. I can't work up there alone. How do you expect me to carry materials up there and do my job? I need someone to help me. Get me someone quick or else I'm leaving. This job ain't worth dying for. You guys are the ones who talk about safety. It's in the contract. This is bullshit." Dan responded coolly, "Calm down, Al, I'll get you another guy. Just take it easy." Alberto, shaking his head, said "You know I work hard, Danny. I don't want to start trouble. But this is too much." Dan answered, "OK, Al. I'll send someone right over."

Construction workers plainly believed that they were far more concerned with safety than management was. Their antagonism toward, and derision of, management was most obvious during safety meetings, which were held every few weeks. At one meeting, a superintendent for the electrical engineering contractor began by stating, "Remember, safety is our first concern." Instantly, the workers jeered in response. "Yeah, that's bullshit." An Anglo Carpenter commented to those closest to him, "Shit, I'd rather get to work than sit here and listen to this." The supervisor in charge of one meeting had to chastise workers three times to "keep it down."

To management, it seemed as if the workers were unconcerned with safety, since they frequently ignored management-imposed safety rules, such as commands for everyone to wear a hardhat at all times. Jim, an Anglo Carpenter, did not wear a safety hat because, he maintained, it caused him to lose his balance when climbing or on a scaffold. Miguel, a young Latin, explained that "they [hardhats] do no good. They're hot and get in your way. They're a hazard." At one meeting, a supervisor threatened, "If you don't wear your hardhats here, you have no business working for this company." The rule, however, was never enforced. Similarly, Jack, a young Anglo Carpenter, commenting on why he did not wear a mask for dust and fumes, claimed, "You know, us Carpenters are ignorant. Anyway, if you had to do this shit for a living, ten years off your life is a blessing." Another Carpenter declared that he did not wear gloves because "they get in the way. Shit, you can't feel what you're doing. That's downright unsafe."

Nevertheless, at one safety meeting, after management discussed its safety rules, the supervisor asked for complaints. The workers quickly obliged: debris not cleaned up, unsteady makeshift ladders to the upper storeys, unclean Port-o-Lets, and no water coolers around the site. After another meeting, workers asked no questions but spoke among themselves of safety issues, particularly the "trash," ceiling insulation sprayed on during working hours. Jim commented, "We should not have to be contaminated by that shit. It should be sprayed on at night and cleaned up before we get here. It could kill us. Who knows what's in that stuff."

The dangers, of course, are real. Accidents do occur. In one two-day period, three Carpenters were injured, one requiring twenty stitches on his sliced hand. During break one morning, Miguel and Ignacio came walking toward Steve and Jim. Ignacio was holding the side of his head. Jim asked, "What the hell happened to you?" "Miguel dropped the fucking screw gun on my head," Ignacio responded. Miguel added, "It was an accident, man." "Well, are you gonna live?" Jim asked. Ignacio retorted, "Fuck you, beer belly." And both laughed. Ignacio complained, "My head feels like a fucking Yo-Yo. Goddam, I'm lucky I wore my hardhat or I'd be dead right now." Manny claimed, "Yeah it saved your freaking life." Jim, who never wears a hardhat, changed the focus. "Shit, you know what this means, guys, don't you? You got it, another safety meeting." After everyone sat down, Jim added, "Hey, Ignacio, you shouldn't have worn your hardhat. You could be getting workers' comp right now. Instead, you got to work like the rest of us slobs; what a pea brain." Everyone else seemed more concerned with Ignacio's health and ignored Jim's comment.

This incident reveals some underlying elements of construction workers' response to the dangers of their trade: individual autonomy and different ethnic responses to danger. First, as Ignacio stated, people should wear hardhats, "It's for their own good. But if they don't wear them, that's their problem." To the men, the key issue was that it should be the worker's choice. The foreman or supervisor should not tell the workers what to do.

Second, workers from different ethnic groups respond differently. In a nonrandom sample of Latins, Anglos, African Americans, and Haitians observed the day after a safety meeting five of ten Anglos, seven of ten Latins, ten of ten U.S. African Americans, and ten of ten Haitians were wearing hardhats. In short, African Americans obeyed management completely, Latins usually, and Anglos only about half the time.

Anglo workers openly criticized their supervisors, who were all Anglo. When Jim and Steve were erecting a wall frame, Steve was cutting 35-foot metal studs to 34 feet six inches with a chop saw, a 20-pound, two-foot-by-one-foot heavy-duty circular saw. It was heavy work turning the 150-pound studs while sitting, then, after cutting them, lifting them into place while Jim, on a scaffold, screwed the tops onto a metal crossbeam. Steve was exhausted by mid-morning, and Jim commented that they needed three people on the job. "That's it. It's ridiculous that you're working like a dog when we could get another guy out here and do the job in half the time." Jim got off the lift and told Steve to wait. About ten minutes later, Jim came back with Dan, the supervisor. "We need another guy out here. This kid is killing himself for nothing. With three guys, one could cut, the other could lift the studs, and the third would be on the scaffold." Dan nodded his head and said, "You don't need three guys to do this job." He then went over to the chop saw and said, looking at Jim, "This is how you do it." Dan grabbed a stud, barely able to lift it off the ground, placed it on the chop saw, cut it, then dragged it over to the lift, hoisted it up over his head, and attached it to the hook on the lift. Jim was obviously not impressed: "Sure, Danny. That's what the boss does when he wants to show that he's right. But do that for eight hours a day and see if it works." Dan's whole face turned red. Before leaving, he loudly declaimed, "Just make sure you make it work." Jim, turning to Steve, responded, "Danny's pissed, but I don't care. He knows he's wrong, but he's just too stubborn to admit it." Then after a pause, "That fucking redneck." A week later, Dan passed by and asked Jim if he needed a third man. Jim replied, "Danny, don't trouble yourself. We're doing fine." After Dan left, Steve angrily asked why Jim didn't request a third person. Jim responded, "I wanted to bust his balls. Dan's stubborn. He always wants it his way. If he can get a ten-man job done by busting one guy's ass, he'll do it." The next day, they had a third man on the job.

In contrast, Latins seldom criticized supervisors to their face, but they disparaged them frequently behind their backs. While Steve, Domingo, and Al were working on a door frame and soffit, Dan passed by to inform them that he wanted the entire structure reframed; the dimensions were off to the left by two inches. Domingo and Al merely nodded their heads and replied in English, "OK Dan." After Dan left, Domingo and Al started their criticism in Spanish, "That dick! First he tells us he wants it this way. Then he tells us he wants it that way. Why can't he make up his mind. They [the foremen] never get anything straight." They recounted the incident to every other Carpenter they encountered that day and continued to insult Dan and the other foremen for the remainder of the day. They did, however, rebuild the door frame and soffit.

In south Florida, the birthplace of the contemporary language restriction movement in the United States (Castro 1992), language use is the focal point of considerable conflict. Language is a metaphor, an emotionally charged emblem of identity and power that can easily antagonize management. At one nonunion construction site, managers posted a sign inside their office declaring that any telephone conversations must be held in English. At the unionized site where Steve worked, a Haitian Carpenter who spoke virtually no English was fired because he worked too slowly; he stapled studs on only one wall in two days, a job that should have taken one day at most. He had worked alone, and Steve observed him looking around as if to find someone to explain to him how to stable the studs properly. But there were no Haitian carpenters to help. Another time, two Latin sheetrockers were applying sheeting to the studs with three-quarter-inch screws. The supervisor, Dan, came up to them after they had spanned half of a hundred-foot wall, to tell them to use one-inch screws. Despite his efforts at using sign language, Dan could not get his point across. His face became red with frustration, and he shouted that everyone should have to understand English if they wanted to work there. Finally, Ed, a bilingual carpenter, intervened and translated Dan's orders. The sheetrockers understood and began taking down the sheeting. Dan thanked Ed and left.

In short, non-English speakers did not confront management, but antagonized management when they could not complete a job as management wanted it. Spanish speakers commonly had co-workers available to assist them with translations. Haitian Creole speakers, at least those who were Carpenters, were not so lucky. If they did not learn English or Spanish, they were likely to be fired. English speakers, both Anglos and bilingual Latins, had the advantage of understanding management's directives and the ability to resist and defy them verbally.

While English-speaking ability permitted workers to argue with management directives, race, more than language, determined workers' responses to management. Haitians and African Americans were the most respectful and careful with supervisors. They usually did not speak with any supervisors or even other workers, except when it related directly to work. For example, Dan, the supervisor, would tell Daniel, a Haitian Laborer, to get studs for Domingo and Steve. Daniel would respond with a nod and "OK." He would never question what size studs or the safety of moving them or indicate that he was in the middle of doing something else. Never once did Steve observe African Americans publicly questioning management's rules about safety or anything else.

While language differences often alienate management, their effect among workers is more mixed. First, English deficiencies are not as common or as detrimental as one might expect. Joseph, a Haitian Carpenter who spoke perfect English, noted, "If you speak the language, that's your first step to making it. You can't advance without knowing the language." Virtually all construction workers understood and spoke enough English to get along, although they spoke among themselves in their native languages. An Anglo Carpenters Union business agent, David, conjectured that language was not as much a problem in construction-related industries because the workers know a specific trade or craft; it is their skill that earns them money.

Second, language in and of itself does not cause conflict. The inability to communicate one's needs and intentions does. At a worksite, if one can find a common language, cooperation usually follows, and the potential for hostilities and tensions is reduced. Many times, Steve observed a Cuban Carpenter unable to find the right word in English "signing" or miming for a tool and receiving it from an Anglo co-worker.

Even more common were multilingual interactions. While walking to the third-story bay windows, Steve noticed Frank, an Anglo, address Alberto, an older Cuban sheetrocker, in Spanish. "Hey joven!" Alberto responded in English. "Hey Frankie." A few minutes later, Alberto was hugging another Anglo Carpenter, saying in English, "How's the kids?" The Anglo responded in English, "They're fine, buddy. How's Marie?" At a lunch break, seven Cubans and one Anglo were eating together. They were all talking about the Anglo's girl friend as one of the bilingual Cubans simultaneously translated for the Anglo.

Haitians are even more likely to engage in multilingual conversation. Daniel, the Laborer's foreman, would give instructions to another Haitian Laborer in Creole. But to the older Cuban Carpenters, he spoke Spanish, while he spoke English to Anglos, including the supervisors. One day, Alberto walked up to an unknown Haitian Laborer and put his arm around him. The Haitian responded in Spanish, "*Que pasa*, man?"

Still, language can cause a chasm between members of different ethnic groups. As one Anglo Carpenter put it to a Cuban co-worker, "Just shut up. I can't understand a word you're saying." Moreover, there is a generation gap between Latins that is reflected in language use. Younger, bilingual Cubans frequently use English as a form of authority and status over older Cubans, who only speak Spanish. One day, for example, when Steve was working with Fred and Ignacio, Alberto asked in Spanish for advice about framing a wall on the second floor. Fred and Ignacio gave him their opinions, but they did so in English.

Nevertheless, Spanish has penetrated so deeply among all workers that being monolingual in Spanish is seldom an obstacle, especially for relations among co-workers within the Carpenters Union. In contrast, Haitian Creole is truly a minority language spoken solely among native speakers. Haitians have responded to this reality by learning both English and Spanish.

WORKERS VERSUS UNION BUREAUCRATS

Carpenters extended their antimanagement sentiments to union bureaucrats. Jack, an Anglo and the Carpenters Union steward, proclaimed, "We should start a civil case against the union for violating our contract. The members didn't want to take a wage cut, but we got it anyway. Shit, you can't take your grievances to the contractor or you get on the shit list. The union doesn't do shit about this. We fucked ourselves in a lot of ways. We gave away our bargaining power—the right to strike." Jim, another Anglo carpenter added,

"The union is just going down hill…. Reps are only in it for themselves. They only care about securing their own ass. That's the only incentive they have to protect the union. They protect the union, they guarantee themselves a job." Jack added, "They know what we want, but they're not on our side. When are you guys gonna face that fact? They're not working with us. They're working against us." Bill, another Anglo, declared, "You got that right. I'll tell you what. I'm sick of this shit. If they negotiate us out of one more benefit, I'm out of here." Mark, an older Anglo, shook his head and insisted, "Come on, guy. You're an old-timer just like me. We're both lifers. We'll be buried with hammer in hand."

One time, Jim, the union steward, found himself battling both management and the union as he tried to protect a young Nicaraguan who had been working as a sheetrocker for four years, having been paid as a journeyman the last two years. When the subcontractor found out how young the Nicaraguan was and that he had not passed the apprenticeship program, he wanted to reduce him to apprentice wages. The Nicaraguan spoke little English and could not understand what the supervisor was saying to him. When Ignacio, a bilingual Cuban-American Carpenter, translated, the Nicaraguan threatened to walk off the job. Jim claimed, "They're really trying to fuck that kid. Look at this kid. He's getting screwed. He's got a family to support. That's the problem we got down at the hall; we got a bunch of chicken shits who are afraid to stand up for what is right." Later the same morning, addressing Dan, the supervisor, Jim asserted, "Hey, Danny, this kid's been working for you for about a year now. All that time he was getting paid journeyman's scale. He's doing good work. So what's this shit that you're trying to pull. I know it's the [union] hall's fault, too. They fucked up. They couldn't even get the kid's work status right. But shit, just because the system's a pile of shit doesn't mean this kid should get the shaft. It really burns me up. The hall is so full of shit. Shit, you don't get to be an apprentice for four years before you start putting up rock. You can learn that shit in a few months. I bet none of these guys [other Latin sheetrockers] ever worked for such shit wages."

ETHNIC AND RACIAL TENSIONS

Ethnic and racial tension pervade Miami. Race riots convulsed the city three times during the 1980s. We have indicated how Anglos sought to exclude Latins from construction unions, how Latins subsequently transformed the industry, and how African Americans remain the industry's worst-paid workers, on the lowest-prestige rung. We might expect, therefore, that relationships among construction workers would be infused with tension and resentment and predominantly segregated by ethnicity and race. While these characteristics are present, they do not dominate construction workers' interaction. The situation is more complex. Workers transform their alienation from the policies of employers and their own union representatives into a strongly class-based view of society, viewing themselves as thoroughly working-class with both lower earnings and less prestige than others. Domingo, an older Cuban Carpenter, advised Steve, "Don't get into this trade, there's no future in it for you. You make no money. You get no respect." And, John, an older Anglo Carpenter, added, "Can't make a decent living at this shit anymore, not even piece-meal work pays. Whatever you do, don't do this. There is no future in this. You get paid shit. You get cut up." Much of the time workers manifest solidarity as workers, regardless of race and ethnicity. As quoted at the start of this chapter, Frank, a beginning young Cuban American Carpenter, stated, "Yeah, there's always going to be prejudice, but it's not that bad here. Everyone's in the same boat. Everyone gets sweaty, dirty, and smelly."

Bob, an African American born and raised in Miami, refrained from criticizing any group. In response to comments that Miami must have changed a lot in his lifetime and that there were many more Latins now, he replied, "Hold on, Steve. Even when I was a kid there were plenty of Latins down here. They used to come from Cuba to invest their money and travel. It's just a media thing to make it seem like just recently all these Cubans are coming in. They have always been here.... I've seen the world ten times over [referring to his time in the navy]. What's funny is that no matter what anybody tells you, people are more alike than they are different."

Morris, an African American, commenting on nonunion immigrant workers, maintained, "Shit, I don't mind. They're trying to make a living anyways they can. They don't take away our jobs, shit. It's supply and demand. If you can work and no one else will do the job, go for it. There's a lot of work out there anyway.... The problem is all those greedy contractors who hire those nonunion guys."

Nevertheless, unionized workers brandished union symbols such as union T-shirts and bumper stickers: "I'm proud to be union." Moreover, they strongly believed in "buying American." Steve's survey of the construction workers' parking lot revealed sixty-four American-made cars (including fifty-one pickups), one beat-up Toyota pickup, one Subaru, and one Honda Accord, the last owned by a Haitian who carefully covered it every day when he arrived at work. A fellow worker told Steve that in the past workers had "egged" foreign-made automobiles.

Miami's unionized Latin construction workers assuredly do not fit the stereotype of immigrants as docile and complacent in the workplace. As one Anglo union business agent described them: "Man, are they radical. You can show them a contract and talk to them about language but if they think that an injustice has been done, they figure it's the union's job to undo it. They always want the union to step in and fight. They drive me crazy" (Grenier 1992). In spite of the ideology and objective reality of workers' autonomy, individuals become acquainted and can become friends regardless of ethnic differences. As one Anglo Carpenter stated about a Cuban co-worker, I've known that son-of-a-bitch for years; we're brothers in wood." Jack, another Anglo, stated, "I know a lot of Cubans." Pointing to David, an older Cuban, Jack added, "I've worked with him for years. We borrow each other's shit all the time."

Borrowing "each other's shit," (i.e., tools) is a mark of trust and cooperation, When a tool is requested, the borrower presumes a level of trust. The lender is expected to give the tool to the person who asks on the condition that it will be returned in the same condition or replaced if lost or broken. Occasionally, the lender does not fully trust the borrower and asserts the primacy of autonomy, as Steve discovered one day when he needed some channel-lock pliers to loosen and replace his chop-saw blade. He asked an Anglo pipe fitter to loan him his channel locks. The pipe fitter stared at Steve and replied, "What would you do if I didn't bring my own tools with me—you'd have to go out and buy your own, now wouldn't you?"

More important than ethnicity in regulating social interaction is a worker's trade affiliation. As briefly discussed earlier, immigrants have unevenly penetrated the construction industry, producing an ethnic segregation within the industry by trades. At the worksite where Steve conducted fieldwork, this segregation was further emphasized by the spatial dispersion of workers across the massive site, which was larger than many city blocks. Interaction among people of different trades was thus minimal and largely coincidental to one's work.[4] But even when cross-trade interaction did occur, trade affiliation seemed to take precedence. For example, two African Americans, one a Carpenter and the other a Laborer, were engaged in conversation during a break. A Haitian Laborer approached the African American Laborer and asked a brief, work-related question. The African American Carpenter quietly slipped away and did not come back even after the question was answered, even though it was still not time to return to work. Instead, he joined a group of fellow Laborers, all African Americans.

Among Anglos, stories are told of how things used to be better before the Cubans came aboard. Anglos, however, are not the only ones who assert that Cubans fundamentally transformed Miami. Cubans are just as likely to take credit. Ethnocentric remarks such as "the Cubans made Miami" are common, not only among Cuban Carpenters but throughout the Cuban community.

CONCLUSIONS

Immigration has fundamentally transformed Miami's construction industry, but not entirely in expected ways. Immigrants have penetrated the industry and contributed to denunionization and a decline in wages. But the unions themselves are probably more responsible for their loss of power than the arrival of immigrant workers. Not only did Anglos exclude Cubans from the unions through the 1980s but unionized Cuban workers are apparently even more radical than their Anglo counterparts.

There are, nevertheless, ethnic differences in responses to management control. Anglos are more likely to resist and confront management verbally, and at unionized sites management is most likely to be Anglo. Latins criticize management covertly, while African Americans and Haitians ostensibly obey management directives. In short, race and ethnicity fundamentally determine relationships. Not only do they affect responses to management, but nearly everything else, thus producing an uneven penetration of immigrants into the construction industry. Immigrant Blacks, for example Haitians, occupy the same low position, Laborers, as African Americans. White immigrants, for example Cubans, have the most varied positions. In the 1960s and 1970s they created an informal sector in the construction industry. The peculiarly favorable characteristics that Cubans enjoyed in the United States helped convert these informal firms into formal ones that began to take control of the new housing market. Subsequently, large influxes of immigrants in the 1980s produced a reemergence of informal labor practices in construction at the same time that other Latins gained entry into unionized work, particularly among Carpenters. By the late 1980s, Latins occupied all levels of the construction trade occupational hierarchy from poorly paid informal workers to owners of large firms that exercise significant political influence in Miami. In contrast, Anglo construction owners have not proven to be the primary beneficiaries of immigration and the associated deunionization of the construction industry. Indeed, their activities have been increasingly limited as Cuban firms gain control.

The workers themselves, at least those unionized workers we came to know well through participant observation, inhabit a paradoxical world. Social-class differences are fundamental, especially between management and labor, where management from their viewpoint includes not only company supervisors but also their own union representatives. Among themselves, workers seemingly inhabit a world permeated by contradictions between profound solidarity and cruel contrasts associated with an ideology of individual autonomy. Solidarity prevails not only in contexts where workers are opposed to management but also surrounding worker-safety issues. Harmony during workdays also predominates as long as workers abide by their unwritten rules of "not messing with each other's shit" and reciprocity in access and tool sharing. Although all construction workers are relatively autonomous in their work, and those engaged in outside work move from job to job, workers still create and maintain friendships as they work with some of the same people in different jobs. The trade segregation, which seems to dominate informal relationships, implies that workers in integrated unions are far more likely to interact and come to know each other personally. Among the Carpenters this included not only tolerance but also genuine interethnic friendships that overcame language differences. The higher-prestige, higher-paid licensed trades remain predominantly Anglo, and the workers in those trades act in the most ethnocentric and exclusionary fashion as they attempt to intimidate minorities.

NOTES

1. While the proportion of Blacks dropped from 19.4 percent in 1970 to 16.6 percent in 1980, the absolute numbers of both Blacks and whites increased as the total construction labor force grew during the 1970s from 36,000 to almost 50,000, according to U.S. census figures for Florida in 1970 and 1980.

2. When referring to a particular union or member of that union, we have chosen to refer to it as a trade and to capitalize it: for example, Laborer and Laborers Union. Some would not consider unskilled Laborers to have a "trade," but our research reveals that they view their work, and especially union work, differently.

3. While the ethnic composition has been transformed dramatically, construction in Dade County remains an utterly male-dominated industry. During more than six months of fieldwork, we found only three female construction workers, two U.S. African Americans and one white American with one U.S. African American doing "inside" work and the other two on the "outside."

4. A similar pattern of ethnic segregation also appears among Carpenters engaged in "inside" work. Fieldwork among the unionized "inside" shops revealed a tendency for Anglos to hold management positions, except in the few firms owned by Latins. Moreover, the few remaining Anglo Carpenters tended to dominate the higher-skilled jobs. Even when Latins had skilled positions, they still tended to work with other Latins.

REFERENCES

Applebaum, Herbert A. 1981. *Royal Blue: The Culture of Construction Workers.* New York: Holt, Rinehart and Winston.

Castro, Max. 1992. "The Politics of Language in Miami." In *Miami Now!* edited by Guillermo Grenier and Alex Stepick. Gainesville: University of Florida Press.

Grenier, Guillermo, 1992. "The Emerging Voice of the Working Class: Ethnic Solidarity and the Cuban-American Labor Movement in Dade County." In *Miami Now!* edited by Guillermo Grenier and Alex Stepick. Gainesville: University of Florida Press.

LeMasters, E. E. 1975. *Blue Collar Aristocrats: Lifestyles at a Working Class Tavern.* Madison: University of Wisconsin Press.

U.S. Bureau of the Census. 1963. *Census of Population, 1960.* Vol. 1, *Characteristics of the Population, pt. 11, Florida.* Washington, D.C.: Government Printing Office.

_____. 1973. *1970 Census of Population, General Social and Economic Characteristics, Florida. Final Report.* Washington, D.C.: Government Printing Office.

_____. 1983. *1980 Census of Population, General Social and Economic Characteristics, Florida.* Washington, D.C.: Government Printing Office.

16

THE POLITICS OF LANGUAGE IN MIAMI

Max J. Castro

THE LATE TWENTIETH CENTURY HAS WITNESSED the rapid growth of the Hispanic and the foreign-born population of the United States. The cultural, linguistic, political, and economic impact of Hispanic growth and of the "new immigration"—related but distinct phenomena—is already being felt acutely, especially in certain areas of the country. Increased cultural and linguistic diversity has been one obvious major consequence. Reactions to this diversity by the culturally dominant population have ranged from a celebration of pluralism and multiculturalism as the essence of American society to the rise of a new nativism.

The decade of 1970 to 1980 saw the reversal of a long trend toward the "Americanization" of the U.S. population. The antibilingualism/English Only movement made its appearance on the historical stage in 1980 in Miami, where the new trend was being manifested most dramatically. In the 1980s an Official English movement was organized on a national scale.

In this chapter I look at the consequences of immigration and Hispanic population growth in Miami, focusing on linguistic diversity and the range of reactions to it by different sectors of the resident population. In Miami the new immigration and Hispanic population growth have been virtually synonymous and especially dramatic processes. While the experience of Miami may not be uncritically generalized to other locales or to the nation as a whole, developments in Miami have often prefigured national trends. Miami had the first bilingual public school program in the modern period (1963) and the first English Only referendum (1980). In the 1990s Miami is certain to become the first metropolitan area in the United States of more than two million people with a Hispanic majority (Wallace 1991:1A).

I address several questions. (1) Why did Miami pioneer the national trend toward bilingualism and biculturalism *and* give birth to the backlash movement against it in the form of the 1980 antibilingualism campaign? (2) How did different segments of the resident population respond to the challenge of Hispanic immigration, and why? (3) What has been the net effect of these responses? (4) What are the implications of the experience in Miami?

The explanation for Miami's seemingly contradictory role as a harbinger first of pluralist and later of nativist trends in late twentieth-century American society lies in the radical, rapid, and profound nature of the ethnic transformation that has occurred since 1959. This transformation has posed an extraordinary challenge to the resident population of the city. The responses to that challenge have also been extraordinary and have varied across a wide spectrum, from an unusual level of accommodation to various forms of resistance and rejection. The nature of the response has been influenced by social and racial differences among the resident population as well as by the characteristics of the incoming population. Language has been a key issue through which battles over power and identity have been fought, feelings of displacement and alienation have been expressed, and xenophobic and ethnocentric sentiments have been politically organized. Below I discuss why the Hispanic

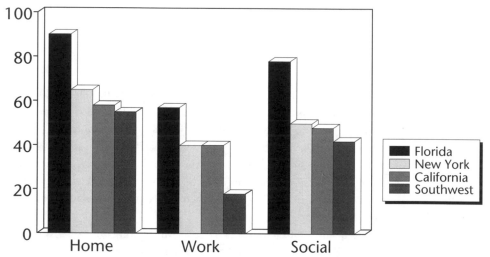

Fig. 16.1. Reported use of Spanish by Hispanics in selected states and regions, 1984. *Source*: Strategy Research Corporation 1984, 90-93.

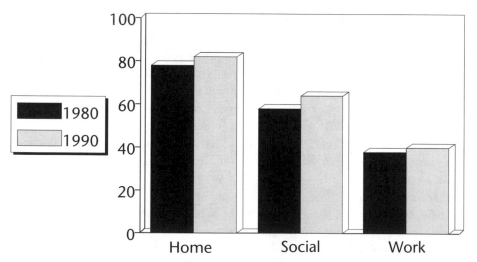

Fig. 16.2. Use of Spanish as most frequent language of Hispanics in south Florida, 1980 and 1990. *Source*: Strategy Research Corporation 1988, 40-41.

challenge in Miami has been so formidable that the expectation of immigrant subordination has been violated, calling forth among other responses a movement to reclaim Anglo linguistic and cultural supremacy.

THE FORCE OF NUMBERS:
A LIGHTNING LATINIZATION

The extent and speed of immigration and Latinization in Miami between 1960 and 1980 is exceptional. The Hispanic population grew from a small minority in the 1960s (5.3 percent in 1960) to a significant community (23.6 percent in 1970), overtaking the black American population (15 percent in 1970) to become the largest minority in the city (see fig. 1.2). Despite a slowdown in Cuban immigration during the next decade, in the 1970s the Hispanic minority continued to grow in absolute and relative size (to 35.7 percent of the area's population in 1980) (Metropolitan Dade County 1983:4). By 1980 the demographic trend was clear: Hispanics were fast becoming the predominant population in Miami. By that year the city of Miami, the largest of twenty-seven municipalities in the Miami metropolitan area, was one of only three cities in the United States of more than 250,000 with a Hispanic majority (U.S. Bureau of the Census 1984). Not only were there suddenly many more Hispanics in Miami, but most of them were recently arrived foreigners who maintained their customs, allegiances, and cultural traits, especially language.

The linguistic impact of Miami's new Hispanic immigrant population was dramatic. Obviously the number of native Spanish speakers rose greatly, but also Spanish was spoken more extensively than in other cities with a large Hispanic population and in more diverse settings (see figs. 16.1 and 16.2). A study by the Cuban National Planning Council found that in 1977, 91.9 percent of Cubans in Miami spoke only Spanish at home and an additional 4 percent spoke mostly Spanish (Díaz 1980:48). More importantly Spanish also became a language widely spoken outside the home in the worlds of business and leisure. A 1984 market research study found that Florida Hispanics were more likely to speak Spanish than English not only at home, but also at work and at social functions. In other markets, Spanish dominated only in the home environment (Strategy Research Corporation 1984). This meant that non-Hispanics encountered Spanish more frequently and pervasively in Miami than in other cities. In Miami, Spanish had become a public as well as a private language; the city had become de facto bilingual.

A RADICAL BREAK

The dramatic ethnic succession just described was especially radical because it represented a sharp break with Miami's previous history. Despite its geographic allocation, Miami grew up as a decidedly Anglo-dominated city with a large and oppressed black population, a substantial Jewish minority, and an insignificant Hispanic presence (Porter and Dunn 1984). While the roots of the Hispanic presence in Florida were inscribed in the very name of the state, Hispanic Miami is definitely a post-1950s creation.

Miami was founded in 1896 long after the end of Spanish rule in Florida, and it became a city after the first major Cuban influx into the state in the latter half of the nineteenth century (this influx produced important settlements in Key West and Tampa) and before the second great Cuban influx in 1959. In the intervening years, Cuban immigrants to the United States, like their Puerto Rican and Dominican counterparts, were more likely to be destined for New York City than Florida (Boswell and Curtis 1984). Consequently in 1950

Hispanics made up only about 4 percent (20,000) of greater Miami's population, a figure that increased only to about 5.3 percent (50,000) by 1960. Not only was Miami an over-whelmingly Anglo-dominated city in every way, but it was becoming even more so in the 1950s. While the Hispanic population increased by about 30,000 to a total of about 50,000 between 1950 and 1960, the non-Hispanic, white population increased by 337,548 to 747,748, or 80 percent of the total population (Metropolitan Dade County 1983:4).

Thus, unlike other cities where Hispanics currently make up a large proportion of the population (San Antonio, El Paso, and even Los Angeles), before the process of Latinization began in 1959 there was a scant Hispanic legacy or demographic presence in Miami. As a result of this history, the Latinization of Miami that occurred beginning in 1959 would not be experienced by much of the resident American population as a historical continuity with Florida's Hispanic past and Cuban connection. Rather, for a significant proportion of the resident population Latinization would be experienced as a traumatic rupture; an alien (and alienating) invasion; and ultimately as a "takeover," a transgression against the expect-ed relation of domination/subordination between native and immigrant, newcomer and established resident, American and foreigner, Anglo and Hispanic. When the *Miami Herald* conducted a poll in November 1980 about the Hispanic influence in Dade County, most non-Hispanics did not see Latinization in a favorable light (see fig. 16.3).

AN EMPOWERED COMMUNITY

What was so unusual about Spanish in Miami was not that it was so often spoken, but that it was so often heard. In Los Angeles, by contrast, Spanish remained a language only barely registered by the Anglo population, part of the ambient noise: the language spoken by the people who worked in the car wash, trimmed the trees, and cleared the tables in restaurants. In Miami, Spanish was spoken by the people who ate in the restaurants and

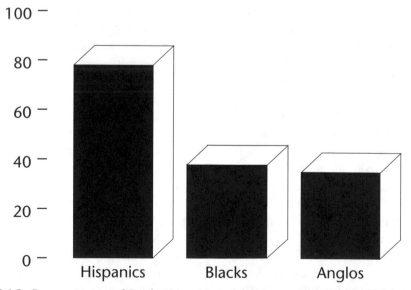

Fig. 16.3. Percentages of Dade County residents agreeing with "The Latin influence helped this county's economy and made it a more enjoyable place to live." *Source*: Browning 1980, 11A.

owned the cars and the trees. On the socioauditory scale, this contrast made a considerable difference (Didion 1987:63).

What made the newcomers to Miami a special challenge to the natives was not merely (or basically) the power of numbers. Unique among Latin American immigrant groups and established Hispanic minority communities in the United States, Hispanics in Miami (and particularly Cubans) were establishing not only a surpassing demographic and cultural presence, but also a strong economic base. The number of Hispanic-owned businesses in the area zoomed from 3,447 in 1969 to 24,898 in 1982 (Cuban American Policy Center 1988). More importantly some of these businesses were relatively large. They were not confined to typical ethnic retail businesses such as restaurants and small stores, but included manufacturing, construction, insurance, real estate, banking, advertising, and export-import firms (Portes and Bach 1985). The structure of this Latin economy in Miami was not only diverse but integrated, with forward and backward linkages among the individual enterprises (Wilson and Martin 1982).

The Hispanic enclave economy in Miami provided not only a source of employment and economic development for the community, but also a resource for political empowerment and a sphere of cultural and linguistic maintenance. While Cubans and other Hispanics did provide a source of labor and consumers for Anglo businesses, and Hispanic businesses traded with Anglo enterprises, the Hispanic enclave economy also competed with Anglo businesses, often successfully.

Speed, numbers, historical discontinuity, and economic empowerment meant radical change for Miami's resident population. How did it respond? In Miami the responses of some key educational, bureaucratic, political, business, and other institutions and the elites that controlled them have generally been characterized by an evolving accommodation to the new cultural and linguistic reality within the framework of Anglo dominance. I term this approach enlightened assimilationism. In contrast the response of a significant proportion of grass roots whites has more often been characterized by expressions of nonacceptance of the new reality, including flight and attempts to reestablish the expected hierarchy. The response of the black community has differed from the responses of both the elites and the white grass roots.

ENLIGHTENED ASSIMILATIONISM

In the 1960s and 1970s, key institutions in Miami adopted significant policies in the area of language that represented a substantial departure from policies adopted at that time by their counterparts in other parts of the country in which large populations of Hispanic immigrants or native minorities lived. In general the policies adopted in Miami tended to be more accommodating of the linguistic and cultural background of the newcomers.

The three most significant policies in this regard were the institution of bilingual education in the Dade County public schools in 1963, the declaration of Metropolitan Dade County as officially bilingual and bicultural in 1973, and the creation of *El Herald* in 1976.

Despite the presence of larger and earlier established Hispanic concentrations in New York City, California, and the Southwest, it was in Dade County in 1963 that the first bilingual program in a U.S. public school in the modern period was founded. The pioneer program at the Coral Way elementary school, while clearly aimed mainly at teaching English to native Spanish speakers, also attempted to maintain Spanish-language skills among Spanish speakers and to teach Spanish to native English-speaking students. This concept of two-way maintenance bilingual education was subsequently implemented in some other schools in the Dade County system. The Dade County bilingual program, while limited, was a harbinger and a model for programs that would be adopted later in other parts of the country.

A decade later, in 1973, the Dade County Commission (which at the time did not contain any Hispanic members) took the unprecedented step of declaring the county officially bilingual and bicultural. The declaration specifically identified Spanish as the second official language and created a division of bilingual and bicultural affairs. The reasons cited for the resolution included the fact that "a large and growing percentage of Dade County is of Spanish origin . . . many of whom have retained the culture and language of their native lands, [and therefore] encounter special difficulties communicating with governmental agencies and officials." The resolution also held, significantly, that "our Spanish-speaking population has earned, through its ever increasing share of the tax burden, and active participation in community affairs, the right to be serviced and heard at all levels of government" (Metro-Dade County Board of County Commissioners 1973).

Another unprecedented concession to the new linguistic reality was made by the *Miami Herald*, when it began publishing a daily Spanish-language edition, *El Herald*, in 1976. The *Miami Herald* thus became the only major metropolitan daily in the United States to publish a daily edition in Spanish, despite the fact that Miami is only the third largest Hispanic market in the United States, following Los Angeles and New York (Strategy Research Corp. 1984:131). By creating *El Herald*, the *Miami Herald*, a leading business institution, civic actor, and editorial voice in Miami, made a decision based largely on business considerations, but which had important symbolic and political implications. For whatever reasons, the Miami establishment had found it necessary not only to listen to the newcomers, but also to speak to them in their native language.

Thus, within the first two decades of massive Hispanic immigration, three leading institutions in Miami—the public school system, the largest governmental entity, and the leading communications media corporation—had made substantial commitments to some level of bilingualism and biculturalism. Why did these institutions—and the political, bureaucratic, and business elites that controlled them—adopt the path of enlightened assimilationism?

The genesis of each of the three instances of accommodation cited above was specific to Miami and Dade County. The immigration of thousands of Cuban teachers and of other professionals who could be retrained as teachers was key in the early institution of bilingual education in Dade, as was the presence in Miami of Anglo educators who had experience with and sympathy for bilingual and foreign-language education. The looming prospect of a large Hispanic vote and growing Hispanic economic clout were undoubtedly factors in the decision to declare the county bilingual and bicultural. The consumer power of Dade Hispanics and the low rates of subscription to the *Miami Herald* among Hispanics were key to the creation of *El Herald*.

More generally the reason for enlightened assimilationism in Miami was that unlike most other Latin immigrant groups, Cubans came largely from urban, middle-class, relatively educated backgrounds. By the 1960s Cubans were swiftly acquiring the economic power that, in the language of the Dade County resolution, "earned them the right to be serviced and heard" by politicians and newspaper publishers. Cubans had more resources and power than most immigrant groups in bargaining with native elites to preserve their linguistic heritage, and as exiles planning to return to their country they had more motivation to do so. Also there was no essential class conflict or radical difference in worldview between the newcomers and native elites. Often the newcomers were drawn from the same class and from the same professions as native elites and could speak the same (class/professional) language. Elites often had sympathy for these mostly white, middle-class refugees from communism. The background of the newcomers sometimes made it relatively easy for the elites to adopt enlightened assimilation. The policy of providing education bilingually as a transition to English appeared rational and efficient because the immigrant group, drawn from the middle class, contained in its rank both the potential consumers of bilingual educational services (students) and the potential suppliers (teachers).

The "right to be serviced and heard" meant that businesses and politicians sought to obtain the newcomers as clients. Cubans provided a good labor force for many businesses and excellent consumers as they sought to rebuild their previous economic status. Although the growing number of Cuban enterprises brought unwelcome competition for some smaller Anglo entrepreneurs, many Anglo businesses, such as wholesalers, profited from the proliferation of small Cuban businesses. Many larger Anglo businesses and professional elites were not adversely affected by the competition (particularly during the early period) and when they were, they often sought to counter it by catering to the clientele in their own language. The *Miami Herald* created the Spanish edition because its market penetration—the proportion of households that subscribes to the paper in the market area—was lower in Miami than other cities in the Knight-Ridder market due to low rates of subscription among Hispanics.

In practice and by international standards, bilingualism in Miami's educational, governmental, and media institutions in the 1960s and 1970s was quite limited. True bilingual education as pioneered in the Coral Way elementary school was carried out on a very limited scale in the Dade County public school system as a whole. Bilingual education in Dade County mostly concentrated on transitional programs. Metro-Dade County's official bilingual/bicultural declaration clearly defined Spanish as a *second* official language. In practice Spanish did not function co-equally with English in local government. Rather, official bilingualism meant merely that certain county documents were translated into Spanish, and a limited range of services was provided bilingually. *El Herald* was an insert provided upon request at no cost to subscribers of the *Miami Herald*, had only a fraction of the staff and budget of the English-language paper, and had no editorial independence. It was consciously and explicitly conceived as a Spanish-language *American* newspaper, and it largely consisted of translations from the English paper. Yet in contrast with the undiluted assimilationist policies just then coming under challenge throughout the United States, key institutions in Miami in the 1960s and 1970s responded to the huge and growing Cuban presence and emergent economic power with substantial concessions to the linguistic and cultural characteristics of the immigrant population.

The enlightened assimilationist policies adopted by the elites appeared to many rank-and-file whites to deepen and extend the process of Latinization by reducing the cost of nonassimilation, institutionalizing Spanish in key institutions, and providing vehicles (media, schools, and government) for maintaining and socially reproducing the immigrant language and culture. Practically and symbolically the official recognition of bilingualism and biculturalism further upset expectations among large sectors of the Anglo population about immigrant/Hispanic cultural and linguistic subordination and assimilation to the dominant culture. It seemed that rather than assimilating promptly, these newcomers from Cuba and other parts of Latin America were "taking over." In the face of this perceived "takeover," some Anglos who did not identify with the accommodationist path chose to abandon the field, and others attempted to reclaim the turf.

THE ANTIBILINGUAL REFERENDUM:
THE LANGUAGE OF RESENTMENT

"The presence of so many clever, industrious, and frugal aliens, capable of competing successfully . . . with the native whites constitutes a political and economic problem of the greatest importance." So read, in part, a 1927 study of Japanese and Chinese schoolchildren in Vancouver, Canada (Portes and Rumbaut 1990:210). These same fears surfaced in Miami much later in the century.

If key Miami institutions and elites adapted to the Hispanic challenge through accommodationist policies, some other sectors of the population responded decidedly differently. Flight has been probably the most common manifestation of rejection of the growing Hispanic influence. It is clear from much anecdotal evidence that the Hispanic phenomenon has been one reason that the Anglo population of Dade County has been declining since 1970. In 1990 there were 161,748 (21 percent) fewer non-Hispanic whites in Dade County than in 1960. During this period the total population of the area more than doubled, the black population tripled, and the Hispanic population increased nineteen times (Metropolitan Dade County 1983; Wallace 1991).

The paradigm of a more organized and active resistance was the antibilingualism movement. That movement arose in Miami in 1980 as a response to growing Hispanic numbers and empowerment. The antibilingualism movement aimed specifically at rolling back official bilingualism/biculturalism in Metropolitan Dade County and substituting English as the only language of government.

Miami thus became the birthplace of the contemporary English Only movement in the United States. It happened in November 1980, when voters in Dade County (Greater Miami) approved a landmark ordinance that reversed the policy of official bilingualism and biculturalism established by the Board of County Commissioners in 1973. The measure, passed overwhelmingly, prohibited "the expenditure of any county funds for the purpose of utilizing any language other than English or any culture other than that of the United States" (Section 1) and provided that "all county governmental meetings, hearings, and publications shall be *in the English language only*" (Section 2; emphasis added) (Metro-Dade County, Board of County Commissioners, 1980).

Arising as it did not only against the Hispanic upsurge but also against the elite policy of accommodation, the antibilingualism campaign did not emerge from any established interest group. Rather, it seemed to spring spontaneously from mass sentiments. The account that appeared in the *Miami Herald* on the day after the election suggests an instance of collective behavior, akin to a panic or craze: "It began as an idea batted around on a late-night talk show last July, and that swiftly gathered irresistible momentum. . . . Marion Plunske heard Emmy Shafer on a WNWS radio talk show on July 8. The two women started their campaign the next day and the Citizens of Dade United registered as a political action group on July 21. From the start, the campaign seemed to run itself. In just over four weeks the group had gathered 44,166 signatures, nearly twice as many as they needed. Exulting in their strength, they brought another 25,767 signatures to the supervisor of elections on Sept. 16" (Browning 1980:11A).

The antibilingualism movement, led by nonelite whites, was actively opposed by the city's white corporate and civic elite, signaling the differences between the elite accommodationist approach and the rejectionist implications of the movement. According to the *Miami Herald*, "by late October, Shafer reported she had received only about $10,000 in campaign contributions from about 1,100 people, an average of $8.06 per contributor." In contrast, the Greater Miami Chamber of Commerce alone spent $50,000 on newspaper and television advertisements in its campaign against the ordinance, called "Together for Dade's Future" (Browning 1980:11A).

In spite of the active opposition of the white elite, support for the antibilingualism ordinance was widespread among virtually all subgroups of the white population, with 71 percent of non-Hispanic whites supporting the referendum. A *Miami Herald* study concluded that "little else besides ethnic group—not age, nor sex, nor education, nor choice of presidential candidate made much difference in how people voted on the ordinance."

If the ethnically dominant population was solidly behind the referendum, the minorities—both Hispanic and black—did not share the enthusiasm. Among blacks only 44 percent supported the antibilingual referendum (Browning 1980:11A); among Hispanics a mere 15 percent favored it.

What explains the massive white rejection of the elite accommodationist policy and the lack of black support? The explanation involves both material interests and symbolic issues. An economist has remarked that the higher one goes in the elevator in a particular major bank in Miami that occupies a downtown skyscraper, the less Spanish is heard.[1] While white elites often were relatively secure from Hispanic competition and often shared similar class interests, this was not necessarily the case for other sectors of the population. Smaller Anglo businesses were no doubt more vulnerable to competition than national and multinational corporations. In the labor market, studies have shown that bilingual requirements for employment—which affect a substantial number of jobs in Miami—are concentrated in entry-level positions.[2] The fact of having to know a "foreign language" in order to qualify for a job in "our own country" was particularly galling to many Anglos, symbolizing a reversal of roles.

In contrast to whites' massive support, blacks, despite what the *Miami Herald* at the time described as "their history of cool relations with Latins in Dade" (Browning, 1980:11A), did not join in support for the antibilingualism ordinance. The split black vote was no doubt the result of several contradictory factors. It is generally argued that blacks have suffered most from Hispanic/immigrant economic competition in Miami (Porter and Dunn 1984). If this were the case, and if economic interests were the only factor, one would expect blacks to have supported the referendum massively. On the other hand, if the referendum was seen as an expression of white racism against a minority group, one might expect massive black opposition. In fact, blacks were divided on the issue, with a majority opposing the antibilingualism ordinance (56 percent) and a substantial minority supporting it (44 percent) (Browning 1980:11A).

What explains the pattern? Black workers, overrepresented in entry-level positions, might be expected to have faced disproportionate Cuban/Hispanic competition. Yet several indicators suggest that from 1970 to 1980, demographic and economic displacement related to the Hispanic presence was felt more keenly by whites than by blacks. The black population of Dade County rose by 52,367 between 1970 and 1980, while the white population dropped by 3,792 (U.S. Bureau of the Census 1984). In the city of Miami, the number of black employees increased by 25 percent between 1977 and 1985, while the number of Anglo employees dropped by 36 percent. The number of black employees classified as officials, administrators, and professionals more than tripled in the same period (City of Miami 1985:24, 28).

Ideologically one might expect that blacks did not identify as closely as whites with the Anglo cultural dominance that was being threatened. One might also expect that some blacks did see a component of racism, prejudice, or discrimination in the antibilingualism movement. The *Miami Herald* survey of voters found that "nearly half the blacks who voted against the ordinance said they believed it to be an insult to Spanish speakers that would hurt relations between Latins and non-Latins." In contrast "only about one non-Latin white voter in four said he or she thought the vote was an insult." (At the other end of the spectrum, more than 65 percent of Latin voters saw the ordinance as an insult.) (Browning 1980:11A).

The antibilingualism movement was a vehicle for the expression of mass native white resistance to Latinization and was a political project aimed at symbolically reestablishing Anglo dominance. The *Miami Herald* reported that over half of the non-Latin, white voters who supported the antibilingualism ordinance would be pleased if it "would make Miami a less attractive place to live for Cubans and other Spanish-speaking people." Over 75 percent of the persons in this same group of voters said they would like to leave Miami if it were practical (Browning 1980:11A).

The level of alienation of Anglo voters in Miami and the intensity of their anti-Hispanic sentiments is interesting in light of the nature of the Hispanic population of Miami. Miami Cubans, who in 1980 made up 70 percent of all Hispanics in Miami, were mostly middle income, conservative, and Caucasian; they had low rates of crime and dependence on public assistance, high rates of labor force participation, and growing rates of naturalization and political participation (Llanes 1982; Boswell and Curtis 1984; Pedraza-Bailey 1985; Portes and Bach 1985; Portes and Mozo 1985; Metro-Dade Planning Department 1986; Pérez 1986; Masud-Piloto 1988). Media coverage of the sudden arrival in Miami in the spring of 1980 of tens of thousands of Cubans (some of them with criminal backgrounds or mental health problems) as a result of the Mariel boatlift undoubtedly tarnished the public image of what might otherwise have been considered a "model minority" (Portes, Stepick, and Truelove 1986). But it was the very success of the Cubans and not the presence of some social deviants among them that produced a backlash. The backlash against bilingualism in the United States began in Miami specifically because Miami had been a pioneer in bilingualism and because Hispanics in Miami were an increasingly large and successful group.

The antibilingualism campaign elevated language to preeminence as an issue of open interethnic struggle in Miami. The vote also marked the beginning of a backlash against the trend toward linguistic pluralism in the United States. In the 1980s this backlash crystallized around the English Only/Official English movement.

Language became a key issue in a battle that was essentially about ethnic dominance and cultural hegemony because language choices reflect relations of power and because language is a key constituent of culture, identity, and nationality. Opinion polls have shown that Americans overwhelmingly believe that to be a true American, one must know English

(Citrin 1988). That the government itself accepts bilingualism is seen by many Americans as a surrender of a key constituent element of nationality to an alien influence. For these reasons, language proved to be an issue upon which xenophobic and ethnocentric campaigns could be built, even in the post-civil rights era. In Miami beginning in 1980, language would serve as a symbolic battlefield upon which battles over power, culture, and identity would be waged. In a short time, other states and cities across the nation would follow.

IMPLICATIONS:
THE LIMITS OF SUCCESS

As an electoral campaign, antibilingualism was wildly successful. Emmy Shafer and her Citizens of Dade United proved that an English Only campaign hastily organized by a political novice could triumph in the face of opposition by the established Anglo civic leadership, the English-language press, the majority of black voters, and one of the largest and most powerful Hispanic communities in the United States.

What were the direct and indirect local and national implications? Were the narrow and overt objectives accomplished? Was the larger (and latent) agenda of the movement (that antibilingualism would make Miami a less attractive place for Cubans and other Spanish speakers) fulfilled? Did antibilingualism work as a solution to the Hispanic problem?

The vote did succeed in reversing the institutionalization of Spanish in county government and forestalling the potential institutionalization of other languages, such as Haitian Creole. The most direct effect of the vote was the elimination of translations of public documents and the elimination of a range of bilingual services provided by the county. Clearly the clients affected by these changes were among the most vulnerable in the immigrant population: the elderly; the poor, who had to make use of now monolingual county services, such as the public hospital; the newly arrived; and the uneducated.

The vote also had some consequences regarding the county's ability to support certain cultural activities because the antibilingualism ordinance encompassed both language and culture. The ordinance prohibited "the expenditure of any county funds for the purpose of utilizing any language other than English or promoting any culture other than that of the United States."

More indirectly the vote also likely had a chilling effect on the development of bilingualism in other public institutions, notably the public school system. Although the referendum had no legal effect on the Dade County public schools, and bilingual education is mandated by federal laws and regulations, the school board is elected by the same countywide constituency that voted decisively for the antibilingualism ordinance in 1980. Since that time and up to the present, even school board members enthusiastically in favor of expanding bilingual education have been extremely reluctant to champion its expansion.[3]

The enduring political deterrence effect of the antibilingualism vote is suggested by what has happened to efforts to repeal the ordinance. On two occasions in the 1980s, George Valdes, then the only Hispanic commissioner on the board, declared his intention to present a motion to repeal the antibilingualism ordinance. Valdes was dissuaded each time by lack of support for repeal among fellow commissioners and on one occasion by an appeal to desist from Hispanic leaders worried about stirring up community strife for what, at that juncture, might still prove a losing battle.

Hispanic leaders were not mistaken in believing that repeal would be divisive. Following one of Valdes's announcements and at the urging of a radio talk show host, callers jammed the phone lines at the county commission. Valdes himself received bomb threats. In 1984 Valdes did manage to secure commission approval to amend the ordinance to exempt medical services at the county hospital and other medical facilities; essential services to the elderly and handicapped; the promotion of worldwide tourism; and emergency police, fire, ambulance, medical, rescue, and hurricane-preparedness services. But in order to secure the agreement of the English Only forces not to oppose the changes, Valdes had to include in the ordinance a declaration that English is the official language of Dade County as well as make provision for a program for English-language training for county employees. The cumulative effect of political deterrence, Hispanic caution, and the elimination of some of the worst aspects of the ordinance has been that repealing the antibilingualism ordinance has virtually disappeared from the Hispanic political agenda in Dade County since the mid-1980s.

One reason why Hispanic leaders may have been willing to give up (or postpone) the repeal fight is that, except for a limited number of county staff directly charged with administering bilingualism, upwardly mobile and younger Hispanics were hardly affected by the repeal of bilingualism. The impact for older Hispanics was cushioned by the existence of a strong set of parallel ethnic institutions. A more important reason is that, despite the consequences outlined above, the antibilingualism movement has failed in its broader agenda of stopping Hispanic growth and advancement. Demographically, politically, economically, and (arguably) culturally and linguistically, Latinization has accelerated since 1980.

In the 1980s, fueled by the Cuban Mariel boatlift, massive Nicaraguan immigration, and significant contingents of immigrants from other Latin American countries, Hispanics overtook whites as the largest population segment in Miami and were nearly a majority by the 1990 census (see fig. 16.2) (Wallace 1991). Clearly the antibilingualism referendum utterly failed to make Miami a less attractive place for Hispanics.

Hispanics also continued to advance economically in the 1980s. With about 5 percent of the country's Hispanic population, Miami has almost half of the largest Hispanic-owned businesses in the United States. The rate of business ownership among Miami Hispanics (43 per 1,000) far exceeds that in other large metropolitan areas, such as Los Angeles (14 per 1,000) (Boswell and Curtis 1984). Beyond the ethnic business enclave, Hispanics made important advances in private Anglo-owned corporations and particularly in top public sector positions. From the mid-1980s to the early 1990s, Cubans were appointed to top administrative posts in several key institutions, including Octavio Visiedo as superintendent of Dade County's public schools, Modesto Maidique as president of Florida International University, Marty Urra as president of the South Florida AFL-CIO, Xavier Suarez as mayor of the City of Miami, and Joaquín Aviño as manager of Metropolitan Dade County. Clearly antibilingualism failed to prevent continued Hispanic economic advancement.

If stemming the Hispanic tide in politics was a hope of the antibilingualism movement, the post-1980 era has brought very bad news. Building on demographics and economic development, the 1980s also saw major Hispanic advances in electoral politics and to a significant but somewhat lesser extent, into the higher spheres of the community power structure. Beginning in the early and mid-1980s, Cubans won an increasing number of elective offices in municipalities with large Hispanic populations, including the mayor's office in the two largest cities in the metropolitan area, Miami (Xavier Suarez) and Hialeah (Raul Martinez), and in newly created single member state legislative districts. While Hispanics currently occupy a single seat on both the Metro Commission (Alex Penelas) and the Dade

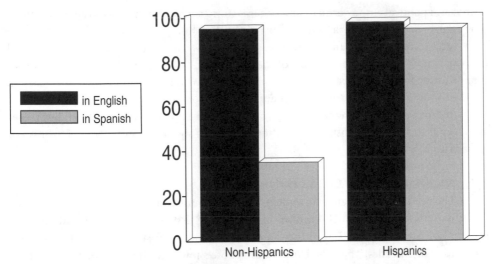

Fig. 16.4. "Very important" for children to read and write perfectly by language. *Source*: **Strategy Research Corporation 1988, 42-43.**

County School Board (Rosa Castro Feinberg), the most important governmental bodies in Dade County, their votes are increasingly essential to the electoral prospects of any candidate. Finally in 1989, Republican Ileana Ros-Lehtinen became the first Cuban-American and the first Hispanic woman to be elected to the U.S. Congress (Malone 1988).

During this period Hispanics for the first time began to play a significant role on boards of directors of key civic organizations. Hispanics for the first time chaired such organizations as the Greater Miami Chamber of Commerce, the Dade Community Foundation, and the Dade Public Education Fund.

Even in the areas of culture and language directly addressed by the ordinance, antibilingualism failed to stop the trend. In the 1980s the Calle Ocho festival, a street festival in celebration of Latin culture, grew to become a huge event with national and international prominence. Also in the 1980s, a Cuban-American film enthusiast, Natalo Chediak, created the Miami Film Festival, which includes many Spanish-language films. In the world of popular music, the Miami Sound Machine put the city on the map to a distinctively Latin beat.

If legislating away or marginalizing the use of Spanish was a key intention of the antibilingualism effort, that hope was certainly dashed. A study by Strategy Research Corporation (1989) found that a higher percentage of Hispanics in Miami spoke Spanish at home, on the job, and on social occasions in 1989 than in 1980.

The ineffectiveness of antibilingualism to banish Spanish to the private sphere does not mean that Miami Hispanics eschew English or even that the place of Spanish is secure in Miami indefinitely. In 1980 fully 94.3 percent of Cuban-Americans born in the United States (more than half of whom live in Miami) reported they spoke English well (U.S. Bureau of the Census 1989). A study by David E. Lopez (1982) found that for 80 percent of U.S.-born Cubans, English was the main language. While these data are for Cubans in the United States, there is no doubt that even in Miami, English tends to replace Spanish as the dominant language intergenerationally. Continuing immigration to Miami masks this intergenerational process. It is an open question whether massive migration, Hispanic economic and political empowerment and other factors (such as Miami's geographic location) may change the context so as to retard or reverse this shift.

A recent market study throws further light on the contrasting views of Anglos and Hispanics in Miami on the question of language. The data suggest that Hispanics almost unanimously prefer bilingualism over either Spanish or English monolingualism (see fig. 16.4). About one-third of Anglos also appears to favor or accept English/Spanish bilingualism. The battle over language in Miami is not about English versus Spanish but rather about English monolingualism versus bilingualism and about the eradication of Spanish or its survival.

NATIONAL IMPLICATIONS

The 1980 antibilingualism campaign in Dade County was a spontaneous, local affair, but it had important national implications. It was the first reversal of the trend toward a measure of language pluralism in the United States and the first political battle over language in many decades. The 1980 Dade County vote showed for the first time the extent of voter support for language restrictionism and for the politics of anti-Hispanic and anti-immigrant backlash. The campaign also provided the method—the referendum—that could and would later be used with tremendous success to institute English Only measures in other states and cities. The Dade County campaign foreshadowed both the ethnically polarized and bitter nature of language battles of the 1980s and the use by both sides of the theme of unity as a centerpiece in future campaigns. It showed the impotence of white leadership and elite groups to effectively oppose such a movement, a pattern that would later be repeated in California and virtually every other state and locality in which the issue has been put to the voter.

In the wake of the Miami vote, the prospects for a well-organized and -funded language restrictionist movement on a national scale must have seemed bright indeed. In 1981 a national English Only movement was launched with the introduction of the first Official English measure in Congress by Senator S. I. Hayakawa. Hayakawa would go on to found U.S. English, the flagship organization of the movement, in collaboration with John Tanton. In the 1980s, U.S. English would succeed in getting many states to pass Official English measures. The organization targeted mainly those states that have large Hispanic populations, seeking to symbolically reaffirm through the ballot Anglo political, cultural, and linguistic hegemony. In California, Florida, Arizona, and Colorado, the organization used its resources to put state constitutional amendments on the ballot. U.S. English won four important victories, although the Arizona amendment subsequently has been declared unconstitutional.

Miami had been a leader in a limited form of bilingualism and biculturalism in the 1960s and 1970s; in 1980 it provided a blueprint for their undoing. The 1980 antibilingualism movement provided the form that a nativist, anti-immigrant, anti-Hispanic national movement might take in a post-civil rights America. In an America where avowed racism had become taboo, language provided a deniable vehicle for the expression of ethnocentric fears and resentments. In Miami in 1980, two-thirds of Anglo voters thought antibilingualism would not hurt relations between Hispanics and non-Hispanics, while 65 percent of Hispanics said it would hurt relations (Browning 1980:11A).

The Miami case also has shown something about the successes and limitations of the type of politics embodied in the antibilingualism movement. Successful in reversing the trend toward bilingualism in government and slowing it down in the public schools, the movement was powerless to stem the larger demographic, economic, political, and cultural forces at work in Dade County. In the face of such forces and of the opposition of both significant white elites and minorities, the antibilingualism movement has been unable to legislate away Latin culture and language. The wish expressed by Anglo voters who supported antibilingualism that the ordinance make the area less attractive to Spanish speakers utterly failed to accomplish this end but did reveal the subtext of the movement (a subtext easily read by the victims).

The history of the national Official English movement so far has reflected much of the pattern observed in Dade County. After spectacular successes in referenda in several states with large Hispanic populations and in the legislatures of some states with small Hispanic populations (and in helping create a climate hostile to bilingual education throughout the 1980s), the Official English movement appears to have stalled. The efficacy of Official English measures has been far more limited than proponents had hoped. In California, courts have ruled that the constitutional amendment passed in 1986 is essentially symbolic. In Arizona, where a highly restrictive constitutional Official English amendment barely passed in 1988, a court has found the measure unconstitutional. In Florida, where an Official English amendment was passed in 1988, Cuban-American Republican legislators from Miami struck a deal with Democratic leaders that effectively blocked the enactment of any enforcement provisions (Castro, Haun, and Roca 1990). The end of the reign of William J. Bennett, an opponent of bilingual education, at the U.S. Department of Education meant the end of the period of greatest federal hostility to bilingual education.

More broadly the 1980s saw very rapid growth in the Hispanic population of the United States and substantial political gains (U.S. Bureau of the Census 1990). In light of growing Hispanic numbers and electoral strength concentrated in key states, neither political party has been willing to adopt Official English as a goal. In 1988 George Bush blocked the inclusion of Official English in the Republican party platform, and Michael Dukakis delivered part of his acceptance speech at the Democratic convention in Spanish. So far Official English measures have also stalled in Congress. In 1988 U.S. English was torn apart by the resignation of its president, Linda Chavez, and some prominent board members, including Walter Cronkite, after a memo with anti-Hispanic undertones written by U.S. English cofounder John Tanton was made public.

CONCLUSION

As in Miami, English Only/Official English advocates elsewhere have found that it is far easier to enact measures than to implement them. They have also found that the very Latinization that they seek to arrest makes it difficult to implement their broader agenda. Politicians and business persons nationally have been too intent on capturing the growing number of Hispanic votes and Hispanic dollars to heed the English Only message.

But the battle is far from over, in Miami or in the nation in general. Because English Only/Official English measures have proven insufficient to curb Latinization, the conflict has partially shifted to other arenas. Bilingual education in particular is likely to continue to be a focus of attack, for English Only advocates see it as an institution through which a U.S.-Hispanic culture and consciousness can be created and transmitted. Immigration policy is a second important arena insofar as it provides a steady stream of additional and unassimilated Hispanics. In frustration over the relative impotence of the antibilingualism ordinance, one English Only advocacy group in Miami reached the conclusion that the main problem is immigration and sought a moratorium on immigration.

Nationally less draconian measures in this direction have already been adopted. The Immigration Reform and Control Act had as its main objective the curbing of undocumented immigration, mostly from Latin America. More recently many bills to reform legal immigration have been proposed in Congress. These measures would reduce the weight of family reunification in the immigration preference system, with the effect of reducing Latin American immigration.

As we approach the end of the century, the growth and development of the Hispanic population continues in Miami and the nation despite these efforts. As the process continues, the battle over language in Miami is a harbinger of battles yet to come over what this trend will mean for the identity of a community and a nation.

NOTES

1. Kenneth Lipner, economist, Florida International University, Miami, personal communication with author.

2. Findings are from the Equal Opportunity Board of Metropolitan Dade County, Marcos Regalado, director, which has conducted two unpublished studies of job advertisements appearing in the *Miami Herald*. Personal communication from the director.

3. Anonymous member, Dade County School Board, personal communication.

REFERENCES

Boswell, Thomas D., and James R. Curtis. 1984. *The Cuban-American Experience: Culture, Images and Perspectives*. Totowa, N.J.: Rowman and Allanheld.

Browning, Michael. 1980. "Antibilingual Backers Celebrate Early." *Miami Herald*. November 5: 1A, 11A.

Castro, Max J., Margaret Haun, and Ana Roca. 1990. "The Official English Movement in Florida." In *Perspectives on Official English*, edited by K. L. Adams and D.T. Brink, 151-60. Berlin and New York: Mouton de Gruyte.

Citrin, Jack. 1988. "American Identity and the Politics of Ethnicity: Public Opinion in a Changing Society." Paper presented at the eleventh annual meeting of the International Society of Political Psychology, Secaucus, N.J., July 1-5.

City of Miami. 1985. *Affirmative Action Annual Report*. City of Miami: Department of Internal Audits and Reviews, Affirmative Action Division.

Cuban American Policy Center. 1988. *Miami's Latin Business*. Miami: Cuban American National Planning Council.

Díaz, Guarioné M., ed. 1980. *Evaluation and Identification of Policy Issues in the Cuban Community*. Miami: Cuban National Planning Council.

Didion, Joan. 1987. *Miami*. New York: Pocket Books.

Llanes, José R. 1982. *Cuban-Americans, Masters of Survival*. Cambridge, Mass.: ABT.

Lopez, David E. 1982. *Language Maintenance and Shift in the United States Today*. Los Alamitos, Calif.: National Center for Bilingual Research.

Malone, Joseph. 1988. *The Second Half of the 1980s: Voters and Votes: Emphasis on Hispanic Influence 1985-1987*. Metro-Dade Elections Department.

Masud-Piloto, Felix. 1988. *With Open Arms: Cuban Migration to the United States.* Totowa, N.J.: Rowman and Littlefield.

Metro-Dade County. 1983. *Dade County Characteristics.* Miami: Department of Human Resources.

_____. Board of County Commissioners. 1973. Agenda Item no. 7(g)(3). Resolution no. R-502-73, Declaring Dade County a Bilingual and Bicultural County.

_____. 1980. Ordinance no. 80-128, "Ordinance Prohibiting the Expenditure of County Funds for the Purpose of Utilizing Any Language Other than English or Promoting Any Culture Other than that of the United States; Providing for Governmental Meetings and Publications to Be in the English Language . . . Effective . . . November 4, 1980."

Metro-Dade County Planning Department. 1984. *Profile of the Black Population.* Miami: Research Division, Metro-Dade Planning Department.

_____. 1986. *Hispanic Profile: Dade County's Hispanic Origin Population 1985.* Miami: Research Division, Metro-Dade Planning Department.

Miami Herald. 1980.

Pedraza-Bailey, Silvia. 1985. *Political and Economic Migrants in America: Cubans and Mexicans.* Austin: University of Texas Press.

Pérez, Lisandro. 1986. "Immigrant Economic Adjustment and Family Organization: The Cuban Success Story Reexamined." *International Migration Review* 20, no. 1 (Spring): 1-20.

Porter, Bruce, and Marvin Dunn. 1984. *The Miami Riot of 1980: Crossing the Bounds.* Lexington, Mass.: D.C. Heath and Company.

Portes, Alejandro, and Robert L. Bach. 1985. *Latin Journey: Cuban and Mexican Immigrants in the United States.* Berkeley: University of California Press.

Portes, Alejandro, and Rafael Mozo. 1985. "The Political Adaptation Process of Cubans and Other Ethnic Minorities in the United States." *International Migration Review* 19, no. 1 (Spring): 35-63.

Portes, Alejandro, and Rubén G. Rumbaut. 1990. *Immigrant America: A Portrait.* Berkeley: University of California Press.

Portes, Alejandro, Alex Stepick, and Cynthia Truelove. 1986. "Three Years Later: The Adaptation Process of 1980 (Mariel) Cuban and Haitian Refugees in South Florida." *Population Research and Policy Review* 5: 83-94.

Stepick, Alex, Max J. Castro, Marvin Dunn, and Guillermo Grenier. 1990. "Changing Relations among Newcomers and Established Residents: The Case of Miami." Final report (unpublished) to the board of the "Changing Relations Project." Miami.

Strategy Research Corporation. 1984. *The U.S. Hispanic Market.* Miami: Strategy Research Corporation.

_____. 1988. *The 1989 South Florida Latin Market.* Miami: Strategy Research Corporation.

U.S. Bureau of the Census. 1984. *1980 Census: Detailed Population Characteristics.* Release PC-80-1-D1-A. Washington: U.S. Department of Commerce.

_____. 1989. *The Hispanic Population of the United States: March 1989.* Current Reports, Series P-20, No. 444. Washington: United States Government Printing Office.

Wallace, Richard. 1991. "South Florida Grows to a Latin Beat." *Miami Herald*, March 6: 1A, 22A.

Wilson, Kenneth L., and W.A. Martin, 1982. "Ethnic Enclaves: A Comparison of the Cuban and Black Economies in Miami." *American Journal of Sociology* 88 (July): 135-60.

17

APARTMENT RESTRUCTURING AND LATINO IMMIGRANT TENANT STRUGGLES: A CASE STUDY OF HUMAN AGENCY

Nestor P. Rodriguez and Jacqueline Maria Hagan

HOUSTON'S 1982–1987 RECESSION created a severe crisis in the city's apartment housing market. As thousands of unemployed, middle-class tenants left Houston, landlords in the city's western sector restructured apartment operations to rebuild renter populations with new Latino immigrants. Fieldwork in a large apartment complex found that changes made by management to attract Latino immigrants helped these newcomers develop survival strategies. When the recession ended, evolving relations between new immigrants and other tenants helped resist, and cope with, a second restructuring process implemented by apartment management to attract higher-income renters. Throughout Houston's west side, settlement and coping activities of new Latino immigrants have changed the material and symbolic environments.

Houston's economic recession in 1982-1987 contained a dramatic downturn of the city's booming real-estate industry. The sharp decline of manufacturing, construction, and service industries affected all sectors of the city's real-estate market (Feagin, 1988). Apartment capital in the city's west-side, apartment-complex industry was particularly hard hit as thousands of unemployed office workers left the city. Facing the out-migration of middle-income tenants, apartment-complex owners and managers in the west side drastically lowered rents and adopted several other changes to attract new Latino immigrants in order to rebuild their renter populations. In the subsequent economic upturn in the late-eighties, west-side apartment landlords developed a second restructuring process, i.e., the upgrading of apartment complexes to attract higher-income (Anglo) tenants, which reduced the presence of immigrant tenants.

The two processes of apartment restructuring in Houston's west side affected the opportunities for new-immigrant settlement and the development of subsequent relations between new Latino immigrants and established residents. Taking a human-agency perspective (M. P. Smith, 1989) in this paper, we use fieldwork observations to describe (1) how new Latino immigrants used the first apartment restructuring process to develop household survival strategies, and (2) how new Latino immigrants used evolving relations with established residents to cope with measures implemented by landlords in the second apartment restructuring process. While other studies have focused on the way capitalist actors (bankers, real-estate investors, developers, etc.) influence urban growth (e.g., see Feagin and Parker, 1990; Gottdiener, 1985), we focus on these two developments to illustrate that the actions of more ordinary women and men may also become a medium for urban change.

Our ethnographic setting is Arboleda (pseudonym), a large apartment complex in Houston's west side. As in many other large apartment complexes in the city's west side, Arboleda became a setting where new Latino immigrants, individually and at times collectively with established residents, appropriated, resisted, and accommodated to broad social-structural changes that impeded their trans-residential community. Through their social actions, i.e., through their "agency," new Latino immigrants modified materially and symbolically many apartment-neighborhood environments in Houston's west side.

RESEARCH IN ARBOLEDA

The ethnography of social action at Arboleda that we present in this paper is derived from two years of fieldwork at the apartment complex and from our continuing contact with several tenant households at the site. As part of a national study of evolving relations between established residents and new immigrants, in 1988-1989 we observed interaction between Anglo, African-American, and Latino established residents and Mexican and Central American new immigrants at the apartment complex. While our observations covered all areas of the complex (apartment units, patios, swimming pools, tennis courts, parking lots, and a restaurant), we especially focused on intergroup interaction in Building 5 (the back building) of the complex's five apartment buildings. Building 5 contains 132 of the 625 apartment units in the complex and has the most heterogeneous tenant population (Anglos, African-Americans, Mexican-Americans, new immigrants) and the greatest new immigrant concentration in the complex.

To facilitate the fieldwork, Jacqueline Hagan became a tenant in Building 5 several months prior to the study. On a daily basis she interacted with established residents, new immigrants, apartment managers, maintenance workers, and security guards at the complex. She gained acceptance among Latino immigrants in the building by translating their notices, employment forms, and other English-written materials into Spanish and by developing friendships with several immigrant households. Her closest informants in the complex included six new-immigrant and four established-residents' households in Building 5.

In the first year of fieldwork at Arboleda, we focused on different levels of inter-group relations between established residents and Mexican and Central American newcomers and on the household survival strategies of the immigrants, who were almost entirely undocumented. In the second year, when Arboleda management adopted measures to upgrade the apartment complex to attract higher-income tenants, we shifted our focus to the immigrants' responses to these measures affected and to subsequent intergroup relations among the tenants.

ECONOMIC CRISIS AND
UNDOCUMENTED LATINO IMMIGRATION

Once viewed as depression-proof, Houston's energy-centered economy entered a dramatic five-year recession in the spring of 1982. When an over-supply of oil in the world market lowered oil prices by 10 percent and, more importantly, the oil-price expectation by 50 percent (B. Smith, 1989), Houston's industrial sector suffered an immediate crash that saw more than 40 percent of the area's manufacturing workforce laid off. The decline of business services and construction in the second phase of the recession (1985-1986) also added to the area's loss of 200,000 jobs. At the height of the area's economic crisis in the summer of 1986, the unemployment rate stood at 13 percent.

The economic crisis severely depressed the real-estate sector which had enjoyed phenomenal expansion in 1975-1982. In this seven-year period, builders doubled the city's office space and added 20,000 units to the area's housing market (B. Smith, 1986). Real-estate development achieved such a high momentum that even after the onset of the recession area builders constructed over 200 office buildings and towers and more than 97,000 housing units (Feagin, 1988; B. Smith 1989). By 1986, however, the recession had clearly enervated the real-estate industry as 485 real-estate firms failed and foreclosures averaged 3,000 per month (Feagin, 1988). In the area's housing market, the number of vacant residential units rose from 86,961 in 1981 to a high of 220,709 in 1985 (B. Smith, 1989).

Out-migration of unemployed workers and over-construction lowered the area's apartment occupancy rate. The rate plummeted from a high of 99.4 percent in 1982 to a low of 79.8 percent in 1984, rising to 81.5 percent when the economic downturn bottomed-out in 1987 (Bivins, 1991). Many of the apartment vacancies occurred in the city's west and southwest sides, areas of white, middle-class growth where real-estate investors and developers had constructed over a thousand large apartment complexes.

The recession thus threatened to decimate the area's apartment-complex industry. For many west-side apartment landlords desperate to rebuild their tenant populations, a temporary solution soon came in the form of undocumented Latino immigrants.

While Houston has long experienced undocumented Mexican immigration, in the late 1970s this immigration accelerated and was complemented in the early 1980s by undocumented Central American immigration. Fleeing political and economic turmoil in their homelands, the new Central American immigrants entered the city in torrents. In contrast to Mexican immigrants who for decades had settled in west-side immigrant enclaves, the Central American newcomers settled mainly in the city's western half. By the mid-1980s, this part of the city contained the largest number of the over 100,000 undocumented Salvadorans, Guatemalans, Hondurans, and Nicaraguans who had settled in the Houston area (Rodriguez and Hagan, 1989).

Central American immigrant settlements in the western half of the city became a major source of low-wage labor for the area's service sector. Many undocumented Central American immigrants found cleaning jobs in restaurants, retail stores, office buildings, and in other business places. Many undocumented Central American immigrant women also found domestic work in middle-class, Anglo homes. The undocumented Central American men who remained unemployed formed street-corner laborer pools as an employment agency of last resort (Rodriguez, 1987).

Large-scale influx of Central Americans and other undocumented Latinos into Houston during the 1980s presented two anomalies: labor immigration in a context of economic decline and, in the case of the city's west side, Latino immigrant settlement in a mainly white, middle-income area several miles removed from established immigrant enclaves. The former anomaly speaks to the ability of undocumented immigrants to develop social strategies for economic survival and to the endurance of the secondary labor market in times of economic decline. The latter anomaly speaks to the effectiveness of apartment-complex restructuring strategies temporarily implemented by landlords to rebuild tenant populations.

IMMIGRANT-TENANT PROBLEMS AND INTERGROUP RELATIONS AT ARBOLEDA

Arboleda is part of a nationwide apartment-complex chain headquartered in Los Angeles. Built in the seventies in Houston's west-side sector of booming white, middle-class neighborhoods and business centers, Arboleda was designed for middle-income, white-collar workers, whose numbers grew with Houston's business expansion. For these tenants, the apartment complex offered maid and laundry services, heated swimming pools and Jacuzzis, tennis courts, and a beauty salon and bar-restaurant in the complex. Monthly rents of $500-$600 and an adults-only rule kept the tenant population young, middle-class and mostly Anglo.

Almost overnight, however, Houston's recession depleted Arboleda's tenant population. The complex's occupancy dropped by over 30 percent as unemployed tenants left the city or sought cheaper housing elsewhere. In the same manner as many other west-side apartment landlords, Arboleda's management responded to the crisis by lowering rents as much as 50 percent for some units and by restructuring its pattern of relationships with tenants to attract arriving Latino immigrants.

The apartment restructuring strategy involved advertising in Spanish, hiring bilingual rental agents and maintenance workers, and printing all apartment notices and bulletins in English and Spanish. Furthermore, Arboleda management developed an amicable, almost sympathetic relationship, with the new Latino immigrant tenants. Management looked the other way when immigrant families moved in with children, which violated the complex's adults-only policy, or when immigrant households expanded beyond the size allowed by rent contracts, which was usually two persons per bedroom. Management also allowed maintenance workers to give discarded apartment furniture to immigrant households. Finally, management ignored several informal business activities that immigrants developed in the apartment complex. The most conspicuous of these activities included an automobile repair shop run by a young Guatemalan on one of the complex's parking areas and the regular assembly of small-truck caravans that transported goods sent by Central American immigrant tenants to families back home. Often the Guatemalan mechanic repaired the battered trucks used for the caravans on the complex grounds.

To maintain and attract more middle-income tenants (which had long been synonymous with white tenants), Arboleda management placed most of its new Latino immigrant renters in the back two apartment buildings, especially in Building 5, away from the visibility of the front entrance. The apartment's rental agents expressed this conscious effort in their comments that the visibility of "those people" (Latino immigrants) would discourage "other people" (Anglos) from moving in. The concern to segregate Latino immigrant tenants in the back of the complex was also demonstrated when Hagan asked to rent an apartment. At first she was shown only apartments in the front three buildings; it was only after her insistence that she was shown an apartment in Building 5.

Table 17.1	Arboleda's Buldilng 5 Housedold Population by Ethnicity and Size							
	Cen. Amer.	Mex.	Mex. Amer.	Other Latino[a]	Anglo	African Amer.	African	Other[b]
Household Size								
1-2	9	11	4	8	7	9	2	2
3-4	18	16	0	3	0	0	0	9
5-6	12	7	0	1	0	0	0	0
7-8	1	0	0	0	0	0	0	0
n	40	34	4	12	7	9	2	11
% of total	33.6	28.6	3.4	10.1	5.9	7.6	1.7	9.2

a. "Other Latino" includes tenants from the Caribbean and South America and ethnically heterogenous Latino households.
b. "Other" includes ethnically mixed households containing Anglos or African Americans.

An alternative census count we conducted in Building 5 in June-July 1990 shows the household composition of the occupied units in the building during the enumeration (Table 1). Homogenous Latino immigrant households accounted for over two-thirds (68.9 percent) of the 119 occupied apartment units in the building. Anglo, African-American, and Mexican-American households accounted for less than a fifth (16.8 percent) of the households in the building. In terms of total population, Central American and Mexican immigrants accounted for more than three-fourths (76.0 percent) of the 350 tenants in the building. For many of these immigrants Arboleda was their first home in the United States.

IMMIGRANT HOUSEHOLD SURVIVAL STRATEGIES

Arriving in Houston with little or no money and with undocumented status, the Central American and Mexican immigrants in Arboleda organized several household survival strategies common among low-income groups (e.g., see Mullings, 1987; Browning and Rodriguez, 1985). The greater distribution of Central American and Mexican immigrants in larger households (see Table 17.1) illustrates the strategy to reduce living costs (rent, food, utilities, etc.) by increasing the number of income earners in the household. Many of the Central American and Mexican households with three or more members consisted of workers in their late teens or in their twenties living in one-bedroom apartments.

The Latino immigrant's use of household arrangements as an agency of economic survival substantially altered the apartment complex's household pattern of earlier middle-income tenants. In the alternative enumeration, no Central Americans and less than 10 percent of Mexicans in Building 5 resided in households of single individuals, while this household size predominated among Anglos, African-Americans, and Mexican-Americans in the building. The most complex household arrangement found in the apartment building, i.e., a household composed of a couple with children and related *and* nonrelated individuals, only involved Central Americans and Mexicans. The second most complex level of household arrangement, i.e., a couple with children and related or nonrelated individuals, also only involved Central American and Mexican immigrant tenants.

The apartment household of Pablo and Maria Ixtecoy, who immigrated from the western highlands of Guatemala, illustrates how household-centered social strategies helped undocumented immigrants survive economically in their new environment. After arriving in Houston with little money, Pablo and Maria moved into a Mayan household in a one-bedroom unit in Building 5. When the original members of the household moved out, Pablo and Maria took in four male and one female new Mayan immigrants who were relatives and friends of Pablo. Pablo found cleaning jobs for the four men in a nearby supermarket where he worked. Maria also helped Ana, the new female household member, find part-time, domestic work in the neighborhood where she cleaned homes. Working in the same maintenance crew, Pablo and the four other men did each other's jobs when one of the men was not able to go to work. Maria and Ana also covered for each other when one of them could not go to work. Covering for each other at work was especially important when one of the household members left to visit family back home. When Maria left for three weeks to visit her family in Guatemala, Ana temporarily took over her domestic job and carried out her share of cooking, cleaning, and other household chores in the apartment. By sharing living expenses and covering for each other at work (and at home for Maria and Ana), the household members survived relatively well even as the broader environment suffered through economic decline.

For the new Latino immigrants, complex housing arrangements also provided socio-cultural resources to facilitate their accommodation in U.S. society. Living in households with more experienced immigrants was especially useful to rural-origin newcomers to learn how to enter an urban labor market. Several of the Central American households in Building 5 had members who came from a mainly peasant background and who had never travelled long distances beyond their homes before migrating to the United States. Among the immigrant women, living in complex households also helped them to obtain information on how to use modern home appliances, operate the washers and dryers in the building's laundry room, and how to negotiate through a host of social institutions (e.g., churches, clinics, and schools).

To be sure, the distinction of economic and socio-cultural household agency among immigrants is only an analytical one. In reality, the same process of household formation and maintenance is at once economic, social, and cultural (and political as we occasionally observed among Central Americans in other apartment complexes). For example, the organizing of birthday and wedding celebrations by households involved the economic activity of sharing expenses, the cultural activities of preparing traditional dishes and, among Mayan immigrant women, wearing traditional garments, and the social activities of reuniting relatives, friends, and co-workers for the event.

EVOLVING INTERGROUP RELATIONS

The clustering of Latino immigrants in the back two buildings of Arboleda separated these newcomers from the concentration of Anglo and other established residents in the front buildings. Other factors such as ethnicity/race and language differences also formed boundaries between the immigrant and established-resident tenant groups. The passage of the Immigration Reform and Control Act (IRCA) in 1986, however, created documentation needs among undocumented immigrants that brought a number of Latino immigrant and established-resident tenants together in Arboleda.

Many undocumented Latino immigrants in Arboleda applied for legal resident status under IRCA. The legalization program of IRCA required that applicants present documents to establish their personal identification, medical-health condition, U.S. employment history, and to prove that they had resided in the United States since before January 1, 1982. Many of the undocumented immigrants in Arboleda held jobs in the informal labor market where work-related documents such as paycheck stubs and W-2 income tax forms were impossible to obtain. Residential documentation in the form of rent contracts and receipts and utility payments was also difficult to obtain, since many immigrants concealed their presence from apartment managers because they lived in households whose size violated lease agreements. In addition, a number of immigrants resided in apartments where the lease and utilities were still under the names of immigrants who had left the complex. To avoid detection and thus avoid paying apartment and utility deposits, new immigrants had moved into these apartments and continued to pay the rent and utilities in cash under the name of the original tenants.

In the absence of readily available forms of documentation, immigrants relied heavily on affidavits provided by neighbors and co-workers. In over a dozen cases, established residents at Arboleda wrote affidavits stating they had been long-time neighbors and friends of immigrant applicants. Sensing the urgency of the opportunity for immigrants, some established residents even lent money to immigrant neighbors to pay for the legalization application fee. In one case, a Mexican-American tenant in Building 5 not only provided his immigrant neighbor with an affidavit and a loan for the application fee, but also accompanied him to the local office of the Immigration and Naturalization Service (INS) for the final interview to determine legalization. In several other cases, established residents in the complex tutored, free of charge, immigrant neighbors to help them pass the English exam of the legalization program. James, an African-American, for example, tutored Santos, his Guatemalan neighbor, and received Spanish lessons from Santos in return. These types of legalization-related exchanges strengthened relations between established residents and new Latino immigrants and made a number of established residents more sensitive to the needs of their immigrant co-tenants.

COPING WITH APARTMENT CHANGES

As Houston's economy pulled out of the recession in the Spring of 1988, Arboleda's management implemented the first measure to "upgrade" the complex and make it more attractive for potential middle-income tenants. The measure was to enforce the previously ignored adults-only policy, and given the high number of immigrant families with children in the complex, the measure was primarily aimed at the Latino tenants. To search for children among the large number of Latino immigrant households in the complex, management offered $50 to its maintenance and security workers for every apartment unit they found housing small children. An Anglo security guard and a Mexican-American maintenance worker reported several households with children, but two maintenance workers, an African-American and a Mexican-American, opposed the measure and aligned themselves with the immigrant families. The two apartment maintenance workers alerted immigrant families with small children when "management spies" (as they labeled other apartment employees) planned to be in the back apartment buildings.

Despite the efforts of the two sympathetic maintenance workers, management succeeded in evicting over 20 households in less than a month after reenforcing the adults-only policy. The evictions, however, became slower and more difficult for management to carry out when the immigrant families gained the support of other tenants, apartment employees, and in one case, of a business employer. The case of Marcelina, a Mexican immigrant tenant with a nine-year-old son, illustrates the collective effort to resist the apartment management's quick eviction attempts. After receiving a notice that her family had to move out of the apartment in three days, she stayed at home fearing to leave her son alone. Since her husband was working temporarily in another city, she turned to another tenant, to a Mexican-American maintenance worker, and to her employer (the owner of a nearby restaurant) for help. Together the group approached management and argued her case. Management reconsidered and agreed to give evicted families thirty days to leave the complex. (The Supreme Court later ruled adult-only apartment policies to be illegal.)

In the summer of 1988, Arboleda management implemented a second upgraded measure that created problems for the Latino immigrant tenants in the complex. The measure was the construction of a security steel fence around the complex and around the visitors' parking areas of the back two buildings. Management distributed instructions for operating the fence gates and issued two gate cards per apartment unit. In contrast to the past practice of printing notices in English and Spanish, the instructions for operating the gates were written only in English.

Several Latino immigrants approached Mexican-American apartment employees and bilingual Anglo tenants for assistance in translating the gate instructions into Spanish. Two Anglo tenants met with management and complained that the instructions needed to be translated into Spanish. An apartment manager responded that a bilingual translator was no longer available nor would be hired in the future. When a Mexican-American tenant offered to translate the notice, the apartment manager refused. During a second meeting between tenants and management, the decision was made to hold a meeting with Latino immigrant tenants to explain how to operate the new security fence system. A bilingual Anglo and two Mexican-American tenants conducted the meeting which over 100 immigrant tenants attended.

Issuing only two gate cards per apartment also caused problems for most Latino immigrant households. Two gate cards were simply not enough for immigrant households containing several adult members with different work schedules. The problem of insufficient gate cards was soon overcome through informal tenant strategies. For example, tenants entering or exiting the rear parking areas regularly slowed down at the gate to allow immigrant tenants on foot time to walk through. Parents and friends also asked children to squeeze through the bars of the fence and press the gate switches from the inside. Several months after the installation of the security fence, a group of tenants found that the rear gate switch could be activated by simply raising the gate a few inches off the ground. After this became a regular method of entering and exiting the rear buildings, management responded by having its security guards periodically pass by the gate. The immigrant renters without gate cards and immigrant visitors simply waited for the guards to pass out of sight and then continued to operate the gate with their popular strategies.

Conversations with established residents in the back building indicated they generally supported the immigrants' gate coping strategies because they felt management should have passed out more gate cards to the larger households and because they viewed the security fence as an inconvenience for visitors to the back apartment buildings. Though several established residents in the back buildings knew who were the immigrants that regularly sabotaged the rear gate switch, they never acknowledged this to the security guards who inquired every time the gate had to be repaired. Instead, the established residents took the side of the Latin immigrants.

A third upgrading measure that united established residents and new Latino immigrants in Arboleda involved the apartment's laundry facilities. The washers and dryers in the laundry room in Building 5 usually were in a state of disrepair, causing the building's tenants to use the laundry rooms in the other buildings. When new washers and dryers were installed in the front buildings, established residents in Building 5 complained to management about the deteriorating conditions of the laundry room in their building. Management responded that there was no use in repairing or replacing the washers and driers in Building 5 because the immigrants would only vandalize them again. When management refused to reimburse immigrant tenants for money lost in the broken-down washers and driers in the building, some immigrants responded by jamming washers and driers in the other laundry rooms with foreign coins. After threatening to press charges against anyone caught vandalizing the apartment's laundry equipment, management closed down the laundry room in Building 5. Established-resident tenants in the building discussed the problem with their immigrant neighbors and sympathetic maintenance workers and selected a small group of tenants to confront management. The Anglos in the group threatened to move out of the complex if management did not repair the laundry facilities in their building. After several confrontations, management finally agreed to renovate the laundry facilities in Building 5.

Arboleda management continued to implement upgrading changes in 1990. In the summer of 1990, it started to paint and renovate the front apartment buildings, presumedly leaving the back sections of mainly immigrant renters for last. As part of its restructuring strategy after the 1982-1987 recession, management raised rents in the complex by an average of $100 in just the first half of 1990. Facing higher rents, some Latino immigrant tenants moved to smaller and thus cheaper units in the complex, while other immigrant tenants moved in with other immigrant households in the complex or left the apartment complex for cheaper rents elsewhere in the city.

Our alternative census enumeration in Arboleda's Building 5 in the summer of 1990 indicates that large numbers of Latino immigrants still reside in the complex. Our finding that many of the immigrant tenants in Building 5 were undocumented, and thus new immigrants, indicates that the complex continues to be a viable setting for immigrant survival strategies. Arboleda management's upgrading measures also brought success. In the game of apartment real-estate investment, the real goal of upgrading apartments is not simply to draw higher-income tenants but to use these tenants to make apartments attractive to buyers. Arboleda owners accomplished this goal when they sold the apartment complex in the spring of 1991.

NEW LATINO IMMIGRANT-RELATED CHANGES
IN THE WEST SIDE

Through their settlement and survival in west-side apartment complexes, Latino immigrants, as well as other new immigrants, have significantly altered the west-side social landscape. Retail centers in the west side now contain a variety of businesses (night clubs, restaurants, supermarkets, etc.) that cater primarily to the area's new immigrant population. Public and other social organizations in the west side have also been significantly affected by the new immigrant settlement. Several public schools, for example, in the 1980s saw their student population change from predominantly Anglo to predominantly Latino-immigrant, creating new pedagogical challenges for administrators and teachers. In places of worship, religious leaders also now experiment with social and language programs to incorporate newcomers into their memberships. Yet, this new urban change has not gone uncontested.

Established-residents groups in several west-side neighborhoods have undertaken actions to limit the changes that new immigrants bring to their areas. In one community, Anglo parents successfully countered a decision to redraw school boundaries which would have created in one school a majority Latino student body from nearby apartment complexes. The parents had the school system implement a student distribution plan that buses the immigrant students to schools with an Anglo student majority. In another community, established residents and apartment owners united to establish a police substation and to have the police department undertake a campaign against vagrants, vandals, and other supposedly criminal persons in the heavily-immigrant apartment complexes in their neighborhood. The "clean up" campaign includes INS raids in the complexes.

In spite of efforts such as these, some of the material and symbolic changes that new Latino immigrants have produced in the west side have gained permanency, especially as in some instances the changes have been incorporated into mainstream institutions. Two cases illustrate this development. One case is an elementary school in an upper middle-class, Anglo neighborhood where the school staff has adopted a *Cinco de Mayo* celebration ("Fiesta Field Day") almost completely without Latino involvement, given the absence of Latino parents in the upper-income neighborhood. While the celebration includes a variety of American games (baseball, three-legged races, dunking booth, etc.), the paintings in the signs and posters used to decorate the event symbolize Latino themes.

The second case involves the opening of a new health clinic in a southwest neighborhood. Since their arrival in large numbers in the west side in the early 1980s, new Latino immigrants had to depend on public health facilities located almost ten miles away. While some immigrants relied on private physicians for medical care, many others unemployed or with no health plans sought medical and health services at public hospitals and clinics (Urrutia-Rojas, 1988). Pregnant immigrant women especially sought prenatal care at public clinics. Occasionally physicians, nurses, and other health professionals offered immigrants free health services in makeshift clinics in the parking lots of churches and apartment complexes in the west side. Prompted by the findings of a health survey among Latino immigrants in a large, apartment district (see Urrutia-Rojas, 1988), in 1990 over a dozen members from Houston public and private community organizations came together forming a task force to locate a health clinic for indigents (mainly new Latino immigrants) in a southwest corridor of the city. After more than a year of lobbying elected officials and established community leaders, the intergroup task force persuaded the City of Houston to contribute $500,000 to a public-private venture to open a health clinic in the southwest corridor. In the clinic's opening day on May 31, 1991, the speeches by the mayor and other public officials indicated that the city's established political structure had finally recognized the new immigrants as part of the west-side community.

DISCUSSION

Economic restructuring has played a central role in the development of capitalist societies (Sassen, 1988; Henderson and Castells, 1987). Previous works have focused on how restructuring impacts the social structure within the manufacturing, primary sector of capital (Beauregard, 1989; Morales, 1983). Our fieldwork in Arboleda shows that restructuring also produces significant changes in the social-structural environment of the real-estate, secondary circuit of capital. Arboleda management's initial restructuring strategy to partially rebuild the renter population with new Latino immigrant tenants became the context for undocumented immigrant-survival strategies, and evolving intergroup relations. These developments later became sources of individual and collective intergroup resistance against upgrading measures adopted by management as a second restructuring strategy, aimed this time to attract higher-income tenants.

Facing a variety of constraints related to their undocumented and new immigrant status and to the decline of the city's economic environment, the Latino newcomers at Arboleda developed household social strategies to appropriate living space within the complex. By letting relatives, friends, and co-workers move into their households, the immigrants enhanced the apartments' use-value while their exchange value (rent) remained unchanged. But the undocumented Latino immigrants appropriated more than apartment space; they also appropriated the apartment environment in the back two buildings and through social actions, such as their informal business activities, reconstituted the symbolic dimension of the buildings' social space. The buildings, which once symbolized the affluent life styles of young, middle-income professionals, now represented the new Latino immigrant community experience in Houston.

Appropriation of apartment space and building environment constituted but one "aggravation" in the apartment complex as a setting of capitalist space (see Lefebvre, 1979). The struggles over the rear gate and the laundry facilities in Building 5 constituted two more. To an extent, the rear gate represented managements' attempt to reclaim the environment of the rear two buildings, to bring it "under control." But what management saw as endangered profit-making space, the Latino immigrants saw as community space, *their* community space. In addition to causing problems for households who needed more than two gate cards, the security fence significantly restricted the daily visits by relatives and friends coming from surrounding apartment complexes. That is, it restricted an important social resource for community nurturing. The immigrants' regular sabotaging of the rear gate switch thus represented attempts to maintain control of access to their community space.

In a similar way, we believe, the struggles over the laundry facilities in Building 5 represented a community-related issue but at a broader level, since it drew the active involvement of several established-resident tenants in the building. The laundry room in Building 5 was more than just a shared physical space where tenants came together to wash and dry their clothes. Over the course of our fieldwork, the laundry room became a common *social space* where different groups of women (Anglo, African-American, Latina) chatted, exchanged stories, and looked after each others washing load or small children if one had to leave the laundry room momentarily. Moreover, the laundry room had helped to promote a degree of community solidarity as the immigrants who "fixed the driers to work for free" taught their established-resident neighbors how to do the same. The whole laundry room episode demonstrated the significance that common space can have in the formation of intergroup solidarity.

Our description of resistance to upgrading measures at Arboleda should not be taken to mean that the complex has turned into a hostile environment where management and tenants daily confront each other. Arboleda is generally a tranquil setting where immigrants and other tenants in the back section pursue household and community activities much like residents in other working-class neighborhoods. What has changed at Arboleda, and is directly related to the immigrants' presence, is that in contrast to earlier days some issues now thrust the complex's back section into contested terrain. Management can no longer assume that its apartment policies will be automatically accepted in all sections of the complex.

As we have described above, new Latino immigration in the 1980's has significantly affected the social environment of Houston's west side. The change that this immigration has produced is greater than the emergence of Latino ethnic enterprises and the penetration of new Latinos into mainstream institutions (educational, health, religious, etc.) in the area. The immigration of Latinos, and other populations, affects the very social structure of the west side. Immigration has deepened the infusion of ethnic/racial and class dimensions into the social-structural foundation of the area, creating new possibilities for contention in the area's future growth. What this amounts to is that settings beyond apartment complexes will also become contested terrain in the west side, especially as the large number of legalized immigrants acquire more experience in the city's political-economic arenas.

CONCLUSION

The Arboleda immigrant experience, as well as the greater west-side immigrant experience in Houston, demonstrates the relationship between macro-structural change (Houston's recession and later upswing) and the everyday actions of women and men of appropriating, resisting, or accommodating in order to survive in constraining social structures. These social actions accomplish more than economic survival—they change materially and symbolically the urban environment. Thus, social actions of ordinary women and men undertaken in response to structural conditions become an agency for urban change. In this vein of thought, people are not simply objects of impersonal structural forces but are historical actors in the production and transformation of urban space.

ACKNOWLEDGEMENTS

We are thankful to Robert A. Beauregard, Joe R. Feagin, Mark Gottdiener, and Robert Parker for their comments on an earlier version of this paper. We are also thankful to Robert L. Bach for the many discussions we had with him on new evolving intergroup relations. Finally, we are especially thankful to the tenants and staff at Arboleda who shared their stories and lives with us. The Changing Relations Project (Ford Foundation), the Research Methods Section of the U.S. Bureau of the Census, and the College of Social Science at the University of Houston provided support for the research presented in this paper.

REFERENCES

Beauregard, Robert A. (Ed.) (1989) *Economic Restructuring and Political Response.* Newbury Park, CA: Sage.

Bivens, Ralph (1991) Apartment rents up 17%, but rise is expected to ease. *Houston Chronicle*, April 3, 1991, Section A, page 1.

Browning, Harley L., and Nestor Rodriguez (1985) The Migration of Mexican Indocumentados as a Settlement Process: Implications for Work. In George J. Borgas and Marta Tienda (Eds.), *Hispanics in the U.S. Economy*, 277-298. New York: Academic Press.

Feagin, Joe R. (1988) *Free Enterprise City: Houston in Political and Economic Perspective.* New Brunswick, NJ: Rutgers University Press.

Feagin, Joe R., and Robert Parker (1990) *Building American Cities: The Urban Real Estate Game.* Englewood Cliffs, NJ: Prentice Hall.

Gottdiener, M. (1985) *The Social Production of Urban Space.* Austin, TX: University of Texas Press.

Henderson, Jeffrey, and Manuel Castells (1987) *Global Restructuring and Territorial Development.* Newbury Park, CA: Sage.

Lefebvre, Henri (1979) Space: Social Product and Use Value. In J. W. Freiberg (Ed.), *Critical Sociology: European Perspectives*, 285-295. New York: Irvington Publishers.

Morales, Rebecca (1983) Transnational Labor: Undocumented Workers in the Los Angeles Automobile Industry, *International Migration Review*, 17, 570-596.

Mullings, Leith (Ed.) (1987) *Cities of the United States.* New York: Columbia University Press.

Rodriguez, Nestor P. (1987) Undocumented Central Americans in Houston: Diverse Populations, *International Migration Review*, 21, 4-26.

Rodriguez, Nestor P., and Jacqueline Hagan (1989) Undocumented Central American Migration to Houston in the 1980s, *La Raza Studies*, 2, 1-3.

Sassen, Saskia (1988) *The Mobility of Labor and Capital: A Study in International Investment and Labor Flow.* Cambridge: Cambridge University Press.

Smith, Michael Peter (1989) Urbanism: Medium or Outcome of Human Agency?, *Urban Affairs Quarterly*, 24, 353-357.

Smith, Barton (1986) *Handbook on the Houston Economy.* Houston: Center for Public Policy, University of Houston.

Urrutia-Rojas, Ximena (1988) Health Care Needs and Utilization among Hispanic Immigrants and Refugees in Southwest Houston. Master's Thesis, The University of Texas Health Science Center at Houston, Houston, TX.

INDEX ❦